People and Communities in the Western World · VOLUME II

The Dorsey Series in European History

VOLUME II

People and Communities
in the Western World

Edited by

GENE BRUCKER
University of California, Berkeley

1979 **DD** **THE DORSEY PRESS** Homewood, Illinois 60430
Irwin-Dorsey Limited   Georgetown, Ontario   L7G 4B3

Cover: Gustave Caillebotte, *Paris, A Rainy Day,* Courtesy of The
   Art Institute of Chicago.

ISBN 0-256-02186-4
Library of Congress Catalog Card No. 78–59217
Printed in the United States of America

1 2 3 4 5 6 7 8 9 0 K 6 5 4 3 2 1 0 9

Preface

This collection of essays by 12 historians is designed primarily as a supplementary text for courses in the history of Western Civilization. The 14 chapters in these two volumes describe particular societies at particular moments in time; each chapter is a sharply focused study of one community for which records have survived and which, if not "typical," does illustrate some general features of human experience in its time and place. Some of the chapters are biographical in approach, exploring a particular social milieu through one individual's life experience. Others concentrate instead upon a rural village or a town, whose contours and experience illuminate some of the larger issues that are treated in Western Civilization texts. By analyzing in some depth and detail a particular community in (for example) the Ancient Near East or in the Roman Empire, the chapters provide students with a richer and fuller account of the social, economic, political, and cultural structures that existed in the various periods of Western history, from the earliest civilizations of the Fertile Crescent to the 20th century.

Each chapter can thus be viewed as a "case study" of an important historical theme in Western history, and can serve as a focus for a discussion section in large lecture survey courses. The rural village of Cuxham in medieval England is the subject of Chapter 5 in the first volume. The description of this peasant community will help the student to understand more clearly the concepts and terms that he or she encounters in the textbook and in lectures: feudalism, manoralism, serfdom. In the second volume, which is devoted largely to aspects of European modernization, the student will read about life in Paris in the early years of the French Revolution (Chapter 2) and about the experiences of factory workers in Moscow and St. Petersburg prior to the outbreak of the Russian Revolution (Chapter 5). In these chapters, the concepts of urbanization and industrialization are illustrated by the experience of particular communities and social groups as are, too, the tensions and conflicts created by these phenomena.

This book has had a lengthy and complex history. The concept for the work emerged from conversations and correspondence with editors and executives of the Dorsey Press. Early visions and versions were refined after thoughtful scrutiny by historians who have taught courses in Western Civilization: J. Kim Munholland, University of Minnesota; William B. Cohen, Indiana University; Robert A. Nye, University of Oklahoma; Charles Trinkaus, University of Michigan; John Coverdale, Northwestern University; and Edward Peters, University of Pennsylvania. I benefitted from their counsel, and from that of scholars who read drafts of most chapters: Carol J. Thomas, University of Washington; Steven Ozment, Yale University; Gerald Strauss, Indiana University; and Edward Peters, University of Pennsylvania. I wish to thank my colleagues who wrote the chapters, and the members of the staff of the Dorsey Press, who assisted me in transforming an idea into a book.

December 1978   **Gene Brucker**

Contents

A French Peasant Community in the Old Regime
GERALD CAVANAUGH   10

Peasants and Society: Some General Views. Living Conditions of the Peasantry. Fiscal Burdens of the Peasantry. The Seigneurie. Beauvais: History and Topography. Beauvais' Social Structure. The Poor of Beauvais. The Beauvaisis. The Rural Society of the Beauvaisis.

Paris of the Great Revolution: 1789–1796
RICHARD MOWERY ANDREWS   56

Paris and the French Monarchy. Parisian Elites and the Old Regime: Nobility and Clergy. The Social and Political Structure of Revolutionary Paris. The Faubourgs: Myths and Realities. Economic Structures. The Inner City: *Human Density. Social Compression. Promiscuity and Abrasiveness of Contact.* Violence and Suspicion. Politics and Terror in Jacobin Paris. Reaction, Popular Resistance, and Repression of the Military. The Consolidation of the New Bourgeois Order, 1796–1815.

List of Maps

List of Illustrations

Introduction

*T*he essays in this book all attempt to answer questions posed by John Hale, in the preface to his Renaissance Europe: The Individual and Society, 1480–1520. *Hale's purpose in writing that book (he tells us) was less to describe momentous events and personalities, or to record significant dates, than "to suggest what it was like to have lived then." How did people of that age perceive the world in which they lived? How did they earn their livelihood? How were they organized socially, and how governed? Finally, "what part did religion play in their lives, and what cultural and intellectual satisfactions were open to them?"*

The nature of the historians' discipline, and of the material dealt with, incline them toward concreteness and specificity. Though recognizing the necessity of generalizing about their data, of fitting it into a coherent and comprehensible format, it is done with some reluctance, and with a sense of having violated historical reality. Historians who have written textbook surveys of Western civilization are faced with this dilemma in its cruelest form. They must sacrifice detail and particularity to the exigencies of the panoramic vision. How did people live, work, think, feel, in earlier civilizations? These questions must be treated briefly and sketchily in synthetic texts whose authors describe, in a few pages, such vast topics as the civilization of Egypt through 20 dynasties and 2,000 years: the Mediterranean world under Roman rule during a half-millenium; the

1

varieties and complexities of European experience during the age of the French Revolution. History instructors use a variety of supplementary materials — interpretive essays, biographies, sources, "problems" — to give their students a deeper understanding of the past. These essays have a similar objective: to enrich the reader's understanding of mankind's historical development by focusing upon discrete communities within the span of a lifetime or a generation.

The strong interest in social history — in the collective lives of our ancestors — represents a significant shift from the dominant concerns of historians and their audiences during the 19th and early 20th centuries. Prior to World War II, historians in America and Europe were most concerned with politics and with the men who governed politics. Written history had a distinctly elitist flavor; it was intensely concerned with great men and great events. But in recent years, historians have tended to concentrate more upon the experience of groups instead of individuals, and to explore a broader range of problems concerning these groups: the history of the family, for example; of peasants; of the urban poor; of slaves. This shift in historical perspective from politics and elites to "masses" is due to several factors. Historians have become more aware of the significance of group experience and of the forces, particularly the material ones, that shape that experience. Moreover, the current generation of historians is more widely read in, and more sympathetic to, related disciplines: geography, sociology, anthropology, and economics. They have studied Durkheim and Weber, Malinowski and Evans Pritchard; they have used methodological tools expropriated from these social science disciplines — for example, computers — to explore historical terrains. And finally, teaching historians have become more concerned with problems of social history because their students have evinced a strong interest in these issues. To a greater degree than ever before, their interest in the past is conditioned by their sense of its relevance for their own problems, personal and social.

The choice of topics for these volumes has been influenced, first, by the availability of sources; and second, by the historical value of the subject, as a microcosm which illuminates the larger cultural world to which it belongs. The survival of significant collections of sources has dictated the selection of several essays in the first volume; for example, that of Nineveh as an archetypal community of the Near Eastern world; and Karanis, a town in Roman Egypt whose society can be recreated from the papyri which have been dug up *from the sands of the Nile. As we move forward in time, historical sources become more abundant, and the choices more difficult. Some topics—imperial Rome, for example—seemed too large to be treated adequately within this format. The majority of these essays focus upon urban societies, although two chapters are devoted to rural communities: in England about 1300 A.D., and in France four centuries later. The authors of some essays have focused upon individuals, not prominent historical figures (except the earl of Essex) but obscure men and women like the Carolingian peasant Bodo, whose life Eileen Power described with such empathy and sensitivity in her* Medieval People *(1924).*

The first volume of essays embraces a time span of two millenia, from about 700 B.C. to the end of the 16th century after Christ. Three chapters are devoted to the ancient world of the Near East, of Greece and Rome; the last four essays explore European societies during the Middle Ages and the Renaissance. The Assyrian city of Nineveh, which figures prominently in the Old Testament book of Jonah, is the subject of the first essay. The Greek world is represented by Athens, during and after the Peloponnesian War (429–404 B.C.). The Roman world is portrayed, not by the capital city (an enormous and intractable subject) but by Karanis, a small rural community in Egypt, in the second century A.D. Seventh century Toledo is the subject of the next essay: a case study in the confrontation of classical and barbarian cultures, in the western regions of the Roman world. The preponderantly rural character of life during the medieval centuries is illustrated by the chapter devoted to an English peasant community—Cuxham in Oxfordshire—in the 13th and 14th centuries. This agrarian world produced the food surpluses and raw materials which fueled the growth of towns throughout western and central Europe. One of the most renowned of these urban centers was Florence, the Renaissance city par excellence, *and the subject of the penultimate essay in the first volume. The last chapter is devoted to the life of an English nobleman, the earl of Essex, whose career illustrates the pervasive importance of the nobility in the society of early modern Europe.*

The essays in the second volume of this collection examine discrete European societies during the last three centuries. This is the age of the great revolutions which have radically transformed European—and world—history. The essays are all concerned with one or another aspect of that process of "modernization," which has culminated in the urbanized, industrialized, "mass" society in which we now live.

The first essay establishes the background for these momentous changes: it describes a traditional, almost static, society in and around Beauvais, a town in northern France in the late 17th and early 18th centuries. A century later, that very traditional society was convulsed by the French Revolution; the second essay examines Paris between 1789 and 1796: from the beginnings of the Revolution through the Terror to the establishment of the Directory. Industrialization is the theme of the next chapter: an analysis of economic and social change in Sheffield, a major center of the iron and steel industry in 19th-century England. The essay on 19th-century London examines a distinctive feature of the contemporary world: the emergence of the metropolis. Industrialization and urbanization wrought great changes everywhere in 19th-century Europe, but in no country were these developments more disruptive of the traditional society than in Russia. The chapter on industrial workers in Moscow and St. Petersburg examines the changes in life-styles and mentalities of peasants who had left their rural villages to work in the factories of those cities. The next chapter on Milan ends with the rise of Fascism, a distinctly Italian response to the problems which modernization and war had posed for every European society that had been involved in the holocaust of 1914–18. That theme is also the subject of the final chapter, which is focused upon the Ruhr valley, one of the most highly industrialized regions in Europe, in the years after World War I which culminated in Adolf Hitler's rise to power in Germany.

Chapter 1

*I*n history textbooks written a generation or more ago, the critical moment in Europe's transition from the medieval to the modern age occurred around the year 1500. In the last decade of the 15th century, in 1492 and 1494 respectively, Columbus had discovered the New World, and Vasco da Gama had sailed around southern Africa to India, thus opening up the age of European discovery and colonization. In 1494, a French army had crossed the Alps to conquer the Kingdom of Naples, an event which inaugurated a new era of European political history, in which powerful and dynamic states competed with each other for the hegemony of Europe. Those voyages—and the armies organized and led by kings—were subsidized by European financiers and merchants, who were prepared to exploit the new opportunities for market and wealth opened up by the explorers in Asia and the Americas. This "Renaissance" age was also a time of momentous change in patterns of thought and belief. Humanist scholars had rediscovered classical antiquity, and had found in that past age a deep concern with man's life in this world (as contrasted with the medieval preoccupation with salvation and the life hereafter), that appealed to their minds and senses. Finally, the early years of the 16th century witnessed the outbreak of the Reformation that shattered the religious unity of Europe and inaugurated an age of confessional diversity and cultural ferment.

Two key concepts, growth and progress, underlie this traditional

5

scheme for describing and explaining Europe's historical development since the 16th century. *Growth* and *expansion* were perceived as characterizing every phase of European life, from population and the volume of trade to literacy and cultural activity. In response to demographic expansion, agricultural productivity increased, and so did commerce and industry. To control their territories, often enlarged by conquest, and their populations more effectively, governments increased the size of their bureaucracies and armies, and consequently, the taxes which they levied on their subjects. To the fact of *growth* was linked, in this traditional interpretation, the idea of *progress*. Not only did Europe become larger (in a demographic sense), richer, and more powerful, but she developed a more complex social and political order, and above all, a more sophisticated culture. The most distinguishing feature of that culture was its secular orientation and, particularly its scientific interest, as reflected in the discoveries and achievements of Copernicus and Galileo, of Descartes and Newton, of Vesalius and Harvey. The culmination of this continuous trend of growth and progress was the civilization that achieved maturity in the 19th century, when Europe dominated the globe with her military and economic power, and when her technology enabled her people to maintain that supremacy, and to provide them with a standard of living unprecedented in human history.

This image of Europe, as following an uninterrupted path toward ever greater wealth, prosperity, and power, does not satisfy contemporary scholars, who are more inclined to stress the difficulties and the pitfalls, the "crisis," that characterized the history of this civilization as it passed from its "medieval" to its "modern" phase. The centuries after 1500 were not an age of uninterrupted growth and prosperity, nor one in which men were better able to control their lives and their environment, than their ancestors had done. The generations of men who lived in the early modern period, between 1500 and 1800, were as conscious of breakdown and failure — of their societies and economies, of their governments and their systems of belief — as they were of advance and progress. Instead of looking forward to a future bright with hope, they were more inclined — at least before the 18th century — to look back with nostalgia to a golden age of the past, when life was less hazardous, more pleasant and serene.

This mood of pessimism was particularly intense and widespread during the 17th century, and for good reasons. The 1600s were truly years of crisis. Europe's population, which had grown rapidly since the late 15th century, stabilized by 1650 and even declined in some areas, as a consequence of plagues and famines, of the ravages of war, of economic dislocation. Epidemics of bubonic plague periodically swept through European cities and villages, killing thousands of inhabitants who had no defense against this terrible disease. The population of Mediterranean regions—Italy, southern France, the Italian peninsula—fell by as much as one fourth in the first half of the 17th century. Between 1618 and 1648, Central Europe was devastated by the armies of Catholic and Protestant princes during the Thirty Years' War, contributing to a sharp decline in that region's population and productivity. Europe was still, in the 17th century, predominantly a society of peasants who gained a precarious living from cultivating the land, and who were particularly vulnerable to the economic vicissitudes of these years. The rural poor were the first to suffer, and often to die, in times of famine, plague, and unemployment; they were overworked and malnourished, and they had no monetary reserves to tide them over the bad times. Even under optimum conditions, when crops were bountiful and grain prices low, the landlord, the tithe collector, and the tax official took a substantial portion of the peasants' income.

The dramatic manifestations of this crisis were the revolutions which broke out in this century, and particularly during the middle decades, in the 1640s and 1650s. These upheavals were of varying magnitude and significance, in most instances of only local scope and short duration, but occasionally—as in England—spreading to an entire country or region. Peasant rebellions, inspired by opposition to tax burdens, occurred frequently in southern and western France. Urban revolts were less common but not unknown, the most significant being the uprisings in Palermo (in Sicily) and in Naples in the 1640s. Earlier in that decade, in 1640, the province of Catalonia in Spain had revolted unsuccessfully against its monarch, while to the west, the Portuguese were able to achieve their independence against the Spanish crown. In France, a revolt (called the Fronde) of dissident nobles and officials against the monarchy broke out in 1648, upon the death of King Louis XIII. After some initial successes, this challenge to the monarchy was crushed, and France under King Louis XIV became the model of royal absolutism in Europe. In England, resistance to the crown had a very different outcome. Civil war broke out in 1642 between King Charles I and a group of parliamentary and Puritan opponents. The royal armies were defeated in battle; the king was beheaded in 1649; and for a decade England was governed by Oliver Cromwell and his associates. The restoration of the monarchy in 1660 brought a measure of peace to that troubled realm.

If there is a common denominator in these upheavals of this "century of discontent," it is the feeling shared by the rebels and dissidents that their rights had been violated, and their status threatened, by those who governed them. This sentiment inspired the rebellious French peasants who attacked the officials sent by the crown to collect new or heavier taxes; it also motivated the judges of the French courts (parlements) who feared that the absolutist monarchy was intent upon limiting if not destroying their authority, and their rank. Everywhere in Europe, so it seems, men felt threatened: by events which they could not control, by the concentration of power in the hands of distant rulers whose orders seemed arbitrary and capricious. And in their responses to these fears, men were very conservative. They fought to preserve the traditional order of things, the familiar systems and routines. This pervasive conservatism helps to explain why change—whether economic or political or intellectual—was so slow and gradual and so bitterly resisted, in the 17th century. Men looked backward, not forward, for comfort and security; they had learned not to harbor extravagant hopes for the future.

These generalizations about European experience in the 17th century are of only limited value and applicability, since the conditions of life varied so greatly from district to district, and from decade to decade. While (for example) a formerly rich and productive region around the German city of Magdeburg was desolated by the ravages of the Thirty Years' War, the Dutch province of Holland enjoyed an unprecedented boom in these years. Dutch merchants and shippers expanded their activities over the entire globe, and amassed huge profits from their business enterprises. The growth of commerce, and of the cities that organized and promoted trade, also stimulated Dutch manufacturing and agriculture. The economic balance of power shifted decisively in this century from the Mediterranean to the areas in northwestern Europe adjacent to the North Sea, and particularly Holland and England. By 1700 the Mediterranean had become an economic backwater while in the north, the foundations were being laid for the economic and social revolution that would transform the face of Europe.

At some point between these extremes of stagnation and dynamic growth was the kingdom of France, the largest and most populous state in Europe in the 17th century. Within the boundaries of that kingdom, some 20 million Frenchmen lived and worked. Since the age of Charlemagne (d. 814 A.D.), this rich and populous region had played a key role in European history: as conqueror and colonizer of neighboring lands and peoples; as creator and exporter of economic, social, and political institutions (for example, feudalism); and of cultural forms (for example, scholasticism and Gothic architecture). During the 17th century, and particularly during the long reign of King Louis XIV (1648–1715), French power and influence in Europe was at its height. The visible symbol of this monarchy was the royal palace at Versailles, a grandiose and resplendent structure built at great cost to house the royal family, and the courtiers and nobles who flocked to this court. The cost of building and maintaining this huge monument to royal power, and the hierarchial social order of which it was a part, was borne by millions of French peasants. The quality of their life, so different from that enjoyed by their masters at Versailles, is described in this chapter on Beauvais and its rural hinterland.

Chapter

1

A French Peasant Community in the Old Regime

*GERALD CAVANAUGH**

PEASANTS AND SOCIETY: SOME GENERAL VIEWS

In that delightfully irreverent survey of English history, *1066 And All That*, the authors offer a digression entitled "The Peasants Revolt" in which they conclude that, among other things, "The Pheasants' Revolts were . . . purely educational movements and were thus easily suppressed."[1] The pheasants-peasants, thus briefly mentioned and quickly disposed of, then fade from the pages of history. As satirical as this account is, it bears a clear resemblance to the actual treatment rendered peasants in historical writing. Although historians have long held that throughout the period from 1500 to 1850 in western Europe the great social questions centered on the peasant or agrarian problem, not much of their attention has been directed to the peasants, their unique problems, and the role they have played in history. This state of neglect is now clearly past. In recent years the peasantry has emerged as a proper subject for historical research and the literature concerning the peasant world has expanded enormously.

The present essay is in every sense of the word introductory to that subject, with special reference to 17th- and 18th-century France. It is designed to acquaint undergraduate readers and other students with the historical realities of peasant society and to illuminate the peasant situation by focusing on one representative French peasant community in the old regime. We must expressly note that the vast majority of

---

* Formerly of the University of California, Berkeley.

people in preindustrial France (and Europe) were peasants. How these people lived, what they ate, how they dressed, what they believed, what they thought of their society whose economic basis they provided, are all subjects of intrinsic interest, the moreso as they are reflections of a world now alien to us—"The world we have lost," as one historian describes it.[2] Indeed, few of us today know much about farmers to say nothing of peasants, although recent crises in world food supply have reminded us of our continuing dependency on the soil and its products. In the old regime no reminders were necessary. The clear numerical and economic preponderance of the peasantry entailed political and social, and thus historical consequences. As noted above, the basic social and economic problems of preindustrial Europe were agrarian in nature. Historians now accept that the study of peasant society is prerequisite to any understanding of what we call the "old regime." This holds especially true for the old regime in France.

Seventeenth- and 18th-century France was a complex social entity: monarchical, hierarchical, corporate, and Catholic. It was also, and primarily, a nation of peasants who in 1700 constituted at least 15 million of the nation's approximately 20 million inhabitants. This peasant population was the very foundation of the French state and society. They produced through their labors most of the wealth of the kingdom, in the form of foodstuffs, wine, textiles, and building materials. They cultivated the land under an archaic and vastly complicated system of land tenure and by means of an ancient and inadequate technology. They were, by and large, victims of a cruel paradox: the primary producers of cereal grains, they were yet constantly threatened by a shortage or even lack of bread. Why this should be so is a matter to which we shall return.

The French peasant world in the old regime was a complex entity about which it is hazardous to generalize. "La France" writes one historian, "c'est diversité." Climatic, geographic, and, broadly speaking, historical differences led to variations in the pattern of peasant life: throughout the old regime peasants of, say, the Vendée, in the west of France are clearly differentiable from, for example, peasants of the Nord, in northeastern France. Nevertheless, allowance once made for variations, we may perceive an essential similarity both in the peasant social structure and in the general course of the rural history of France before the Revolution. The undeniable regional-historical differences in the French peasant world may legitimately be seen as variations on a single sociological and technological theme.

In their studies of contemporary peasant societies anthropologists have helped historians to perceive this unity in diversity and they have provided conceptual and theoretical formulations that form the basis for our definition of the peasant. "Peasants," wrote Arthur Kroeber,

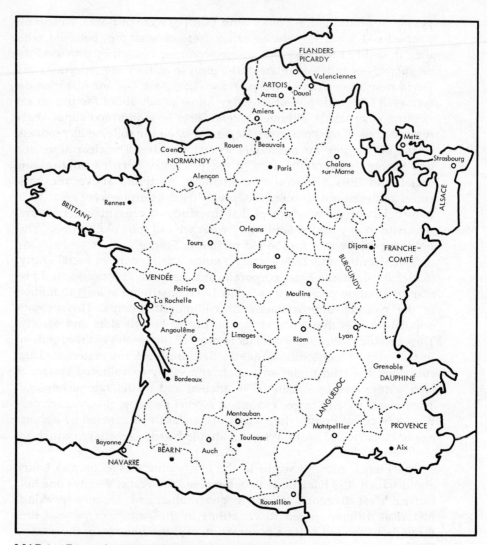

MAP 1. France in 1700: Administrative districts.

"constitute part societies with part cultures. . . . Peasants are definitely rural—yet live in relation to market towns; they form a class segment of a larger population which usually contains also urban centers. . . . They lack the isolation, the political autonomy, and the self-sufficiency of tribal populations; but their local units retain much of their old identity, integration, and attachment to soil and [religious] cults." Kroeber's formulation includes the elements basic to any definition of the peasants but it has been refined and extended by other anthropologists. Thus, Eric Wolf notes that "it is the crystallization of executive power which serves to distinguish the primitive from the civilized, rather than whether or not such power controls are located in one kind of place or another." The state, not the city, Wolf writes, is essential to the definition of a civilization. With the appearance of the state, food cultivators make the transition to peasants. Thus (Wolf continues), "it is only when the cultivator becomes subject to the demands and sanctions of power-holders outside his social stratum—that we can appropriately speak of peasantry." As we shall see, the peasants' special relationship to the French state, especially in terms of the state's fiscal demands, was a primary concern of royal officials.

A further refinement of the Kroeber definition is offered by George M. Foster:

> Like most anthropologists, we agree that peasants are primarily agriculturalists, but we also believe that the criteria of definition must be structural and relational rather than occupational. For in most peasant societies, significant numbers of people earn their livings from nonagricultural occupations. It is not *what* peasants produce that is significant; it is *how* and *to whom* they dispose of what they produce that counts. When settled rural peoples subject to the jural control of outsiders exchange a part of what they produce for items they cannot themselves make, in a market setting transcending local transactions, then they are peasants. We see peasants as a peripheral but essential part of civilizations, producing the food that makes urban life possible, supporting (and subject to) the specialized classes of political and religious rulers and the other members of the educated elite. This elite carries what Redfield called the "Great Tradition," which gives continuity and substance to the sequences of advanced culture, and which lies in contradistinction to the "Little Tradition"—which characterizes villagers themselves.[3]

Historians have evolved or adopted essentially the same definitions and have distinguished the same general features for peasant societies in old regime France. The peasants lived in subordinate and usually passive relationship both to the state with its bureaucratic apparatus and to the cities with their juridical and market imperatives. Everywhere in France, peasants produced the material wealth essential for the maintenance of urban society. Everywhere, the peasants were "conservative," clinging tenaciously and with good reason, as we shall see, to their customary ways, lagging behind developments in the world of the "Great Tradition," maintaining their "Little Tradition," their "part culture" with little change over the centuries. And everywhere, the peasants were despised (and feared) by the city dwellers: "Jacques Bonhomme has a strong back and will bear anything," went the French saying. The essayist, La Bruyère, more sympathetically described his peasant compatriots:

We see certain ferocious animals, male and female, swarming over the countryside. They are ghastly, burned black by the sun; they cling to the soil, at which they doggedly scratch and dig. They can speak, and when they stand up, they appear human, and indeed they are human. At night they slink into their dens for their meals of black bread, water, and roots. They spare other men the pain of sowing, cultivating, and harvesting: for this, they surely should not lack the bread they themselves have made. (*Les Caractères ou les Moeurs de ce siècle*, "De l'homme," 128).

La Bruyère's concern was not shared by most of his contemporaries. The peasants continued to be reviled and then ignored, except for purposes of exploitation.

LIVING CONDITIONS OF THE PEASANTRY

The plight of the peasants and the effects of their traditional and complex relationship to the land and to the larger society comprised the so-called agrarian problem of old regime France. It was a problem which taxed the ingenuity and vexed the patience of Louis XIV's ministers. Their attempts to master it or at least to ameliorate its effects constitute a great part of the administrative and social history of "the splendid century," indeed of the whole of the 17th and 18th centuries and beyond. So complicated and refractory was the agrarian problem that not even the French Revolution could find or force a solution to it.[4]

Despite the regional and local diversity which characterized agrarian France in the old regime, two generalizations may be offered: (1) almost all peasants owned at least some land and (2) almost all peasants owned insufficient land to feed their families and were impoverished. This second fact largely explains the paradoxical situation of most of the peasants, the producers of grain, being chronically threatened by a shortage of bread. As for landownership itself, only a small proportion of peasants possessed land in absolute right, free from any seigneurial claims (*franc-alleu*), but in most cases proprietory arrangements were both extraordinarily complex and preclusive of absolute possession. Even so, the reality of "possession" is undeniable. This meant, in fact, that such peasants "owned" their land but in law and custom owed dues, fees, and services to the *seigneur* who retained, if only in theory, rights of "eminent domain," that is to say the seigneur could take back the land if he properly compensated the peasant proprietor. Legal conflicts involving these peasants thus rarely touched upon proprietorship but rather upon the payments due the seigneur.

Since most peasants did not own enough land to support themselves they entered upon engagements to work farms belonging to greater landowners, whether richer peasants, absentee bourgeois and noble seigneurs, or the Church. They had no property rights at all to the land they thus worked and in most cases they enjoyed only a precarious tenure, strictly regulated and with a clearly-defined time limit. Some of these peasants might earn a decent income from their leased lands but in general it was the *propriètaire* who profited. All of these proprietary and leaseholding arrangements varied from place to place throughout France. In Normandy, Picardy, and the Paris basin, large farms, *la grande culture*, predominated and the great landowners there took an active role in the management of their estates. This agriculture was "commercial," intimately involved in market transactions and characterized by extensive "bourgeois," that is, urban, ownership which made much use of *laboureur-fermiers* as stewards and of day laborers to work the land. Most of France, however, consisted of *la petite culture*, areas of unenclosed land divided into innumerable small plots subject to the enormous variety of leasehold and proprietary arrangements noted above. What seems clear, however, is that for most peasants the idea of "tenure," under whatever arrangements, was more compelling in the *ancien régime* than the idea of "propriété," simply because most peasants owned far less land than they rented or leased.

It has been calculated that to attain self-sufficiency, a peasant growing grain required 30 acres of land in good harvest years and 65 acres in bad years. Very few peasants owned such large plots of land. Pierre Goubert notes that in the Beauvaisis area, at which we shall soon look more closely, only about 10 percent of the peasantry were self-sufficient; the remaining 90 percent had far less than the necessary amount of land. Peasants who engaged in the cultivation of grapes (viticulture) could be economically independent, if the market were favorable, with as few as eight acres of land but even with this limited acreage only a minority of the peasantry attained autonomy. Those who were not self-sufficient exploited numerous ways to raise extra income: when they could, they leased land from other landowners; they worked as woodsmen, cutting down trees and selling the lumber; they did day labor on the bigger farms; they served as drovers or carters, transporting livestock or goods to neighboring towns; they worked in the rural textile cottage industry, if it were available, as in the environs of Beauvais; or as casual laborers in river or sea ports, if they were close by; they migrated seasonally to cities where work was available; they became poachers or smugglers, both respectable trades among peasants who were forbidden to hunt and who had to pay exorbitant taxes on necessary commodities; they engaged in petty theft, or turned to begging. They found some relief in these expedients but never enough to keep themselves out of debt.[5] This pattern appears to have obtained throughout most of France. The "profile" of the rural social structure thus reveals not a pyramid but rather a rectangle enclosing a stratified mass of more or less poor peasants, with a small outcropping at the top representing those few well-off *fermiers* and *laboureurs*. As noted above, this meant in effect that most peasants, although they produced the grains, had to buy most of their bread: they lived, as Pierre Goubert writes, "with one eye fixed on the price of bread."

And bread was their staff of life. It constituted the great bulk of the peasants' diet which was characterized by the predominance of starches from cereal grains, a rarity of protein foods, and a deficiency of vitamins. Meat was rarely eaten because most peasants did not own enough cows, pigs, or chickens to make them a part of their normal diet. In his well-researched "Projet de Capitation," (1700) the great Marshal Vauban justified a rather heavy tax on livestock because "in the countryside only the well-off farmers have livestock." Milk, butter, cheese, and eggs were thus for most peasants luxuries; the commonest vegetables were turnips, beans, peas, lentils, and onions, with cabbages to be found in some few provinces. Parsley and cicely were the only condiments in general use. Vauban describes the monotonous diet and poor nutrition of the inhabitants of one area he studied closely:

> All among those called *bas peuple* eat only bread made of mixed barley and oats from which they do not even remove the bran — this bread may be lifted from the table by grasping the oat chaff mixed into the bread and extending through the crust. The people also eat some fruit, most of it very poor in quality and growing wild; they sometimes have a vegetable from their gardens, cooked in water with a little rapeseed or walnut oil, without or with just a pinch of salt. Only the well-off eat rye bread mixed with barley and wheat.
> The wines here are mediocre and . . . the common people rarely drink them, nor do they eat meat more than three times a year. They use salt rarely. . . . It is not surprising then that people so badly nourished have so little physical strength and endurance. Furthermore, their strength is sapped by the elements since they are ill-clad, three-fourths of them being dressed, winter and summer, in torn and ragged rough linen and shod in wooden shoes with stockings. Those few who have leather shoes wear them only on Sundays and holidays. . . .
> It is impossible to push the limits of misery further and, as we might expect, the consequences are grave. In the first place, the people are rendered weak and sickly, especially infants, many of whom die for lack of proper nourishment. Second, the men are sluggish and discouraged. . . . Third, such conditions breed liars, thieves, men of bad faith, always ready to bear false witness provided they are paid, always ready to get drunk as soon as they have the money: voilá, the character of le Bas-peuple who, I remind you, constitute seven-eighths of the population. ("*Description géographic de l'élection de Vezelay.*")

Vauban was describing the people of a rather poor area, but his report accords well with the picture drawn by modern scholarship of peasant life throughout France.

The world of the French peasant was "une Arcadie besogneuse," a depressed rural slum, we today might say. Average life expectancy among the peasants (and their urban cousins) probably did not exceed 27 years. One out of every four babies born died before the age of one year; two out of every four died before reaching puberty. The following tables document what was by no means untypical of life expectancy and infant mortality in the old regime; the information on Louis XIV's family indicates how impotent in the face of disease were even the richest families.

In such a situation a man of 43 years was regarded as a dotard, a "barbon," and a woman of that age was considered very old. The population was at the same time very fecund and very fragile, never or rarely limiting conception by artificial means. Peasant mothers breastfed their infants and this practice tends to suppress ovulation and thus reduce the chance of conception. Chronic malnutrition and actual shortages of food reduced fertility periodically. The death of one parent—a not un-

Infant Mortality in the Old Regime

The Faburel family
(Drawn from the parish register of population,
Le Coudray–Saint-Germer)

Madeleine	born in May, 1673 died in June, 1674
Jean	born in October 1674 died in October 1674
Marie	born in September, 1675 died in September, 1675
Catherine	born in February, 1677 died in January, 1680
Jean	born in February, 1679 died in January, 1680
Marie and Louise	born in January, 1681 died in January and February, 1681
Marie	born in October, 1682
Laurent	born in September, 1685
Jean	born in October, 1689

The children of Louis XIV

1. Boy — born 1661 — lived to maturity
2. Girl — born 1662 — lived six weeks
3. Girl — born 1664 — lived five weeks
4. Girl — born 1667 — lived five years
5. Boy — born 1668 — lived three years
6. Boy — born 1672 — lived five months

Louis XIV also fathered 11 "illegitimate" children of whom 7 died in infancy. Later in life he lost his only son, his grandson, and his elder great-grandson within the space of a few months.

Infant Mortality in the Beauvaisis (from the Parish Register of Auneuil)

I. Thomas and Antoinette Alepée: Married July 11, 1662

Name	Baptized	Deceased	Married
Marie......................	July 18, 1663	Dec. 13, 1663	
Anne	April 26, 1665		Aug. 6, 1701
Françoise.................	Sept. 9, 1667	March 2, 1733	July 17, 1691
Marie......................	May 26, 1669	Oct. 27, 1669	
Simon.....................	Feb. 18, 1671	Sept. 14, 1671	
Louis	March 15, 1675	Sept. 13, 1676	
Jean.......................	July 5, 1678	April 24, 1679	
Marguerite (I)	July 28, 1680	Dec. 31, 1748	Jan. 31, 1708
Marqueritte (II)	July 26, 1682	Oct. 6, 1784	Dec. 7, 1706
Antoinette	May 20, 1684	May 23, 1684	

II. Jean and Jeanne Gallot: Married May 17, 1718

Name	Baptized	Deceased	Married
Jean.......................	Jan. 1, 1720	Dec. 8, 1758	Jan. 14, 1755
Louis	Jan. 9, 1722		July 7, 1754
Marie-Jeanne	Nov. 28, 1723		Oct. 1, 1764
Pierre.....................	March 16, 1726	May 5, 1727	
Jean-Étienne	Dec. 27, 1728	Feb. 17, 1729	
Jacques	March 10, 1732		Jan. 10, 1758
Therèzé..................	Aug. 30, 1735	Sept. 13, 1735	
Françoise................	March 11, 1738		June 14, 1763

From Pierre Goubert, *Beauvais et le Beauvaisis*, pp. 83–84.

common event—interrupted the reproductive cycle; there were many more miscarriages, natural abortions, and stillbirths than in modernized countries today. Late marriages reduced the child-bearing range of potential mothers: a woman marrying for the first time at age 24, would in the course of her married life normally have two or three fewer pregnancies than an 18-year old bride. These factors kept the population stable. They were mightily assisted by the three great scourges of the common people: famine, plague, and war.

Famine years—and these were periodic, for example, 1629–30, 1636–37, 1648–51, 1660–62, 1693–94, 1709–10—were almost always accompanied by epidemics. Deprived of even their subsistence diet, the poor succumbed to plague, smallpox, and other diseases whose contagion was heightened by the movement of masses of peasants turned beggars (and sometimes brigands), driven across the countryside by their quest for food. Mortality was greatest among the very old, the infants, and young children. Those who survived the crisis experienced relatively better times until the next disastrous harvest, when a similar round of misfortunes would inevitably follow. "Just as the cemetery was in the center of the town," Pierre Goubert writes, "so death was in the midst of life." The peasants accepted their lot fatalistically. Buttressed by their religious faith, they passively contemplated death with a morose stubbornness that drove the few and ineffectual provincial doctors to distraction. It was a fatalism interspersed, however, by moments of blind, raging revolt. Living as they did, with constant fear of death and disease, exposed to the elements, chronically malnourished, experiencing brutishness as a daily condition and bearing a cruel burden of debts and taxes, peasants periodically cast off their passivity and rose up in revolt. Marc Bloch's view is particularly apt here: "Agrarian revolt is as natural to the seigneurial regime as strikes, let us say, are to large-scale capitalism." Typically foreshadowed by food shortages or by an outbreak of disease, or by both, exacerbated by heightened tensions generated by the sharpened struggle for subsistence, the peasant uprisings were most commonly directed against the royal tax collector, the tax farmers' agents, or the seigneurial steward. In the first half of the century there is evidence that nobles and even bourgeoisie directly participated in revolts against an intrusive royal government whose demands were seen as a threat to their own local power and influence. After 1660, however, such participation was a distinct rarity and after 1685, although conditions in the countryside worsened, peasant revolts themselves decreased in incidence and intensity of violence. Marshal Vauban, who was much concerned with the condition of the people, believed the peasants remained docile out of reverence for the king and fear of punishment. Historians, noting the improved instruments of social control—i.e., the army and mounted police—available to the monarch by that time, rather stress the latter quality: "Governmental repression (la terreur)," Pierre Clement writes, "prevented or crushed" these revolts. In any event, they accomplished little for the peasants. They might occasionally cast off their passivity but not until 1789 did they cast off their heavy social yoke. "Almost invariably doomed to defeat and eventual massacre," Marc Bloch has written, "the great insurrections were altogether too disorganized to achieve any lasting result." For the vast majority of peasants, La Bruyère's searing portrait, noted above, reflected only too accurately their actual state.

FISCAL BURDENS OF THE PEASANTRY

These natural calamities were aggravated, as La Bruyère implied, by social inequities. Having little or no economic margin as a buffer in hard times, the mass of the peasants were constantly and increasingly debt ridden. "The poor people (Vauban wrote) are crushed by the weight of the loans, in kind or in money, extended to them in their need by the rich who, though they call their loans "gifts" to evade the law, extort from them a usurious rate of interest . . . and who either keep them permanently in their debt or invoke the bailiff to strip them of their property. Many other vexations are inflicted on these poor people but I refrain from describing them, for fear of offending people." With no governmental mechanism to provide low cost short-term loans, the poorer peasants were forced to mortgage their tiny holdings whenever bad harvests or extraordinary expenses left them with too little to pay their taxes, tithes, and seigneurial dues. Nobles, ecclesiastics, and wealthier peasants all extended credit to, and quite regularly, foreclosed on the small peasant landholder. Such foreclosures did not necessarily drive peasants off the land. Sometimes they reduced the small peasants' holdings; sometimes they turned the small landholder into an agricultural day laborer; only occasionally did they entail the removal of peasants. The total area of land under cultivation might in some cases diminish but larger farms could more easily be assembled, common lands be reduced, and labor more cheaply be obtained. Urban creditors, however, were the main beneficiaries of this aspect of the rural economy. The bourgeoisie of the towns and cities which dotted the rural landscape viewed peasant and, indeed, noble financial difficulty as an investment opportunity. It was one that paid off. Bourgeois landholdings and bourgeois power and influence in the countryside were advancing in the last decades of the 17th century and they were to continue that advance throughout the 18th.

With all their debts, the peasants yet bore the heaviest burdens of royal taxation, church tithes, and seigneurial dues, as well as service in the army and the militia. The peasants, a contemporary observer noted, were "convinced that they will garner only the least and worst share of the fruits of their labor." He concluded that their apathy and alienation were products of a society and its economy which failed to provide returns sufficient to motivate them to improve their lot. The remarks of a modern sociologist, Barrington Moore Jr., on the peasantry and modernization are apt here: "For peasants living close to the margin of physical existence, modernization is clearly too risky, especially if under the prevailing social institutions the profit is likely to go to someone else. Hence an abysmally low standard of living and set of expectations is the only adjustment that makes sense under such circumstances." Such attitudes underlay what is usually derided as peasant "conservatism," that tenacious clinging to traditional ways. But properly to understand this conservatism requires an awareness of the psychological as well as the material environment of the peasant world. Opportunities to improve one's position were limited in most cases to the point of practical impossibility. All worldly "goods" — property, food, money, power, life itself—were seen as finite in quantity, always precariously enjoyed, and chronically in short supply. Deficient tools, plows, and scythes; insufficient draft animals; a lack of pastures which entailed a shortage of livestock and consequently a shortage of manure which in turn meant that potential pasture had to be cultivated in order to "rest" other cultivated land: all of these factors created a vicious circle which enveloped the peasants. The "image of the limited good" which anthropologists have isolated as a typically peasant world view[6] was one shared by the French peasants of the old regime. But this concept was not limited to peasants. The mercantilist theories of Colbert, Louis XIV's chief minister, also reflected the realities of peasant life: a static economic world in which men naturally assumed that one man's (or one nation's) gain was another's loss because, obviously, the world's goods were constant in amount and unexpandable. Mercantilist thought, in a real sense, is preindustrial, peasant economics writ large.

One of the major causes for the peasants' conviction that they could never improve their lot was the glaring inequity of the tax system, especially as it concerned the *taille*. This direct tax was the greatest of the fiscal burdens borne by the peasantry. Originally a seigneurial levy imposed by lords on serfs and leaseholders, by the 15th century it had become a permanent royal tax. Depending upon the region, the taille was levied either on the arbitrarily estimated wealth of the individual peasant or on the more rationally calculated value of the peasant's real property and harvest. In either case the problems of administering the tax were enormous. By the end of the 17th century, the taille (in one observer's words) "had fallen into such a state of corruption that the angels in heaven could neither correct its abuses nor prevent the poor from being oppressed by it."

The problems relative to the taille were extensive and tenacious. Both the assessment and the collection of the tax engendered inequities. Again, the situation and its concomitant level of inequity varied from place to place. Pierre Goubert finds, for example, that in the Beauvaisis the administration of the taille was not so abusive or discriminatory as contemporaries and later critics charged. Nevertheless, it seems clearly established that in general the heaviest burden fell on the poorest peasants, who constituted the great majority of the rural population. The "privileged" in French society—and this included ecclesiastics, wealthy bourgeois landowners, and well-off peasants (*coqs de paroisse*) as well as nobles—almost always escaped paying their fair share of taxes. The assessed amount in each parish or *élection* was made up by squeezing the lower peasantry. In those areas of France where the tax was levied on real property (*taille réelle*) the assessment was, in theory, more equitable than in areas of the *taille personnelle*. In the former case land and productivity surveys (*cadastres*) provided some basis for accurate assessment of income: those with property whose productivity was known could be taxed. Even then, however, the rich and the privileged avoided their proper share of the tax burden. In the first place noble land was not *taillable*. In the second place the cadastres on which the tax depended were generally ancient, poorly drawn, and misleading. In the absence of an effective government bureaucracy, fraudulent income reports were the rule. Although frauds were perpetrated by the poor landowners as well as the rich, the latter had much the better of the game.

In areas of the taille personnelle, the peasantry suffered even greater injustice. Without a cadastre, even the most imperfect one, an equal assessment of the tax was impossible. Here, too, nobles and other "privileged" were exempt from the taille. Locally elected or appointed assessors-collectors (*asséeurs collecteurs*) arbitrarily estimated the worth and income of their neighbors — taxpayers. Since the property holdings and agricultural productivity of the peasant were unknown to the assessors, the "person" of the taxpayer had to be assessed by whatever means available. This was what made the tax both *personnelle* and arbitrary. In most areas the assessment task was an unenviable one, since the assessor-collector was personally responsible to the crown for bringing in the tax money assessed of his parish, and it was the parish that was assessed, not the individuals in it. To save himself, the collector concentrated his efforts on his neighbors who were obviously productive and thus could pay. This tactic could only have deleterious results, driving the efficient farmers into fraud or decreased production. If his fellow taxpayers would not or could not pay their share, the collector had to advance the money. If he were ruined by or defaulted on this expenditure, the government constrained the principal inhabitants of the parish to pay the designated tax, even if they had already paid their share of the burden.

The responsibilities of the job were thus onerous and frightening. The estimates of income and the assessment of taxes put forth by the asséeurs collecteurs were influenced by self-interest and by the intervention of powerful individuals in the parish. "Nothing was easier for a collector," Esmonin has noted, "than to underestimate the property of a taillable friend in order to cut his taxes or to overvalue that of an enemy in order to overcharge him." As might be expected, "the poor and lower sort of people," in John Locke's words, bore the extra burden sloughed off by the well-placed.

The well-informed Marshal Vauban summarized the situation well:

> For a long time now people have perceived and complained that landed property renders a third less than it did 30 years ago especially in those areas of the *taille personnelle*. Few people, however, have taken the trouble to examine in depth the causes of this diminution which will be felt more and more unless the proper remedy is applied. Little study of the countryside is necessary to understand clearly that the *taille* is one of

the causes of our difficulties. Not that it is always too high a tax but rather because it is assessed disproportionately, not only in bulk, from parish to parish but even from individual to individual. In a word, the *taille* has become arbitrary, having no proportion to the property of the individual. The tax moreover is extracted harshly and at such great cost that a quarter of the receipts are eaten up. It is even customary to push the collection of the levy to the extent of taking down the doors of houses after having sold off the fixtures inside. I have seen collectors demolish homes to get the beams, joists, and planks which, to levy the *taille*, were then sold, and at five or six times less than they were worth.

It may seem unduly harsh as well as uneconomical so to extract a pittance from the poor, but Vauban's testimony is corroborated by other observers. So too is his description of the social and political biases which operated in the fiscal administration. As he writes:

The authority of powerful and respected persons often moderates the imposition on one or several parishes, so that their taxes are below the just amount. Consequently other neighboring parishes are overcharged. This is an inveterate abuse not easy to remedy. These powerful individuals are rewarded for their protection. Their lands and those of their relatives and friends are increased in value by the exemption from the *taille*. It is common to see a farm of three to four thousand *livres* income assessed for only forty or fifty *livres* while another of four to five hundred *livres* income will pay one hundred or even more; the result is that land remains uncultivated [for fear of the confiscatory tax].

Vauban concludes with an analysis of why the peasants will not bestir themselves to improve their lot. Hard work, thrift, innovation, and reinvestment of any surplus are foolhardy because they are totally unremunerative as the system works:

It is the same whether between relatively well off farmers (*laboureurs*) or between poorer peasants (*paisans*): the stronger oppresses the weaker. Things are reduced to such a state that those who could use their talents in many skills or trades to improve their own and their family's style of life prefer to do nothing; those who could care for one or two cows, and some sheep or lambs, with which they might improve their farms, are obliged to deny themselves the chance in order not to be overwhelmed by the *taille* the next year when the collector sees that they have increased their livestock or improved their yield. It is for this reason that a man and his family not only live very poorly, going almost naked and consuming very little, but further that they neglect their land, working it at half its potential, for fear that if it yielded what it could, being cultivated and fertilized, it would only serve as the occasion to double their *taille*. It is thus manifest that the primary cause of the depression in property values is the deficiency of cultivation and this deficiency derives from the manner of imposing and collecting the *taille*. (*Projet d'une dixme royale.*)

Barrington Moore, Jr., echoes Vauban's conclusions when he observes, of the relationship in general of peasants to the state:

> What then did the government do for the peasant? Modern Western sociologists are perhaps too prone to dismiss as impossible the answer that it did practically nothing, which I suspect is the correct one. They reason that any institution which lasts a long time cannot be altogether harmful to those who live under it (which seems to me to fly in the face of huge masses of both historical and contemporary experience) and therefore undertake a rather desperate search for some "function" that the institution in question must perform. This is not the place to argue about methods or the way in which conscious and unconscious assumptions determine the questions raised in any scientific inquiry. Nevertheless it seems more realistic to assume that large masses of people, and especially peasants, simply accept the social system under which they live without concern about any balance of benefits and pains, certainly without the least thought of whether a better one might be possible, unless and until something happens to threaten and destroy their daily routine. Hence it is quite possible for them to accept a society of whose working they are no more than victims. (*Ibid.* p. 204.)

Such views are appropriate both to the peasants' usually passive acceptance of their lot and to their intermittent but furious revolts.

The heaviest fiscal burden, the taille, was not the only one borne by the peasants. In 1695, a new tax, the *capitation,* was added to the taille; in the 18th century the *vingtième* (5 percent) was to appear. These were direct taxes which in general only the peasants paid at their full rate. Indirect taxes, which fell on all consumers, completed the list of exactions levied by the royal government. The *gabelle,* a tax on salt weighed heavily on most peasants (though some areas of the kingdom were exempt) and was detested above all other taxes by those who were subject to it. The *aides,* sales taxes levied on playing cards, alcoholic beverages, and (in some areas) on bread and meat, were almost as unpopular as the gabelle. "They render consumption more expensive (Vauban wrote) and consequently lower it. In a word, this method of taxation hurts both the subsistence of men and the flow of commerce."

The tax collector and the army or militia recruiter were the only agents of the national government with whom the peasants ever came into contact. Life in the countryside centered on local affairs, local attachments. The parish and the seigneurie enveloped the peasant and defined his horizons. In this narrow compass, too, the mass of the peasants bore the cost of maintaining the social mechanism. Church tithes—*la dîme*—were usually levied on grain and vineyard harvests and less generally on livestock and on garden produce. All land—noble, ecclesiastical, and common—was subjected to the dîme. Again, however, nobles were able to obtain a much lower rate of assessment than did the commoners. The peasants themselves rarely paid as much as the 10 percent implied in the term. The rate varied from place to place and even within the same community. This meant that in some areas the dîme might be relatively light while in others it was one of the heaviest dues paid by the peasant. The *dîme ecclesiastique* was consequently the source of many complaints and provoked much contention. Since the Church's claim on the harvest had priority even over the taille, peasants could be caused great inconvenience in the gathering and disposition of their crops if the dîme collection were delayed. Still, although the dîme was unpopular among the peasants it appears they were willing to pay what they regarded as a just contribution toward the cost of maintaining the Church.

The Catholic Church was one of the most powerful institutions at the national level in France, "the eldest daughter of the Roman Church." With its own hierarchy, bureaucracy, tax and fiscal agencies, law courts, educational and charitable institutions, and sacramental powers it played a very important role in matters of state and society. At the local level its role and influence were even greater. The *curé*, the parish priest, was always numbered among the elite which led and governed rural society. Because of his superior education, his respectable revenues, and his control of the sacraments he naturally assumed a position of leadership among his peasant parishioners, especially if the seigneur was a nonresident, as many of them were. Living close to the soil himself, he could sympathize with both the plight and the aspirations of his flock. Curés are known to have led the peasants in violent resistance to government policies. They defended the common property of the village against seigneurial pretentions. They were influential in village affairs, having both the talent and time necessary for sustained involvement in administrative detail. They were the prime contact with the great world beyond the peasant community. But, as in all such cases, this position of power generated ambivalent feelings. As a receiver of the tithe, as exempt from the taille and vingtième, as a defender of ecclesiastical property and privileges, the curé was frequently at odds with his parishioners. Curés usually came from bourgeois or better-off peasant families and their social attitudes and economic actions reflected their backgrounds. It was not uncommon for curés to make small loans at interest, thus violating both common and canon law, and to strive to increase their personal and institutional property holdings, inevitably at the expense of the peasants. As Pierre de Saint-Jacob has noted: "In the eyes of his peasant parishioners, the village priest was a rich and privileged man."

Nevertheless, on balance the relationship between the curé and his parishioners appears to have been a good one. The parish church was the center of village social and political life. The bells of the parish church (and each parish prided itself on the distinctive sound of its church bells) summoned peasants to meetings of the village assembly; the curé customarily presided over such assemblies; and in most conflicts between the peasants and the seigneur or the royal bureaucracy the curé took the part of his parishioners. Even the dîme, the heaviest ecclesiastical tax, did not draw extraordinary hostility upon the curé for the peasants well knew that it was the hierarchy not the parish priest who benefited from it. The "grievance petitions" presented to the Estates-General in 1789 complain not so much of the dîme itself but rather of the inequities in its administration and of the diversion of the money so raised from its legitimate ecclesiastical purposes. This complaint was an old one in the 17th century.

What the peasantry protested most fiercely, however, were exactions uncompensated by any discernible benefits or services. The state might plead the cost of defense and administration; the Church provided services open and obvious to all the faithful. Not until the Turgot ministry in the 1770s did the central government's general attitude of unconcern toward the plight of the poor change. Turgot's plan of a national system of workshops for the unemployed, limited at it was, at least officially recognized the poor as victims of circumstances beyond their control and announced the government's responsibility to assist them. In the 17th century as Pierre Goubert notes, "the physical existence of their millions of subjects did not constitute one of the concerns of the king and his government." Until the second half of the 18th century when the State began to take some part in providing for "social services," hospitals, orphanages, foundling homes, organized charity, education, and whatever "culture" peasants acquired were all supported by the Church, along with its primary sacramental functions. The seigneurie, in contrast, too often took much from the peasants and reneged on its responsibilities to them.

THE SEIGNEURIE

The seigneurie was a complex social and spiritual organism rooted physically in the land. Seigneurs had originally been noble but by the 17th century the seigneurie, with all its rights and privileges, could be and very often was in the hands of commoners who had bought the land. There was no longer any strict connection between nobility, noble land, and the seigneurie. In 1695, for example, when the feudal levy, the arrière-ban, had been invoked to muster the provincial nobility into military service, complaints reached the king that most of the seigneurs who appeared for duty were poor and badly equipped, being "attorneys, notaries, barristers and other professionals" (that is, commoners), who had bought "petits fiefs." Ecclesiastical corporations — abbeys, monasteries — possessed seigneuries as well. The seigneur — noble, priest, or commoner — retained many useful and honorific rights which guaranteed his domination of both individuals and the community. Local justice was administered by the seigneur through his own agents. This juridical function was the heart of the seigneurial system and a source of great power: "The seigneurial judge," Abel Pointrineau writes, "by virtue of his police powers, controlled every aspect of social and economic life." It was also a source of income, derived from fees connected with the numerous lawsuits and regulatory matters which fell within the seigneurial jurisdiction. More directly, the seigneur received income from fees and dues that were his by right of contract or custom: a percentage of the selling price of land which changed hands within the seigneurie (*lods et ventes*); a share of the harvest of those who owned or leased seigneurial land (*champarts*); fees charged for the use of the seigneurial winepress, or oven, or flour mill (*banalités*); claims on the free labor of peasant tenants (*corvées*). The list of such rights is impressively long.

The honorific rights pertaining to the seigneurie were at least as highly valued as the monetary. The seigneurie symbolized local leadership; the seigneur, noble or common, derived unquestioned social power from the position. Precedence in public ceremonies, a choice pew in the parish church, distinctive garb, a monopoly on the conspicuous sword, the gratifications of social deference and public hommage all figured among the honorific rights accorded to the seigneur by law and custom. To be sure, these rights were not entirely without responsibilities. Seigneurs did fulfill a socially useful role that was sometimes thrust upon them, sometimes willingly undertaken. They did, on occasion, assist their peasants in bad times with credit and capital; they intervened when the royal *fisc* appeared too harsh in its exactions; they often adjudicated conflicts fairly in which they themselves had no interest. In general, however, the return to the peasants in services did not compensate for their burden of seigneurial rights, dues, and fees. In the 18th century, during the so-called seigneurial reaction, that return was to lessen while the burden grew. By 1789, in Georges Lefebvre's view, "For almost every peasant, to be free meant to be rid of the seigneur; freedom, equality — two words for the same thing that was the very essence of the Revolution."

Within the seigneurial jurisdiction, the peasant village — the *communauté villageoise*, the *communauté d'habitants* — formed the social basis of the countryside. The seigneurie was indeed an area of land but the village was even more closely defined territorially: "Every true peasant society," Saint-Jacob writes, "has its *finage*, its territory in which it is at home." In the village community the peasant, as it were, lived and moved and had his social being. The village was at once the clearly defined place of habitation and the mechanism which directed the exploitation of the adjoining finage: the land, forests, waterways, pastures, and common lands. Individualism was socially unacceptable and therefore, throughout most of the old regime, a rarity. The family, not the individual, constituted the social atom; community action, not individual action, was evoked at all times in response to the exigences of life. The village was organized to exploit as effectively as possible, within the context of immemorial custom, the resources of its territory. This meant that the individual family farm although privately owned, had to be worked in accordance with traditional village procedures. Any departures from tradition had to be approved by the village assembly. The village was also committed to the defense of its collective rights against the assaults of neighboring communities, the seigneur, the Church, and the State. The sense of peasant solidarity, fostered alike by village leaders and social mores, was strengthened by a clear awareness of a collective vulnerability to famine, plague, flood, fire, and other natural calamities. It was further enhanced by a reflex action against what Pointrineau describes as "the strange and dangerous world 'outside' where people spoke an unknown language and from which emanated only injunctions and demands."

Under the royal and seigneurial legal jurisdiction the community administered itself: it was the village assembly that symbolized the life of the group. The assembly regulated matters relative to the taille, to public works, and to all the myriad problems which affected the community. It levied taxes, contracted debts, and in general supervised the physical and spiritual life of the village. A rough democracy characterized the administrative and electoral procedures of the community but the village was far from being an ideal, egalitarian society. There was much family egoism, intense conflict over the distribution of fiscal burdens and social prestige, and deep suspicions and animosities between neighbors, within the village. From the seigneur, "premier habitant," down to the street beggars a social hierarchy was clearly observed, its extent and complexity varying according to the size and economic concerns of the village. In any case, the village leadership was a preserve of the wealthier members of the community. Although by the end of the 17th century we may discern a weakening of the ancient structures and attitudes which formed and oriented the peasant village, it remained a viable and vigorous corporate entity. In the 18th century, a great expansion of the capitalistic system of market relationships was to occur, pervading and transforming the traditional peasant economy. The vast expansion of viticulture is a signal example of this process. Wine production by definition is capitalistic in organization and the 18th century is *par excellence* the century of expanding viticulture. The demographic advances of the 18th century which created new and powerful pressures on the available land hastened the expansion of viticulture because the cash yield per acre-man-hour of such cultivation is from three to ten times as great as that from any other kind of farming or gardening. Viable smaller plots of land in grapes allowed the larger peasant population to survive, if but barely. These economic and demographic changes and their social effects were to erode the traditional values and institutions of the rural community.

But in the 17th and early 18th centuries, the system still worked and still evoked in its members affection and passionate loyalties. Within this peasant world of seigneurie, parish, and village, the labors necessary for the support of the other groups in French society — the church, the nobility, the bourgeoisie — and to the maintenance of French predominance in Europe were accomplished. Despite the enormous social inequities and technical inadequacies they suffered, the French peasantry produced practically every year a surplus of agricultural products. French wines, grains, salt, meat, and leather goods (and, increasingly, French textiles woven primarily by peasants engaged in rural industry) were sold everywhere in Europe. The stubbornly pursued labor of the peasant masses joined to the natural productivity of the soil provided wealth enough for France to seduce her monarch into dreams of European hegemony. But that wealth was produced at great social cost: those whose labors provided for all citizens benefited the least.

Nevertheless, dysfunctional (to use the modern term) as the system no doubt was, it worked. We may simply note that the population of France, whose total area expanded only slightly, increased from about 20 million in 1700 to about 27 million in 1789. The existing archaic technology underwent no real improvement in the 18th century, as we shall see, and yet it sufficed to provide for those increased numbers. Famines and food shortages in the 17th century and perhaps more so in the 18th (given the rise of commodity speculation) were only rarely completely "natural" in origin: food was almost always available, but only to those who had money. The brilliant court of Louis XIV and the urban society of Enlightenment France was made possible by the taxes drawn from the peasants. It bears repeating that they got very little in return. But perhaps this is a conclusion forced upon us by our general perspective: it is time to look more closely into the matter, concentrating now on a specific community: Beauvais.

BEAUVAIS: HISTORY AND TOPOGRAPHY

As we shift our perspective from the general peasant situation to the more specific environment of Beauvais, we may be able more concretely to answer the question of "what was it like to have lived there and then?" We may be better able to grasp the social texture of men's lives, the political, religious, economic, psychological — in short, the old regime social context in which men and women lived. To gain a clearer appreciation of that social context as it impinged upon the Beauvaisiens is the purpose of this part of our chapter.

It must be emphasized at the start that Beauvais and its environs is not a "typical" old regime community. Rather, it exemplifies that frustrating but inescapable fact, always necessary to recall, that "France, c'est la diversité." Further, the town itself seems to be one entity, the countryside another. And yet, we must agree with the area's master historian, Pierre Goubert, that the town cannot be understood without reference to its surroundings, "which it vitalized and from which it drew life," nor can the countryside be understood without reference to the town, "to which the countryside gave so much, from which it received so little." A dual urban-rural perspective imposes itself upon us. I shall therefore attempt to present life in Beauvais as it might have been experienced by a wealthier, well-placed townsman, a bourgeois merchant. Such a type might be expected to have wider connections within his urban-rural community and a deeper awareness of events and developments around him. An "ideal-type" peasant being difficult to fashion, we shall have to adopt a more general approach to the countryside. This being said, we may now proceed with a description of the city and its hinterland.[7]

Beauvais and its environs (le Beauvaisis) comprised a finely articulated administrative, seigneurial, rural, industrial, commercial, and financial network. The town itself, about 45 miles northeast of Paris, about 60 miles from the Channel, was rather large by old regime standards, having a population of about 13,000: there were perhaps 20 towns in France larger than Beauvais. Like most towns of any importance in the old regime, Beauvais had gained exemption from the taille, the heaviest direct royal tax. This was a benefit to its wealthier citizens especially; the town did pay indirect taxes on articles of consumption: the aides and the gabelle. These were sales taxes, thus regressive and more onerous to the poor. The diocese of Beauvais included about 200 parishes and about 100,000 people: such, approximately, was the area and population of the Beauvaisis (see map and note). Between town and country ran numerous economic, fiscal, and social currents, most of which were generated by town needs and concerns, and were more beneficial to the town than to the country.

1. Cathedral of
   St. Pierre
2. Therain River
   and tributaries
3. Canals
4. Market place,
   pillory and
   town well
5. City hall
6. A cemetery
7. Vineyards
8. Gardens

MAP 2. Beauvais in the early 17th century

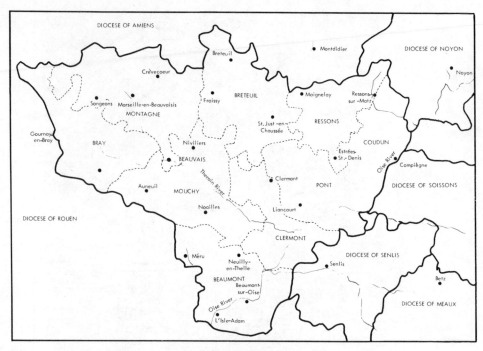

MAP 3.   Diocese of Beauvais and subdivisions

That town, home, and business center to our merchant-observer—
let us call him Gabriel Motte—was an ancient place. Prehistoric Celtic
dwellings once marked its site; ancient Romans had occupied it, built
it up, canalized and tamed the Thérain river. In the third century A.D.,
they put up the first of the many walls the town was to have. In the
sixth century, a Benedictine abbey was established in the town; in
the 11th century a market and sanctuary for Jews was added. By the
14th century the town had grown to its maximum area of about one
square kilometer. It was enclosed by walls that, frequently repaired and
improved at much expense to the community, were to define and
defend it into the 18th century. The river with its network of small
canals and locks provided both the town's water supply and its first
line of defense: until the border rectifications of the late 17th century,
Beauvais was a "frontier" town, always in danger of enemy incursions.
The Thérain river, it must be noted, was not navigable for commercial
purposes, an unusual situation in that large towns almost always enjoyed access to navigable rivers or to the sea. All efforts to improve the
waterway broke down because of a lack of money and because vested
interests opposed the improvement. The canons of the cathedral in

Beauvais, for example, owned all of the water mills in the town and any regularization of the river's course would have doomed their mills. They thus resisted all plans to render the Thérain navigable. Without a serviceable waterway, Beauvais and its hinterland was a relatively isolated area. There were roads connecting the various parishes and hamlets within the diocese, but they were generally in execrable condition and not suitable for the rapid movement of goods or even of news: there was no direct mail from Paris to Beauvais until 1738. Fewer than a dozen Beauvaisiens journeyed to Paris each year.

Within Beauvais' enclosed square kilometer lived over 11,000 people —another thousand lived in the three *faubourgs*, suburbs beyond the town's walls. Had our townsman, Gabriel Motte, taken the trouble to walk through Beauvais he might have noted that the only large plaza in the town covered two and a half acres of land; that there were 17 churches and a vast episcopal palace; 10 religious establishments, some with extensive grounds; 3 gardens whose produce was consumed by the bourgeois merchant companies; 6 cemeteries (just as in the midst of life there was death, Goubert notes, so in the center of towns there were cemeteries); several livestock yards; and 1 large open sewer. Altogether this meant that the population density of the town was close to 20,000 per square kilometer. Houses were generally of wood and thus open to infestation by rodents and insects. Most people's accommodations were tiny, crowded, and without adequate light and air to say nothing of plumbing: chamber pots provided essential services and water was drawn directly from the river system or from the few noisome wells. Beauvais had not one fountain and no really potable water. Stagnant pools and open sewers abounded. As might be expected, the poorer parishes of the town were the most crowded and insalubrious. The 12 parishes of Beauvais were distinguishable along economic lines. Two were wealthy: Saint-Sauveur, wherein the wealthiest bourgeoisie resided, and Basse-Oeuvre, wherein ecclesiastics and judicial officers lived. Five parishes were defined as poor, while the remaining five were without a dominant character.

M. Motte, however, rarely walked the streets of Beauvais: they were unpaved and thus either muddy or dusty and at night, dark: there were no street lights until 1765. In any case the streets were narrow and littered with refuse and excrement. The courts continually and vainly forbade Beauvaisiens "to throw, by day or night, excrement, filth, urine, and trash, into the streets." (Inns, cafés, and restaurants without toilets had to provide at least a "vessel" for their patrons' use, which receptacle had to be emptied into the river but once a week.) Chickens and pigs ran about in front of many houses rooting amidst the daily refuse cast out by butchers, fishmongers, and bakers. To this general atmosphere must be added the stench emanating from the town cemeteries. Graves were constantly being opened in order to make room for new burials. The largest cemetery was reorganized every 12 years, the smallest every year, the others every 3 or 4 years. Graves were shallow and in certain badly maintained cemeteries, dogs and rodents ran about and pigs foraged, while butchers' carts passed by at night with suspicious slowness. Even the wealthier classes complained of the stench and it is not surprising that when forced to enter the streets they held to their noses perfumed handkerchiefs or flowers (nosegays).

A more pleasant sensation excited the ears of Beauvaisiens. With its 12 parish churches, its cathedral chapters, monasteries, convents, abbeys, and houses of charity, all of whose religious duties and public commemorations were marked by the ringing of bells, Beauvais was "une ville sonnante," alive with the sound of its more than 135 great bells and its dozens of smaller chimes. These bells rang out from institutions which were supervised by almost 500 priests, monks, and nuns. This proportion of ecclesiastics to the general population was typical for an episcopal town in that area of old regime France. The Church, that is, Catholicism, was pervasive in the lives of all the people, rich and poor. In Beauvais as elsewhere in France, the Church registered baptisms, sanctified marriages, and defined through its calendar the days of work and of rest. Those Beauvaisiens who knew how to read and write learned their first lessons from priests who taught from the Bible and other sacred literature; those who were illiterate recognized and employed the sacred signs and symbols, the Cross, for example, and the Lamb of God. The parish curé maintained a careful watch over his parishioners' behavior; in time of need it was to the curé that the people applied for help. In normal times, the curé, the Church that is, could respond to their needs because ecclesiastical revenues were ample.

BEAUVAIS' SOCIAL STRUCTURE

The Bishop-Count of Beauvais was one of the few nobles in Beauvais, a notably "common" town. He was also the seigneur, the landlord of almost everyone in Beauvais. Throughout the Beauvaisis, ecclesiastical seigneuries predominated as well. This meant great income to the Church in rents, fees, and commodities. It meant also that the Bishop-Count and his fellow high churchmen were political and economic leaders of the town and diocese, not least because the Bishop-Count managed to purchase from the king certain secular offices which further strengthened his position. (Students should understand that in order to raise money the royal government *sold* public offices, e.g., "Inspector of Manufactures" and "Secretary to the King." Some of these offices conferred immediate and transmissible nobility upon the purchaser and his family. The whole system is known as "venality of office," and it lasted until the French Revolution swept it away.) The double dignity of the Bishop-Count, his noble status, which stood out sharply in "common" Beauvais, his ecclesiastical revenues, his directorship of the Hospital, the Foundling Home, and the Poor House (the so-called *Trois Corps*) assured him a dominant place in Beauvais society.

Gabriel Motte well knew that his Bishop-Count stood at the summit of Beauvais society and politics. Motte, a cloth merchant, belonged to the town's elite because Beauvais, in addition to being an episcopal seat, was also a commercial and cloth manufacturing center: almost one third of the population, for example, were weavers and their families. The cloth merchants dominated the town's economy and shared with the bishop its social and political leadership. Of the 3,000 families in Beauvais 300 were "bourgeoises." This was a "bourgeoisie" in fact, not in law, being simply the wealthiest commoners in the town. (The term "bourgeois" means literally a town dweller, one who enjoys the "rights of the city." In Beauvais any person, rich or poor, who managed to live in the town for one year automatically became a "bourgeois." The term, however, was used then and is so used here primarily with reference to the wealthier citizens.) About 60 of these bourgeois families were connected with royal, municipal, and ecclesiastical office. Some 150 families drew their incomes from family legacies, rents, and interest on loans and government bonds. The merchants comprised the remainder of this "bourgeoisie" — from 80 to 100 families. This group was the dynamic portion of the bourgeoisie, drawing its income primarily from the manufacture and sale of woolen cloth and linen fabrics. Beauvais and its environs produced each year ten times the amount of fabric that it consumed by itself, more than 300,000 pieces of wool and linen. The supervision of such production and of its transport to, and sale in, such markets as Paris, Lyons, and (in the 18th century) Spain and the Indies was the work of these merchants. They supervised almost all aspects of the production and distribution of the commodity that supported the town's economy. This meant that they collected the raw wool and linen from peasants and then distributed it to weavers in town and countryside. They gathered the finished cloth, woven to their specifications. They built and operated linen-bleaching works, and managed retail outlets and wholesale warehouses. They maintained national and international market connections. They had to overcome the execrable road system and to master the challenge of old regime weights and measures, the varying rates of monetary exchange, and the vicissitudes of both market and fashion imperatives. To the extent that they succeeded in all of these operations, the cloth trade and their families prospered.

But there was more to the bourgeois estate than the cloth trade. Such families, great and middling, also served as agents for the collection of the taille and tithe; they were merchants in grain, wood, and livestock as well as in cloth; they loaned money on the collateral of wages or bonds; they were discreetly usurious; and they were often imperious creditors who initiated foreclosures in courts they themselves ruled. Their children monopolized the religious orders and the cathedral chapters; their relatives controlled the courts and legal institutions; they engrossed most of the best lands within a ten mile radius of Beauvais; they played an important role in the agricultural, pastoral, and forest economy of the Beauvaisis. Because their role and importance in the countryside was so great and pervasive, Pierre Goubert could conclude that "whoever studies the countryside inevitably ends up in the nearest town . . . where the great fortunes are, fortunes drawn from rural rents, rural investments, rural dues and fees, rural cloth production. The town lived and prospered because of the countryside, often to the detriment of the rural inhabitants: not the entire town prospered but the narrow and solid group of the great bourgeois families."

These families, all involved in the cloth trade and other enterprises and always anxious to improve their social status, nevertheless displayed many different characteristics. Gabriel's grandfather had been a rude, pushy, social upstart manifesting a taste for magnificent display typical of the parvenu: these traits were perpetuated, if less intensely, in the family. The Motte family was reported to be vain, of bad character, only moderately honest, and intermittently involved in "scandals." Other bourgeois "founding fathers" displayed different traits: simplicity, economy, restraint in dress and in all forms of display, probity in business and in private life. Still, regardless of different personal and family traits, all of these bourgeois families gave decisive direction to the Beauvaisis cloth trade while at the same time they undertook to secure their own social and political advance.

In 1700 Gabriel Motte's family was rich, its wealth being drawn mainly from commerce but also from investments in land. It was active in the town's affairs, socially respected in spite of its occasional failings, and well represented among the directors of the economic, administrative, judicial, religious, and charitable organizations of Beauvais. (It should be noted, too, that most of the rich in Beauvais paid little in direct taxes because of the town's exemption from the taille and because of their rank and the offices they held.) In these and other matters Gabriel Motte's family was typically bourgeois and Gabriel clearly belonged to the elite. As such, whenever he glanced down upon the masses of people in Beauvais, he did so from a relatively exalted position.

THE POOR OF BEAUVAIS

Of those masses below him more than one half were officially designated as poor, living in good times at the subsistence level. Jewelers, goldsmiths, grocers, druggists, master weavers, innkeepers, butchers, masons, tailors, tanners, carpenters, drapers: these were some of the trades practiced by the better-off members of the urban poor. They were gathered together in "corporations and communities of the arts and trades" which were supposed to regulate such things as apprenticeships and access to masterships. There were many irregularities in the operation of their regulations, however, and many professions—for example, the building trades—simply ignored them. The usual working day in summer was from 5 or 6:00 A.M. to 8:00 P.M.; in winter, from 7:00 A.M. to 8:00 P.M. At best, the working day was never less than 12 hours long, and sometimes it ran to 14. More than one half of all the workers in Beauvais were directly involved in one aspect or another of the cloth trade; almost all of them were too poor to pay taxes. Among those in the trade who were better-off were the *fabricants*, the master drapers and serge-weavers. They brought the poorer workers into their workshops or distributed material to them in their homes. These masters supervised the transformation of raw wool and linen into cloth ready to be used. There were about 250 such fabricants in Beauvais, each employing an average of 7 workers, with the range being from 1 to 20. The relationship of workers and masters was much more capitalistic than familial, based on impersonal economic imperatives rather than on personal considerations. To the workers, the fabricants appeared to be powerful, autonomous masters but in fact even the wealthiest of them feared and envied their social and economic betters, the merchants such as Gabriel Motte. Successful fabricants transformed themselves into merchants as soon as possible; poorer and unlucky fabricants dropped into the workers' ranks. In any event, they performed the critical task of training and supervising the work force.

The workers usually entered the cloth trade between the ages of 10 and 15 as apprentices. Most often such apprentices were sons of cloth workers but there was a great movement of rural youngsters into the trade as well. About one quarter of the apprentices never completed their training: they were too incompetent, or too sickly, or they simply ran away from masters who worked them too hard. Those who remained often found their period of apprenticeship lengthened because of sick leaves and indebtedness to the master. The long working hours and unwholesome working conditions were exacerbated by disputes over wages and by the threat of unemployment. Wages were supposed to be officially regulated, with both a minimum and a maximum scale; fabricants, however, were often able to evade these regulations, to the workers' cost. Another ruse was to pay the workers in truck, that is, in commodities not easily converted into cash. And in times of economic crisis workers would be dismissed, just as modern workers are, but without any unemployment compensation.

Given such conditions, in "normal" times, i.e., good times, 6 percent of all workers received poor relief from the Church. In bad times, following one or two poor harvests, the price of bread would rise precipitously thus reducing the workers' real salaries. In times of "subsistence crises"—and these occurred many times in the course of an adult's life—the price of bread could double, triple, or quadruple. We must emphasize that bread was the single most important food, and almost the only food in the workers' diet. One of the more common definitions of the "poor" was: "those who have insufficient bread to live." With food draining off so much of everyone's income, a commodity glut would develop, and rather quickly fabricants would lay off their workers who would then be reduced to penury and thus exposed to starvation and disease.

Such was the pattern that emerged during the great *mortalité* of 1693–94, when because of poor harvests, the price of bread quadrupled. The cloth trade felt the effects immediately. Merchants stopped their orders; fabricants reduced their work force; the workers were thrown upon the charity of Church and town. But despite conscientious efforts to feed the poor, the charitable institutions were overwhelmed by numbers. They possessed insufficient resources to counter a crisis whose roots penetrated deeply into the economic and social structure of the region. The workers and their families, a true proletariat, went hungry. In a weakened state, crowded into their dirty, airless, infested apartments, they succumbed to disease, the old and the very young dying first. Only the young adults were capable of holding on. In such crises even the family of Gabriel Motte might suffer, not from hunger but from disease, the so-called revenge of the poor. In the two wealthy parishes of Beauvais the death rate doubled in 1693–94. In the poorer parishes, however, the death rate quadrupled symmetrically with the price of bread, the key to the whole crisis. With the possible exception of the crisis of 1709–10, there was never a time when bread was unavailable. The shortage was almost always economic rather than material. In the absence of any thoroughgoing distribution system to insure fair shares to all, prices allocated supplies. Inevitably, the poor suffered—and died. Elite bourgeois like Gabriel Motte found little injustice in, and felt no remorse over, this situation. In the first place, the economic segregation of the town somewhat masked the problem: the poor, crowded within their working class ghettos, were hidden from view. In the second place, when disease threatened the town, the rich would flee to their more salubrious country homes. Further, Christianity itself proclaimed that poverty was ineradicable, that man inhabited a "vale of tears and sorrow," that suffering was a just punishment for sin, and that to the faithful—heaven would be adequate recompense. Finally, there was a growing belief—perhaps merely a psychic defense mechanism—among the elites that the poor were lazy and shiftless, preferring to live amidst disease and squalor. Like their peasant cousins, the urban poor (when they were perceived at all) were seen as animals, and intermittently dangerous animals as well. For in the early stages of a subsistence crisis, as prices rose and wages fell, the workers would assemble and their complaints would often turn into threats. The authorities would respond first with palliatives, then, as the crisis worsened, with armed force. Against the army or bourgeois militia, the workers, unorganized and leaderless, had no chance. In the eyes of the elite, however, they remained the "dangerous class."

In 1695, the crisis having passed, fabricants began to complain of a labor shortage, a natural enough result of the previous year's mortality. The price of bread fell rapidly as a decent harvest came in; jobs were again available as the bourgeois merchants placed new orders for cloth; the cloth workers reattained their subsistence level, perhaps for a while an even higher standard of living. But it only signified a renewal of the cycle into which the workers were locked: misery and near misery interspersed by regular periods of calamity: high prices, scarcity, famine, and epidemics. Not until after 1750, when, coupled with good weather and ample harvests, improved urban hygiene and better systems of relief were initiated, did that cycle change.

Such was life in the ecclesiastical-capitalistic town of Beauvais. The town encompassed a wide variety of people in a highly stratified social environment, with a few rich elite at the top, in the middle some masters and professionals, and many poor at the bottom. The town generated great wealth, in the form of cloth, which its merchant elite dispatched at a profit to distant markets. But the town drew great wealth to itself— from its rural hinterland to which it gave little in return. Into that environment we must now enter.

THE BEAUVAISIS

One tenth of the population of the town of Beauvais was in fact rural in profession or orientation. That proportion included several middling peasants (*laboureurs*), along with many coopers, vintners, threshers, blacksmiths, and agricultural laborers. Beauvais thus retained many features of a rural community. This was inescapable inasmuch as the surrounding countryside constantly impinged upon the town and contributed greatly to its economic welfare and to the wealth of its great bourgeois families.

The rural area proper to Beauvais, the Beauvaisis, manifested two distinct agricultural economies. To the north and east of the town lay the plains of Picardy. These lands were cultivated to the greatest possible extent. There were few forested areas, wastelands, meadows, vineyards, or common lands (i.e., lands open to use by all members of the community): four fifths of the total area was of necessity under the plow and devoted to the production of those grains used primarily for bread, i.e., wheat, rye, oats, and barley. It was, therefore, an area of "monoculture" depending almost entirely upon its grain for subsistence. The productivity of its farms was mediocre and only in years of exceptionally good harvests was it able to offer any grain for sale elsewhere than in Beauvais itself. In bad harvest years, the town absorbed most of its production and the poor peasants were left to their own devices, which very often, meant death.

A land of grain, it was also a land of sheep. No other livestock existed in significant numbers. Where there were, say, 40 cows and 30 horses there would also be 1,000 sheep. Nor were there any appreciable numbers of pigs and chickens. In the absence of meadows, pastures, and common lands, there could not be large herds of cows and horses; in the absence of forests, wherein pigs might root for themselves, and because both pigs and chickens eat grain and thus compete with humans for food, there could be no herds or flocks of such animals. The heavy tax on salt further precluded large herds of swine because it was too expensive to salt the meat. Sheep, however, abounded because they neither competed with humans for food nor needed vast meadows upon which to graze. Even so, the area did not raise enough sheep to supply the Beauvaisis wool trade; most of Beauvais' wool came from other regions. This relative lack of larger livestock affected the productivity of the soil. With no livestock, there was no manure for fertilizer; this meant soil depletion and thus the necessity of letting one third of the land lie fallow each year (the so-called "triennial" system). Since most peasants were too poor to keep livestock through the long winter months, they lacked fertilizer for their soils and were forced to farm extensive lands which produced only mediocre returns. They were thus locked into a stagnant, enclosed rural economy.

The area to the south and west of Beauvais was in many ways in sharp contrast to all this. Grain production here concentrated on wheat and rye. There were numerous pastures, meadows, and common lands, many of them enclosed. There were thus significantly greater numbers of horses and cattle than in the north. Peasants in the area included milk products in their diet and realized some cash income from the sale of dairy products and livestock. There were many forests and copses in the area which provided work, firewood, and lumber to the peasants; charcoal burners provided further profits and jobs. Fresh water fish were plentiful and there was a lively trade in salt fish, a food especially marketed in Paris. The area also supported a thriving wine and brandy trade as well as lace-making and mother-of-pearl button manufacturing. People in this region were very much involved in market relations with the world beyond their borders.

The two areas of the Beauvaisis thus stood in sharp contrast to each other in many ways. "A rural area in which only grains grow," Pierre Goubert writes, "one without pastures and almost without trees, is one in which life is hard and food shortages always threaten. A region with pastures, however, means an easier and happier existence." With its mixed economy of grain and livestock and with its numerous secondary resources, this southern area of the Beauvaisis was both more productive of goods and more resistant to the impact of famine and disease.

There were, however, many basic similarities between the two regions. In both areas, there was an extreme parceling of land, with tiny plots marked off by stones and, more rarely, by trees. In both areas, the exception to this rule were the lands owned by the Church: these were always large, consolidated farms. Both areas were dotted with small communities devoted to the cooperative working of the soil, which soil was always and everywhere worked on the triennial system of rotation. Both areas were primarily grain producers, the southern region being a "mixed" economy only in comparison to the mono-cultural work. And, finally, both areas were populated mainly by poor peasants; all told, peasants (90 percent of the rural population) owned but 40 percent of the land. Ecclesiastical property (20–25 percent), noble lands (20–25 percent) and bourgeois holdings (10–15 percent) engrossed far more, and usually better land.

There was another supremely important similarity. Both regions produced large quantities of woolen and linen fabrics, prepared by rural workers in their own homes: 37 percent of all woolen cloth produced in France came from the Beauvaisis and adjoining areas. In certain areas of the Beauvaisis there were far more weavers than farmers. This is not to say that such weavers were any less "peasant" in their environment and outlook. Certainly, too, there were far more rural weavers and other cloth workers than "urban" workers, many of whom were rural migrants in the first place. That cloth manufacturing flourished in the countryside was due to certain economic, demographic, and political conditions. Farm work is essentially seasonal, with short but feverish periods of labor interrupted by longer slack periods.

Peasants seasonally had time on their hands and could thus work as weavers, bleachers, and carders. Further, the urban cloth trade and its labor force were regulated, sometimes very effectively. Rural manufacturers were exempt from such regulation and this impelled merchants to exploit the freer atmosphere and cheaper labor of the countryside. Such labor was cheaper because in proportion to agricultural production much of the countryside was overpopulated: three fourths of the peasantry possessed insufficient land to be economically independent. Many thousands of peasants thus became cloth workers to eke out their livings. It should be noted that in this as in so many other matters, the initiative and direction came from Beauvais: the town, as usual, dominated and exploited the countryside.

Thus, the Beauvaisis was marked by an archaic system of agriculture which rarely produced more food than it needed for itself and for the dominant town, Beauvais. Periodically, it produced insufficient food, and shortages, even famines would occur, striking mainly at the poorest peasants. The cloth trade provided a vital economic support to the peasants and this trade, more rural than urban but still urban directed, constituted a major industry. Despite poor roads, no seaports, and no navigable rivers, the industry reached out beyond the region to national, and international markets. The area was one of small farmers, peasants, intimately involved with the commercial economy of the cloth trade. They were a numerous and mostly poor peasantry, burdened with children (most of whom soon died), impotent in the face of famine and disease, and lacking adequate land, tools, and livestock. All too often they evoke La Bruyère's searing portrait of the peasant. They merit a closer look in their rural social context.

THE RURAL SOCIETY OF THE BEAUVAISIS

Like all but the most primitive of human societies this rural society was highly complex. There were nobles, professionals, artisans, and priests as well as peasants (the vast majority, however) in the countryside. The peasants themselves were a stratified social group. The poorest among them were called *manouvriers*. Representing about two thirds of the peasant population, they shared with beggars the lowest rung on the social ladder. Manouvriers only rarely owned significant property or livestock and most often they worked for others at seasonal, common, and unremunerative tasks. They performed essential work but rarely were they able to improve their economic status. In the southern Beauvaisis, an enterprising manouvrier would occasionally be able to parlay the common pastures and a few cows and sheep into a small flock. He would then be a *manouvrier-fermier* (a title, by the way, he would insist on). He would then be eligible to pay taxes: one of the reasons we know so little about the poorest peasants is that the authorities left them out of their accounts since they paid no taxes. Through tax records, we know rather more about the Horatio Algers among them but then as now few individuals were able to break out of grinding poverty. Another avenue of upward social mobility lay open to those who could seize upon opportunities in the cloth trade. Some few were able to turn themselves into rural master artisans: *manouvriers-sergers*. But these success stories, too, were rare.

Above the manouvriers in the peasant social scale were the so-called *haricotiers*, a middling sort of peasant quite numerous in the Beauvaisis. The haricotier typically owned a few parcels of land, rarely more than 20, usually about 12 acres, which he worked with the aid of a mule. He commonly had some livestock, especially sheep. He lived in a thatched mud hut, with a garden and sometimes a few fruit trees outside. The haricotier leased lands from other landlords to supplement his own holdings: very few such peasants owned enough land to be independent of others and only in years of bountiful harvests (which were quite unusual) were such peasants truly free of the necessity to work for others and to borrow money to keep going. Like the manouvrier, the typical haricotier was debt-ridden. Since these two types together comprised the great majority of the peasants, it is clear that most peasants were thus economically dependent and in debt as well.

Rural artisans, grape growers (*vignerons*) and truck gardeners (*airiers jardiniers*) completed the middling ranks of the peasantry. Rural artisans — weavers, coopers, tailors, wheelwrights, blacksmiths — were always peasants, usually haricotiers originally, who in effect were "moonlighting" and thus able to support a higher standard of living. Grape growers — vignerons — besides owning some land of their own often supervised for a set wage the vineyards of bourgeois and ecclesiastical seigneurs. Theirs was a very specialized employment and they stood out as a group among the other, more traditional peasants. Grape growing — their own and others — some grain production, and gardening (beans and cabbages planted between rows of vines) sufficed to maintain these vignerons, almost all of whom lived close to the town of Beauvais, where the wine was consumed. It should be remembered that just as the peasants often lacked the bread they themselves produced, so the vignerons rarely drank any wine. Only the very wealthy could afford to drink wine (or eat wheat bread). Peasants had to make do with cheaper intoxicants.

Similarly, most of the airiers lived in the eastern faubourgs of Beauvais, on tiny plots of land which were valued as much as four times that of land in grain. These commercial gardeners raised sorrel, lettuce, cabbages, carrots, and beets for the urban market, that is, for the tables

of the rich. A small number of gardeners raised artichokes and aspara-
gus, most of which were marketed in Paris (home of the *very* rich).
All of these middling peasants — haricotiers, artisans, grape growers,
gardeners — remained clearly distinguishable from the rarest type: the
independent peasant.

These rare birds — in the Beauvaisis they were called, in ascending
order, laboureurs, gros fermiers, and *receveurs de seigneuries* — comprised
at most ten percent of all peasants. They were the wealthiest and best
equipped peasants: a laboureur — the least of them — by definition possessed two horses and a plow. Laboureurs usually owned substantial
land outright (30 acres for the average middling laboureur), and they
farmed or managed other lands as well. They were able to ply other
trades as well as artisans, and, because they had horses, as carters and
grain dealers. These secondary occupations enabled some of them to
rise to the level of the great fermiers and receveurs, those who stood at
the top of the peasant hierarchy.

Such relatively well-off peasants worked their own substantial lands
but more important were the farms they leased from others (fermiers)
and the seigneuries whose cultivation they supervised and whose
revenues they received (receveurs) to pass on to the seigneur. Such
peasants owned much equipment and many horses, which they rented
out to less fortunate peasants. They possessed considerable numbers of
cattle and sheep. The receveurs were the most fortunate of peasants.
They sometimes worked as many as 250 acres, with a dozen horses and
with hired plowmen. They exploited vineyards, forests, and herds of
livestock. They were creditors to the other peasants and this meant,
among other things, that they were assured of a docile labor supply
and a certain social precedence: they were the *coqs de paroisse*. These
receveurs were necessarily literate and quite sophisticated estate managers and masters of commercial relations. They saw to it that their sons
were as well educated as rural conditions allowed. They formed a
closed social elite based on wealth and intermarriage. Their aim
always was to increase the lands they owned and leased, and in this
they were largely successful. By 1789 they had engrossed appreciable
amounts of both church and peasant lands in the Beauvaisis. In 1700,
they already stood far above most other peasants in the rural hierarchy.

Such was the peasant social pyramid: at the bottom, beggars and a
mass of poor peasants, with insufficient or even no property; a small
middling group, and a few well-to-do. (This is a profile which matches
that of the town of Beauvais itself.) With its archaic techniques and
technologies and its extreme parceling of the land (which precluded the
application of modern methods) this peasantry was rarely able to produce much of a food surplus even in good years; in bad years famine
threatened. Furthermore, given the landholding patterns, with ecclesi-

Courtesy Museum of Fine Arts, Boston.

FIGURE 1.   Peasants in front of a house, after Louis Le Nain. The house here depicted is rather more substantial than the typical peasant dwelling, but Le Nain has captured the poverty and resignation of peasants amid their few material possessions.

astical, noble, and bourgeois seigneuries engrossing most of the land, peasants rarely received the first fruits of the harvest. These went to the landlords and to the state. King, clergy, and seigneurs (noble and common) collected taxes, rents, tithes, dues, fees, and services right off the top, as it were. The taille levied on a haricotier, for example, could amount to 20 livres, the equivalent of the production of about four acres of land. Since most haricotiers owned only about ten acres of land, the taille alone took almost one half of the income from their own land. To this tax was added the gabelle, the indirect taxes (aides), and, periodically, a special tax (the so-called *franc-fief*) on any land that once had been noble. Together, these taxes took about 20 percent of the peasants' total income.

The church took its tithe even before the state had extracted the taille. The task of collecting the tithe was contracted out by the church to secular, bourgeois agents. The tithe could be as high as 18 percent in some places—where it sparked revolts in the old regime and where in 1789 the peasants were to take their revenge. Normally, however, the tithe was about 8 percent of the peasants' gross income; to the tithe were added other ecclesiastical dues and local fees so that peasants usually paid at a rate of 12 percent to the church. This left them with about 68 percent of their gross income.

Other demands reduced that percentage still further. Rents especially were high and in bad years poorer haricotiers might have to turn over part of the harvest from their own property to pay the rent on leased property. Seed grain, too, had to be put aside for the next year, and then there were the inevitable losses of livestock from accidents and disease. With these deductions, peasants were left with less than half of their gross revenues. They survived but often just barely, and most of time, on the border of misery and increasingly in debt.

The poorest peasants were always in debt simply because to live out the year they needed advances in money, tools, and seed. Peasants without horses and plows (i.e., the majority) were indebted to those who provided such essentials. In bad years all but the wealthiest peasants had to borrow for seed and to pay rents that fell due. Finally, when his creditors became frightened and threatened to foreclose on a peasant's land, he would often take out, as it were, a second mortgage at the usurious rates offered by bourgeois speculators. In this way a small number of people actually held the peasants' land through loans, on which they levied high rates of interest. Sometimes richer peasants enjoyed this advantageous position but more often it was the prerogative of townsmen. In such ways did the Beauvais bourgeoisie come to control peasants' lands, collecting rents, recovering debts, and insinuating themselves into dominant positions in the countryside as well as in the town. It is the trail from rural debtor to bourgeois creditor, to paraphrase Pierre Goubert, that leads one studying the countryside into the town.

With such a mass of peasants populating or, rather, overpopulating the countryside it requires a special effort to note the various other social types which inhabited the rural world. The high churchmen, the noble grand seigneurs, the rich bourgeois landlords, it is true, were rarely to be seen about their country properties: they were absentee landlords. There remained however the parish curés, lesser nobles, and village-dwelling professionals (notaries and estate managers), and tradesmen (innkeepers, millers, bakers). Notaries were especially important and numerous in the countryside. They had some legal training and were instrumental in drawing up the many and varied leases and contracts that bound peasants and seigneurs. They at times were as influential as the curé in interpreting the "outside world" to the peasants. Innkeepers, millers, and bakers were influential and powerful members of rural society. As well as possessing equipment necessary to peasant life — mills and ovens — they were often moneylenders and pawnbrokers to the needy, at usurious rates of interest.[8]

All of these types — curés, lesser nobles, village tradesmen and professionals — were more or less "privileged" by virtue of their juridical status or official capacity. They made up the rural elite.

Perhaps most influential in the Beauvaisis were the curés. They were true native sons but never sons of the soil. Three fourths of all the priests in the diocese were native Beauvaisiens. Many of them came from bourgeois and professional families. In 1700, there seems to have been not one priest who derived from a worker's family, no doubt because each priest had to possess a guaranteed annual income of 50 livres. Similarly, most curés of peasant stock were sons of well-off laboureurs; there is no evidence of any priests emerging from the ranks of the haricotiers and manouvriers. The curés were thus drawn from the upper and middling ranks of society.

This is reflected in their standard of living. There were no poor country curés in the Beauvaisis. Besides the revenues attached to their parishes, most of the curés had their personal incomes. All of them benefited from gifts offered by wealthier peasants and from the many dinners which followed religious celebrations. In a world where food was never taken for granted, an invitation to dinner was an economic as well as a social boon. Curés also managed ecclesiastical properties and their personal property as well. They were deeply involved in the peasant world and in many ways they reflected peasant concerns and values. They were socially and economically closest, perhaps, to well-off laboureurs and fermiers. There is much evidence that they felt a great solidarity with their peasant flock, interpreting the news from the "outside" to them, and protecting their interests, even to the extent of leading them in open revolt against unjust measures. They also educated them: the Beauvaisis was a rarity in the old regime, a countryside in which the majority of men could read and write. Literacy was more widespread in northeast France than elsewhere so that in this matter the Beauvaisis was typical of that region. One further point: although the curés in general preached an austere Catholic theology, their peasant parishioners still maintained pagan and superstitious beliefs difficult to root out. Witches, warlocks, and the "evil eye" were accepted as threatening realities by most peasants. The curés, a respected elite in the peasant world, had little influence in these matters.

As for the lesser provincial nobility, they had fallen to a relatively low social state. In the first place the very notion of nobility had become obscured. "Noble" lands had passed into nonnoble hands to such an extent that the terms "fief" and "seigneur," which originally had implied noble status, no longer meant anything of the sort. Further, nobility itself was purchasable, at fixed prices, by any commoner with sufficient cash; certain offices, also for sale, carried nobility as well. In such a confused situation, further muddied by their frequent intermarriages with rich commoners, the old landed nobility tended to decline. They were also being overwhelmed economically. The European inflation of the late 16th and early 17th centuries had eroded noble fortunes and the extended religious wars of the 16th century had drained both wealth and blood from the nobility. Perhaps most important as a factor in their decline was the nobles' refusal or inability to alter their mode of life. Strict economy and enlightened administration of one's estate were "bourgeois," not noble virtues. Only a minority of the nobles adapted themselves to the new imperatives.

This opened the way for the ubiquitous bourgeoisie. Through marriage alliances, foreclosed loans and venality of office, they both joined and defeated the old nobility while they exploited and controlled the peasants. It was a long and slow process, apparent in 1700 and still continuing in 1789 as the old regime entered upon its death throes.

For the peasant masses, however, it made little difference that a new elite was forming over them. As they had been subject to, and exploited by, the nobility, so they were subject to, and exploited by, the new bourgeois—notables, who in any event did little to alter traditional ways of doing things. What remained constant in the countryside, were the great seasonal rhythms of peasant life, with the peasants sowing and harvesting, and in between supplying the bulk of the woolens and linens in the cloth trade, doggedly attempting to wrest surplus food from a niggardly nature and seeking, usually unsuccessfully, to rid themselves of their debts. The town, the rich bourgeoisie, meanwhile continued its domination of the Beauvaisis. Despite its heavy burdens the peasantry maintained itself, and France as well. In rural communities (such as Beauvais and its environs) were accomplished the tasks necessary to secure the fabric of French society in the age of Louis XIV. That the Sun King's name should appear only at this point in our narrative indicates the relative unimportance of political matters when we view history from this social perspective. Beyond Louis XIV, as Pierre Goubert put it, there were 20 million Frenchmen. It is to them in their traditional occupations, in their relatively unchanging social context that we must look if we wish to understand the old regime in France.

NOTES

The works of many historians inform this essay and it is proper to list a few of them inasmuch as numbered references were kept to a minimum in the text.

Pierre Goubert's splendid study *Beauvais et le Beauvaisis de 1600 á 1730* (Paris, 1960) was the first of a series of regional studies that have appeared in France over the last 15 years. Among the best to follow Goubert's thesis are Pierre de Saint-Jacob, *Les paysans de la Bourgogne du Nord au dernier siècle de l'Ancien Régime* (Paris, 1960); René Baehrel, *Une Croissance, la Basse-Provence rurale (fin du XVIIᵉ siècle—1789)* (Paris, 1961); Abel Pointrineau, *La vie rurale en Basse-Auvergne au XVIIIᵉ siècle* (Paris, 1965); and Emmanuel Le Roy Ladurie, *Les Paysans de Languedoc* (Paris, 1966), English translation, *The Peasants of Languedoc* (Urbana, Ill., 1974); Roger Dion's *Histoire de la vigne et du vin en France des origines au XIXᵉ siècle* (Paris, 1959) is indispensable as are Edmond Esmonin's *La taille en Normandie au temps de Colbert* (Paris, 1913) and Pierre Deyon, *Amiens, capitale provinciale; étude sur la société urbaine au XVIIᵉ siècle* (Paris, 1967). There are many other titles that deserve mention. For a full bibliography students should consult Pierre Goubert, *The Ancien Régime. French Society, 1600–1750* (tr. Steve Cox, New York, 1974).

1. Walter Carruthers Sellar and Robert Julian Yeatman, *1066 And All That. A Memorable History of England* (New York, 1931), pp. 43–44.

2. Peter Laslett, *The World We Have Lost. England Before the Industrial Age* (New York, 1965).

3. These definitions are drawn from George M. Foster's essay "What Is a Peasant?", in Jack M. Potter, *et al*, eds., *Peasant Society: A Reader* (New York, 1967), pp. 2–14.

4. Armando Saitta and Albert Soboul describe the study of the peasants and their problems as "the backbone of the history of France in the old regime and of postrevolutionary France." See their preface to Georges Lefebvre, *Les paysans du Nord pendant la Révolution française*, 2d ed. (Bari, 1959), p. vi. On the inability of the Revolution to solve the agrarian problem see Georges Lefebvre, "La Révolution française et les paysans," in his *Études sur la Révolution française*, 2nd ed. (Paris, 1963), pp. 338–67.

5. The often neglected role of women in what Olwen Hufton calls "an economy of expedients" is outlined in her excellent article, "Women and the Family Economy in Eighteenth Century France," *French Historical Studies* IX (1975), 1–22.

6. See George M. Foster, "Peasant Society and the Image of Limited Good," in Jack M. Potter, *et al.*, eds., *Peasant Society*, pp. 300–323. The quotation from Barrington Moore, Jr., is from his *The Social Origins of Dictatorship and Democracy. Lord and Peasant in the Making of the Modern World* (Boston, 1968), p. 423.

7. What follows is drawn almost entirely from Pierre Goubert's magisterial thesis, *Beauvais et le Beauvaisis de 1600 à 1730. (Contribution à l'histoire sociale de la France du XVIIᵉ siècle)* (Paris, 1960), and from his complementary essay,

Familles Marchands sous l'Ancien Régime: les Danse et les Motte, de Beauvais, (Paris, 1959). For purposes of comparison I drew upon Pierre Deyon's superb study, *Amiens, capitale provinciale; étude sur la société urbaine an XVIIᵉ siècle* (Paris, 1967), and other relevant works.

    8. Students may recall the nursery rhyme, "Three Men in a Tub"—the butcher, the baker, the candlestick maker—the last line of which reads, "Turn them out, knaves all three." This is a reflection of the popular attitude toward village tradesmen who perform necessary tasks and to whom most of the poor are indebted. In times of popular revolt, urban and rural, such tradesmen were commonly objects of collective aggression: they would be lynched and their equipment destroyed. Nursery rhymes often reflect our common peasant ancestry. The tale, "Stone Soup," recalls the peasants' impotence before the "outside world." When but three royal soldiers appear in the community, panic ensues as the peasants hasten to hide their livestock, food, and women (in that order) but the soldiers nevertheless attain their end—a feast—by playing upon the peasants' ignorance, credulity, and desire to get something for nothing. Similarly, "The Pied Piper of Hamelin" is a folk description of the plague, with rats dying first (as they do when bubonic plague strikes) and the children being "carried off" (as is demographically accurate). The explanation for the catastrophe is typical: God's punishment for the breaking of a sworn contract. People observed the rats dying first as the plague descended but no connection was made between rats, fleas, men, and the disease. Not until the 19th century did European scientists develop the germ theory of disease. Until then the matter was left to Heaven and God's inscrutable providence.

BIBLIOGRAPHY

Bloch, Marc   *French Rural History: An Essay on Its Basic Characteristics* (Berkeley and Los Angeles, 1966).

Blum, Jerome   *The European Peasantry From the Fifteenth to the Nineteenth Century,* Publication number 33, Service Center for Teachers of History, *American Historical Association* (Baltimore, 1960).

Dakin, Douglas   *Turgot and the "Ancien Régime" in France* (London, 1939; reprinted, New York, 1965).

Goubert, Pierre   *Louis XIV and Twenty Million Frenchmen* (New York, 1970).

——   *The Ancien Régime. French Society, 1600–1750* (New York, 1974).

Hufton, Olwen   *Bayeux in the Late Eighteenth Century* (Oxford, 1967).

Laslett, Peter   *The World We Have Lost. England Before the Industrial Age* (New York, 1965).

Potter, Jack M.; Diaz, May M. and Foster, George M. eds.   *Peasant Society: A Reader* (Boston, 1967).

Chapter 2

*T*he society of the ancien régime *in France was a very complex structure that had evolved gradually over the centuries, shaped by the collective experience of many generations of Frenchmen, and in turn influencing and conditioning the ways that people lived, worked, felt. It was not a uniform or monolithic system; each region, each district, each village possessed its own particular features and characteristics. Just as the wine made from the grapes of one small vineyard in Burgundy will have a distinctive taste and bouquet, discernible to the connoisseur, so too was each French community unique, and different from its neighbors. The differences might be due to variations in the physical environment (topography, soil, climate); or in the patterns of land tenure and cultivation; or to the proximity of roads, markets, large cities; or even to such human factors as the genial or rapacious character of the local* seigneur. *These variations notwithstanding, the social order of the* ancien régime *did have certain general characteristics of which two, poverty and privilege, were of especial significance. Most Frenchmen were peasants, tillers of the soil; and most peasants were very poor, earning barely enough to feed their families. By their labor, these peasants supported a small minority of privileged individuals — landlords, clerics, bureaucrats, nobles, affluent townsmen — who enjoyed a comfortable living standard, and who firmly believed that*

51

the system under which they lived and prospered had been ordained by God.

One other noteworthy feature of this society was its static character, its resistance to change. The population of France (and indeed of Europe as a whole) did not grow significantly between about 1600 and 1720 but remained quite stable, though with some short-term fluctuations, at about 20 million. The French economy was predominantly agrarian, and the productivity of the land increased very little, if at all, from the 16th to the early 18th century. All of the land available for cultivation had been put to the plow, and no major technological advances were made to improve the low yields, and thus to increase the food supply. Other segments of the economy, such as commerce and industry, did not expand much during this period, lacking any sharp stimulus from a European economy that was chronically depressed, and hampered by a very primitive transportation system. The French economy of the ancien régime has been succinctly and aptly described by Pierre Goubert as "a patchwork of rural provinces with traditional attitudes, archaic techniques, chronic shortage of currency and poor communications, where the struggle for daily bread remains the overriding consideration and every human grouping strives to be self-supporting." (The Ancien Régime. French Society, 1600–1750: New York, 1973, p. 68). These realities fostered a conservative outlook in every social group. The thoughts of the poor focused exclusively on survival, and on avoiding penury and starvation; the well-to-do struggled to keep what they had, including their legal and social privileges, and to avoid any risk that might reduce them to poverty.

But changes did occur in this conservative, tradition-bound society, as a consequence of external pressures and events and, to a lesser degree, of policies formulated by the state. French kings and their chief ministers, men like Richelieu (d. 1642) and Colbert (d. 1683) worked indefatigably to govern the kingdom effectively: to force recalicitrant subjects to obey the crown; to raise armies and navies to enhance French power in Europe and on the high seas; to raise money to pay for those troops and ships, and for the court at Versailles. It has been estimated that the taxes imposed upon the French people increased five-fold between 1600 and 1650; thereafter, the amount continued to grow, though at a reduced rate. Since the nobility and many townsmen were exempt from the primary direct tax, the taille, the peasantry bore the brunt of this fiscal burden. A *veritable army of royal officials was formed to collect these taxes, to administer justice and to enforce royal edicts. To a much greater degree than ever before, these officials intruded into the lives of ordinary Frenchmen. They levied the* taille *and the salt* gabelle, *imposed tolls on commerce, regulated the currency, and supervised the production of manufactured goods. They recruited troops for the king's armies and sailors for his fleet. They censored printing and the theatre and scrutinized the religious beliefs of Frenchmen of high and low estate. These bureaucrats were hated and feared, and occasionally their exactions and interference provoked local rebellions. But the institutions and techniques for exercising control over the French populace were never abolished nor reduced in scope; they became the foundations of the modern, centralized nation-state.*

This large, expensive, and cumbersome bureaucracy was, by modern standards, extremely inefficient. The ability of the king and his ministers to implement their policies was hampered by the primitive systems of communication and transport, by the venality and incompetence of lesser officials who had bought their posts and could not be removed from them, and by the resistance of many Frenchmen to royal authority. The most striking feature of government, as of the society, was its inequity. Depending upon their social status, profession and residence, Frenchmen were assessed taxes at different rates (or paid none at all), were tried in different courts, enjoyed different rights and privileges, and (in the lower ranks of society) suffered different kinds of disabilities. The arbitrary character of this system is illustrated by the notorious lettre de cachet, *an official document that authorized the imprisonment of any French subject, who could be held indefinitely without trial, and without ever knowing the reasons for his detention.*

The intensified activity of the absolutist state did stimulate certain segments of the French economy. To cite one example, the maintenance of a large standing army created a market for cloth (uniforms) and leather (shoes), as well as for metals (cannon and muskets) and building supplies (fortifications). The construction and supplying of ships for war and commerce brought prosperity to such ports as Brest and La Rochelle, and the overseas trade in slaves and sugar, encouraged by the state, was the source of great mercantile fortunes. But the most significant economic fact of the prerevolutionary period was the dramatic growth in population that began in France (and elsewhere in Europe, in varying degrees) during the mid-decades of the 18th century. This demographic expansion has been charted by specialists, though its causes are still largely unknown. Between 1720 and 1789, the population of France increased from 20 to 26 million; perhaps one third of that swollen number was so poor as to require some assistance for survival, even in years of good harvest and moderate prices. The French economy could not absorb the surplus population; the charitable institutions operated by the church were overwhelmed by this mass of destitute humanity. Poverty was the main social problem of the French government in the 18th century, and the most glaring illustration of its weakness and ineptitude. In many regions of France, bands of vagrants wandered through the countryside, robbing and terrorizing the rural populace, contributing to that mood of fear and suspicion that was an important element in the early stages of the French Revolution.

On the eve of that revolution, in the 1780s, France was a cauldron of social discontent. Every group in society—nobility, clergy, burghers, peasants—was dissatisfied with the status quo. In the countryside, tensions increased between peasants and their lords, and between peasants and the inhabitants of the towns. The peasantry sought a reduction of rents, feudal dues, and taxes, and the preservation of their traditional forms of community. Landlords, whether they lived on their estates or in towns, were eager to increase their revenues from the land: by raising rents, by encroaching upon the common land of rural villages, by resurrecting old feudal exactions. The most privileged group in France, the nobility, was also the most insecure in the eighteenth century. Fearful of losing their perquisites and prerogatives, the nobles sought to strengthen their position, in particular, by obtaining a monopoly of certain administrative and military offices. They resented the intrusion of nonnobles (rotouriers) into the government and the army, while the latter in turn became increasingly hostile to the idea of a social and political order based on privilege. Providing an ideology for these "bourgeois" (merchants, industrialists, lawyers, notaries, scientists) were the so-called philosophes—men like Voltaire, Diderot and Condorcet—who denounced the inequities and absurdities of the ancien régime and agitated for its reform.

Social and intellectual ferment was most intense in Paris, France's largest city and ancient capital. The population of Paris had grown substantially during the 18th century, to about 650,000 in 1789. Many of its immigrants were impoverished rural folk, seeking a livelihood that they could not earn in their native villages. Within its boundaries, Paris embraced the whole spectrum of French society. Though the king and his court were located at Versailles some 15 miles away, many great nobles and officers of the crown maintained residences in Paris, as did wealthy financiers, contractors, and merchants. In the great hotels of the old nobility, one could hear aristocrats complaining about the mismanagement of the royal government, and the challenges to their rights and privileges. In the fashionable salons frequented by the city's intellectuals, the conversations might touch upon the failures of the monarchy, but they would range more widely, to attack the foundations of the political and social order, which appeared to be breaking down. Employed in these affluent households were thousands of domestic servants, while additional thousands of artisans and shopkeepers catered to their needs, and to those of other Parisians. At the bottom of the social hierarchy were the miserables, living from hand to mouth, many resorting to crime and prostitution to feed themselves. In no other city in France was the contrast between the great and the lowly, the rich and the poor, so starkly visible as in Paris.

That city was the main setting, the arena, for the great revolution of 1789.

Paris of the Great Revolution: 1789– 1796

*RICHARD MOWERY ANDREWS**

PARIS AND THE FRENCH MONARCHY

"The King reigns at Versailles; public opinion rules in Paris." This adage was current from the late 17th century until October 1789—when its ambivalence was resolved by the massed Parisians who forcibly escorted the royal family from Versailles to a gilded semi-imprisonment in the Tuileries Palace on the Seine. The adage pithily expressed the complex relations that had existed between a monarchy which claimed sovereign authority over all the realm of France and the one "imperial" City of that realm, the City that had lodged and largely created the first French kings, the Capetians of the early Middle Ages. In the 17th and 18th centuries, these relations were especially complex. The pretentions of an "absolutist" state were incompatible with the sophistication and pride of Paris, whose active mass of inhabitants retained, or rapidly acquired, an awareness of their ancient and living power.

In the 1660s, Louis XIV, his court, and ministers permanently fled from the tumultous pressures of the City, and to Versailles. This was an artificial town. For all the Baroque grandeur and calculated magnificence of its Chateau and rituals, in Parisian sensibility Versailles always remained disincarnate, somewhat grotesque, and insulting—"a speck on the ass of Paris," according to popular slang. With the death of the "Sun King" in 1715 and the advent of the Duke of Orleans'

Regency, the political center of gravity shifted back to the City. Between 1713 and 1740, Paris became the cultural, sumptuary, and erotic capital of Europe. For Parisians, it had never ceased to be the political capital of France. Already by the accession of Louis XVI in 1774, Versailles had become a decaying shell of sovereign rule: all vital forms and activities of government—bureaucracies, banking, tax collection, courts of law and public executions, decisive intrigues, and subornments—were centered in the metropolis on the Seine. Well before 1789, during most of the 18th century, each major confrontation between royal policy and Parisian collective will had been won by the latter: (*a*) the protracted struggle between the pro-Jesuit episcopacy, supported by Louis XIV and Louis XV, and the dissident Jansenist clergy, sustained by the bourgeoisie, populace, and "Parlement" (high law court) of Paris, which ended with the dissolution and dispossession of the French Society of Jesus in 1764; (*b*) the equally acerbic and prolix battle between the Crown and the Paris "Parlement" over the issue of the court's right to approve or reject Royal edicts before promulgating them, a battle lost by the monarchy in 1774; and two years later, (*c*) Parisian sabotage, by brutal rioting and savant economic pressures, of the Royal attempt to abolish craft guilds and end regulation of the grain trade.

Between July and October 1789 Parisians saved the National Assembly and the Revolution by successfully resisting the obstructionism of the Old Regime monarchy and the threat of its regiments. On August 10, 1792 they destroyed the remaining authority of the monarchy by frontal assault on the Tuileries Palace and its Swiss Guards batallions (with over 600 killed and wounded among the assaillants), then forced the National Convention to try to execute Louis XVI for betrayal of his oath to the Constitution of 1791 and for treasonous conspiracy with the Austrian Hapsburgs. But contrary to royalist propaganda, and much historiography, Parisians were neither anarchic, antimonarchical, nor even republican in collective sentiment; they became republican by necessity in 1792. The events of 1789 and 1792–93 were not aberrations, brutal ruptures of continuity in French history. In fact, they were moments of a continuity, and are intelligible only within a millenial tradition of relations between the monarchy and the City. Since the 10th century, almost all French kings had depended upon the support or, at very least, the acquiescence of the Parisians. Brilliant, successful reigns had depended profoundly upon alliance with Paris: the more intelligent of French monarchs—Philip Augustus, Louis IX, Francis I, Henry IV, Louis XIII—had respected this fact, lavishing embellishments, patronage, and flattery on the City and its inhabitants. Since the late 17th century, there had developed an ever-widening chasm between court and city; it was temporarily bridged by the Constitution of 1791 (which displaced sovereignty from the monarchy to the Nation, and made the king a chief executive whose ministers were responsible to an elected legislature), but that reconciliation was destroyed by Louis XVI's breaches of contract and of faith with the city and the nation. The French monarchy had originated not through divine right, but in secular investiture by Paris; it ended in 1792–93, and finally in 1848, when Parisians withdrew that investiture.

During the second half of the 18th century, Paris reached a near-apogee, in its long history, of demographic, economic, cultural, and political force, in relation to both the state and the realm of France. In these respects, it bore comparison with only one other Occidental city, Hanoverian London — the city of Parliament, Newgate judges and Tyburn hangmen, of Johnson, Hogarth and Blake, of the Thames docks and Exchange Alley. (Contemporaries, before and during the Revolution, were conscious of this fact: chroniclers on both sides of the Channel obsessively — and uniquely — compared these two urban giants.) With a population of some 650,000 in 1789 (more than twice that of Lyons, second city of France), Paris was surpassed demographically only by London and Naples. As a center of international banking, its only serious rivals were London and Amsterdam. It was the undisputed capital of Europe in all forms of luxury manufactures. Paris was a major port, linked by the Seine with the great harbor at Le Havre and, by the fluvial network of the Yonne, the Aube, the Marne and the Burgundy Canal, with the interior of France. Most provisioning of the City in its vital staples of grain and wines was by river; one can gauge the magnitude of this traffic, and of Parisian drinking habits, by the fact that in the 1780s the City consumed an annual average of 141,400,000 gallons of wine. Paris was also the site of convergence for the finest and most extensive highway system in Europe, and the principal destination for products (dyes, sugar, spices, coffee, silks and calico) from the French colonial empire, and for much of the vast profits from the African slave trade. Both quantitatively and qualitatively, it was the premier city of the Continent in literary production and consumption. Its resident population, down to even the lower ranks of the City's massive petty bourgeoisie, was reputedly (and probably) one of the most literate in Europe. Each of the 52 parishes dispensed elementary instruction for modest sums. There were also, as of early 1792, more than 700 lay schoolmasters, tutors, and semipublic writing teachers throughout the City: shopkeeper and artisan families pooled funds to hire for their children the inexpensive services of these local "literati"; this practice had substantially expanded during the closing decades of the Old Regime, to the detriment of the Parisian clergy and their ideological authority. As the demographic registers of 1793–94 disclose, the great majority of adult male residents either born in the

City, or who had resided most of their lives there, since 1750 could, at very least, sign their names. Learning enjoyed considerable general prestige, and its local purveyors would play important roles in the City's revolutionary assemblies, clubs, and committees. Louis-Sébastien Mercier, the great chronicler of the late 18th century Parisian life, did not exaggerate when he wrote in 1787: "In each building there is always someone known as 'the philosopher'; if a merchant's shop-boy or a solicitor's clerk utters a few striking propositions beyond the ordinary run of ideas, he becomes 'the philosopher.'"[1]

With its scores of academies, "collèges," University faculties, salons, of bureaucracies, chancelleries, administrative corporations and courts of law, 18th century Paris daily generated, and widely diffused, a prodigious quantity of print. It was a City of scribblers and of legalistic formulas. In 1789, Paris harbored almost 2,000 men of the law; the number of bureaucrats and clerks was considerably greater. These institutions and their activities, not classrooms, formed the genuine cultural infrastructure of public literacy in Paris of the later 18th century; all resident and producing classes were variously, and continuously, exposed to the written word. This infrastructure rapidly and massively expanded from the very inception of the Revolution; from 1790 until 1794, the successive governments of the Revolution constantly multiplied bureaucracies, offices, and personnel at all administrative levels; between April 1789 and April 1793, more than 800 new journals and newspapers came into existence throughout France, most of them published in Paris, and the number of newshawkers and pamphlet vendors ("colporteurs") regularly working the streets of Paris in mid-1792 was placed conservatively at roughly one thousand. The image (still current in many texts and historical works) of the typical "sans-culotte" militant of a Paris Section in 1792–94 as essentially a brutish illiterate is thoroughly false, a product of counterrevolutionary myth and not of Parisian realities. The typical Parisian militant and Section official of the Republic possessed at least the elements of formal culture. Most importantly, through a prolonged osmosis with his environment, he had acquired a large arsenal of political and administrative rhetoric and formulas. This, and not sheer physical numbers or simple revolutionary ardor, is what made him so consistently formidable.

PARISIAN ELITES OF THE OLD REGIME: NOBILITY AND CLERGY

The nobility were more strikingly visible in 18th century Paris than they were genuinely numerous or powerful there. Estimates of the number of noble families in the Paris of 1789 vary from 2,000 to 6,000, and the imprecision of these figures is quite significant. Most of these families — including the "nobles of the robe" who controlled the great bureaucracies and courts of the Old Regime — were only seasonally resident in the City, and drew revenue principally from landed estates in the provinces. Only 800 chose to vote in the assembly for election of delegates from the City's Second Estate in April 1789, as against 11,700 electors in the assembly of the Parisian Third Estate. For all the ostentation of their public appearance, patronage of literary and artistic activity, consumption of luxury products, employment of domestics, and contracts for construction and embellishment of town houses, the aristocracy remained essentially peripheral to Parisian economy and internal government. Many formed a debtor class, which rarely paid; they owned only a small portion of Parisian real estate; they were geographically self-segregated, concentrated principally in the *faubourgs* Saint-Honore, Saint-Germain, the "Marais," and the "Isle Saint-Louis"; they were barred from investing in the commerce and manufacturing which sustained the City; their collective arrogance and sensitivity in matters of caste privilege had notably intensified since the 1770s. All of these realities were observed by the bourgeoisie and common people of Paris, who by the 1780s looked upon the aristocracy as parasitic and deeply resented their monopoly of supreme offices in bureaucracies, courts, the Church, and the Army. The only categories of the Third Estate with which the nobility in Paris had extensive social and economic intercourse were the *milieus* of tax farmers, money changers, international bankers, and speculative financiers. And these milieus were detested by the bulk of the Parisian bourgeoisie and laboring classes, as usurers, frauds, engineers of fiscal instability and commercial depressions, agents of foreign powers and rivals, speculators in popular misery. Between 1789 and 1792, the nobility provided the majority of staunchly royalist deputies in the Constituent and Legislative Assemblies. But already by mid-1789, most Parisians had come to perceive the aristocracy as a kind of dangerous collective excrescence, neither Parisian nor even French. (Exceptions were consistently made for individuals of proven patriotism and revolutionary loyalty, and there were several ex-nobles among the deputies elected by Paris to the National Convention in 1792.) During the years 1791–93, the nobility emigrated almost *en masse* from Paris, and many of them from France — to join the coalesced, invading armies of Austria, Prussia and England. Their emigration produced no general dislocation of Parisian economy and society. But their violent repudiation of the City, the Revolution and the Nation gave to Parisians a major psychological weapon, providing the Revolutionary City with its most emotionally-charged, cohesive, and tenacious image of hatred, betrayal, and combat, the indispensable negative image which dialectically clarified republican virtues and purposes: "L'aristocratie!"

From the closing decades of the Old Regime through the Revolution, the relations between Paris and the Church were particularly complex, multiple, and involuted. In the 18th century, Paris remained the ecclesiastical capital of France: 3 cathedral chapters, 52 parishes, 40 monastic establishments and more than 100 convents. As of 1789, there were 3,500 members of regular orders—Benedictines, Dominicans, Lazarists, Franciscans, Cistercians, Carmelites, Ursulines—and a total ecclesiastical personnel in all functions and roles of between 6,000 and 8,000. The number of ecclesiastics periodically resident in the City at any given time was much greater, because of the density of "colleges" and seminaries. Foreign visitors (especially from Protestant countries) were struck by this pullulating swarm of clerics, and often compared Paris, in this respect, to Rome and Madrid. The Church was responsible for charitable relief of the poor—a herculean task during the late 18th century—and administered the great hospitals. It tenaciously retained monopolistic control over higher education, in the "collèges" and the Sorbonne. Throughout the "Île-de-France" and within Paris it was a great landowner. The "Chapter" of Paris possessed full seigneurial rights over important grain-producing domains in the "Île-de-France." And the "dead hand of the Church" (in contemporary bourgeois parlance) held approximately one fourth of income-producing real property in Paris *intra-muros*. From this, it drew an annual revenue of 2,840,000 *livres* as of 1789. Most significantly, fully 2,227,000 livres of this sum belonged to monastic and conventual establishments.[2] Like the nobility, the Church was not subject to taxation under the Old Regime.

The Church was powerful within the City, but far from hegemonic in any sense. Its moral and ideological authority, over both the propertied and popular classes, was in continuous decline across the 18th century. Its prelates and magnates had made the colossal mistake of dogmatically and coercively supporting the pro-Jesuit and pro-papal policies of the monarchy from 1713 to 1764, against the more democratic, Gallican, and pro-Jansenist sympathies of the Parisian bourgeoisie and lower classes; there had been excommunications, expulsions, imprisonments, riots, and deployments of royal regiments. The Clergy of Paris were not a *bloc:* still in 1789 they were riven by internal conflicts and hatreds, both social and ideological. The upper echelons of the hierarchy were aristocratic, conservative, and extremely opulent. The median and lower ranks—especially the parish clergy—were largely recruited from the Parisian middle and petty bourgeoisie, sharing the attitudes and interests of these classes. Many of them in the poorer parishes—such as Saint-Médard, Saint-Ambroise, Saint-Laurent—were obliged by the poverty of the benefice to depend on the active support of parishioners and to live vocations of conscientious service and *misericordia*. In 1790, the majority of the parish clergy of Paris took the oath to the Civil Constitution of the Church, which established the new regime of state control of the Church, nationalization and sale of its properties, election of curés and bishops by parishioners, and their remuneration by fixed salary scales. Most of the upper ranks of the hierarchy were among the more than 40 percent of the City's ecclesiastics who refused the oath.

Parisian anticlericalism of the later 18th century, in its roots, forms and intensities, is a difficult and still-debated historical question. The visible majority of Parisians enthusiastically supported the great Church-State reforms of 1790–91. The bourgeoisie invested heavily in nationalized Church properties—these properties, not those of the *émigré* nobility, formed the most important transfer of wealth in Paris during the Revolution. The popular classes readily accepted the election of curés. Very few Parisians regretted the old episcopacy, or the monastic and conventual orders. The secularization of poor relief and the creation of free public education were consensual demands of Parisians, whereas the pressures for civil marriage, divorce, and burial were minoritarian. The symbolically violent "dechristianization" movement of 1793—whose consummate episode was the procession through Nôtre Dame Cathedral during which a prostitute draped in Grecian robes was proclaimed "Goddess of Reason"—was even more minoritarian. It was very short-lived, regarded as grotesque and politically dangerous by most Parisian authorities and the government of the Republic. Early in 1794, the "ultras" principally responsible for the movement were tried and executed as cryptoroyalists.

Beneath the material dispossessing of the Church, the discrediting of religious dogma and the decline in observant practice, the ritualism and moral sensibility of Catholicism remained deeply rooted in Revolutionary Paris. In 1793–94, during the great crisis years of the Republic —when Parisians, almost alone, had to face civil war in the Vendée and Brittany, the treasonous secession of Lyons, Marseilles, and Bordeaux, and the invading armies of the European powers—this ancient ritualism and sensibility welled up to create unmistakable and powerful syncretisms. There was a public cult of "Martyrs of Liberty" (the most famous were Lepeletier de Saint-Fargeau, Chalier of Lyons, and Jean-Paul Marat) who were commemorated throughout Paris in ceremonies and oblative images—medallions, engravings, paintings, busts, and monuments. Meetings of assemblies and clubs were often moments of intense communion. They followed liturgical patterns: singing of the "Marseillaise" and the "Ça Ira"; readings of letters from volunteers with the armies in the Vendée, on the Rhine or the Spanish frontier (letters replete with details on the Satanic behavior of the counter-revolutionary forces) and of proclamations by the government, the voice of orthodoxy; passing of the hat for "patriotic donations"; mutual denunciations, self-justifications and confessions, followed by either suspension of membership, ostracism, or exoneration and reconciliation; and, at least once weekly, a lengthy sermon on some theme of republican virtue. On the occasion of military victories, solemn processions wound through Paris, converging on the National Convention and the "Place de la Concorde." These were republican *Te Deums*, and they were followed in the evening by "fraternal civic banquets," by drinking and dancing, in each Section of the City.

This syncretism is equally visible in the very moral style of Parisian Jacobin republicanism: the passion for solidarity and unanimity, and the intolerance of dissent; the readiness to pronounce anathemas and to purge; the public moral apotheosis of the laboring poor, for their "simplicity" of life and their generosity; the immense respect for self-sacrificing loyalty, and for politically efficacious casuistry (especially when the two were combined). In these matters of sensibility, there were profound complicities between the bourgeois elites of Republican Paris and their laboring constituents and troops. These complicities operated at the expense of the French clergy; but, one suspects that at deep cultural levels they did not operate at the expense of French Catholicism.

THE SOCIAL AND POLITICAL STRUCTURE OF REVOLUTIONARY PARIS

The political history of the Parisian Revolution, the chronicle of events and legislative acts, has been written many times, and to a current point of saturate redundancy. (This ceaseless and repetitive production is one of the more puzzling sectors of contemporary historical publishing.) That history will not be recounted in this essay. Rather, we shall attempt to probe beneath the political history of the revolutionary City, to examine certain fundamental structures and themes of Parisian social and civic life at the close of the 18th century. Such an itinerary is necessarily sinuous and convoluted: in the later 18th century Paris was one of the most compactedly mysterious cities of the Occident, internally, and externally in relations with the French nation and the French state. Sinuous and convoluted: for we shall also attempt to explore the subjectivity of protagonists. History is never intelligible merely through material structures. Its quintessence is experience.

In the 18th century, Paris was dominated economically by the propertied elites of its Third Estate, by the manifold categories and hierarchies of its bourgeoisie. This had been so long before 1789. In perhaps its most important social meaning within the long history of the City, the Great Revolution was the period during which this dominion became full and political hegemony, an hegemony established in two modes: negatively, at the expense of monarchy, aristocracy, and the Church; positively, over the lower classes of the City. It was the successful mobilization and regimentation of lower class energies and numbers which allowed the propertied elites of revolutionary Paris to dominate each national government from 1789 to 1794 —Constituent Assembly, Legislative Assembly, National Convention —and thereby to influence decisively the course of the French Revolution.

Louis-Sébastien Mercier had insisted in 1787 that the torrential popular violence and depredations of the 1780 riots in London (the "Gordon Riots," later given immortality by Dickens in *Barnaby Rudge*) would be impossible in Paris, for the "empire" of the Parisian bourgeoisie over the lower classes was too powerful.[3] He was essentially correct.

Each major and successful insurrectionary movement of the Parisian Revolution—July 13–14 and October 4–5, 1789, August 9–10, 1792, May 31–June 2, and September 5–6, 1793—was largely orchestrated, led, and politically capitalized upon by vital segments of the Parisian bourgeoisie. The movements which failed had been either opposed or boycotted by the politically majoritarian forces of that bourgeoisie. The significant exception to this pattern was the prison massacres of September 2–5, 1792. This movement—convulsively spontaneous, ferociously violent, and brief—involved only a few hundred executioners, and occurred in the context of the Revolution's supreme crisis, with a seemingly invincible Prussian Army only 150 miles from Paris. It was a prolongation of the assault on the Tuileries Palace, and a response to the sweeping incarcerations of royalists in ill-guarded prisons by municipal order, and to the news of the fall of the fortresses of Verdun and Longwy. It occurred at the moment of departure from Paris of masses of volunteers, marching to meet the Prussians in the Ardennes. The Revolutionary bourgeoisie of Paris was mutedly complicitous in these massacres, although incapable of preventing them: they morally condemned the movement, politically excused it, and never allowed such an outburst of popular terror to recur. And in 1793–94, contrary to certain legends, there was no devolution of local authority in Paris to the lower classes, nor even uniformly to the petty bourgeoisie. To understand the lines of force which determined the internal history of the Parisian Revolution, we must examine the socioeconomic and political geographies of the City.

Between 1789 and 1795, the legislative peregrinations of voting rights were complex, but the suffrage can be divided into two principal forms and periods: the "censitary" period, of the constitutional monarchy, from 1789 to August 1792; the republican period, of relatively democratic suffrage, from August 1792 to the autumn of 1795. The censitary regime comported three categories of citizenship: (1) passive (those who enjoyed civil liberties but were ineligible to vote); (2) active (adult males aged at least 25, resident in their municipality for at least one year, and paying a minimum direct tax equivalent in value to three days of labor, who could vote in primary assemblies but could not become electors or hold office); (3) eligible (persons who met the above stipulations, but who in addition paid a direct tax equivalent to ten days of labor, and could therefore become electors or hold administrative office). In 1791, the property qualification for high legislative office was raised further, to a property or income equivalent of 150 days of labor. In the immediate aftermath of the 10 August Insurrection, the property qualification (and thus the distinction between active and eligible citizenship) was abolished; henceforth, all adult males resident for one year and aged 25 were eligible to vote and hold office; the Constitution of 1793 reduced the age requirement to 21.

The censitary suffrage was intended to exclude from political rights the poor and transient populations. As the Table reveals, within the economic demography of Paris in 1790–91, it embraced even the lowest levels of the petty bourgeoisie and artisan classes: some 75,000 persons enjoyed the status of active citizens. The disproportion between them and "eligible" citizens was not great: in the Sections of Inner Paris, there were only one-third more éligibles than actifs; in the faubourg Sections the numbers within the two categories were equal. The percentages of augmentation of the body politic during the republican period varied widely throughout Paris: in the poorer Sections the increase was from three to four fold; in most, it rarely more than doubled.

The Table (which should be studied with the map) discloses the rough statistical outlines of the socioeconomic and political geographies of Paris during the Revolutionary years. The numerical bulk of the City's population, some two thirds, resided in the Inner City. The majority of its politically active population, from 1790 to 1794, also resided there; although the faubourgs gained considerably in political importance—as measured by the technical right to vote—with the extension of the suffrage in 1792, their body politic never rivalled in magnitude that of the Inner City. They harbored a majority of the

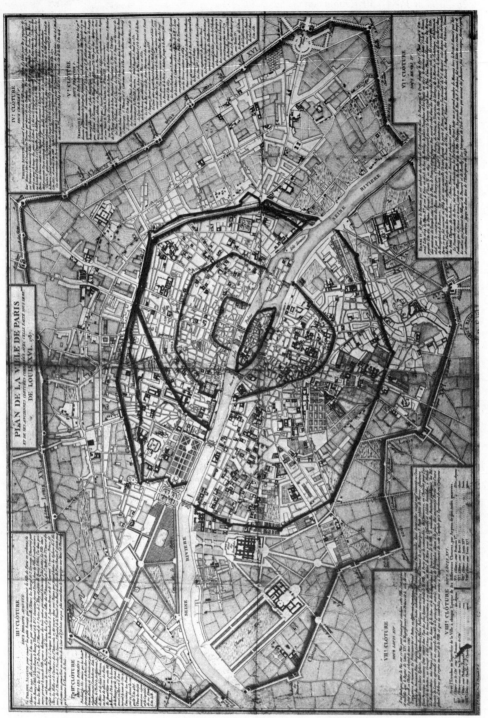

MAP 4.   Paris in 1787 (From Howard C. Rice, Thomas Jefferson's Paris, Princeton University Press, 1976.)
The concentric rings on this map represent the administrative expansion of Paris since the Roman period. The next to last was the official boundary of the City at the beginning of the 18th century. The final boundary – the customs wall of the Royal General Tax Farm – was constructed in 1785–87; incorporating the faubourgs, it made them subject to customs duties. This wall and its toll houses were burned by the people of Paris in mid-July 1789.

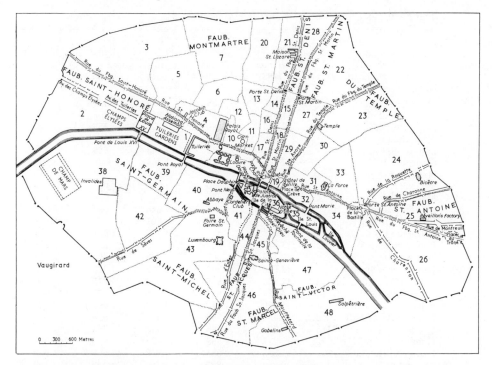

MAP 5.   Revolutionary Paris in Sections (From Georges Rude, The Crowd in the French Revolution, Oxford, at the Clarendon Press, 1959.)

PARIS SECTIONS: 1 TUILERIES 2 CHAMPS ÉLYSÉES 3 ROULE 4 PALAIS ROYAL 5 PLACE VENDÔME 6 BIBLIOTHÈQUE 7 GRANGE BATELIÈRE 8 LOUVRE 9 ORATOIRE 10 HALLE AU BLÉ 11 POSTES 12 PLACE LOUIS XIV 13 FONTAINE MONTMORENCY 14 BONNE NOUVELLE 15 PONCEAU 16 MAUCONSEIL 17 MARCHÉ DES INNOCENTS 18 LOMBARDS 19 ARCIS 20 FAUB. MONTMARTRE 21 POISSONNIÈRE 22 BONDY 23 TEMPLE 24 POPINCOURT 25 MONTREUIL 26 QUINZE VINGTS 27 GRAVILLIERS 28 FAUB. SAINT-DENIS 29 BEAUBOURG 30 ENFANTS ROUGES 31 ROI DE SICILE 32 HÔTEL DE VILLE 33 PLACE ROYALE 34 ARSENAL 35 ÎLE SAINT-LOUIS 36 NOTRE DAME 37 HENRI IV 38 INVALIDES 39 FONTAINE DE GRENELLE 40 QUATRE NATIONS 41 THÉÂTRE FRANÇAIS 42 CROIX ROUGE 43 LUXEMBOURG 44 THERMES DE JULIEN 45 SAINTE-GENEVIÈVE 46 OBSERVATOIRE 47 JARDIN DES PLANTES 48 GOBELINS

City's indigent poor; yet of this social category, there were also 30,203 among a total population of 409,077 within Inner Paris.

The major sociographic distinction in late 18th century Paris was that of the Inner City and the faubourgs; yet the differences between these zones were relative, matters of gradation and densities. Of equal importance, and in political terms, was the extraordinary diversity in distributions of aggregate population, voting population and indigent poor which characterized Inner Paris at the close of the century. The quarters of the Inner City formed a kaleidoscope of all classes,

The Paris Sections: Political and Social Statistics

Section (name and number)	Population (end 1794)*	Indigents (mid-1794)†	Active and Eligible Citizens, 1790‡	Merely Active Citizens, 1790§	Voters, 1793‖
Inner Paris					
Tuileries (1)	15,148	508	1,078	424	–
Palais Royal (4)	11,377	1,365	1,847	807	5,031
Place Vendôme (5)	13,428	784	820	353	3,540
Bibliothèque (6)	9,930	510	1,068	316	–
Louvre (8)	12,691	522	1,148	816	3,318
Oratoire (9)	12,846	365	1,201	592	3,869
Halle au Blé (10)	11,640	200	1,061	638	–
Postes (11)	12,567	900	949	664	3,224
Mail (12)	9,500	370	936	354	3,139
Molière-Lafontaine (13)	9,424	355	843	372	2,670
Bonne Nouvelle (14)	14,860	1,807	801	777	4,181
Ponceau (15)	16,648	521	1,157	1,322	4,356
Bon-Conseil (16)	13,818	642	940	777	5,281
Marchés (17)	13,146	502	608	605	2,724
Lombards (18)	14,811	561	1,077	1,322	3,490
Arcis (19)	11,800	855	693	815	–
Gravilliers (27)	24,774	1,616	1,335	1,070	–
Réunion (29)	16,320	1,219	1,093	1,085	4,378
Homme-Armé (30)	10,481	358	937	636	–
Droits de l'Homme (31)	12,321	1,265	918	781	–
Hôtel de Ville (32)	12,231	4,258	623	820	3,347
Indivisibilité (33)	11,836	855	958	678	3,599
Arsenal (34)	10,264	845	701	645	3,142
Île Saint-Louis (35)	4,862	1,180	430	362	1,614
Cité (36)	11,402	767	693	869	–
Pont-Neuf (37)	5,126	158	586	304	883
Fontaine de Grenelle (39)	12,554	792	1,048	1,052	4,127
Quatre Nations (40)	21,601	1,401	1,623	1,723	–
Théâtre Français (41)	14,400	846	1,636	981	2,418
Thermes de Julien (44)	12,394	1,246	1,053	856	–
Panthéon-Français (45)	24,977	2,630	1,663	1,510	–
The "Faubourgs"					
Champs Elysées (2)	9,000	977	387	317	–
Roule (3)	11,377	1,365	526	424	–
Grange Batelière (7)	10,920	1,031	418	200	–
Montmartre (20)	10,104	1,567	276	198	–
Poissonnière (21)	8,435	1,847	491	279	1,886
Bondy (22)	12,404	1,856	563	673	–
Temple (23)	11,988	1,340	754	665	2,950
Popincourt (24)	10,933	3,930	493	533	2,594
Montreuil (25)	13,479	4,211	444	664	–
Quinze Vingts (26)	18,283	6,601	818	937	–
Nord (28)	11,630	1,938	532	795	–
Finistère (48)	11,775	4,951	704	450	3,783
Jardin des Plantes (47)	15,125	3,946	857	793	–
Observatoire (46)	13,193	2,803	1,112	601	4,212
Luxembourg (43)	16,663	773	1,060	991	4,651
Croix Rouge (42)	16,744	2,037	906	1,001	4,494
Invalides (38)	10,401	1,662	344	634	2,440

The Paris Sections: Political and Social Statistics (continued)

Section (name and number)	Population (end 1794)*	Indigents (mid-1794)†	Active and Eligible Citizens, 1790‡	Merely Active Citizens, 1790§	Voters, 1793‖
Total: Inner Paris..............	409,077	30,203	31,524	24,326	
Total: "Faubourgs"	212,454	42,835	10,685	10,155	
Total: All Paris.................	621,531	73,038	42,209	34,481	

Note. The Sections listed in the category of "faubourgs" include those most, or a large portion, of whose surface was comprised within the boundary of 1785–87, not within the wall of Louis XIV. "Inner Paris" lay within the wall of Louis XIV.

* Albert Soboul, *Les Sans-culottes parisiens en l'an II: Mouvement populaire et gouvernement révolutionnaire, 2 juin 1793 – 9 thermidor an II*, Paris, Clavreuil, 1958, pp. 1091–92.

† Ibid.

‡ Marcel Reinhard, *Nouvelle histoire de Paris: La Révolution, 1789–1799*, Paris, Hachette, 1971, pp. 415–16.

§ Ibid.

‖ Soboul, *Les Sans-culottes Parisiens*, pp. 1093–94. As the table indicates, an official computation was not made in all Sections in 1793–94.

.onditions, and levels of human density. The urban core of Paris, the quarters *intra-muros* (within) were also its political core.

THE FAUBOURGS: MYTHS AND REALITIES

The faubourgs were incorporated to Paris only during the 18th century. Until the creation by royal decree of the new customs wall of the General Tax Farm in 1785–87 (one of the most unpopular and politically maladroit acts of Louis XVI's reign), the bulk of these vast expanses had existed outside the administrative dominion of Paris. After incorporation, they still shaded almost imperceptibly into the outlying rural *banlieue* of the "Île-de-France." In their aggregate, by comparison with Inner Paris, the Sections of the faubourgs were socially crude, only semiurban, and poverty-stricken. In 1792, 20 percent of their population was officially indigent (as against 13.5 percent in Inner Paris); in 1790, only 10.5 percent of their total population was eligible to either vote or hold office (as against 14 percent in Inner Paris). Topographically, the faubourgs were sprawling and chaotic. Demographically, they were very unevenly settled and would remain so until late in the Restoration. The mass of their populations inhabited zones around the great arterial routes leading into Paris. The rest were scattered over a somber landscape of vegetable farms, stock pastures, stone quarries and river hutments. And yet, the faubourgs were bound in multiple ways to the life of Inner Paris.

These were regions of a continuous human flux and reflux. They provided the employers and the revolutionaries of the Inner City with a massive, but volatile, reserve of unskilled labor. The northern faubourgs were inhabited by large numbers of the seasonal building laborers who worked for entrepreneurs of Central Paris. The southern faubourgs of Saint-Victor and Saint-Marceau provided the bulk of the City's river and dock proletariat. Paris depended for much of its daily consumption of vegetables on the farm women and carters of the faubourgs. These areas were initial way stations for provincial immigrants to the City, and they also notoriously served as places of hiding and refuge for its pariahs—the unemployed, debtors, pursued felons, lunatics, and the diseased and, during the Revolution, political suspects from Inner Paris.

Several activities vital to the Parisian economy but repugnant to the City's resident population were largely relegated to the faubourgs: stone quarrying and cutting; curing and tanning of hides; lead, saltpeter, and acid manufacturing (lethal trades); crude smelting and forging; laundry washing (especially of infected hospital linen and rags); maintenance of the Great Sewer which stretched from the faubourg du Temple to the Seine at Chaillot. In one of their most important material and social relations to the Inner City, the faubourgs harbored the great *guingettes*, which combined the qualities of cabarets, gaming dens, and large pleasure gardens with orchestras and dancing; "La Courtille," "Les Porcherons," "La Nouvelle France," "La Petite Pologne," "Le Gros Caillou." (In Marcel Carné's great film, "The Children of Paradise," there are scenes which recreate with stunning accuracy the world of the guingettes during the late 18th and earlier 19th centuries.) On Sundays and holidays much of the Inner City's laboring classes streamed out to the guingettes where wine, food, music, restorative adventure, and equally restorative violence were cheap and plentiful, thus perpetually reforging links with the laboring masses of the faubourgs and the outer banlieue. Louis-Sébastian Mercier and his bourgeois contemporaries understood, but deplored, the weekly Sunday night spectacle of "veritable regiments of drunks returning to the City from the faubourgs, staggering, pounding on the walls . . ."[4]

Before and during the Revolution, for Parisian bourgeois and magistrates, the poor of the faubourgs were objects of suspicion and fear. Their relative primitivism, high illiteracy, recency of arrival, dispersion and baseness of labor made them appear mysterious and dangerous. The poor of Inner Paris were numerous and restive, but they were also compacted, observable, and more easily manipulated. Parisian authorities of the Old Regime and the Revolution were obsessed with identifying persons and groups so as to predict—and hopefully to preempt or control—their behavior. For this reason, authorities of Central Paris perceived the poor of the faubourgs as fluid and seasonal, almost anonymous, and therefore undisciplined.

The wretchedness of dock-workers, hod carriers, quarriers, and laundrywomen ("viragos," especially feared for their muscularity, wooden bat, and aptness to riot) was indeed half-concealed in the labyrinths of the docks and depots of the faubourgs Saint-Marceau and Saint-Victor, or behind the "Montagne Sainte-Genevieve" and over the marshy plain which stretched from the rue Mouffetard to the village of Moutrouge. To the north, in the faubourgs Saint-Martin, Saint-Denis and Roule, there was a universe similar in its murk and desolation: stock and slaughter pens, penurious vegetable farms, refuse and carrion dumps, quarries—many of whose denizens easily slipped into the nocturnal vocation of highwayman. In both urban mentality and fact, the faubourgs were principal zones of passage and habitation for the thousands of beggars, vagabonds, and petty thieves which daily infested the streets of Paris. During the 18th century, it was equally axiomatic that whenever the masses of the faubourgs Saint-Victor and Saint-Marceau streamed over the bridges of the Seine to join comrades of Central Paris and the faubourg Saint-Antoine, this signified a major riot or insurrection.

For Parisians of the Inner City, most of the faubourgs were thus zones of sinister penumbra. Yet, despite these fears and realities, the poor of the faubourgs never spontaneously invaded and violated Inner Paris. They marched either when summoned by their own elites allied with those of the Inner City, as in July and October 1789, July 1791, August 1792, or May and September 1793, or as support waves drawn by the gravitational pull of general popular movements which had originated within the Old City, as in the prison massacres of September 1792, the grocery riots of February 1793, and in the spring of 1795.

Throughout the faubourgs, even the most socially primitive, there were thousands of relatively solidly implanted tradesmen and small and middling master-entrepreneurs, principally in metallurgy, building construction and related trades, carting and hauling, and woodworking and furniture making. This class formed the pre-Revolutionary social elites of most faubourgs; it was the class which also dominated and regimented the political life of most Sections of the faubourgs. Precisely because of the precarious and seasonal character of employment in these regions, the economic and subsequent political power of this entrepreneurial class was locally very considerable. Because of these local elites, their power, roles, and interests, the populace of the faubourgs never became anarchic in relation to Central Paris. Among the Revolutionary elites of each of these Sections, there were members of the Jacobin Club and deputies to the Municipality and Commune. These linkages were active expressions of a deeper reality, the general mutuality of interest joining the productive bourgeoisie of the faubourgs with that of central Paris: desire for local self-government and for a preponderant influence over the State; hatred of the nobility, and of bankers, financiers, and currency speculators; skepticism regarding the Church; desire for property aggrandizement; the need to ensure labor discipline without having to increase wages substantially themselves, and therefore to force the State to guarantee the provisioning of Paris in vital staples at cheap prices; ardent enthusiasm towards the opening of civic careers to those of talent, and modest capital.

During the second half of the 18th century, until the depression of the late 1780s, the faubourgs had been zones of relative economic opportunity for immigrants or natives possessed of energy, skills, and even small capital. The revolutionary elites of the faubourg sections were composed in their majority of men whose socioeconomic careers during the last decades of the Old Regime had been on the ascent, both locally and in relation to the general Parisian economy. It is anachronistic to describe them (as Albert Soboul and George Rudé have done) as a declining petty bourgeoisie fighting a rear-guard action against the concentration of manufacturing and commercial capital: this is to view them distortedly from a late 19th or 20th century historical vantage, and to ignore their collective biographies, their local stature and its meanings.

At the end of the century, Saint-Antoine was the most "classic" of the great faubourgs; it is the one which created for itself the most brilliant legend of revolutionary militancy; it was also the most internally homogeneous and closely linked to the Inner Parisian economy among the faubourgs. In addition to a swelling mass of semitransient laborers, most of them recent immigrants, its three Sections—"Quinze Vingts," "Montreuil," and "Popincourt"—contained in 1790 at least 5,000 resident craft workers; this was a dense and redoutable mass whose combative potential became manifest under the walls of the Bastille on July 14, 1789, in the cannon-raked courtyard of the Tuileries Palace on August 10, 1792, and in each of the great subsequent *journées*. The bulk of these laborers worked within the dominant sectors of Saint-Antoine's economy: principally, woodworking, furniture-making, carpentry, and building construction; secondarily, metallurgy and rough textile manufacturing. Of the 80 men who formed the genuine and official elites of these three Sections—who concerted the faubourg's participation in general movements and who led—61 were masters of these trades, and many were heads of ateliers and chiefs of enterprises. They could command labor, votes, and loyalties. They had coalesced as a local social elite well before the Revolution—in a region without aristocratic presence or a large mercantile or manufacturing bourgeoisie, with relatively few members of the liberal professions, and a mass of immigrant laborers. Their scale of direct employment in ateliers was small by modern industrial standards (from 10 to 20 apprentices and journeymen), but through subcontracting and piecework they could provide sustenance to many others.

In the later 18th century, the artisan elite of the faubourg formed a rather exclusive, but not thoroughly closed, universe of extended families and clans, which were bound by solidarities of marriage and trade association. Five of these "dynasties" — each of them surmounted by an aged patriarch — were extremely prominent in the revolutionary politics of the faubourg: the Rebours, Caumont, Bertrand, Chauvin, and Damoye. The last of these, the Damoye clan, was a figuration in dramatic extreme of the general social characteristics — energy, ambition, cunning, power to command — which made the artisan elite of the faubourg Saint-Antoine both locally formidable and, in moments of crisis, so very useful to the revolutionary authorities of Central Paris.

In 1733, the elder Damoye, founder of the dynasty, had emigrated on foot as an adolescent from a village in the north, near Beauvais, to the faubourg Saint-Antoine. Apprentice, journeyman, master, then merchant-manufacturer, during the following two decades he ascended the hierarchy of the trade of carriage-maker and ironmonger. About 1770, he purchased a group of buildings at the Porte Saint-Antoine (in the most urbanized and expanding area of the faubourg), including no. 2 Porte Saint-Antoine where he had lived, as a neighbor of the Chauvin family, since 1735. The alliance with the Chauvin dynasty, hat-manufacturers on the rue du Lappe, had long since been sealed. The second generation of the Damoyes was characterized by a dual expansion — of manufacturing and commercial enterprise and of real estate aggrandizement in the faubourg. In 1773, Antoine-Pierre, eldest son of the *père* Damoye, married the daughter of a master-merchant of the faubourg; her dowry was 25,000 livres; his father added 40,000 to this sum. The other sons directed the family carriage-making business, which passed from a capital value of 10,577 livres in 1775 to 279,913 in 1793. Antoine-Pierre Damoye, officially a master carriage-maker like his father and brothers, made extensive further investments in real estate and established a major carriage renting and wagon hauling enterprise in the faubourg. In 1790, his personal capital assets were officially evaluated at 250,000 livres.

Elector of the district's Third Estate in 1789, officer of the Municipality of 1791–92, deputy to the Insurrectionary Commune of August 1792 from the Section "Montreuil," an executive administrator of the Paris "Department" in 1793–94, member of the Jacobin Club: until 1795, Antoine-Pierre Damoye was a principal leader of the revolutionary faubourg Saint-Antoine. From the first years of the Revolution, he bought nationalized Church, royal, and aristocratic properties.

In an act which comports for us immense historical symbolism, and as if personally to crown a *faubourien* dynastic triumph or to render homage to its solidarities, in 1793 Antoine-Pierre Damoye purchased for his large family the *chateau* of an *émigré* aristocrat, with its landscaped gardens and extensive farm lands. This chateau was in the Oise — about 20 kilometers from the peasant village which the père Damoye had left on foot in 1733.

The wealth of the Damoyes was exceptional in the faubourg Saint-Antoine. But the civic stature of Antoine-Pierre Damoye was based on local affinities which bridged possible chasms of economic class. This family, and its counterparts among the other revolutionary "dynasties" of the region, were respected because they incarnated certain virtues cherished by the artisan petty bourgeoisie of the faubourg: (a) continuity with the difficult and generic years of mid-century when the distinctive social personality and possibilities of the faubourg were forged by perseverant labor; (b) continuity with the social defiance of the père Damoye who had walked out of a feodated seigneurial village at the age of 14; and (c) continuity with a subsequent two thirds of a century of loyalty to the faubourg; in the case of Antoine-Pierre Damoye, civic courage and loyalty (he shouldered a musket under the walls of the Bastille), and efficaciousness in representing the faubourg's interests among the revolutionary authorities of larger Paris. For these values and these energies were shared by Damoye's comrades among the revolutionary elite of the faubourg. Three of them witness for scores of others.

Marien Chappuis had immigrated, as a journeyman tailor, to the Porte Saint-Antoine in 1771, from the Allier in central France; he became a master tailor and protegé and friend of the Damoye family. After this initial success and implantation, in the late 1770s and 1780s his four sisters followed him to Paris, and married young artisans and tradesmen of the Montreuil quarter who were either friends or social analogues of Chappuis: Joseph Haut, cabinet-maker; F.-P. Boudin, wood-turner; A.-A. Cottereau, tradesman; J.-M. Vacret, stocking-weaver. Here, the nucleus of an extended clan had been formed before 1789: from the inception of the Revolution, Chappuis, Boudin, Cottereau, and Vacret became militant cadres of the Section, officers of its militia force, and in 1793–94, revolutionary commissioners. The social trajectory of P.-J. Gilles, master marble cutter, was similar. In 1783 he had arrived in the faubourg from the village of Montatour in Brittany, and was lodged by a relative from earlier immigration, a wineshop owner on the rue de Charonne. In 1790, Gilles, now a master of the trade, was joined by his younger brother, apprentice marble-cutter. During the Revolution, he became one of the Section's most energetic revolutionaries and then police commissioners. Charles Balin, of the neighboring Quinze-Vingts Section, was native to the faubourg; son of a cabinet-maker, in 1789 he was a 29 year old journeyman cabinet-maker. Member of the prestigious "Society of the Vanquishers of the

Bastille" (composed of veterans of the assault); company captain; and justice of the peace of his Section: Balin was a principal militant leader of the "Quinze-Vingts," and a principal target of the purges of 1795. Then, his ascendent conservative enemies said of him:

> A powerful, sonorous voice allowed him to dominate the assemblies, which he frequently presided over. Author of all the petitions, member of all the deputations, all the illegal actions of the Section are in large part his work.[5]

In characteristically Jacobin accents, Balin answered from prison: "I was poor before the Revolution; I am still; my conscience is pure." This was the respected, laborious and productive "poverty" of the faubourg, and Balin added that he was born and had lived his entire life in the region, "where for nearly a century my family has existed, with a spotless reputation."[6] Damoye, Chappuis, Gilles, Balin, and their comrades were all bound in self-conscious solidarities of faubourien pride of achievement, and community of aspirations in relation to the region, the larger City, and the Revolution.[7]

Their examples would be multiplied by hundreds in the faubourgs. Throughout these Sections, the schema of revolutionary leadership resembled that of the faubourg Saint-Antoine: coalitions of older and more successful entrepreneurs, young and energetic artisans and tradesmen, and local clerks and "literati." Physically robust, easily belligerent and even violent in dealing with opposition from both social inferiors and superiors, this petty bourgeois leadership remained very close to the world of manual labor, and its members proved themselves adept at regimenting and manipulating the energies of the genuine and dangerous poor of the faubourgs.

In several of the great journées of the Parisian Revolution, the participation of the faubourg Sections—serried battalions marching into Central Paris—was spectacular in its mass and visibility, and this participation reanimated an older legend of the volatility of these populations. Yet, during the course of the Parisian Revolution, the initiative, program, and organization of major political movements was always provided by quarters of Central Paris, those of the "Halles," the rues Saint-Denis and Saint-Martin, and Latin Quarter. Zones of leadership, these classical quarters also provided masses of insurrectionary troops. Satellites to the economic and social life of the late 18th century Paris, the faubourgs were also satellites to the politics of the revolutionary City.

ECONOMIC STRUCTURES

During the second half of the 18th century, the Parisian economy embraced six principal sectors of activity: administrative bureaucracies and the law; finance and banking; commerce in food and drink; luxury production (including printing and publishing); clothing, fabric, textile, and accessories manufactures; building construction and related trades. Most of these sectors, in their density and importance, were predominantly concentrated intra-muros.

Although there were dense concentrations of bureaucrats and men of the law resident in the Latin Quarter, the faubourg Saint-Germain and the "Cité," bureaucracies, the law, finance, and banking were highly localized geographically in western Paris, from the "Grange-Batelière" to the Tuileries and from the Louvre to the "Place Vendôme" (Sections —Tuileries, Palais Royal, Place Vendôme, Bibliothèque, Mail, and Molière et Lafontaine.) This was the most secularly monumental, metropolitan, and wealthy region of Paris, the site of the major organisms of state and their personnel, and of finance and banking, both before and during the Revolution. In their aggregate, its propertied classes were the most politically and socially conservative of the revolutionary City.

The "Halles," the ancient and great central market area near the rue Saint-Denis, remained the core of the immense Parisian economy of grains and foodstuffs. The great convoys of these provisions arrived here, to be sold by a mass of wholesalers and retailers. Highly structured, regulated, and internally disciplined, with a remarkable stability of roles and commercial population, the "Halles" were one of the most "perennial" quarters of Paris. Its population of small-scale food tradesmen and tradeswomen (the renowned *poissardes*, or fishwives) were daily barometers of relations between the City and the provisioning world of rural France, and thus of real or imminent shortages and price increases. They enjoyed enormous influence among the Parisian laboring classes and petty bourgeoisie, and, when they chose, over organs of government. Since the 14th century, most major seditions involving the popular classes had originated in the "Halles." This was not a region of indigence or of social dependence. Louis-Sébastien Mercier and Restif de la Bretonne, the two great anatomists of Paris at the end of the century, respected the people of the "Halles" and appreciated their political sophistication. In the 1790s, the civic dynamism of this people was sustained and powerful, but always focused on the fundamental question of subsistence provisioning of Paris. Their contribution to the Revolution in 1789 was less the assault on the Bastille, than the march on Versailles in October. The Sections of this zone initiated the movement which led to the overthrow of the monarchy in August 1792, but provided very few executioners in the prison massacres of September. The Terror which they propelled in 1793 was limited, directed at grain merchants, financiers, food wholesalers, hoarders, and speculators, a terror conceived by them as the only possible means of ensuring the provisioning of the City. Until the summer of 1795, the principal Sections of the "Halles" — Marchés, Halle au Blé, and Bon Conseil — were among the most politically militant and efficacious in Paris.

During the Revolution, Paris contained almost 3,000 wineshops, cabarets, taverns, and cafes, with their greatest density in the central and arterial quarters of the rues Saint-Denis and Saint-Martin. There were some 600 bakers and 1,000 grocers throughout the City. These tradesmen (and especially tavern and wineshop owners) varied enormously in wealth and scale of enterprise. Collectively, they had considerable authority over other groups of the petty bourgeoisie and the poor, and their extension of short-term credit — largely because of daily proximity (artisans and laborers usually lunched in the taverns, and also filled the wineshops after work). Barometers of popular attitudes, tavern-keepers and wineshop owners were also informal regulators of political discourse. In each Section, they provided the City with revolutionary cadres.

The scope of luxury production in Paris was the widest in Europe: gold and silver work, jewelry, sword and gun-making, enameling, engraving, fine chiseling, ornamental painting, monumental sculpture, watch-making, crafting of optical and precision instruments, bookbinding, dry-point etching, and every form of material embellishment technically possible in the 18th century. The thousands of these craftsmen (in 1788 there were more than 600 master goldsmiths and jewelers alone) had made Paris the sumptuary capital of the Occident. They were represented locally in practically every quarter of the City intra-muros, but were particularly numerous and socially prominent in four regions: the Latin Quarter, the "Cité" Island, the rue des Lombards, and the opulent zones of the Palais-Royal and the Place Vendôme. In this sector of the Parisian economy, as in most others, the hierarchies of class and scale of production varied widely, from genuine master-manufacturers to myriads of precariously self-employed artisan tradesmen with miniscule boutiques.

The building and related metallurgical trades, and textile, clothing fabric, and accessories manufacturing and commerce employed by far the largest work forces in late 18th century Paris. In structure, they were also the most socially pyramidal of all sectors of the Parisian economy: at the base, tens of thousands of unskilled or semiskilled proletarians, many of them only seasonally employed and at piece-rates, and journeymen with little chance of ever becoming independent masters; legions of tenuously independent small masters and tradesmen, who themselves worked on the building site, in the atelier or the sewing-room with their handfuls of laborers; hundreds of median entrepreneurs with substantial work forces; and, at the summit, several scores of industrial-style entrepreneurs, also often merchants and shippers (in the textile, fabric, and accessories sector), with relatively stable work forces numbering into the hundreds.

As of 1791, there were approximately 2,000 individual enterprises of the building, metallurgical, and woodworking trades: somewhat over half of them were distributed throughout the "inner" regions of the faubourgs, and the rest were heavily concentrated in the constricted and thickly populated central and northern quarters of the Right Bank. The economic magnitude of textile, clothing, fabric, and accessories production and commerce was even greater — if one includes the multitude of nonproducing shops (*boutiques de modes,* of all qualities) and the hundreds of dealers in old clothes, used fabrics, and haberdashery. (The laboring classes of late 18th century Paris rarely purchased from the boutique de modes or were measured by the tailor. They bought from the old clothes dealer, and for this reason were immediately recognizable — especially in evenings of diversion, on Sundays and holidays — by the frayed and bizarre discordances of their costumes.) This production was more geographically localized, both in enterprises and work forces, than the building trades: principally in the central region of the Right Bank. In the four principal Sections of the rues Saint-Denis and Saint-Martin — Lombards, Bon-Conseil, Ponçeau, and Gravilliers — there were, in 1791, at least 235 of these enterprises. They surmounted and periodically gave sustenance to a massive population of workers locally resident (and transient) in furnished rooms, lodging houses, and garrets.

For decades, these two sectors of the Parisian economy had experienced mounting prosperity, a reflection of the general growth cycle of the French urban and rural economies which began at mid-century. This prosperity was ended by the commercial crisis which began in 1786–87, a crisis which deepened during the 1790s. It was in these two sectors of the Parisian economy that the social questions of discipline of the laboring classes, unemployment, popular subsistence, crime, and commercial survival were most acute, and from the very advent of the Revolution.

Genuine economic sovereignty, as expressed through control of production and labor, was held in late 18th century Paris by some 50,000 artisans, merchants, and tradesmen. Within this mass, socio-economic conflicts and cleavages, just as hierarchies of wealth and power, were extensive; and yet, so also were fundamental solidarities of interests and aspirations.

For Parisians, the Revolution of 1789 occurred at the temporal intersection of economic, political, and social crises. These matters were not simply material. They were human and moral, and experienced within the unyielding physical strictures of a very ancient City.

THE INNER CITY

Human density, social compression, promiscuity, and abrasiveness of contact: these themes described, and largely determined, the quality of collective existence and of social relations in Inner Paris of the 18th century. They profoundly illuminate the social and political history of the Parisian Revolution.

Human Density

Approximately two thirds of the City's population of 650,000 lived in the Inner City, and the majority of these inhabited the extraordinarily constricted area of the medieval quarters of the Center—on the Right Bank, along and off the rues Saint-Denis and Saint-Martin, and on the Left Bank along and around the rues Saint-Jacques, Montagne Sainte-Geneviève, de la Harpe. There was an average of 900 to 1,000 persons per each 2.5 acres in Central Paris, one of the most important population densities in urban Europe of the late 18th century. The quarter of the "Lombards," near the "Place de Grève," could be walked from east to west in less than seven minutes, and from south to north in no more than ten. This rectangle harbored 11,500 persons in 1789, and then 13,500 by 1794. The region of the "Montagne Sainte-Geneviève" on the Left Bank contained almost 25,000. During the second half of the 18th century and far into the 19th, it was the ancient quarters of Central Paris (whose topography and physical infrastructure had barely changed since the Renaissance)—and not the faubourgs—which had to absorb most of the relentless increase in the population of Paris, an increase due principally to raw provincial immigration.

Social Compression

In 18th century Paris spatial segregation by economic class was minimal. The very wealthy tended to cluster in the quarters of the Palais-Royal, the Tuileries and the faubourgs Saint-Germain and Saint-Honoré. But even these pockets of affluence were not genuinely isolated. The poor, although particularly numerous in the faubourgs, were almost ubiquitous, varying only in their mass and the gradations of their misery. In the quarter of the Hôtel-de-Ville, they formed one third of the population. The adjacent quarters of the rues Saint-Denis and Saint-Martin contained the City's most important concentration of cheap lodging houses and furnished rooms, which harbored thousands of semiresident proletarians. The depths of popular misery were in the faubourgs, but the aggregate of the City's laboring classes, like the majority of its propertied classes, lived in Inner Paris. The propertied and the propertyless were locked into mutually close proximity, just as they were bound in a tension-ridden symbiosis. Practically each quarter possessed social hierarchies ranging from wealth to poverty. Generally, class segregation was more vertical than horizontal, a matter of more or less expensive and spacious rentals within individual apartment buildings. Within individual quarters, the wealthier and more respectable would at most, monopolize certain streets or portions of them. Building contractors on the rue Saint-Martin lived only a short distance from the lodging houses of "sleep merchants" where their laborers bedded down on straw mats, often four to a room. Textile manufacturers on the rue Greneta owned and inhabited buildings whose attic garrets were occupied by piecework seamstresses, *grisettes* who frequently doubled as prostitutes.

Promiscuity and Abrasiveness of Contact

All of the massive sources from late 18th century Paris—literary, pictorial, administrative, and archival—attest to this reality, a reality whose principal arena was the street. In its social life and relations, 18th century Paris was an intensely "public" City, to an extent difficult of imagination for a mid-20th century urban dweller in America or Europe (except perhaps for those in slums or ghettos.) The streets of Inner Paris were narrow and labyrinthine, filled by a thick, slow, and frequently clogged circulation of pedestrians, hand-carts, wagons, hackney-coaches, carriages, and horses, a circulation in which all classes mingled daily. Most retail commerce in foodstuffs did not occur in shops and over counters, but in open market places and on the streets. Below the level of luxury craftsmanship, almost every type of commodity produced in Paris was also sold in some form—new, used or stolen—on these streets. There were thousands of ambulant vendors of objects and services—caged birds, mirrors and window-glass, bowls and plates, magic lanterns, flowers, vegetables, parasols, old shoes, boots and clothes, amulets, medallions and palm-readings, rabbit and cat skins, milk and curds, pigeons and chickens, dentistry and medicine ("empirical" doctors of the *carrefours*), coffee, strong drink, and shaving water, song-sheets, brochures, almanacs and pornographic engravings. This was the provisioning of Paris by the *petits métiers de la rue*. Most of these trades had their distinctive cries, which formed a strange and wondrous music: shrill, lancinant, undulant, sometimes guttural, and occasionally Gregorian in the melodiousness and resonance of the chant. (Parisians of all classes lived amidst a din of human and animal noises, which slackened only late at night.) The bulk of money-changing, especially of coin (both genuine and counterfeited), also occurred on the street—around the "Bourse," along and off the rue Vivienne, and in the arcades of the "Palais-Royal."

Paintings, etchings, and engravings of late 18th century Paris eloquently and loyally convey to us this intense traffic and trafficking of life. In these *tableaux* all classes are distinctly recognizable by dress and gesture, and yet are inextricably mingled in the congested flow. All are simultaneously, in varying styles and intensities, spectators, participants, and accomplices: the bishop peering from his stalled carriage at two brawling carters whose collided wagons have jammed the narrow exit from the "Pont Nôtre-Dame" to the rue Saint-Martin, who addresses them, not in language of Christian desistment but in shouts of enraged impatience and encouragement; the aristocrat whose galloping horse has sprayed with mud some market-women of the "Halles," who is rapidly unhorsed, fights (but does not dare draw his sword), submits to the judgment of the crowd, pays and then resumes his progress at slow trot, amidst general laughter and cheers; the "empirical doctor" on the "Place de la Contrescarpe" who spots a passing bourgeois, quietly sics his trained dog, and then cauterizes the bite with a hot iron (standard treatment for possible rabies before Pasteur) for coin and in the center of an appalled and delighted crowd; the hotly pursued criminal or deserter emerging from an old clothes dealer's shop on the rue du Louvre, still tugging at one leg of his newly acquired breeches and identity.

Paris was also the European capital of print, in the daily fabric of its social exchanges, a preeminent City of spoken discourse, of "la parlotte." Like an indispensable wellspring, the language of the popular classes irrigated that of their bourgeois masters—a fact which would be amply registered in revolutionary discourse.

Most streets had their resident story-teller, the "diseur de bonne aventure." Their tales divided roughly into three genres: thinly veiled political satire; picaresque episodes of social inversion through sexual conquest (the stable-boy who becomes majordomo of the *chateau* by seducing the countess, or the apprentice who marries the widow of the master); and especially military exploits, for many of the "diseurs" were ex-soldiers. Only the more seriously injured or least clever of disabled and homeless veterans retired to the Royal—and then Republican—military hospital at the Invalides. The others spun artful tales on street corners and in wineshops for small coin, food, and drink. They were venerated fixtures of Parisian landscape, even for magnates of birth or intellect. The Duke of Orleans, the great chemist Lavoisier, the naturalist Buffon regularly paused or detoured to listen, occasionally to interpellate, and always to pay. In the 1780s the American War was an extremely popular subject, and redskins a major fascination. (If the number of actual veterans of Rochambeau's expeditionary force had equalled that of claimants among "diseurs de bonne aventure," the British would have been overwhelmed within a week.) During the Revolution, the embroidered imagery shifted to charges at Jemappes, Hondeschoote, and Fleurus, and to the conquest and looting of Northern Italy by the "Little Corporal" and his army. For his famous, fabulistic, and cynical painting of Bonaparte riding over the Saint-Bernard Pass like a republican Hannibal, Jacques-Louis David was lavishly paid by the state. This painting merely traduced on canvas what was being spoken for small coin, with far less cynicism, in Parisian streets and wineshops by disabled veterans who knew the truth.

Because of this promiscuity, this constant traffic and trafficking of life, the streets of 18th century Paris were potent. They easily generated chance encounters which transformed lives. Incidents of this fact are plethorically recorded in literature, autobiographies, and police documents. Let us observe one composite incidence of this transformational power.

On a Saturday evening in November 1792, a 20-year-old journeyman carpenter strolled to the rue Saint-Denis in search of pleasure. He wore a napped white woolen jacket of military cut, recently purchased from an old clothes dealer on the Quai de la Féraille. Unlike the dealer, the journeyman had failed to notice, or to understand, the faint outlines of stitch-marks on the sleeves of the jacket—traces of removed insignia. In the dense nocturnal flow of the rue Saint-Denis, he crossed paths with a young captain of the Fifth Infantry Regiment of the Line, briefly on leave from the mud of the Austrian Netherlands. After quick, intense, and accurate scrutiny, the captain gently accosted the journeyman and the following conversation occurred:

> Excuse me citizen, but haven't we met before?
>
> No, I don't think so, I don't recall.
>
> You're from Normandy!
>
> Yes, Argentan. Do you know it?
>
> Argentan! It must have been there! What a splendid town, the finest cider and the most appetizing girls in France! How I enjoyed my stay there! Citizen, my comrade and I would like to offer you a "chopine" [the pewter pint of rough red wine]. We're strangers to Paris, soldiers on leave, and it's always a pleasure to clink pints with a brisk and hearty Norman. Argentan, imagine that!

The captain was then joined by his "comrade," the smiling, gnarled, and thoroughly experienced sergeant who had accompanied him on leave to Paris. The three entered a wineshop. After a few "chopines," the captain excused himself and proceeded to more refined pleasures in the elegant brothels and gaming dens of the "Palais-Royal." But the sergeant remained with the journeyman and with many "chopines," finally to guide the drunken hand of a provincial immigrant onto the signature line of a printed form entitled: "Army of the French Republic, Fifth Infantry Regiment of the Line." The following day, the captain, sergeant, and recruit departed—with numerous others—for the canister-swept and blood-swarmed lines of Brabant. With Parisian artfulness, the captain and sergeant had replaced a genuine deserter. They had also created a pure "sans-culotte," a cannon-fodder volunteer of the Republic, and given a new chapter to the already long life of the white woolen jacket, with faint outlines of stitch-marks on its sleeves.

Superimposed on the material, socioeconomic geography of Paris there was another geography whose thematic coordinants were spectacles; carnality, and a generalized brutality of social relations. Its most important sites were also within Central Paris.

The "Place de Grève," in the dead center of Paris and facing the municipal edifice of the "Hôtel-de-Ville," resumed all of these themes. Here, laborers massively assembled each morning in the hope of being hired by entrepreneurs—mostly building contractors and fabric, clothing, and accessories manufacturers. Striking workers also converged here, before and during the Revolution, to manifest their demands to the authorities of bourgeois Paris in the Hôtel-de-Ville. Immigrant laborers often began their Parisian careers on the "Grève"; many of them, after having slid from unemployment and destitution into crime, had their careers ended here, on the gallows or the wheel. The Parisian Revolution began on the "Grève," on July 13–14, 1789. During those 24 hours the bourgeois leadership of the City in the Hôtel-de-Ville transformed the electoral assembly of the Third Estate into the Commune of Paris, organized a militia in each district of the City, sacrificed the Provost of Merchants to the popular insurgents packed into the "Place," and then channeled the mass of these insurgents into the faubourg Saint-Antoine, to the assault on the Bastille. In subsequent years, when the revolutionary Municipality of Paris wished to show its strength to the national government, it was to the "Grève" that it summoned the City's masses, marshalling them and parading its control over them.

In 1772, the historian Jaillot tersely expressed three of the several meanings of the Place de Grève: "This square serves for public festivals, for the Saint-Jean fireworks show, and for the execution of criminals."[8] The births of "dauphins," heirs to the throne, were lavishly and publicly celebrated here. Each June 23—on the eve of the summer solstice—there was the semipagan Saint-Jean fireworks show on the "Grève," sponsored by the municipality and the monarchy until the Revolution. The pyrotechnic display was followed by a vast, and officially sanctioned, nocturnal bacchanalia of masques and disguisements, drinking, dancing, love-making, molestation, and violence, by a kind of Shake-spearean "mid-summer night's dream" during which law, constraint, and roles were suspended until dawn. While Parisians revelled on the "Grève" and throughout its environs, the illuminated royal barges cruised the Seine, laden with food, drink, and orchestras.

From the late 16th century until the Revolution, it was also on the "Grève" that the State hanged, whipped, and broke on the wheel its malefactors. Hangings were less frequent in 18th century Paris than in Hanoverian London. The penal code of French "despotism," although plethoric and sanguinary, was less murderous than that of English "liberty." Common theft was punished by public whipping and brand-ing (not the rope), yet highwaymen and murderers were broken on the wheel, a prolonged and ornamented death. But Paris, like London, was known as a City of the gallows, the hangman's town. These spectacles of justice were festive rites, cherished by all classes, for differing motives: for the monarchy and the magistrates of Paris, they were sumptuous, didactic ceremonies of power; for the popular classes, they were pre-cious occasions of mockery, of malediction or sympathy, of respite from labor (hanging days were holidays), of adventurous concourse, drunk-enness, and thieving; for the bourgeois and aristocrats who rented windows from apartment dwellers along the "Place," they were sub-jects for diversion, carnal fascination, and conversational judgments.

The revolutionary government suppressed all corporal punishments and replaced the rope and the wheel with the infinitely more humane guillotine. Executions were shifted from the "Grève" to the "Place de la Révolution" (actual "Place de la Concorde"). Parisians had long been addicted to the spectacle of public chastisement, and yet, during the year of the Terror, the crowds at guillotinings were far more disciplined and less sanguinary than those which had flocked to the gallows on the "Grève."

Until as late as 1770, an annual ceremony of exorcism—for those possessed by Satan—was held during the opening days of Holy Week in the "Sainte-Chapelle." These scenes of convulsionary hysterics and ecclesiastical shamanism would have been thoroughly familiar to Parisians of the 14th century. They drew huge crowds and large sums of money. To the northeast, on the perimeters of the faubourgs du Temple and Saint-Antoine, there was the "Place du Combat," near the heights of Montfaucon (site of the medieval gibbet) and the great carrion refuse-dump. From 1778 to 1848, this was the site of weekly animal fights: in a large circus arena, dogs were pitted against bulls, wild boars, wolves, and occasionally panthers.

The streets of the City, before and during the Revolution, swarmed with jugglers, puppeteers, singers of obscene ballads, acrobats, organ-grinders and mimes. Until 1792, they were continuously traversed by often lurid religious processions. In the 18th century, Paris, not London, was the European capital of theater, and especially of street theaters. In the faubourg du Temple alone there were seven of these which each day performed a scatalogical *comedia dell'arte;* there were dozens more, of all qualities, in the region of the Palais-Royal. Eighteenth century Paris was renowned throughout Europe as a City of grand farce. In 1798 when Bonaparte's army took Cairo, the general — in order to maintain the morale and discipline of the troops, many of whom were Parisian or from urban France — urgently requested the government in Paris to send out the following: a ballet troup, a theater company, a marionette show, 100 prostitutes, 25,000 gallons of brandy and 125,000 gallons of wine. In one of the largest squares of Cairo, the Army of Egypt constructed a pleasure garden which closely resembled the great guingettes of the "Courtille" and the "Porcherons."

In 18th century Paris, even madness was trafficked as spectacle. "Bicêtre," the major prison-hospital for the insane, was partially self-financed, for each week the more frenzied inmates were put on show. The performances were announced throughout Paris by street-criers and drew paying audiences from all classes. "Bicêtre" was also a principal station in the careers of thousands of prostitutes in late 18th century Paris. Those arrested (usually for not having paid the police) were sent to the prison of "La Force" on the rue Saint-Martin, where they were tried. On the last Friday of each month those condemned were escorted — in broad daylight and in long convoys of open carts — across all of central Paris to the hospital of the "Salpêtrière" in the faubourg Saint-Marcel. There, a *triage* occurred: the healthy remained in the "Salpêtrière"; the manifestly venereal once more traversed Paris in open carts, to incarceration at "Bicêtre." These processions were festivals of dialogue. Throngs in the streets exchanged brutal, inventive, and joyous *lazzis* (insults) with the tied occupants of the carts.

The Palais-Royal was perhaps the consummate site of that intense *brassage* (abrasive rubbing) of all classes which characterized 18th century Parisian life. It was the most brilliant, lascivious, socially complex, and in many ways mysterious quarter of the City. Although its political role within Paris was immense before and during the Revolution, its history remains to be written. (Most modern historiography of revolutionary Paris has been accomplished by respectable middle-class Marxist academics; they have given only peripheral attention to the "Palais-Royal," for they have visibly found the site to be morally and civically repugnant.)

Louis-Sébastien Mercier described the "Palais-Royal" in these images:

> A point unique on the globe. Visit London, Amsterdam, Madrid or Vienna, you will find nothing comparable. It is called the "capital of Paris." Everything can be found here. This enchanted abode is a small,

luxurious city enclosed by a larger one. It is the temple of voluptuousness, where the brilliance of vice has banished even the faintest traces of modesty. There is no cabaret in the world more graciously depraved. Libertinage is eternal here, its temple open all hours of the day and night and at all prices.[9]

The Palais-Royal was owned, and had been substantially created, by the Orleans family, cadet line of the Bourbon dynasty. During the Regency of the Duke of Orleans early in the century, the "Palais" was granted the legal privilege (shared only with the enclosure of the "Temple") of being placed outside the jurisdiction of agents of the Lieutenant-Generalcy of Police, a privilege which accounted for much of its magnetic splendor and unique social atmosphere. This was a large, unbroken, and self-contained rectangle of buildings and colonnades with an interior of arcaded galleries; it enclosed a spacious esplanade and promenade garden. It was quintessentially public and commercial, open to the poor who were forbidden entry to the more sterile grounds of the Tuileries and Luxembourg palaces. The Palais-Royal was simultaneously opulent and scabrous, exquisitely refined and physically brutal. The embrace of its life was unique: several of the most important literary and political cafes and *salons* of 18th century Paris; a large and affluent residential population (including the Dukes of Orleans); scores of luxury boutiques and a major concentration of trade in erotic engravings and literature (and in sado-masochistic gear) for which the City was recognized throughout the Occident; the most important density of gambling dens in Paris; usurious trafficking of real and counterfeited monies; hundreds of prostitutes of all qualities, specialities, and costs, ranging from the cut-rate *tartares* who solicited under the wooden arcades to the most expensive, artful, and famed *courtisanes* of Europe who lived and practiced in elegant upper-story brothels, guarded by stout doormen in fine livery; frequent masqued balls in the esplanade and garden, during which the fountain would be filled with champagne; duelling, brawling, and practically every form of fraud and bribery. Symbolizing the unique importance of the "Palais" to the City, in the garden there was a cannon which was fired punctually each day at noon. Parisians set their watches to its reverberation, for the cannon of the "Palais-Royal" was considered more reliable than the chimes of Notre Dame.

Choderlos de Laclos, author of the *Liaisons dangereuses* and friend of the Duke of Orleans, had apartments in the Palais-Royal. The Marquis de Sade inhabited the neighboring Place Vendôme, but was also a denizen of the "Palais." His principal novels must be read as allegories of this place.

Closely adjacent to the milieus of banking and finance along the rue Vivienne, to the Jacobin Club on the rue Saint-Honore, and to the national legislature in the "salle du Manège," the Palais-Royal was a major center of political activity, much of it semiclandestine and, between July and October 1789, heavily financed by the prorevolutionary Orleans family. In subsequent years it was dually a site for pro-Jacobin and proroyalist meetings, propaganda, and recruitment.

And finally, there was the river itself, veritable artery of the City's material existence. The Seine, with its some 15 port-docks between the faubourgs du Roule and Saint-Antoine, provided a daily spectacle of massive, picturesque, and brutal labor. The 8 million cords of wood consumed annually by Paris in the 1780s arrived in great flotillas during the summer months, to be stacked on "Ile Louviers." The wood was extracted from the river by hundreds of haulers (*tireurs de bois flotté*) who worked from dawn until dark. Their labor was extremely dangerous and often murderous, for the gangs had to wade the slime and rapid currents of the Seine to manhandle the wood without ropes or hooks. They were considered the most savagely exotic and brutalized category of the Parisian proletariat. Parisians of all conditions came to watch them from the banks and the "Ile Saint-Louis," waiting for the convulsive arching of a body being crushed, the twisting hand of a hauler being dragged under by swift current or suction of the slime, the staccato music of curses, screams and gasps.

Like all categories of the Parisian laboring poor, the haulers who died rapidly were fortunate: the alternative was frequently a prolonged agony of disease and malnutrition in the recesses of the great hospitals. "Above all, do not die in the hospital": until far into the 19th century, this was an axiom among the Parisian laboring classes. After decease, there remained the "Petit Clamart," the vast pauper's cemetery to the southwest of the City. As for the meaning of this site, we must listen carefully to Louis-Sébastien Mercier:

> Here, there are neither pyramids, tombs, inscriptions, nor mausoleums. The place is naked. This earth greasy from burials is where young surgeons come in the night, climbing the walls and carrying off cadavers to submit them to their inexperienced scalpels. Thus, after the death of the pauper he is still robbed of his body, and the strange dominion exercized over him does not cease until he has lost the last traces of human resemblance.[10]

VIOLENCE AND SUSPICION

These sensuous, violent, and socially promiscuous qualities of Parisian life must not be conceived as mere addenda to material structures. They were essential realities of urban culture, attitudes, and behavior, realities which molded revolutionary politics.

Human compression and abrasiveness both exacerbated social tensions and gave them form. For the propertied classes, this meant a permanently self-defensive posture in relations with the propertyless, and an imperative of exercising direct and immediate controls over them. The instinctive fears underlying this imperative were expressed by Restif de la Bretonne on July 14, 1789 as he watched, from the window of his apartment on the Isle Saint-Louis, the laboring masses of the southern faubourgs streaming over the bridges to join with the common people of central Paris: "Now is the moment, or never, to create a national [i.e. bourgeois] militia."[11] For the popular classes, compression meant unique possibilities for using the threat of disorders and violence as a political weapon.

Among Occidental cities in the 18th century, Paris was a choice terrain for contagions of rumors, false or exaggerated news, and "panics" which could quickly generate riotous assemblages. These contagions spread with extraordinary rapidity throughout the City, and were all the more potent because their imagery was obsessively fixed: starvation plots by landowners and grain merchants; "aristocratic plots"; treason within the State and the armies; collective breakouts from the prisons by secretly armed counterrevolutionaries and criminals; infiltration of the City by "brigands" disguised as beggars and vagabonds. In their progress throughout Paris, rumors were usually inflated to grotesque dimensions, becoming horrific spectacles within popular imagination and a macabre form of collective excitation. During the evening of September 1, 1792 the first rumors of an imminent prison breakout by royalists began to circulate in the Paris Sections: within less than 24 hours, before municipal authorities could intervene, the courtyards of the "Abbaye" and "La Force" were filled with *sabreurs*. In June 1793, the news that the Vendée rebels had crossed the Loire and taken Saumur was known in the hauling depots of the rue Saint-Denis before it was announced in the National Convention. The circulation of persons between Paris and the provinces was massive and incessant; most news from the provinces was conveyed by them. During the Revolution, as before, Parisians gave far greater credence to these persons, to word of mouth, than to information proferred by authorities and the press; viscerally, and with reason, they suspected the latter of lying or concealing.

This contagiousness of rumor and collective fears (a derivative of the City's human density) also gave experienced revolutionary elites, possessed of adequate techniques and structures, a powerful means of psychologically manipulating the Parisian lower classes. The sheer compression of Parisian life vastly facilitated political mobilization: this compression was the demographic underpinning of that permanent and tightly woven network of assemblies and clubs which was the secret of Jacobin political success in the City.

The common people of Paris shared with large segments of the City's bourgeoisie a faith in the efficacy of violence as a solution to fears and to social distress. The legal Terror of the Jacobin State in 1793–94 was largely based upon, and drew its political strength from, this popular faith in coercion. For violence, in multitudinous forms, had been endemic to 18th century Parisian life — endemic to definitions of the State, to relations between and within classes, to the aesthetics of spectacles, to the casualness of the street.

Privacy of personal and family life, the insular individuality of the domestic *foyer*, were situations cherished by the bourgeoisie of 18th century Paris. These were precarious and embattled situations, difficult to preserve in this City. And they were not respected as values by the popular classes, who were habituated to intensely public existence in the street, in overcrowded apartments and lodging houses. In 1793–94, the anti-Jacobin bourgeoisie of Paris was almost as outraged by the domicilary searches of the Terror as by its orders of incarceration. In the minds and emotions of the popular classes, for whom distinctions between "public" and "private" life never had the meaning of experience, these searches were normal and imperative measures of public safety, and forms of class harassment and vengeance. Similarly, any type of clandestine identity or political activity was extremely difficult to achieve or maintain in late 18th century Paris, for the residents of each quarter constantly exercised unofficial surveillance. The dismal and predictable failure of the *babouviste* "Conspiracy of the Equals" in 1796 was simply the most dramatic illustration of this fact.

A generalized attitude of suspicion was one of the most politically important consequences of this human compression, promiscuity, and abrasiveness. This attitude was shared by all classes of Paris, since long before the Revolution. Suspicion — of any persons or groups perceived as alien, dissimulant, furtive, unattached to a neighborhood or to a "respectable" trade, of those too recently arrived in the City and the quarter, of those not immediately identifiable and classifiable, of all persons and classes whose conditions and behavior contrasted radically with those of the beholder — was entrenched in the collective psychology of 18th century Parisians. Suspicion — a reflex of self-protection in which fears, myths, and realities commingled — intensified during periods of general crisis and released punitive energies. The notorious "Law of Suspects" of September 1793, the cornerstone legislation of the Republican Terror, codified the pervasive social epistemology of revolutionary Paris. This epistemology was not entirely irrational.

POLITICS AND TERROR IN JACOBIN PARIS

Throughout western Europe, the second half of the 18th century was an era of demographic expansion, an expansion registered with particular force in cities. Across the century, the population of Paris had steadily increased through internal reproduction supplemented by relatively stable rates of immigration. From 60 to 80 percent of the resident population of Paris in 1789 were natives of the provinces; the majority of them had come to the City between 1765 and 1785. During the years 1786–94 the volume of provincial immigration swelled to an unprecedented mass. This migratory wave came principally from northern, eastern, and northwestern France (Flanders, Picardy, Champagne, Burgundy, and Normandy); it was propelled by the commercial and manufacturing depression which began in 1786–87 (for these were textile provinces), bad harvests and, beginning in 1792, the ravages of war. Georges Lefebvre estimated that by early 1789 one of every ten persons in the populous northern provinces was on the road.[12] These roads all converged on Paris. The immigration of 1786–94 comprised some 200,000 persons; they were largely social debris, raw, desperate, unskilled or semiskilled proletarians. The majority of them were uneducated males, either youthful or in the prime of life.

Census records from the Paris Sections disclose the social contours of this immigration. In 1791 there were 128,000 lodging houses in the City, which rented furnished rooms; 74,000 of them were of a slum character. Some 220,000 persons, the mass of them recent immigrants, were miserably and transiently housed.[13] In the Popincourt Section of the faubourg Saint-Antoine only 29.5 percent of the total population in 1793 were native Parisians; 20 percent of the immigrants had been in the City for less than a year.[14] In the Oratoire Section of central Paris, 86 lodging houses contained 1,480 persons in 1791: 1,200 of them were male, mostly laborers and fresh immigrants; of the 280 women, the majority were destitute provincials who subsisted by prostitution.[15] In the Pont-Neuf Section, one of the more socially hermetic and bourgeois of quarters, one-quarter of the population in 1793 were semiskilled immigrant proletarians.[16] With the exception of enclaves in western Paris, this immigration permeated the revolutionary City. It gave to Paris a massive "floating" population, largely unemployed, and furtively mobile across and within quarters: in the densely populated Gravilliers Section, which was a social microcosm of central Paris, more than 50 percent of the adult male population had moved at least once between December 1792 and April 1794.[17]

Their biographies fill the Section police records of Paris from 1790 to 1795: ubiquitous yet "foreign" and marginal, capable of labor but unemployed, these immigrants were prime objects of suspicion and fear by the resident classes of Paris and their elected authorities. They also formed a substantial portion of the City's criminal population. Their disciplining and then mobilization was an imperative for the Parisian bourgeoisie of the revolutionary years.

From 1789 to late 1793, Parisians and the State were confronted with three fundamental and interlocked social problems, each of crisis dimensions: unemployment and labor discipline; price inflation and fiscal instability; adequate provisioning of the City in vital foodstuffs, the question of *subsistances*. Until 1793, the governments of the Revolution were committed to a policy of *laissez faire* liberalism, to non-regulation of the economy by the State. By the spring of 1791, there were almost 120,000 persons in Paris either unemployed or so marginally gainful that they required public assistance, and in an urban economy which was severely contracted. The relief funds allocated by the State were pathetically inadequate, and in the name of economic liberalism it refused the alternative of large-scale public works. The *assignat* was the basis of State and public finances from 1790: this paper money was issued in large quantities to facilitate the purchasing of nationalized Crown and clerical properties (the "collateral" of the National Treasury), and thus hopefully to reestablish the solvency of a bankrupted State and animate the economy. But the legal coexistence of metallic currency and the assignat led to rampant price inflation and deterioration of public finances. Coin was hoarded, exported, or used speculatively to purchase assignats at rates increasingly below their face value, by an extensive Parisian and international structure of exchange agents, financiers, and bankers. By July 1793, the real value of the assignat was only 30 percent of its nominal value. Since mid-1791, Parisian employers had been obliged by the shortage of metallic currency to pay their workers in assignats; their profit margins steadily declined, while the wages of laborers were eroded by price inflation. Basic commodity prices soared during these years; the harvest of 1788–89 had been disastrous; that of 1792 suffered severe disruptions in transport to the cities. With impunity, grain merchants and cultivators speculatively hoarded, refused to accept assignats in payment, and exported grains beyond France. In February 1793, throughout Paris, there were spontaneous popular grocery riots, forced sales of basic goods at tolerable prices.

In the economy of late 18th century Paris, there were three possible ways to ensure provisioning of the City: (1) continual wage increases to meet the spiraling prices of a laissez faire commerce in vital foodstuffs, which would have severely damaged the productive economy of Paris; (2) the purchase of these commodities at their rural sources at the prices of laissez faire commerce, and their resale at far lower prices, creating a deficit which the Parisian resident classes would have to absorb in augmented taxes; and (3) the imposition of systematic price controls on subsistence commodities at their sources in the provinces, a regime of regulation and of economic imperialism of the cities and towns over the countryside. Fundamentally inadequate,

the second of these means was the one employed by the State between
1789 and mid-1793. The last of these means, comprehensive economic
regulation, was one of the most ardent demands of the Parisian common people, and their analogues throughout urban France.

The social and political genius of Paris Jacobinism in 1793–94 consisted in its solution to these interlocked socioeconomic crises. Through
this solution—whose structure we must examine—it mobilized popular
energies and saved the Republic and the Revolution from defeat.

The aspiration to local self-government was one of the most powerful
and consensual forces of the Parisian Revolution. Between 1792 and
1794, this aspiration was essentially realized within the 48 Sections
of the City. The Section was the basic unit of politics and administration, the fundamental arena of militancy, civic creativity, and discipline. Most of the 48 Sections into which the City was divided in
1790 corresponded to distinct and preexistent *quartiers*. For this reason,
the civic life of a Section was animated by persons who knew each
other: both the intensity of faction rivalries and the cohesion within
factions derived from lived oppositions or affinities of residence,
occupation, leisure, family, personal ambitions, and political choice.

Each Section had a general assembly of voters, which usually met
thrice-weekly, and every evening during periods of crisis. The assembly elected all Section officials, deputies to the General Council
of the Commune, and members to the permanent electoral assembly of
Paris (who chose among themselves the executive administrators of
the *département.*) Assemblies were also the principal forums of public
debate; through correspondence and delegations, they communicated
directly with each other and concerted pressures on higher authorities.
The Section possessed the following administrative organs: a civil
committee, responsible for general administration and allocation of
funds; a welfare committee, responsible for poor relief; a revolutionary
committee (after March 1793) which enforced the legislation of the
Terror; a health officer; a subsistence commissioner (after August
1793) who supervised enforcement of economic legislation; a justice
of the peace who arbitrated or tried minor disputes in civil law and
provided legal advice to the poor; the police commissioner, whose
authority included all dimensions of peace-keeping and enforcement
of the criminal law within the Section. Through the offices of justice
of the peace and police commissioner—prestigious and well-salaried
functions whose incumbents were elected for a term of two years—
the Section was largely responsible for its own internal security and
social discipline. All executive officials of a Section were elected, or
dismissed, by the assembly (and not by higher authorities), and their
performance was constantly subjected to its scrutiny. The majority
will of the general assembly was sovereign within the Section, until

October 1793 when the decree organizing the Revolutionary Government made the appointment or dismissal of local officials a prerogative of the Committees of the Convention.

The ultimate force of Section Paris resided in its militia battalions. They varied in size according to the population of a Section; by January 1793 they totalled a force of some 116,000, with an average of 2,400 per Section. All able-bodied resident citizens were obliged to serve at fortnightly intervals within their Sections. Each Section possessed its own arsenal, and a cannoneer company with its own ordnance. The majority of citizens had personal arms, most frequently the pike and sabre. This massive paramilitary force was composed of a remarkably disciplined and enthusiastic citizenry; these battalions of the revolutionary journées were not an armed "mob." Officers were elected by their companies, and each battalion was supervised by a military committee which was responsible to the general assembly. The companies frequently drilled, and proper behavior on duty was rigorously enforced. (Drinking, not shirking or insubordination, was the most serious disciplinary problem.) The Section battalions had four crucially important roles in Republican Paris: they formed an unprecedently large and effective police force which patrolled their Sections under the supervision of the police commissioner, preventing or repressing crime, casual violence, vagabondage, strikes, riots, food hoarding, currency speculation, and political sedition; by rotation they provided units to the Paris National Guard, responsible for policing of the entire département (and whose commander-in-chief was himself elected by vote of Section and, in the banlieue, communal general assemblies); they were, in moments of crisis, a standing reserve for the armies on the frontiers or in the Vendée; they were the indispensable armed citizenry which gave sinew to the will of revolutionary Paris in its relations with the State.

Finally, by the end of 1792 almost every Section of the City had a local "popular society" or political club. These had originally been composed largely of "passive" citizens excluded from voting rights before the Insurrection of August 1792. Officered by left democratic bourgeois and sans-culotte militants, in 1793 the popular societies provided the cadres and troops which wrested control of Section assemblies and committees from conservative and anti-Jacobin elements. These societies were closely affiliated with the Paris Jacobin Club.

In 1792–94, the strategic and intellectual core of this entire political matrix was located not in the Municipality at the Hôtel-de-Ville, but in the Jacobin Club on the rue Saint-Honoré. The montagnard deputies in the National Convention; the principal administrators of the Municipality and the département; numerous executive personnel of the ministries; the majority of the most energetic and influential Section officials and assembly leaders; the general staff of the Paris National Guard and many regular army officers (particularly the younger and more intelligent, those destined to victories): these cadres were either among the some 1,000 members of the Club, or its close allies and clients. Programatically, the Jacobin Club was the source of revolutionary orthodoxy in Paris. Politically, it was the general headquarters for the great popular mobilization which in 1793 purged the conservative *girondin* deputies from the Convention, established a montagnard hegemony there, accomplished the temporary dominion of Paris over the State, and opened the way to the revolutionary government of the Year II (September 1793–September 1794). Structurally, the strength of the Paris Jacobin Club lay principally in its coordinating and transmissive capabilities, which were possessed by no other group or institution in France: in a triangular fashion, it bound together the montagnard legislators in the Convention (most of whom were "Parisianized" provincials), the most politically virile forces within the City, and, through its incomparable network of affiliated societies in the provinces, much of urban and communal France. A center of deliberation, patronage, and unity, the Club on the rue Saint-Honoré legitimated Parisian initiatives against State policies in 1792–93 and alleviated Parisian isolation from the rest of France. It also provided a crucible within which was forged probably the finest governing elite in the history of Paris and in the history of the realm and the nation of France.

Socially, the Paris Jacobins and the montagnard deputies to the Convention represented the median ranges of the French bourgeoisie in the later 18th century, with a significant additive of former nobles who had proven through services and risk a dedication to the Republic. Few had come from opulent families, and even fewer from the world of laboring penury. In this, they broadly resembled the elites of Sectionary Paris in 1793–94. The some 1,500 officials of Section Paris, the sans-culotte leadership of the City, ranged from small-scale artisans, tradesmen, and clerks to substantially established bourgeois of production, commerce, and the professions: very few were recruited from the world of unskilled labor or the *petits métiers de la rue;* more significantly, representatives of the grand bourgeoisie of the Old Regime and the constitutional monarchy — bankers, financiers, notaries, wholesale merchants, magistrates, prominent jurists, wealthy rentiers — were very minoritarian, for most had been purged from Section and Municipal offices in 1792–93. Occupationally, the elites of Sectionary Paris in 1793–94 largely corresponded to the social geography of the City: masters and entrepreneurs of the building and associated trades in the faubourgs, luxury craftsmen in the zones of the "Pont-Neuf" and the Latin Quarter; food, garment, and household goods tradesmen in the "Halles Centrales"; garment, fabric, and accessories manufacturers and tradesmen in the regions of the rues Saint-Denis and Saint-Martin; men of the law, bureaucracies, and liberal professions in the Sections of western Paris.

It was this alliance of Jacobins and sans-culottes which forged the revolutionary government of the Year II, and saved the Republic from economic, political, and military ruin. Although centered in the National Convention, this government, from its inception to its demise, was based on Paris. Breaching with laissez faire liberalism and suspending the exercise of absolute private property rights, the new regime halted inflation, guaranteed the subsistence provisioning of the City, and organized the war economy. The Stock Exchange was closed, the assignat was declared full legal tender and speculation in its exchange rate was outlawed under penalty of death; the hoarding and export of metallic currency were equally outlawed. A general maximum on prices of all commodities vital to popular subsistence and the war effort, accompanied by a maximum on wages (which represented a substantial increase in the buying power of the laboring classes) was established in September 1793: the State and local authorities assumed direct responsibility for provisioning, armed with legal and coercive force. War manufactures and transport were either nationalized or placed under temporary requisition and supervision by public authorities; in Paris especially, these measures led to a dramatic increase in lower-class employment. The most egalitarian system of military service in the history of France before the Third Republic, the *levée en masse*, was instituted: all bachelors aged 18 to 25, regardless of social class, were under requisition, with exemptions granted only to public officials and those engaged in vital war work. These were the great organic measures of "public safety." They were supplemented in 1793–94 by the most socially radical and democratic legislation of the revolutionary era: free, obligatory, and secular primary schools; the beginnings of modern "social security," notably free medical care at domicile, public funds for mothers of large families, pensions for the elderly and disabled, support by public funds for the wives and families of volunteers; total abolition of slavery in the colonies; abolition without indemnity of all remaining seigneurial rights and privileges; the public sale of nationalized properties (notably those of émigrés and persons condemned by the revolutionary Tribunals) in small lots, payable over a period of ten years; a constitutional recognition by the Republican State of its obligation to provide either work or the means of subsistence to all Frenchmen.

For the montagnard leaders of the National Convention and their constituents in Paris and elsewhere, these legislative actions were not cynical expedients for manipulating lower-class hopes and energies in a time of general peril. They were matters of right and purpose, determinant images of a beauteous polity to be created. Through efficacity and these commitments, the regime of the Year II magnetized an unprecedented support among the common people of Paris. In this Paris of 1793–94, there was a strikingly new tonality of civic and social relations: distinctions of wealth, rank, and even talent declined in importance; much of the value structure of the Old Regime was inverted, for now productive manual labor was regarded as preeminently honorable and virtuous; modes of speech, gesture, and even dress became fraternal or egalitarian; "egotism" became one of the worst of epithets and the ideal of *civitas*, of a public and collective endeavor transcending private gain, became a standard of behavior, and a mandatory code for those invested with office.

In Paris, as throughout France, the regime of the Year II was obliged to coercive dissuasion of its opponents, to the use of political terror. Without recourse to terror the measures of 1793–94 could not have been implemented, and the Terror was an overwhelming demand of sansculotte and laboring Paris in 1793. The realities of the Terror in Paris were far less dramatic than the ferocious imagery of repression which has been transmitted to us: the Terror was legal, carefully defined, and organized by decrees of the National Convention; exceptional and defensive, it was to last only until the conclusion of the internal and external wars; in both design and operation it was essentially psychological and dissuasive, not physical and annihilatory (no social group or class, even the former nobility still resident in France, was categorically victimized); its principal means of dissuasion and repression was imprisonment, not the guillotine; suspects under house arrest or in prison retained basic rights to the dignity of their persons (there were no beatings or forced labor), and were entitled to receive visitors, parcels, and to exchange correspondence; those brought before the revolutionary Tribunal were entitled to legal counsel, and there was an acquittal rate of approximately 40 percent among them, until the Law of 22 Prairial Year II (June 10, 1794) which strengthened the repressive role of the Paris revolutionary Tribunal. Between the voting of the "Law of Suspects" in September 1793 and the end of July 1794, nearly 9,000 persons were imprisoned in Paris; between March 1793 and the end of July 1794, 2,639 were tried and condemned to the guillotine by the revolutionary Tribunal (of these, 704 were provincials not resident in Paris).[18] The vast majority of imprisoned suspects were never brought before the Tribunal.

The Parisian Terror was pyramidal in structure: its directing organs were the two great executive committees of the National Convention (Public Safety and General Security) which instructed the revolutionary

Tribunal and supervised local authorities; intermediately, there were the Police Bureau of the Municipality and the Committee of Public Safety of the département of Paris; at the base, of both initiative and enforcement, were the revolutionary committees of the 48 Sections, the most important cadres of the Terror. The "Law of Suspects" gave revolutionary commissioners a wide latitude in the selection of victims; the categories defined words and deeds opposed to the democratic currents of the Revolution (former affiliations with constitutional monarchists, pro-girondin sympathies, seditious remarks concerning any aspect of the regime of 1793–94, relations with families or friends of émigrés, abstention from civic responsibilities, obstructionism of any sort); and most of the categories were made retroactive to 1789. The powers of arrest given revolutionary commissioners were therefore vast, but their application was calculatedly restrained. The strategic intention behind the "Law of Suspects" was not literal punishment, but rather to threaten into silence and acquiescence both real and potential adversaries of the Jacobin and sans-culotte regime. Imprisonment had a dual purpose: preempting the capacities of suspects to damage the Republic by removing them from civil life; protecting them from popular animosities and vengeance. Only two categories of French civil society were subject to automatic arrest: families of émigré nobles and nonjuror clergy. In the case of all arrests, revolutionary commissioners were legally obligated to justify their actions to the committees of the Convention. The revolutionary Tribunal was principally reserved for the more blatant or "exemplary" cases of real or suspected opposition.

Throughout Paris, revolutionary commissioners used their powers to imprison those who had been their political adversaries since 1792 or 1789, and those who challenged their current hegemony. The Sectionary Terror had a pronounced "vendetta" quality, but even this was relatively limited in its numbers of victims. This phenomenon was typified in the "Gravilliers" Section of Central Paris. Its population of almost 25,000 included practically all classes, occupational groups, and tensions of Parisian society; it had a voting population of 2,405 in 1790–92, which was perhaps trebled in mid-1792; since 1791, its political life was characterized by particularly intense conflicts between conservative and pro-Jacobin factions. Of the mass of possible victims, the sans-culotte elite during the Year II imprisoned only some 300 persons: the leaders and principal militants of the former conservative faction (some 50 persons); the leaders of a nascent left opposition (some 15); a score of former priests and persons connected with émigré families; nearly 100 nonresidents of the Section; and an array of persons suspected of economic crimes or guilty of seditious statements.[19] But despite its statistically limited application, the Sectionary Terror of the

Year II (some 80 percent of whose victims were former members of the Third Estate, not nobility or clergy), generated deep hatred among large segments of the Parisian bourgeoisie, hatreds which would become viciously manifest during the Year III.

The cynosure of the regime of the Year II, in Paris and the montagnard Convention, was not the Terror, but the Constitution of 1793. It was written by the Convention and approved by national referendum in the summer (excepting the zones of civil war); the Convention decreed in the fall that its application would be suspended until the war crisis had been surmounted. This was the most radically democratic and decentralizing constitution in the history of France: based on universal manhood suffrage, it vested most political and administrative powers in municipalities and communes, not in higher administrations or the State. Its moral essence was expressed perhaps most clearly in the following articles of its Declaration of Rights: the purpose of social association is the common welfare; government is instituted to guarantee all citizens the enjoyment of their natural and imprescriptible rights; society has a sacred obligation to provide subsistence to all members, through work or aid; resistance to oppression is a natural right; when the government violates individual or social rights, insurrection is a right and duty. The constitution was never implemented.

REACTION, POPULAR RESISTANCE, AND REPRESSION OF THE MILITARY

Within Paris, the alliance of the propertied and propertyless, under the aegis and organizational genius of Jacobin republicanism, emerged from general crisis and was sustained by war. It was also reinforced by a delicious and sophisticated metropolitan arrogance: Parisian arrogance, in dominating the State, in galvanizing provincial France, in successfully defying the "barbaric" Europe of French traitors, Austrian barons, and Spanish *hidalgos*, of priests, mercenaries and London gold. But this alliance could not survive its own splendid triumphs, for from the beginning it had been socioeconomically fragile and always based politically upon contingencies and extremity.

By the summer of 1794, extreme and common danger to the City and to the Republic—incarnated by the armies of the coalition and counterrevolution in the provinces—had been forced back to distant horizons, by defeat and containment. This fact was exploited by the provincial deputies who formed the majority in the National Convention. They had long and silently resented the dominance of the State by the *robespierriste* Committee of Public Safety—which was based on the power of the Paris Sections and Municipality—and of general national politics by Paris. The "Thermidorian Reaction" began on 9 Thermidor Year II (July 27, 1794), in the aftermath of the stunning victory over the Austrians at Fleurus and the revolutionary reconquest of Belgium, with the overthrow, by vote of the Convention, of the robespierriste Committee of Public Safety, and the ensuing execution of its supporters among the Municipality and Communal Council of Paris. During the following months, the montagnard deputies associated with Jacobin Paris were evicted from power and influence in committees of Government and within the Convention. In the spring of 1795, the last of them were proscribed, and several were executed. Over the same period, Parisian cadres were systematically purged from ministerial bureaucracies.

Parisians had largely created the National Convention and the Republican regime of 1792–95: at the closing of the circle, they were among the principal victims of that regime. In its most ostensible form, the Thermidorian Reaction was a revenge of more conservative provincial France (especially of its landowning peasantry and bourgeois) upon Parisian political, ideological and economic "imperialism." But the roots of the Reaction were deep, and the reasons for its success were complex. Most of the repressive measures of the Thermidorian Convention were applied nationally, and not merely against Paris. The following is a chronology of the Reaction's progress before the last great Parisian insurrections of April and May 1795.

In August 1794, the Law of 22 Prairial was abrogated, and the revolutionary Tribunal of Paris "reorganized"; it effectively ceased to function by autumn. Section revolutionary committees were abolished throughout France, and replaced by surveillance committees of *arrondisements* (12 in Paris) with very limited powers to arrest. This meant a de facto end to the Terror and the "Law of Suspects." In September and October, the government ordered a massive and almost unconditional liberation of political suspects who had been incarcerated in 1793–94. They were reintegrated to civil and political rights within their Sections. In October, the government interdicted throughout France any affiliation between political clubs and their right to present collective petitions. In November, it decreed the closing of the Jacobin Club and of the remaining central political clubs in Paris. On December 24, the general maximum on prices and wages of 1793 was abolished, initiating a return to laissez faire policies. This resulted, almost immediately, in hoarding, food shortages, a prodigious inflation of commodity prices, and devaluation of the assignat.

By the early spring of 1795, a form of "civil war" had been raging for months within Paris. The thousands of those incarcerated in 1793–94 — including numerous royalists and constitutional monarchists — had reconquered political power in most Sections of the City, by outvoting, proscribing, and harassing into silence their former persecutors. With the complicity of the Convention, committees of government and the new authorities of Sections and arrondissements, bands of young anti-Jacobin thugs (*muscadins*) roved throughout Inner Paris (but not the faubourgs) beating and intimidating the former cadres of 1793 and their laboring class supporters. The network of clubs and assemblies which had been the strength of Jacobin Paris was practically destroyed. And perhaps most importantly, the vital linkages of political legitimation and mobilization which had bound montagnard deputies within the Convention to militants within the City were severed.

Throughout all of France north of the Loire the winter of 1794–95 was the most severe since 1709. In Normandy, Picardy, Champagne, in Flanders, Burgundy, the Beauce, and the "Île-de-France," the soil hardened to an average depth of two feet. Roots and shrubs shrivelled and disintegrated, trees and orchards shattered in the winds, even bark became inedible. The Seine froze over for several weeks. Entire villages were deserted by migration to Paris. On the perimeters of the "Île-de-France" there were incidents of cannibalism, and a re-surgence of brigandage unknown in scope and violence since the 17th century. Packs of wolves prowled the outer banlieues of the City. Their apparition in the night triggered ancestral and collective images of horror, of *loups-garous* (werewolves) — symbols of sorcery, malediction, sexual impotence, of a grisly death. For Parisians, it was as if all the savagery, both human and natural, latent in the surrounding country-side was being released. This was the winter of *nonante-cinq*. It was remembered long into the 19th century.

During this winter, the abandonment by the government of eco-nomic controls and coercion had catastrophic results for the common people of Paris. Hoarding became general throughout northern, central, and eastern France. The classic provisioning area of Paris shrank to a barren wilderness in which local authorities and populations fought each other, often physically, to retain meager scraps of sustenance. Convoys of grains purchased by government agents (at exorbitant prices) were pillaged before they reached the City; haulers often re-fused to venture beyond the banlieues, even with armed escorts. The daily bread ration for which Parisians formed interminable queues was progressively cut. Starvation reappeared in Paris, and especially among that class of artisan laborers which had provided the human weight of revolutionary militancy in the City. All sources converge in describing their existence during that winter as one of gnawing physi-cal debilitation and erosion. Police records, especially from the faubourg Sections, disclose an ascending curve of suicides and infanticides among this class, and of deaths from sheer cold and exhaustion in un-heated garrets and hutments. As during all periods of extreme dearth, class antagonisms became acute in Paris: the chasm of hatred and fear separating the rich and the poor, widened and deepened.

The first popular explosion occurred on April 1 (12 Germinal); the second, far more violent, ample in its scale and decisive in its failure, occurred six weeks later, on May 20–21 (1–2 Prairial). The insurrections of Germinal and Prairial Year III — the *journées des ventres creux* — were the last great popular movements of the Parisian Revolution, and they were distinguished from previous insurrections by three fundamental characteristics: they were essentially leaderless; the politically majoritarian forces of the Parisian bourgeoisie were actively opposed to them; the Government had long anticipated them and had prepared for them. At their core and from their inception, these were subsistence riots which lacked political organization and a systematic program. The slogans of an implementation of the Constitution of 1793 and a return to the coercive regime of 1793–94 were grafted on to these movements by former revolutionary cadres who never genuinely controlled them. In these journées, more than in any other of the Revolution since July and October 1789, the roles of laboring class women and of the faubourg populations were dominant.

The insurrection of 12 Germinal began in the morning, on the square in front of Notre Dame. By early afternoon, some 10,000 persons — mostly women and unarmed — gathered around and within the Convention. Their overwhelming demand was for bread. The montagnard deputies, who used their presence to propose the liberation of all those who had been imprisoned since Thermidor and a return to price controls, were arrested and imprisoned by decree of the Convention during the following 24 hours. Not a single Section battalion, not one armed and organized unit, marched with the insurgents of 12 Germinal. The battalions of some ten Sections of western Paris — wealthy, staunchly anti-Jacobin, and loyal to the Reaction — arrived in force and dispersed the insurgents. In the weeks following 12 Germinal, the repressive character of the Reaction was accelerated. Some 100 persons — all ex-cadres who had been implicated in the journée — were imprisoned. On 21 Germinal, the Convention decreed the disarming of "all those known in their Sections for having participated in the 'horrors' committed under the tyranny which preceded 8 Thermidor [Year II]." Within the following weeks, approximately 1,600 former militants were disarmed, including the great majority of revolutionary commissioners and veterans of the Parisian Revolutionary Army. The lists had long since been prepared by the new authorities of most Sections. At the end of Germinal, the Government thoroughly and socially reorganized the Parisian National Guard, the Section battalions (from which most of the officers of 1793–94 had been purged): "elite" companies of fusileers and cavalry were formed in each Section; they were composed of volunteers who had to provide their own uniforms, arms, and equipment, that is, of the rich; even members of the cannoneer companies—hitherto the most popular and egalitarian of Section units—had to provide their own equipment. And since mid-Germinal, the government had been gathering formations of the regular army in the environs of Paris; by 1 Prairial (20 May) they numbered some 20,000.

The *grand coup de chien* (in contemporary revolutionary parlance), the general popular insurrection of 1–2 Prairial was more desperate, violent, and ultimate than had been the 12 Germinal. It was led essentially by the Sections of the faubourg Saint-Antoine allied with those of Saint-Victor and Saint-Marceau. In the Sections of central Paris, there were scissions within battalions: some companies marched with the insurrection, others refused. The insurgents once more invaded the Convention. Their demands echoed those of 12 Germinal, but were more detailed and imperative: return to the maximum; liberation of all those imprisoned; rearmings; purging of the committees of government and their replacement by montagnard deputies; implementation of the Constitution of 1793. As on 12 Germinal, a core of Jacobin deputies supported these resolutions (which the Convention cynically voted, to save itself): within a week these deputies were condemned by a specially appointed military commission, and then executed; all of the insurgent resolutions were annulled by 4 Prairial. By 3 Prairial, the movement had degenerated into a confused series of local confrontations, assemblies, harangues, resolutions, and unsuccessful attempts at a general political mobilization. On 3–4 Prairial, a force of some 46,000 troops—20,000 regular soldiers and 26,000 Parisian militia—encircled and invested the faubourg Saint-Antoine, which capitulated.

The Prairial insurrection comported remarkably little murderous violence: practically no shots were fired; one conservative deputy of the Convention was killed (half-accidentally) by the insurgents; and the final confrontation in the faubourg Saint-Antoine between the massed forces of government and those of insurrection did not become a battle. But these journées culminated in an internecine Parisian social violence which exceeded even that of 1793.

Between October 1794 and June 1795, approximately 4,500 former Parisian cadres of 1793–94 were imprisoned. Of this number, some 3,000 were incarcerated between May 23 (4 Prairial) and June 1, 1795. This week was the apogee of the "Counter-Terror" of the Year III. The human remnants of Jacobin and "sans-culotte" Paris were swept from civil existence by this purge.

The proscription was ordered by the government, but the selection of victims and the actual arrests were largely delegated to local Parisian authorities: special commissions of general assemblies; civil committees; arrondissement surveillance committees. Class hatreds, personal vendettas, and most of the social tensions which had seethed within the City since at least 1789 mingled in these local purges. Mercier's "cascade of contempt," a distinctive feature of Parisian social relations in the 1780s, became a torrent of vituperation in the spring of 1795. In these records of denunciation and arrest the word *canailles* (scum) reappears: this had been the most contemptuous epithet of Old Regime vocabulary. Former Section cadres, and even simple militants, became "hyenas," "blood-drinkers," "cannibals," "felons," "murderers," the "dregs of society," or, in the case of Jacobin bourgeois, "class traitors and renegades." Impecunious or disabled "sansculottes" who had been appointed property-guardians in the homes of wealthy suspects arrested in 1793 were imprisoned, as were women who had been active in subsistence movements even before Germinal. The majority of the former revolutionary commissioners of the Year II were incarcerated, as were most of the police commissioners and justices of the peace who were either still incumbent from 1793–94 or had held these offices then. Almost *en masse,* the Section cannoneers of 1792–94 were incarcerated—regardless of their services in the Vendée, against the Federalist secession in the Midi, or on the frontiers.

In symmetry to this internal Parisian repression, to this "settling of accounts" between categories of Parisian civil society, the government voted a general law stipulating that henceforth those arrested for riot or insurrection would be liable not merely to imprisonment, but to deportation for life. One of the most durable legacies of the Thermidorian Convention to bourgeois France—a legacy preserved until the 1930s—were the malarial prison camps of the Seychelles and Guiana.

The journées of Germinal and Prairial Year III possess an epic stature in modern historiography of the Revolution, as they did in 19th century Parisian republican and socialist traditions. The scale of their repression reanimated and transmitted to posterity a deeply-rooted Parisian conviction, an image of the retrograde avarice and brutality of provincial French elites when in alliance with the City's rich. In June 1848 there were still Parisians who remembered and recounted not the successfulness of this repression, but its hatefulness. These journées represented the most stark confrontation between laboring need and propertied self-interest among all the episodes of the Parisian Revolution. They mark a major turning point in the history of the Revolution and of modern France: the emergence of the Army as a force of internal reaction. They gave to Republican posterity the "martyrs of Prairial" (Romme, Goujon, Soubrany, Bourbotte, Duroy, Duquesnoy): these were the "last montagnards," the deputies who courageously supported the insurgents within the Convention on 1 Prairial, and who then refused the illegitimacy of their condemnation by a military commission and the ignominy of the guillotine by committing a semi-public, collective, and "republican" suicide with a single kitchen knife, passed from hand to hand. The journées of Prairial were the genesis of the legendary "Conspiracy of the Equals" of 1796, of the putatively socialist "Babeuf Plot," all of whose major protagonists had been herded together in the cells of *Plessis* and *La Bourbe* in 1795.

The essential reasons for the failure of the insurrections of 1795 —for the success of the Thermidorians and for the consolidation of the Directorial regime which they created with the Constitution of the Year III—lay within Paris itself: in the implacable opposition of the City's propertied classes to the austerity, relative egalitarianism, and quasi-social democracy of 1793–Year II; in the disagregation of that alliance of Jacobin bourgeois and common people which had forged the regime of 1793. Since at least the end of 1793, there had been a steady depletion of revolutionary energies and fissuring of solidarities within this alliance.

War and revolution are the two most passionate and therefore fascinating or (depending on one's sensibility) repugnant styles of collective experience. They share at least one fundamental characteristic: they impose highest rates of attrition among the very best, the scything of the most ardent and intelligent by death, exhaustion, or promotion and absorption into bureaucracies, and the sordid, indispensable compromises of statecraft. As for the mass of men and women, revolutionary militancy can never be a permanent mode of life. Collective militancy is always enveloped by shifting and temporal contingencies: crisis perceived as general; reasonable hopes of success; provisioning (for one cannot eat militancy); broad solidarities and reciprocities; savant leadership; in sum, disciplined coalitions of otherwise latent, dispersed, or even mutually contradictory social forces in the face of extreme and common dangers. These realities—more than any simple class-based reaction emanating from the National Convention in 1794–95—account for the recession and demise of Parisian revolutionary cohesion and militancy.

To a far greater proportionate extent than the inhabitants of any other French city, between 1789 and 1794 Parisians had paid the blood price of the Revolution and the Republic. From 1792 to 1796 they gave to the armies of revolutionary France between 80,000 and 100,000 volunteers and conscripts. In 1793, 30,000 marched to the Vendée, Brittany, and the Midi. Commanders exercised in the new style of Republican warfare—rapid manouvers, large-scale skirmishing with its premium on individual initiative, the massed columnar attack in which officers and troops were mingled and whose success depended on *élan* and solidarities—valued Parisian levies, for their intelligence, ardor, pride, magnificent sense of humor in hardest adversity, for their *gai savoir* and aggressive inventiveness under fire. Egalitarian, argumentative, intractable to rigid discipline, they also demanded and obtained more cunning and valor from their officers than perhaps any other soldiers of the Republic. Because they were highly motivated ideologically, Parisians were the levies preferred by the Jacobin State for its "amalgam" of 1793–94—the admixture of volunteers, conscripts, and line veterans in the new *demi-brigades*, which replaced the regimental structure inherited from the Old Regime. Many of these troops, both volunteers and conscripts, had been recruited from the battalions of the Paris Sections. This recruitment heavily drained the Parisian laboring classes and petty bourgeoisie of their most physically able, combative, and democratically politicized members. Discounting casualties, which were numerous, the great majority of these Parisian levies were still in the ranks in 1795–96, and therefore abstracted from the political life of the City.

The armies of the Republic were in many ways the distillation of its moral essence. Their gradual metamorphosis, from 1794 to 1799, into a quasi-autonomous professional caste reflected the character of the Thermidorian and Directorial regimes, which were dominated by conservative and self-aggrandizing elites. In the spring of 1795, the army was the decisive force behind the Thermidorian Convention's crushing of Parisian radicalism. It was the direct agent of the destruction of the Directorial Republic, in the Bonapartist *coup-d'état* of 18 Brumaire Year VIII (November 10, 1799). This metamorphosis is already visible, in its first signs, during the Year II. The Jacobin State displaced barracks and quartering from the densely populated Sections of Central Paris and the inner faubourgs, to camps on the outskirts of the City; it calculatedly removed the troops from the local influence of Parisian radicalism.

In 1794, Parisian authorities and observers frequently remarked on the arrogance and brutality of soldiers on leave in the City, a behavior particularly conspicuous among the new officer corps promoted from the line or from subaltern rank since 1792. Here, there were pronounced dialectical ironies: the very prestige officially accorded the army by the Jacobin State facilitated the evolution of a caste mentality in its midst; the Jacobin Republic of 1793–94 had refashioned the army as a democratic institution of promotion according to talent, social ascension by prowess (and political favor), and therefore as a principal avenue for individual ambitions. By 1795–96, loyalties within the ranks were being displaced from civil authorities to successful individual commanders. Among officers and men, conquests and occupations meant the decline of civic and defensive attitudes and the rise of an offensive, professional, and predatory ethos. Antiroyalism, anticlericalism, and hatred of the émigré aristocracy remained deeply embedded in the army, but not the sentiments of Revolutionary political radicalism.

From 1795 to 1799, officers of pronounced democratic opinions and affiliations were often dismissed or refused promotion. Others among them sought and found death on the battlefield. Their symbolic figure —who also incarnated the prodigious social and moral creativity of Revolutionary Paris—was Lazare Hoche. Orphaned son of a kennel-keeper at Versailles, he immigrated to Paris in 1784 at age 16 and enlisted as a rifleman in the principal garrison regiment of the City, the French Guards. This was the most Parisian of Royal regiments and it defected to the Revolution in the summer of 1789. Combattant in the assault on the Bastille; passionate autodidact, a democrat, and Jacobin; officer of the Paris National Guard and commander of Parisian volunteers in 1792; commanding general of the armies victorious on the Rhine and Moselle in 1793; commander-in-chief of those which in 1795 defeated the Anglo-Royalist invasion at Quiberon Bay and the main forces of the Vendée insurrection: this career and its unswerving revolutionary loyalties made Hoche the general most beloved of "sans-culotte" Paris, and the one most dialectically opposite to the opportunism of Bonaparte. He was killed in the Rhineland in 1797 at the age of 29, to the relief of the regime's conservative elite and their accomplices among the generals. In his tribute to Lazare Hoche, Georges Lefebvre also composed an epitaph for the passing, moral or physical, of an entire generation of officers which had been created by the energies of revolutionary Paris in 1792–94:

> With Marceau and Kléber, he has remained dear to Republican tradition on account of his gay and generous impetuosity, his youthful lower-class enthusiasm for the Revolution. Around the memory of the soldier-citizen, whom death carried off a few days after the eighteenth of Fructidor, there float those Beethovenian strains which express a regret for a noble hope left unfulfilled. It is to him that the *Eroica* should have been dedicated.[20]

Beneath its obsidional appearance of cohesion and solidarity, Jacobin Paris of the Year II was ravaged by the attrition of self-purges. They began among the montagnard elite in the Convention and rapidly extended to the local, Section base of the City. In the spring of 1794, personal animosities, rivalries of factions and clientele systems, disputes over the questions of extending or diminishing the Terror, economic regulation, property redistribution, and anticlericalism all fused in these conflicts, which destroyed first the internal solidity of the montagnard leadership and then the solidarities binding the Jacobin State to militant Paris. Danton, Fabre d'Églantine, Basire, Chabot,

Delaunay d'Angers, Philippeaux, Delacroix and Camille Desmoulins were purged as moderates or "crypto-royalists" by the robespierriste faction of the Mountain and then executed. Several of these deputies had belonged to the leadership core of Paris Jacobinism since 1792. In April, the putatively "extremist" chief executives of the Paris département administration, Municipality, and revolutionary Army — Chaumette, Hébert, Ronsin, Vincent, Manuel, and Momoro — were condemned and executed. These latter were utterly creations of sansculotte Paris, of its Sections and clubs, and had risen to positions of eminence in the City through their popularity among the thousands of local militants. The execution of the *hébertistes* was followed by the dismissal of their partisans from the General Council of the Commune, the administration of the département and the Ministry of War. During the three months preceding 9 Thermidor Year II, some 150 Section cadres (many of them revolutionary commissioners) were dismissed, and the majority of them imprisoned, by the robespierristes who now dominated the Convention, the State, and the City. In Section assemblies throughout Paris, anti-Jacobins who had been quiescent since 1793 reemerged to manouver within these fissures. At the other social extreme, among the Paris laboring classes, discontent became marked by the late spring: the lassitude engendered by the government's regimentation and then closing of Section political clubs was succeeded by anger over lax enforcement of the maximum on food prices and a reduction of the maximum on wages. The regime whose destruction began in Thermidor had already undermined its indispensable bases of urban support.

Two episodes illustrate this phenomenon of disaggregation within Revolutionary Paris, and the relationship between the purges in the spring of the Year II and the repression of the Year III. In Prairial Year II, Charles-Marie Lion was dismissed as police commissioner of the Ponceau Section (the principal Section of the "Portes" Saint-Denis and Saint-Martin) and imprisoned by the Committee of Public Safety for alleged hébertiste sympathies. A young decorative painter, Lion was an archetypical militant artisan of Section Paris: a delegate to the Insurrectionary Commune of 1792, officer of "Ponceau's" popular club, and police commissioner since late 1792. To replace him, the Committee of Public Safety selected Nicholas Gambette, an inspector of the Municipal Police, a salaried agent of the State without personal or political roots in the Section. Five weeks later, on 22 Messidor Year II, Gambette brutally descended on the fraternal table at 55 rue du Ponceau to arrest the 13 sans-culottes — all former members of the Section's popular society, which had been dissolved — who had gathered to celebrate the victory of Fleurus and what they pathetically believed would be its consequences; an end to the astringent regime of the Year

II; the implementation of the Constitution of 1793; and the advent of its promised new order of popular sovereignty and initiative.[21] These spontaneous banquets had been forbidden by the Jacobin State, precisely for fear that they would generate popular initiatives.

This incident had an almost perfectly consonant echo in Germinal Year III. Until the aftermath of the journées of Prairial, the Porte Saint-Martin, which was very near the rue du Ponceau, was a site of continuous popular agitation and turmoil. For this reason, it attracted numerous of the dispersed and proscribed Jacobin cadres of 1793–94, who vainly sought a lost constituency. Among them, there was Dufourny de Villiers, former member of the bourgeois elite of Paris Jacobinism, chief engineer of the Municipality, political journalist, and President of the Paris départment in 1793–94. At the "Porte" in the afternoon of 22 Germinal he attempted to persuade a crowd of insurgent women and laborers that the cause of their distress lay in the Thermidorian suppression of the Jacobin Club. Faced with derision, Dufourny — still trapped within his elitist formation of 1793–94 — could only respond: "If the Jacobins had remained united they would have triumphed, but the present Jacobin deputies are all cowards, except those under arrest; besides, what destroyed the Jacobins was their acceptance of offices." This crowd of desperate sans-culottes may have included some of those whose banquet had been forcibly disrupted in Messidor Year II; it was certainly composed of their social analogues. According to observers, they reacted with disdain or indifference to Dufourny's exhortation and apologia.[22]

Absorption into bureaucracies and statecraft of the talented and energetic: this was a principal social theme of revolutionary Paris, a theme neglected by historians obsessed with popular insurgency and supposedly autonomous "mass movements." In 1789 and during subsequent years, Paris was a City socially distended in most of its occupational categories, whether manual or intellectual. Competition for survival and advancement was fierce within all social groups. It was also a City which both attracted from the provinces and internally created myriads of déclassés. At the end of the Old Regime and during the early years of the Revolution the bloated social demography of Paris was not due merely to unskilled provincial immigrants. It also comprised great numbers of bourgeois, of persons forced by economic crisis and institutional dislocation to live on the thin margins of social respectability: former clerks, bureaucrats, and lawyers of Old Regime institutions and "corporations" which were suppressed in 1790–91; artisans, merchants, and small entrepreneurs plunged into redundancy, debt, and decline by the general constriction of urban markets (especially in the luxury trades and building construction) after 1788; dependents, in all stations, on the patronage of the wealthy, whose emigration became pronounced in 1792; educated provincials, many of them formerly attached to Old Regime courts and magistracies, who were lured to the City by its political and social effervescence (including a majority of the montagnard deputies to the National Convention). These groups formed a substantial portion of Sectionary Paris, and a majority of its cadres in 1792–94. The Revolution offered them a personal terrain for social and economic redemption, fresh careers in service to the new State and within its vast administrative structure. Their progress followed a uniform pattern: Section office (notably as police commissioner, justice of the peace, revolutionary commissioner or assembly president), militancy in the local popular society, and company or battalion command in the Section militia; ostentatious participation in the journées; membership or favor in the Jacobin or Cordeliers Clubs, the nuclei of patronage systems in revolutionary Paris; election to office in the Commune, Municipality, or Department; appointment to salaried government office in 1793–Year II. With ease, the National State of the Year II recruited a majority of its bureaucratic cadres from Paris, for candidates pullulated throughout the City.

This social phenomenon was of immense political significance. The ultimate political force of Paris had resided in its Section base since at least 1792. By spring of the Year II, the majority of the most capable, experienced, and dynamic of former Section cadres had gravitated to government roles and their imperatives (including approximately one fourth of revolutionary commissioners and a far higher percentage of police commissioners and justices of the peace), and they progressively lost local roots, identities, and allegiances. Government policy, combined with the sheer compression of militant time and ascension (in a space of only two years), meant that this generation of local Parisian leaders had no equivalent successor: its members were replaced during the Year II from above, by State appointment and not local elections, with persons largely subordinate in capacity and energy, who were themselves functionaries in Section committees and not militants. In the ambivalently egalitarian National State created by revolutionary Paris in 1792–94, government offices—including important ministerial functions—were opened widely to former artisans, tradesmen, and entrepreneurs of production; but this process was accompanied by a stifling of democratic initiatives and forces at the constituent base of the regime. During the Year III, this personnel from commerce and production was purged almost en masse from government, imprisoned, and then plunged back into the obscurity of the atelier and the shop. In 1795–96, the State and its roles became once more a monopoly of specialists, of professionals in the arcana and duplicities of administration and the law. A vital proportion of them were also recruited from Paris.

THE CONSOLIDATION OF THE NEW BOURGEOIS ORDER, 1796–1815

The Directorial regime (October 1795–November 1799) thoroughly accomplished that depoliticizing of Paris which had begun in 1794 — the excision from Parisian life of militancy, self-government, local civic pride, and autonomies, and all forms of metropolitan imperiousness regarding the Nation and the State. The Municipality and Commune were abolished, and replaced by 12 arrondisement administrations, each surmounted by a national commissioner. Paris became literally a "canton," whose *bureau central* was supervised by officials of the Executive Directory of the Republic. The Section remained as a mere administrative unit, and the site for periodic convocation of primary assemblies to chose electors. Property-based voting qualifications were reintroduced and with them, distinctions between passive, active, and eligible citizens. Some 17 percent of Parisians enjoyed the rights of active citizenship (essentially the power to vote in primary assemblies for the choice of electors). The severely exclusionary nature of the suffrage was expressed in the qualification for electors, and thus for holding office: an income equivalent to 200 days of labor, a social threshold far higher than that of the *éligibles* of 1790–92. The bulk of the petty bourgeoisie were thereby barred from all offices in the Paris of the Directory. Among those possessed of active citizenship, the rates of abstention from participation in primary assemblies were unprecedentedly high during the Directorial years: the vote had become a hollow ritual, for politics was now a monopoly of oligarchs and professional administrators. The Directory periodically violated its own Constitution, by annulling the election of opposition candidates. The social and institutional gangsterism of the Directorial Republic prefigured that of the Empire.

Economic liberalism; sanctity of private property; enhanced severity in the criminal law; gradual return of the émigré aristocracy and non-juror clergy; repression of neo-Jacobinism and of overt royalist activity; military conquest; increased taxation of the socially modest; profiteering and corruption: these were the principal features of the Directorial regime in Paris and the Nation. The force of this regime resided not in legitimation by elections, but in the police, the army and the bureaucracy. The Ministry of General Police, a national and supreme police, was the Directorial Republic's most important political organ and its principal legacy to the Consulate and Empire. The efficiency of this organ was formidable, for the majority of its personnel were professional bureaucrats who had served in the various administrations of the Jacobin State and its Terror in 1793–94. They knew, often personally, the remnants of democratic opposition, the milieus and styles of royalist intrigue, and the hidden mechanisms of the State and society issued from the Revolution. They were selected for these reasons. With the former regicides who formed the Directorial regime's elite they shared an overarching interest in preventing, at all costs, a restoration of the monarchy; they and their patrons would be its first victims.

In Paris and throughout France, the Directory inaugurated the social and political reign of the *notables*, the class which would dominate across the 19th century. These were the principal beneficiaries of the Revolution, of its great transfer of property and of power: affluent and usually *parvenu* career functionaries, barristers, rentiers, manufacturers, merchants, contractors, bankers, and financiers. The Paris of the Directory and the Empire reflected their image.

The Place Vendôme and its Column, the Pantheon, the Champs-Elysées and the Arch of Triumph, the Austerlitz bridge, the Louvre and Tuileries Palaces which were consolidated in one vast, hermetic ensemble, and, most expressive of all, the Bourse (Stock Exchange): in their adamantine and imperial neoclassicism, these were iconographic sites of the new bourgeois hegemony. This hegemony was financed by epic depredations in France and throughout Europe. During these years, the faubourg Saint-Honoré began the conquest and occupation of the lower-class faubourgs of Roule and Poissonnière, by investment, forced bankruptcies and expropriations. The "Palais-Royal" entered perhaps the most luxuriant and frenzied period of its existence. Its new epoch of speculation, eroticism, and *jouissances* was sustained by a capital expenditure of parvenus which far surpassed the former capacities of the Old Regime aristocracy and bourgeoisie.

From 1796 to 1815, the Paris of labor and small trade was constrained to silence and obedience by police, tribunals, employers, and conscription: its reality was reduced to statistics, enumerable among the cadavers of Marengo, Austerlitz, and Eylau, in the demography of crime, prostitution, and disease. And yet, beneath the silence and obedience, it was precisely during these years that the legend of the *grand soleil de 93* (the "great sunlight of '93")—a memory of glorious hope and prodigious accomplishments, followed by betrayal and repression—matured among the common people of the City. For in the Paris of the Directory and the Empire there was also a moral oligarchy: those who remained enraptured by a vertiginous and generous "wonderment" of collective experience, those who refused to forget or to relinquish democratic beliefs, who endured a feral existence under police surveillance and the threat of execution or deportation, those who witnessed and transmitted a faith. Magnified by these survivors and their progeny, in the 19th century the legend of 1793 dialectically crystallized for popular and radical Paris all that was vicious, despoiling, and illegitimate in the reign of the *notables*.

In this postrevolutionary Paris of the Directory and Empire, one already discerns the rapacious and cruel City of Eugene Süe, Balzac, Flaubert, Daumier and Zola: a bifurcated metropolis of the wealthy and ambitious, the penurious and destitute, of irreconcilably opposed memories. One discerns the sanguinary, tragic Paris of 1848 and 1871.

NOTES

1. Louis-Sébastien Mercier, *Tableaux de Paris*, 12 vols., Amsterdam, 1783–87, vol. 10, p. 23.

2. Marcel Reinhard, *Nouvelle histoire de Paris: La Révolution; 1789–1799*, Paris, Hachette, 1971, p. 404.

3. Mercier, *Tableaux de Paris*, vol. 10, p. 3.

4. Ibid., vol. 12, p. 275–77.

5. French National Archives, F7 4635, dossier Castille.

6. Fr. National Archives, F7 4585, dossier Balin.

7. The preceding discussion of the faubourg Saint-Antoine and its revolutionary personnel is drawn largely from R. M. Andrews, "Réflexions sur la Conjuration des Égaux," *Annales: Économies, Sociétés, Civilisations*, janvier–fevrier, 1974, pp. 73–106.

8. Jaillot, *Recherches critiques, historiques et topographiques sur la Ville de Paris*, 5 vols., Paris, 1772, vol. 3, p. 19.

9. Mercier, *Tableaux de Paris*, vol. 10, p. 230.

10. Ibid., vol. 2, pp. 233–34.

11. Restif de la Bretonne, *Les Nuits de Paris*, Paris, Hachette, 1960 edition, p. 207.

12. Georges Lefebvre, *The Great Fear of 1789: Rural Panic in Revolutionary France*. (trans. by Joan White), New York, Pantheon Books, 1973.

13. Reinhard, *Nouvelle histoire de Paris*, p. 101.

14. Martine Sévegrand, "La Section de Popincourt pendant la Révolution française," in *Contributions à l'histoire démographique de la Révolution française; Études sur la Population parisienne*, Paris, Bibliothèque Nationale, 1970, pp. 9–91.

15. Reinhard, *Nouvelle histoire de Paris*, p. 102.

16. Author's compilations from the registers of identity cards for the Pont-Neuf Section, 1793–95, Fr. National Archives, F7 4803.

17. Reinhard, *Nouvelle histoire de Paris*, p. 103.

18. Reinhard, ibid., p. 290.

19. Author's compilations from the F7 series of the French National Archives, dossiers and registers of arrests for the "Bravilliers" Section.

20. Georges Lefebvre, *The Directory*, (trans. by Robert Baldick), London, Routledge & Kegan Paul, 1965, pp. 84–85.

21. Fr. National Archives, F7 477/24, dossier Lion; F7 4715, dossier Gambette.

22. Fr. National Archives, F7 4686, dossier Dufourny.

Chapter 3

*T*he French Revolution had a profound impact upon the minds and sensibilities of contemporaries throughout Europe and also in the Americas. Literate people avidly read about the Bastille, the beheading of King Louis XVI and Marie Antoinette, the Terror and Napoleon's rise to power. Some sympathized with the revolutionary cause, while others deplored the upheavals which threatened to destroy the ancien régime. The greatest·changes in the political and social order occurred, naturally, in France itself, and in those adjacent regions (the Low Countries, Switzerland, the Rhineland, northern Italy) that were under French control during the revolutionary and Napoleonic eras. A new polity was created in France, built upon the concept of the nation, and upon the principles of uniformity and rationality. In central, eastern, and southern Europe, change was less dramatic than in the French zone of influence, but the ramifications of the Revolution were felt even in the Balkans and in Russia. In some of these regions, serfdom was abolished; in others, governments based upon written constitutions were established, if only temporarily. The political map of central Europe was drastically changed, as dozens of small states were absorbed by their larger neighbors. But the most important legacy of the French Revolution was that complex of ideas expressed in the phrase: **liberté, egalité, fraternité.** Those ideas were the inspiration of revolutionary movements in Europe and in the Americas throughout the 19th century.

113

While the ideals of the French Revolution, spread by republican and Napoleonic armies, were subverting traditional institutions and values on the European continent, a revolution of a very different character, but of equal significance, was transforming the economic and social structure of France's most tenacious enemy, England. This was the Industrial Revolution, which had already begun when the Parisian crowd stormed the Bastille in July 1789. In contrast to the French Revolution, which was so widely publicized, the Industrial Revolution was slow in developing, undramatic, unobtrusive. In its early stages, before 1800, it was scarcely noticed by contemporaries. Not until industrialization had transformed, not only the English economy and social order, but her landscape, was its significance recognized. Now, two centuries later, students of this phenomenon can state confidently that it was the most "dramatically revolutionary" event in human history since the Neolithic revolution of the seventh millenium, B.C.*, when men first began to live together in stable, agricultural societies. (Carlo Cipolla,* The Fontana Economic History of Europe, *III, p. 7).*

The most significant feature of the Industrial Revolution was the utilization of inanimate sources of energy to do the work that had been done previously by men and animals, with some minor assistance from wind and water. It involved, too, the mechanization of the processes by which goods were produced and, as a consequence, a dramatic increase in productivity. Other characteristic features were the investment of large amounts of capital in the industrial process and in auxiliary systems of transportation and communication, and the recruitment of a labor force and its subjection to the discipline of the factory system. Population rose during the Industrial Revolution, and it tended to concentrate in large urban agglomerations. Industrialization was already well advanced in England by the end of the Napoleonic wars in 1815; by the middle of the 19th century, it had transformed the British economy and the society in fundamental and irrevocable ways. During the middle decades of that century, industrialization spread across the English Channel — to the Low Countries, to France and Germany, to Switzerland — and across the Atlantic to the United States. Later, and more gradually and haltingly, the Industrial Revolution came to the more backward regions of Europe: to Italy, to the Iberian peninsula, to the Austrian empire, to Russia, and the Balkans. By the beginning of the first World War (1914), industrialization had left its mark, though with varying degrees of intensity, upon every part of continental Europe.

Why did the Industrial Revolution first occur in England, beginning (so most specialists agree) in the 1780s? The explanation for England's primacy lies, in large part, in her historical experience during the 17th and 18th centuries, which fostered the growth of institutions, attitudes, and circumstances that were conducive to industrialization. For example, the cost of government was appreciably less in England than on the continent (largely due to the absence of a standing army), and as a consequence, more capital was available for private investment in trade, transportation, and industry. The political and social restraints upon business activity, and upon the accumulation of wealth in commerce and manufacturing, were much weaker in England than on the continent. Nor did she have any of the tariff barriers that divided the kingdom of France into several economic units, and that restricted trade between its provinces. English agriculture was more capitalistic, more profit and market-oriented than its counterpart on the continent, and thus better able to increase productivity, and to feed an expanding population. The English system of transportation, both by sea and by inland canals, permitted the movement of goods more cheaply than anywhere on the continent, with the possible exception of Holland. English overseas trade throughout the 18th century was a major source of national wealth, and an important factor in her ability to sell the goods that began to pour from her factories, once industrialization had begun. Finally, the British Isles were very rich in the two raw materials, coal and iron ore, which were essential to industralization.

In the growth of the cotton industry in Lancashire (in northwestern England), the process of industrialization can be seen in its most dramatic form. Cotton cloth was not a major textile industry in England prior to 1750, though some yarn and cloth were produced by spinners and weavers in rural villages. The expansion of the industry was stimulated, first, by a series of technological advances (the spinning-jenny, the water-frame, the cotton gin, the steam engine), which greatly increased productivity; and second, by the sharp rise in demand, both domestic and foreign, for cheap cotton cloth. Statistics tell the story of the unprecedented growth of this industry. One factory worker operating a spinning jenny in 1812 could produce as much cotton yarn as 200 women could with spin-

ning wheels 50 years earlier. In 1785, England imported 11 million pounds of raw cotton, compared with 588 million in 1850; the production of cotton cloth rose from 40 million yards in 1785, to just over 2 billion in 1850. The price of cotton yarn declined from 38 shillings per pound in 1786, to just 7 shillings in 1807. By 1830, cotton cloth accounted for one half of the total value of all goods exported from the British Isles. Statistical data on other industries reveal similar patterns of growth, though not as spectacular as that of cotton. The production of pig iron in Great Britain has been estimated at 17,350 tons in 1740. By 1788, that figure had increased four-fold to 68,000; it had doubled by 1796, and doubled again by 1806 (258,000 tons). In 1848, Britain was producing nearly 2 million tons of iron or 100 times more than a century earlier.

Statistics can indicate the quantitative changes wrought by industrialization: the increase in population and productivity, in the value of imports and exports, in per capita wealth. But figures and graphs do not show how the quality of English life was transformed by the Industrial Revolution. One can glimpse the magnitude of that change if one travels today from the rustic Cotswold district west of Oxford—dotted with ancient, picturesque villages and stone-fenced pastures—to the grimy suburbs of Birmingham 40 miles to the north. This trip, from rural village to industrial metropolis, was made by millions of Britons from the mid-18th to the end of the 19th century. The journey involved a profound change in the ways that these people lived and worked. Instead of the seasonal routines of agricultural labor and the casual, independent life of weavers and craftsmen, the migrants to the industrial towns were subjected to rigorous factory discipline, and to the vagaries of the market. Traditional structures of family and community dissolved in this urbanized, industrialized milieu, and these were not easily replaced by new forms of social organization. Likewise, the old patterns of behavior and belief broke down in this world of factories and slums, from which there gradually emerged a new culture that was appropriate for this environment. In the next chapter, these changes are described for one industrial community, the city of Sheffield in the South Riding of Yorkshire.

Sheffield during the Industrial Revolution

*SIDNEY POLLARD**

PATTERNS OF GROWTH

The location of the city of Sheffield does not, at first sight, seem to be a very favorable one for an industrial center, a pioneering community in the industrialization of Britain. Much of it is built on steep slopes, rising to the bleak, infertile, and inhospitable moorlands in the west, and dropping abruptly to the river valleys which scar the landscape, but also provided at one time the water power for local industries. Only towards the east, as the valley of the Don, the town's main river, broadens out into flatter country, is the terrain easier for the building of factories and steelworks, and for the laying down of lines of communication. How could such an area, a long way from the sea, cut off from easy contact with the rest of the country, dour and infertile, become part of that engine of change, the British Industrial Revolution? How could it contribute to lifting the world out of its traditional framework and set it on the irreversible path towards its modern industrialized life?

It should be noted that the location was not altogether untypical. Much of the new industry, whether textile, metal, or ceramic, settled along distant streams on the slopes of the Pennine range, or, if we think of Birmingham and its surrounding metalworking districts, it gravitated towards areas that were even farther from the sea, though perhaps less mountainous. This was not accidental. The men who built the new

* University of Sheffield.

117

communities looked for water power untrammelled by the rights of shippers who needed the broader, slower rivers of the plains for transport; they looked for labor that was cheap because returns from local agriculture were poor; they looked for freedom from the traditional restraints of the older towns; and they looked for coal and other minerals, which happened to be found in the north and west of the country, away from the richer townships and the more fertile agriculture of the South and East. No doubt, it made economic sense, but it also imposed additional hardships and helped to create the oppressive, inward-looking, culturally deprived, and socially explosive communities which became characteristic of Britain in the Industrial Revolution.

In the middle of the 18th century, at the outset of these momentous changes, the population of the built-up area in the center of the parish of Sheffield was around 12,000; the parish as a whole, which was exceptionally large and contained several quite separate industrial and agricultural hamlets to be joined into one continuous urban sprawl only over the next 200 years, contained perhaps 20,000 souls in all. This represented a fourfold increase over the preceding 60 years; the total was to grow over two-fold in the next 50 years, to treble again in 1851, and to reach 240,000 in 1871, when the change-over to modern industry was completed. Thus a single life span was to see a change from village to town; another from town to city; and a third, from city to a large urban concentration. Growth of numbers and expansion of the built-up area was thus an overwhelming fact of life for the citizens of Sheffield.

Growth of that order of magnitude did not depend merely on an excess of births over deaths, particularly in the unhealthy and insanitary environment of a city in the Industrial Revolution. Death rates were certainly higher in towns than in the countryside, and if towns grew faster than the population at large, they did so because of net immigration. By the time of the 1851 census, 49 percent of the population of Sheffield over 20 years of age, and 36 percent of the whole population, were found to have been born outside the city. In other words, at least half the population was composed of immigrants and their children. Most of the immigrants, as a matter of fact, came from adjacent or nearby counties: the youths to learn the traditional crafts of the city, as they had come from surrounding villages for hundreds of years, or to get the kind of unskilled jobs, like laboring, portering, or serving in inns, which are always available where large numbers congregate; the girls, in equal or possibly even greater numbers, either to go into domestic service, the largest single source of employment in any town, or to marry some lad from their village. Few came from farther afield, and relatively few from Ireland.

Since people died young and much of the population was therefore youthful, and because so many had recently migrated, frequently more than once in their lives, the population of a city like Sheffield in the Industrial Revolution, was mobile, footloose, adventurous, and adaptable. It was not averse to trying out innovations, and not unduly impressed with privileges depending not on merit or ability, but merely on tradition. Over most of the period, therefore, industrialists were highly inventive, politics were turbulent, and in various ways, anti-traditional, but Sheffield's history has certain specific characteristics in these respects which will be discussed below. Here we have to note that these same features also made a large proportion of the population insecure, detached from their social environment, dissatisfied and frustrated. Those who had come from settled communities, and there were many in every new generation, missed the framework of expected behavior and the web of mutual obligations they had known before they reached the city. They had to learn, and accept, not only new skills and disciplines at work, but also to live with the restrictions of a cramped dwelling, to learn the skills of urban shopping, and to build up functional organizations for achieving their social objectives. They had to learn, without precedents or teachers to guide them.

After the regular series of decennial Censuses of population beginning in 1801 when population changes can be established with fair accuracy, the fastest growth periods were the 1820s (1821–31) and the 1850s and 1860s (1851–71). The reasons for this are not hard to find. The first period saw the greatest expansion in the traditional cutlery, tools, and silverware trades after the wartime restrictions had fallen away and Sheffield products penetrated vast new overseas markets, particularly those in North America. The second period saw the great expansion in steelmaking immediately before and after the technical breakthroughs which allowed steel to be mass-produced. In each of the decades 1851–61 and 1861–71 the *net* immigration into Sheffield was in excess of 26,000. Actual immigration was larger, as many skilled men migrated outwards, particularly to the United States. In other words, the explanation for population growth is industrial, and this is significant: Sheffield was first and foremost an industrial or manufacturing city, rather than a trading or marketing center, and, still less an administrative regional capital. Its *raison d'etre* was its industry, and its industrial fortunes dominated the city's fortunes, just as its industrial structure dominated the city's geographical and social structure.

Although mentioned in the Domesday Book of 1086 and in numerous medieval records, Sheffield was of little significance, just one of several small metalworking and farming communities in a peripheral area until the early modern period. Its importance arose only with the growth of its industries, in the 16th and particularly in the 17th century, when a great deal of specialization and improvement in skill and artistic ability took place. The Cutlers' Company of Hallamshire, a somewhat belated gild, was formed in 1624 to preserve and encourage these skills, to limit entry and to represent the collective interests of the men engaged in the local staple industry. Their products were all based on steel:

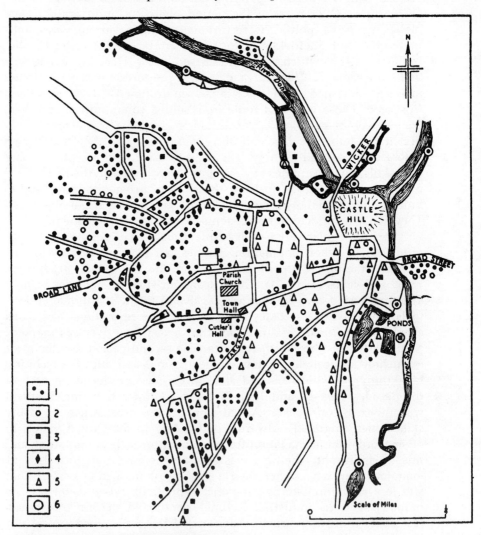

MAP 6.   Industrial Sheffield in 1787

1. Cutlers and edge-tool makers.
2. Craftsmen in trades ancillary to cutlery (bone, leather, &c.).
3. Steel converters, refiners, and founders.
4. Makers of plated and metal goods other than cutlery.
5. Maltsters, makers of textiles and other goods.
6. Waterwheels (shown in combination with other symbols).

knives and forks, edge-tools and scissors, files and razors. They were also based on local resources, such as water power and fuel (first timber, then coal), iron ore, and materials for fireclay and grindstones. Local specialization ensured that ultimately they were also based on skills that were even harder to imitate elsewhere, so that these industries, scattered at one time over many centers, tended to gravitate to Sheffield. Ultimately the town became the supplier to the nation and this special role was possible because local goods, having high value in little bulk, could be carried outwards to the ports on mule or packhorse trains without pricing themselves out of distant markets.

The center of the industry was the master-craftsman. With the growing subdivision of labor, there had crystallized out by the second half of the 18th century such trades as forgers of table knives, grinders of saws or file-cutters. The typical local craftsman worked in his own premises or in rooms rented by himself in a larger building. The grinder, who needed power to drive his grindstone, rented his "trough,"

Courtesy Sheffield City Libraries.

FIGURE 2.   Sheffield knife grinders at work, c. 1866. Though crowded together in one large "hull," each grinder normally rented his own "trough" (the grindstones ran in water) and paid for the power that turned his stone. From the Illustrated London News.

or workplace, in a "hull," or large room, in a "wheel," or building with a central source of power, either a waterwheel or, later, a steam engine. There he worked what hours he pleased on a basis of piecework or subcontract. The orders, and the materials, might come from a factor or merchant, or from a fellow-craftsman, say, the grinder, who then put the work out for its different stages to forgers and finishers. Any one of them might cut his cutler's trade mark, as an advertisement and a guarantee of quality on the finished article. As long as the Cutlers' Company or Gild operated its rights of supervision, the numbers of journeymen and apprentices which any craftsman might employ directly were strictly limited, normally to one or two. These limitations were found to be increasingly irksome by the more ambitious or go-ahead masters, and in long drawn-out struggles which began in the 1770s and ended with an Act of 1814, they managed to get all the restrictive powers of the Cutlers' Company, except the right to grant trademarks, abolished. Henceforth there was no legal limitation on apprenticeship or on the numbers of workers which any man could employ.

For many decades thereafter, however, this change made relatively little difference to the social relationships within the traditional Sheffield industries. It is true that men began to be collected in factory buildings or manufactories, the first full-sized one being the "Sheaf Works" erected by Messrs. Greaves in 1823, working off a single steam engine. But while this move from the more scattered workshops (particularly from the waterwheels strung out along the river valleys), into concentrated buildings in the center of the town had all kinds of consequences for the forms of living and particularly the state of health of the workers concerned, it was not associated with any change in techniques, and therefore not with any fundamental changes in economic relationships. Some workers might now work in a building owned by merchant-manufacturers, but they still pleased themselves as to hours of work, they still paid rent for their work places, and they still reserved the right to work for other masters, though less so as the century proceeded. Limitations on apprenticeship, which gave control both over the rate of expansion of a craft and over the skills of the new generation, was transferred from the defunct gild to the trade unions which took on wide ranging functions in the 19th century. The main changes, increasingly clear with the passage of time, was the widening gulf between manufacturer-employer and workmen, the latter becoming increasingly less likely to become independent masters themselves, and the growing opportunity which this clearer division between masters and men gave to the so-called little mesters. These, the bane of both, emerged in particularly large numbers during slumps, to under-

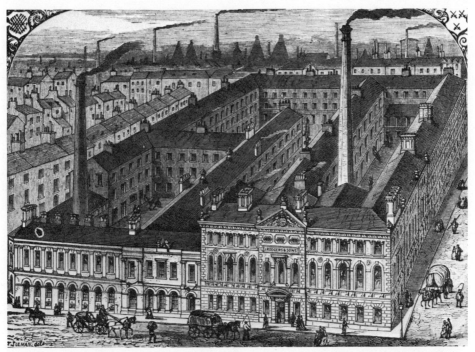

FIGURE 3. Joseph Rodgers' Cutlery Works, 1879. From Pawson and Brainsford's Illustrated Guide. This famous factory is surrounded by densely packed workers' dwellings. Bee-hived shaped cementation steel furnaces can be seen in the background, together with numerous chimneys of steam-engine boilers.

cut wages, undercut prices, and rear up partly-trained and ill-paid young men to undermine the bargaining position of the craft.

On the basis of the cutlery trades, others had been attracted into the town. First, there were the haft and handlemakers, using bone, stag-horn, mother of pearl, and silver plating to decorate the handles of pen and pocket or table knives. It was out of this work that Thomas Bolsover in 1743 developed the method of fusing silver onto a copper base, the "Sheffield Old-Plate," which led to a flourishing local industry of making coffee and tea pots, candlesticks, snuff boxes, and other similar goods, many with splendid artistic design, and collectors' pieces to this day. In turn, this work attracted a silversmithing industry, symbolized by the opening of the Sheffield Assay Office, one of only three in the country, in 1773.

More important in the long run was another ancillary industry, the making of steel. It was about the year 1740, that Benjamin Huntsman developed his crucible method of making cast steel, a product of better quality and greater consistency than the blister steel used until that time. The earliest surviving directory of 1774 lists five firms making it locally, and by the mid-19th century there were around 60 firms. Crucible steel was produced by small groups of four to six men possessing great skill, and turning out 30–60 lbs. from each pot every four hours or so. Its manufacture was therefore not very different in organization from that of the cutlery and tools industry. From the 1830s, however, there came the railways with their need for buffers and springs, and the spread of machinery which required steel for certain parts, as well as the growth of world markets for traditional Sheffield goods—steel wire, files, rasps, and reamers for engineers and machine

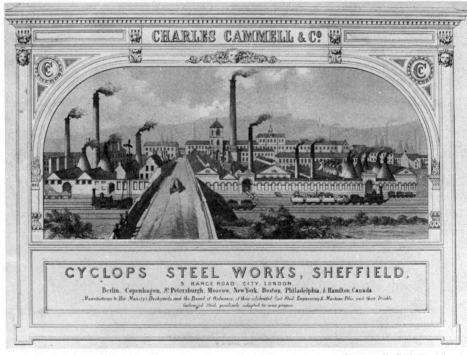

Courtesy Sheffield City Libraries.

FIGURE 4. Cammell's Cyclops Works, c. 1860. From an advertising card. In contrast with Joseph Rodgers, this was a new steel firm which had settled on the only available flat space along the river valley, the railway and the canal to Rotherham, where its factories and furnaces could be laid out more rationally. Cementation furnaces are on the right (as well as the left), and immediately behind them, crucible steel furnaces with their typical square chimneys. In the foreground is the Sheffield —Rotherham railway branch.

builders, as well as armaments. The demand for steel began to take on a new dimension altogether, and traditional methods threatened to break down under the stress.'The first technological breakthrough was the invention of Henry Bessemer's "Converter" for mass producing steel cheaply. His early promise of 1856 led to much disappointment, and Bessemer was forced to set up in business and make steel himself. He settled in Sheffield in 1858, and by 1860 he had successfully proved his method in practice and had persuaded the first local steelmaker, John Brown, to adopt it. Within a few years, vast steelworks mushroomed along the lower Don valley, the only flat area available in Sheffield, using massive capital equipment, and hordes of semiskilled or unskilled laborers, many of them immigrants to the town.

In some sense, therefore, the Industrial Revolution reached Sheffield only around 1860, or a century after its first signs began to be felt in Manchester. Rich manufacturers with large capital resources facing proletarianized workers possessing nothing but their labor power appeared in Sheffield only in significant quantity with the technical revolution in steelmaking. But it would be wrong to deduce from this that the Industrial Revolution had passed Sheffield by altogether in the intervening period. On the contrary, the town was most significantly affected in numerous ways. Sheffield was less than 40 miles distant from Manchester, and less than 40 miles from Leeds and Bradford. Although it had few factories of the classical cotton-mill type, its first steam engine was erected in 1786, and after the peace of 1815, its grinding wheels were rapidly converted to steam power: by 1841 there were 40 waterwheels as against 50 steam wheels, and by 1865, 32 as against 132. It benefited not only from the cheaper food of the agricultural revolution, the cheaper iron and the cheaper textiles and the greater market for its machine-building tools for the Industrial Revolution elsewhere, but it was directly drawn into the same vortex of change itself. Thus the improvements in transport which are a basic ingredient for mass markets and therefore mass production, were felt in Sheffield as much as in Manchester. The first major river improvements to ease water transport out of Sheffield began around 1730, the first Act having been passed in 1726. In the Turnpike era, no fewer than six major roads out of Sheffield were turnpiked between 1756 and 1779 and a total of 22 local turnpike Acts passed (excluding extensions of existing schemes) in the years 1739–1818. Tradition has it that the first trading journey of a Sheffield factor to London was undertaken in 1723, the first to the Continent in 1747; but it is certain that the new transport network, which was national and therefore affected "advanced" districts as much as the more backward ones, though in different ways, was responsible for the growth in local industry, its power to drive out other competing centers and raise Sheffield to a monopolistic position in several branches. The same could be said about other aids to trade and communication, such as a better postal service, a more sophisticated banking system, a great expansion in the number of newspapers. Close to the town, several large ironworks were erected, true symbols of the Industrial Revolution; collieries were sunk all round the district, some large ones, including steam engines, railways, and other heavy and up-to-date capital equipment above and below ground, in Sheffield itself from the 1770s on.

Even as late as 1850, or nearly a hundred years after the beginnings of the British Industrial Revolution as conventionally dated, there were only two British industries in which more than half the labor force worked in true factories: cotton and silk textiles. Everywhere else, industrialization, while it meant some large mills or ironworks or mines, also meant a growth in the number of workshops, of putting-out industries, of more traditional manufacturing methods. Sheffield, far from being somewhat exceptional, was thus typical for its mixed reactions to the new industrialism. It was this mixture itself, this incomplete factory structure, this strengthening of some aspects of the old as well as the destruction of other aspects of the old by the new, which was responsible for the tensions, the movement, the progressiveness as well as the misery of Sheffield as of other typical British towns in the Industrial Revolution.

THE SOCIAL STRUCTURE

There were several special features about Sheffield, as no doubt about every other town. Perhaps the most important, which arose out of the peculiar structure of local industry, was the relative social homogeneity of the population. There were few very rich people, and few abjectly poor, compared with most, in the 18th century. The typical cutlery worker had a small piece of land as well as his trade, and while in bad times anything up to 40 percent of the population might be on poor relief (in 1799–1800 it was still 10,000 out of 31,000 in the Sheffield Township), this was temporary and widespread. In good years, mobility up to the status of master and back down to journeyman was easy and not infrequent, and it was not always the "master" who had the higher or more regular income. In the silver trades, where the highly skilled craftsmen had to be attracted from other towns and therefore offered particularly high wages, it was even alleged that two of the workers kept hunters, whilst the employers had to walk; and several of the men had the hairdresser to attend them with powder at their respective manufactories in working hours. It was only by slow degrees, as the Victorian local historian added piously, "that the employers were able to throw off (this) vassalage . . . and inaugurate a better state of things."[1]

At the top of the social tree, there were no really affluent masters in the early part of the 18th century. Cutlers' Feasts consisted of homely drinking sessions at which present and former master cutlers and other prominent citizens recited popular songs in the local dialect. Apart from the vicar, represented in the latter part of the century by a member of a landed family, a typical Tory squire rather than a curer of people's souls, no one in the town was considered gentleman enough to be appointed magistrate, and in times of troubles, messages had to be sent to the country houses eight or ten miles away to find justices of the peace. The factors, merchants, and bankers who represented the selling side of the expanding local trades, together with some lawyers, were the first to rise above the common herd in wealth, and before long in cultural aspirations, and built themselves larger houses outside the town. This included families like the Parkers, Shores, Roebucks, and Broadbents.

The slower rise of the manufacturers' class, whose growing economic success and security allowed them also to realize their increasing social, cultural, and political aspirations within the community, and behind them the rise of a professional middle class of doctors, lawyers, scientists, and others, forms one of the most significant features of the social history of the town in the period of the Industrial Revolution. Growing wealth and growing numbers, in turn, meant the emergence of wealthier shopkeepers as well as of manufacturers in other than the staple industries. A good cross section of this local elite is provided by the officer corps of the local Volunteers, for they were the local middle class under arms, partly mobilized to meet the somewhat remote danger of an invasion by Napoleon, and partly to be on hand against the more immediate threat of unrest by the lower orders at home.

The Lieutenant Colonel of the Sheffield Volunteers (re-formed in 1803) was a merchant, and the Major was a silver manufacturer. The total officer corps in the period 1803–1807 could be classified as follows:

Merchants and bankers	2
Professions	5 (attorneys, clergy, optician)
Cutlery etc. manufacturers	9
Silver manufacturers	6
Shopkeepers	6
Brushmaker	1
Unknown	3
	32

Colonel of the Regiment, of course, was a neighboring aristocrat, the Earl of Effingham.

As always, what mattered was not so much the absolute level, but the growing differential from the lower orders. No doubt, in some absolute sense, the standard of living of wage earners also rose in this period of around a century. But the uncertainties of life remained for them and earlier memories of poverty were recalled in the widespread distress of the postwar years of 1815–20, and in the early 1840s. There was now also increasing certainty that wage earners would always remain wage earners, and in the process lose whatever social status and political influence they might have had in the old town. In addition, there was formed a class below them, of unskilled workers, without a trade, without a plot of land, suffering from even lower and more uncertain wages. Yet, compared with the textile towns, with their great gulf between factory owner and mill hand, what was significant in Sheffield was the social continuum, and Sheffield has, with some justification, been called a "city of assimilation" in contrast to Leeds and Manchester which have been called "cities of conflict."

Some of the changes and experiences as they affected the townsfolk in this age may be illustrated by the life of Thomas Asline Ward (1781–1871) which spanned almost the whole of the period considered here. Born into the family of one of the largest cutlery manufacturers in the town, he was able to devote his life, not only to business, but also to local affairs, becoming at one time or another, editor, librarian, Parliamentary candidate and political leader, magistrate, and Master Cutler (twice), and holding virtually all public offices of honor, and leading positions in almost every cultural institution of his time. Being successful in business made it possible for him to indulge in much leisure, and to have more sympathy with his workers than was common among masters whose position was less secure. Thus it was characteristic that when the apprenticeship limitations of the Cutlers' Company were abolished in 1814, as noted above, and the trade thrown open, he wrote on May 12, 1814: "I am sure the alteration will be injurious to me individually, for the little mesters will take a multiplicity of apprentices, which I shall not be inclined to do, and will thereby be enabled to undersell those who give handsome wages to journeymen." The fact that he was highly literate and cultured and left an enormous stock of written material regarding his life, makes him wholly untypical, yet in many important respects he provides us with a true image of life in Sheffield in the Industrial Revolution.

Growth of the town and its growing stratification were very evident to him. In 1802, for example, he records a feast given in honor of his twenty-first birthday, when "the workmen, to the number of 100, supped at Mr. Bellamy's, the sign of the Royal Oak in New Street. Father, Brother Saml. and I staid till nearly 12 o'clock. We went at 7. Expense, £10.10s."[2] Personal contact and vigorous survival of archaic relationships of masters and men implied by this entry, at this time, contrast strongly with his plaint 50 years later, in 1852: "Once it seemed as if all the inhabitants of the town were known to me. Now I cannot tell one in ten of all the new owners in these new habitations." The latter referred to middle-class houses standing in large gardens in Broomhall on a salubrious hillside on the western side of the town. "To walk on the Parker Broom Hall, and see the mansions erected on its site is quite a marvel."[3] To know large numbers of individuals in the working-class quarters would no longer even have entered his head.

The physical move from the crowded inner areas to residential suburbs was one of the most obvious outward signs of the social differentiation occurring in the town. Ward himself grew up in his father's house adjoining the works in Howard Street and lived there until the age of 33. The family was sufficiently wealthy also to possess a country villa, "Park House," standing in open country, and inhabited by them in the summer months. In 1814, when Ward married, he moved there permanently. Long before the time of his death it had been swallowed up, like most other houses of this kind, by the urban sprawl of Sheffield, and the further flight of middle-class households to even more distant quarters, ahead of the flood, marked the social progress of many families in this period.

In the mid-18th century the town still had a semirural aspect. There was still much fine woodland nearby, but it was rapidly being cut down. The streets were narrow, but the houses strung out along them had large gardens and orchards behind, affording fresh food and fresh air even to the poorer inhabitants. In any case, the countryside was near, and there were no large works to pollute the air, no steam hammers to drown out private living by their noise. Apart from the grinders, most of whom needed the water power of the valleys and therefore lived in the outlying settlements, the local craftsmen in the cutlery trades, as well as general suppliers like cobblers, carpenters, or printers, worked in their own or their masters' premises that were part of or adjacent to, their dwelling houses. By the hearth-tax returns of 1672, there was a smithy to every 2.2 households recorded. This made for democracy even in living, with no obvious geographical divisions between middle-class and working-class streets, and no need to move households as the family fortunes changed. Only merchants and bankers, and a handful of successful merchant-manufacturers, like the Wards, built villas in somewhat grander style on the open slopes outside the built-up area.

CHANGES IN SHEFFIELD'S TOPOGRAPHY

The main characteristic of the period was growth, and as the town grew it changed its character by that very expansion itself. Distances were extended and began to matter, and land near the center became more and more valuable, too precious to be wasted in gardens and open spaces. Thus the gaps between houses and between streets began to be filled up with closely packed dwellings, run up as cheaply as possible in brick although the area has some fine yellowish sandstone as building material which enhances the appearance of the houses of the gentry, the churches, and even the humble dwellings in the villages. As building spread outward, too, it was laid out at very high density, for the land was sold at a price which only maximum densities could afford.

There was a bonanza for those owning land, the largest owners, like the Duke of Norfolk, preferring to lease rather than to sell. A spate of enclosures followed in order to cash in on the boom: Ecclesall 1779–88 (the first year being that of the Act, the second that of the final award); Brightside 1788–95; Upper Hallam, Nether Hallam, Heeley 1791–1805; Attercliffe 1810–19. In Sheffield township itself no open field land had been left. There developed the notorious "back-to-back" style so common in Pennine towns, of rows of houses built in continuous terraces, backing on to similar rows facing inward into a court which was surrounded by similar double rows on every side. Thus each house abutted on three others, one on each side and one against its back, and the windows and door had to be all in one wall, so that there was no through ventilation. The streets onto which the front houses faced were as narrow as possible, so as not to waste precious building land, and so were the courts into which the inner houses faced (which not only lacked what fresh air there was in the streets, but which also contained the privy middens, and at times the water pumps or standpipes), for the whole complex of buildings contained perhaps 200–400 persons. Few of the courts or streets were properly paved, so that stagnant water, sewage, and droppings from the middens, cleaned out periodically for the sale of manure to nearby farmers, added to the insanitary state of the residential quarters of the town.

A calculation for 1839–41 for Ecclesall Bierlow, the western and slightly better-off quarter, showed the following figures for life expectation at birth:

	Town Areas	Open Country Areas
Gentry and professional classes	46 years 4 months	70 years
Artisans in various trades	20 years 8 months	34 years
Artisans in local staple trades	18 years 11 months	27 years

Class and the unhealthy nature of certain of the local trades, like grinding, had a clear effect; but the effects of the environment are also unmistakable.

Local trades, whether carried on in separate buildings or within the dwellings were carried on in residential streets and courts, so that to the nuisances of overcrowded living were added the noise of hammers, the smell from tanneries or bone cutting shops, the smoke of chimneys and steel furnaces as well as the heavy goods traffic to these works by day and the noise arising from public houses within the terraces at night. Yet Sheffield, all contemporaries agreed, had far superior housing than the textile towns: here were no cellar dwellings; overcrowded, damp, and periodically flooded, as in Manchester or Liverpool, no "wynds" of Glasgow. Sheffielders used their cellars to store coal and food, and had a living room and two bedrooms above (one in the attic) as a minimum. But the back-to-back style was bad enough: when further building of this kind was prohibited by local bylaw in 1864, 38,000 such houses had been put up and were occupied.

Being a hilly town, Sheffield was in some ways easier to keep clean than the agglomerations of the plains. In its village days, a water reservoir was kept at what was then one of its highest points, Barker Pool, and periodically opened to flush the town. Then housewives would

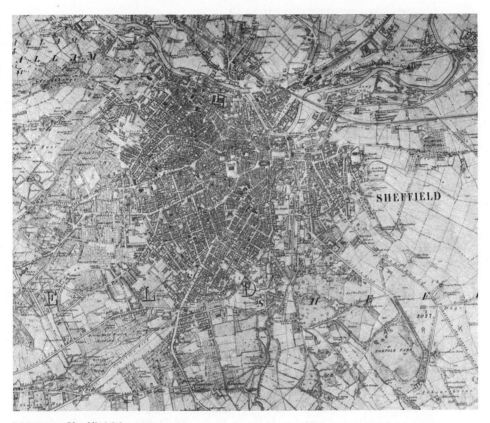

MAP 7. Sheffield in 1851

rush to their front doors to sweep their accumulated rubbish into the flowing stream. However, as the village became a town and this in turn became a city, the unevenness of the terrain meant that some low-lying areas accumulated stagnant water and sewage from a wide area and thus became even more insanitary. Moreover beyond a certain point, the rivers which drained Sheffield and which also carried away its refuse, became unable to cope as the balance between clean and polluted water changed more and more in favor of the latter, while the flow itself continued to be blocked by weirs and dams for the waterwheels lining their course. The mass of 28 decomposing dead dogs found gently floating above Bell Street bridge, and the water discolored and showing chemical reactions, as described at the time of the Social Science Congress meeting in Sheffield in 1865, mark the nadir in this melancholy history. Thereafter better sewage systems and water supplies, paved streets and building regulations achieved a marked improvement. Meanwhile here was one facet of life, and a most significant one, which in the experiences of Sheffielders had shown no progress, but retrogression instead.

The cause of the deterioration lay not in the decline of individual fortunes, for on the contrary, incomes were rising, but in the massing of individuals in the urban community itself. A small conglomeration of houses with poor sanitary facilities is tolerable, but thousands of them compressed together become oppressive. By 1850 there was no open space left in a circle of one mile around the Parish Church: many Sheffielders by that time had to walk $1\frac{1}{2}$ miles to reach green fields and the distances were constantly growing. However, they were more fortunate than most in living in a very hilly area, so that there was no place in the town from which the eye could not feast on some part of Sheffield's magnificent skyline. Within the radius, however, the Churchyard, a source of nauseating pollution to the houses and wells around it, the market place, and Paradise Square, a small opening in the sea of brick buildings used for mass meetings and political demon-strations, were the only spaces not built upon. There were not even any wide roads: unbelievably, Sheffield, a city of 130,000 inhabitants in 1848 had only five streets wider than 40 feet, and four of them were old approach roads—South Street, Broad Street, Shalesmoor and the Wicker.

The claustrophobic meanness of a city of this kind was aggravated by the fact that apart from the churches, there were no buildings of any dignity and size, no square opening in front of them to set them off, no places for citizens to sit or linger. Even the town hall and Cutlers' Hall were small, mean structures. Factories and warehouses were larger, but while some were embellished by pediments or pillars, and others had well proportioned windows, those in the built-up town center were on streets too narrow to allow their frontages to be seen, and their appearance was spoilt by the straggling mass of buildings surrounding them.

Like many (though not all) of the leading towns of the Industrial Revolution, Sheffield had had no corporate existence in earlier centuries. Until 1843 its administration, insofar as it had any, was manorial. There were therefore not even the fine civic and other public buildings or open squares associated with older towns, to provide some dignity and invite imitation. At the same time, there was also no authority to override the numerous private interests making for maximum load on each acre, and insist on wider streets, open spaces or minimum standards of building, though there were the Highway Boards, while the so-called Police Commissioner, set up in 1818, had some civic functions for the inner part of the town. Domination by private interests untrammeled by public responsibility, growing private affluence, and public squalor could therefore hardly go further, and it was largely the example

Courtesy Sheffield City Libraries.

FIGURE 5.   Scenes from Old Sheffield: Market Place, c. 1840, showing the mean streets and houses, even in the town's center. From a trader's card of William Jackson, whose toyshop can be seen on the left.

of cities like Sheffield, and particularly the experiences of the cholera epidemics of 1832 and 1848–49, which changed British public opinion on the necessity for the authorities to curb the unfettered action of private interests.

Slow change began in the 1840s. Some of the larger works moved to the open space in the East, where industrial buildings were less cramped, and the space they vacated was partly now being filled by shops and offices; indeed the highest absolute population figure for the inner town was recorded in the 1841 census, after which people began to move out. What remained unbuilt-over of the private "Park" of the Duke of Norfolk (who was Lord of the Manor and owned much of Sheffield's land and rights over it), was offered to the city as its first public park in 1841. The shattering report in 1848 by two sanitary engineers, J. Haywood and William Lee on the state of the city, describing in relentless detail not only streets and courts but also individual property, led to some localized measures of reform, and the speedy reaction of the city to the cholera in 1849 earned it national praise. Above all, in 1843 Sheffield received an Act of Incorporation, which gave it an elected Town Council with important powers over various aspects of the citizens' lives, and they were greatly added to in the next decades by Victorian legislation. But the benefits, even by 1870, were still limited, and some consequences, such as the enormous costs of compensation for street widening, parks, or civic buildings in central areas because no land had been left free for such purposes when land was still cheap, are still with us today.

By the middle of the 19th century, the sheer extent of the outward sprawl of the building line permitted the townscape to reflect even more accurately the social stratification of the city. First, there was an outer ring of large manufacturers' mansions, set in elaborate gardens, and an inner ring of middle class houses, more closely spaced, but still built of stone and placed in pleasant leafy roads amid gardens of fair size. The best of these districts, like Kenwood, Endcliffe, and Broomhill, laid out around 1830, were found in the cleaner western suburbs, in each case on the southern slopes, with the incidental curious effect that while the proletarian housing on the northern slopes looked out upon the greenery of the middle class suburbs, the latter's view consisted of slate roofs and lifeless brick terraces on the less favored side of their valley. Beyond them, within the more compact inner quarters, there were subtle gradations as well as divisions by industry. In the center and the western suburbs, crowding round the cutlery and tool works, were the workers in the traditional crafts as well as those in the many service trades needed in a town; in the East, surrounding the new steel and engineering works, were the straight terraces of houses of the immigrant steelworkers. The Irish, a small minority in Sheffield, huddled with their domestic animals in the narrow courts of the "Crofts" below

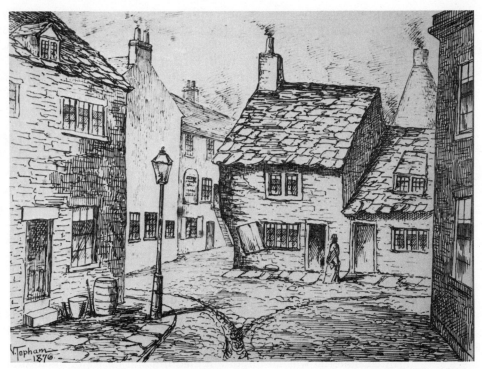

Courtesy Sheffield City Libraries.

FIGURE 6.   Scenes from Old Sheffield: Balm Green, 1876, showing typical crooked streets and poor houses. Drawn by W. Topham.

the Parish Church. In the "Park" a warren of slums on the steep slope facing the oldest part of the town lived the poorest, least skilled, and most casual of the native workers, together with such criminal elements as Sheffield possessed. In the northwest, towards Walkley and Crookes, as also in the southwestern direction of Heeley and Abbeydale, houses had gardens, streets were wide, and the inhabitants, some of whom owned the houses they dwelt in, were among the most steady and respectable, or among the least scrupulous, of local artisans and little mesters, many of them on the way up. Valley sides are steep in Sheffield, and valleys were sharply differentiated, and churches and chapels, public houses and shops, spoke of the differences between them.

EDUCATION AND CULTURE

Within 10–20 miles of the mean 18th-century town were some of the finest great houses of the Augustan age, two of them, Chatsworth and

Wentworth, inviting comparison with some royal palaces by their extent and the artistic treasures which they housed. These two worlds simply did not meet in a material sense, and as late as 1801 Lady Wharn-cliffe's coach stopping in Sheffield excited as much open-mouthed curiosity among Sheffield urchins as their pallor and their tatters excited among the travellers looking out. Culturally, too, they seemed to be separated by an unbridgeable gulf. The grace and elegance, the classical learning and wide European outlook on which the age prided itself might be found in London or the county towns, or in country houses barely ten miles from the center of the town. Sheffield, however, which was neither a center of administration, nor of the law, the church, education or trade, which was without a leisured class, without a professional class, with a culturally deprived artisan community, seemed in traditional terms to be a cultural desert.

The first "assemblies" were held in the town in 1733, and in 1762 were transferred to purpose-built Assembly Rooms in Norfolk Street. Some hesitant signs of "polite society," fostered by a handful of am-bitious wives of middle-class men, then began to emerge. A proper theater was built in 1763 to take the place of rooms at the Angel Inn, and new hotels were put up later in the century, including the fashion-able Tontine Inn (1785), to mark the growth in social activities as well as becoming centers of the expanding stagecoach network.

Printed material was an important medium and indicator of cultural interests. Lister's *Sheffield Weekly Journal* appeared in 1754, containing (in the style of provincial papers of the time) local notices and adver-tisements, some literary effusions and out-of-date news culled mostly from London papers and official announcements. It was not very long-lived, and in 1760 there began to appear Ward's *Sheffield Public Adver-tiser*. This endured until 1793, when it combined with the *Courant*, a Tory paper, only to share in its demise in 1799. From the 1780s on, the local press increasingly reflected political leanings: Joseph Gale's *Sheffield Register*, later changed into the *Sheffield Iris* when it was edited for a time by James Montgomery, the poet and hymn-writer, was the vehicle for Radical and Democratic propaganda but later turned to a more staid liberal stance. It declined rapidly after 1840 and was ab-sorbed by the *Sheffield Times* (established 1846) in 1848. *The Sheffield Mercury*, a vigorous Tory paper, began publication in 1807. *The Shef-field and Rotherham Independent* began as a weekly in 1819, representing the Liberal-Radical tradition, then the strongest element in Sheffield's political makeup, under a directorate including T. A. Ward, who served as editor from 1824 to 1829. Later in the century, under the editorship and proprietorship of the Leader family who had first made their fortunes as silver manufacturers, the *Independent* became one of the leading provincial papers of England, turning into a daily in 1861. It found a worthy opponent in the *Sheffield Telegraph,* the Conservative paper founded as a daily in 1855 by (Sir) William Leng.

The weakness of local publishing reflects the limited cultural interests of the town. In the period 1760–1800 some 120 items which were not local reports or catalogues were published by Sheffield printers. Apart from devotional books and sermons, these were mainly entertaining or of a scientific nature. Many of the titles which local booksellers retailed for London publishers were also of a broadly scientific character. Indeed, apart from such aspects of a popular culture as the songs of Joseph Mather, a filesmith, some of whose songs are still known and sung today, it was science which became the main basis of the town's cultural developments in the first half of the 19th century.

The role of culture and science in the Industrial Revolution has often been misunderstood. Starting from the rigorous separation of the "Two Cultures," the humanities and the sciences, of today, and indeed the further subdivisions between pure sciences and applied technology, and among the separate subjects in turn, we may unwittingly compartmentalize what for contemporaries was a single stream. It is true that for medical men and certain manufacturers, the acquisition of scientific knowledge had immediate business or professional applications, but in the absence of fundamental analytical understanding, which was only then being created, largely by the practitioners themselves, the practical know-how of chemical manufacturers and steel smelters *was* all that was known about "Chemistry" and the practical experience of doctors *was* the largest component of medical science. Fields of knowledge overlapped and were not yet entirely separated from aesthetic appreciation. The coffee pots and candelabra of "Old Sheffield Plate" of breathtaking elegance and beauty, well proportioned and, if ornamented, ornamented with perfect professionalism, were in fact hammered out by local craftsmen wearing the same aprons, living in the same streets, and being entertained in the same public houses as the bulk of the local working classes. If there were designs by professional artists, they were used only as general guidelines to style: the craftsman was still an independent and inventive artist in his own right. To a lesser extent, this also applied to knife and scissor forgers and handlemakers and, later in the 19th century, to the design and ornamentation of iron stoves and fenders, another flourishing local industry. If the transformation of the articles in silver and Old Sheffield Plate (and later electroplate) from the style and elegance of the late Georgian and Regency period to the clumsy ornateness of the Victorian age is any guide, local craft designers were well aware of the artistic trends in their societies around them.

For others, too, lines of division were not easily drawn. A manufacturer of tools, for example, might have an immediate interest only in such questions as the properties of steel or the latest improvements in steam engines. But money was to be made in Sheffield by exporting to such areas as North America, Latin America, or India, which required an understanding of the needs, the social prejudices and, in many cases, the languages of these areas. Thus every important local manufacturing family had some members who had travelled widely, and this in turn created a demand for wider education for practical needs. When the British Industrial Revolution turned, as it did after 1815, from inner colonization and development to the economic penetration, and thereby often the cultural interpretation of other continents, Sheffield men were often in the forefront.

Further, it has recently been shown that for the doctors, pharmacists, opticians, chemists, schoolmasters, and others of this type, membership in the Sheffield "scientific community," which flourished particularly between 1800 and 1840, was a way of legitimizing their own socially uncertain position, confirming their arrival as members of the middle classes. Such status was by no means certain at the beginning, when surgeons still had difficulty in being distinguished from barbers, and it should not be forgotten that one of the two existing medical schools in the town, opened in 1828, was forced to close its doors because of rioters who accused it of body-snatching. The seal was set on the arrival of the medical profession by the knighthood conferred in 1841 on A. J. Knight, a local doctor. For that matter, the industrial-commercial classes themselves still had to establish their own new status, still to capture representation on the bench and in Parliament, for example. It was no accident that so many members of that community were radicals in politics, and nonconformists in religion, particularly Unitarians — or indeed agnostics. The discoveries of science implied a questioning of tradition, just as the rise of the industrial middle classes implied a revision of existing social relationships and ultimately of the political constitution. Aristotelian science and the British constitution alike were vulnerable to a test of utility: commercial expansion and scientific achievements were both, in their different ways, destructive of conservatism, and it was natural for one mind to encompass both liberating forces.

The wide spectrum of motivations, backgrounds, and levels of achievement associated with the developing scientific culture can be discerned from the makeup of the audiences of the itinerant science lecturers who formed one of the most characteristic expressions of that local interest. Some few workingmen were to be found among their audience, craftsmen usually who wanted to understand more clearly the principles with which their technique operated. There were young men, eager to acquire knowledge, ladies of leisure filling their idle hours, eager to be seen at the socially approved functions of the town, or genuinely longing for an understanding of their world. There were also local scientists and *savants* who might know more about the subjects under discussion than the lecturers themselves.

T. A. Ward was associated in a leading capacity with practically every scientific-cultural institution to emerge in the first half of the 19th century. In 1804 he joined the "Sheffield Society for the Promotion of Useful Knowledge." "Each [member] in turn reads a paper on any subject he prefers, except religion and British politics, which, as they might cause disputes, are wisely avoided." This formal anxiety not to appear to subvert the existing social order while encouraging intellectual inquisitiveness which might ultimately have the same effect was typical of the cultural institutions of that period. Equally typical was the topic combining economy, technology, and humanitarianism which Ward describes in the same diary entry for November 8, 1804: "The paper read this evening was by Mr. Sutcliffe, and attended by experiments. It is well known that the white lead manufactory is very pernicious to those employed in it. Mr. S. hopes he has discovered a manner of preparing the article which obviates this dreadful effect and be quite as cheap an operation."[4] Altogether, the 38 topics for discussion balloted for and approved in 1804 may be grouped as follows:

Technology and natural sciences	13		
Medicine	5	Sciences	24
Agriculture	3		
Geography	3		
Psychology	2		
Philosophy, ethics	8	Humanities	14
History	2		
Taste, Literature	2		

Curiously, Ward speaks of this society in his diary as the "Literary and Philosophical Society" in 1804, although a society of this formal name was not established until 1822. "Lit. and Phil." societies, providing a broad spectrum of cultural interests as implied in the title, were a significant feature of leading provincial towns in the Industrial Revolution. Sheffield's appeared very late, but its active forerunner was founded at much the same time as in other towns.

In 1804 T. A. Ward was a subscriber also of the Surrey Street Library, the Surrey Street Newsroom, and the Assembly. In 1809 and again in 1820–27 he was president of the Surrey Street Library. This had been founded in 1771 as a subscription library, and it is known that in 1792 it held 848 works, while in 1825 it held some 4,000. This was a relatively poor showing compared with the circulating libraries run on a commercial basis, largely but not exclusively by booksellers: In 1787 at least two firms are listed in the local directory as "hairdresser and keeper of a circulating library." The first commercial circulating library appears to have been established in 1753 by a bookseller named Richard Smith, and there were several in operation by the 1790s. The largest of these had 3,000 volumes in 1794 and 7,000 volumes in 1806, though of the latter number, some two thirds were "novels, romances, tales."

The occupational breakdown of the 107 out of the 210 members who had passed through the Surrey Street Library membership list and whose occupations are known is significant, and may be compared with a similar list of 503 that can be identified out of some 2,400 who took out prepublication subscriptions of locally published works in the period 1788–96. Fifteen percent of the library members, and between one third and one half of the subscribers were women.

	Library 1771–1802	Subscriptions 1788–1896
Clergymen, schoolmasters	19	39
Doctors, lawyers	19	35
Cutlery and allied trades	22	137
Merchants	9	21
Shopkeepers	13	79
Gentlemen	5	22
Innkeepers and victuallers	20	37
Miscellaneous [mainly other industries]		133
	107	503

Meanwhile, in 1806 the Sheffield Book Society was founded and T. A. Ward became its secretary and librarian in 1808, holding that office until 1863. It was a rather exclusive club, but in the first year of his office, six of his "shopmen" were persuaded to make small payments to the society, "for whom I made a selection of proper and useful books to excite in them a fondness for other employs than drinking and idleness." Second only to his ambition to elevate himself, the new middle-class representative had as his chief aim the task of making the workingman more respectable.

In 1821 Ward joined the New Book Club, from which he resigned in 1826, and in November 1822 he became one of the four vice presidents of the new "Lit. and Phil." Society, Dr. Knight becoming president. In 1824 the Sheffield Mechanics' Library was opened. Although the suggestion for its creation had come from a group of artisans, it was under heavy middle-class patronage, T. A. Ward being a keen supporter. It had 2,000 volumes at its opening, 4,500 in 1841. Less predictably, Ward was elected president of Sheffield Music Hall later in that year. The Mechanics' Institute was set up in 1832, again largely patronized by middle-class supporters, including T. A. Ward and it shared its premises with the Atheneum. The Public Library of 1856 also opened in the same building. Of 154 supporters of the Institute in 1832 whose occupations are known, 28 were medical men, 13 in teaching or clerical professions, 19 in legal or similar professions, and 36 were merchant-manufacturers. Perhaps more striking still, 50 percent of those whose religious affiliation is known were Unitarians, while according to the religious census of 1851 the Unitarians had only 2.7 percent of the church sittings in the city.

As almost everywhere else, however, the expressed hope of teaching science to mechanics, "particularly (those which) are connected with the staple manufacturers of the town" remained largely unfulfilled: the Sheffield Mechanics' Institute quickly settled down to provide either elementary classes for artisans, or vocational courses for clerks and other white-collar workers. It was left to the Sheffield People's College, a pioneering institution founded in 1842 on which the more famous London People's College was based, to provide some genuinely higher education for working men. The college was unique in having at least for a time, its governing body and even its teaching staff, largely made up of working men.

Sheffield had made great strides in one lifetime. From a benighted small town it had grown into a city with some claims to culture, and to being a plural society with its own intellectual initiative. Yet it had still a long way to catch up, not only as compared with the more privileged older towns, in which wealth was spent rather than earned, but even in comparison with a more advanced industrial city like Manchester. The playgrounds and gymnasia, the great libraries, theaters and concerts, the parks and the fine streets with their imposing frontages found there, had to wait for the latter part of the 19th century in Sheffield. By the same token, however, the popular village culture had survived much better in Sheffield, particularly in the outlying hamlets that were only gradually being engulfed in the sea of bricks. This included sports events, among them shooting matches, cricket, and coursing, as well as walking, swimming, and gardening. Popular songs were still being added to by ballads written for special occasions, reflecting not only political views, but also popular attitudes toward industrialization and urbanization.

If the lack of a rich urban tradition had disadvantaged Sheffield in its cultural provision for adults in the 18th century, it was responsible for an equally poor base for the education of the young. There was no wealthy public school, and but a single small grammar school from the Reformation days, eking out an obscure and narrow existence until an endowment in 1603 enabled it to pay two learned men to act as schoolmaster and usher. It was, however, under the control of the Church

Burgesses, one of the two parochial bodies, who administered charities and other funds dating from the middle ages and as such it was formally Anglican in a town of strong nonconformity after 1660. By the later 18th century the teaching was mostly carried on by members of the Anglican clergy on a part-time basis, but it did allow some local middle-class boys to acquire a reasonable education and was undoubtedly the best school available in Sheffield at the time. Leaving out a brief period of glory, when one of the finest nonconformist Academies, preparing young men for the ministry, flourished in Attercliffe in 1686–1718; the newer foundations of the period were the charity schools, usually short-lived affairs, set up to bring the rudiments of education, obedience, and other Christian virtues, and a useful trade, to orphans, pauper children, and others of the lower orders. The Boys' Charity School was founded in 1706 for the "clothing, maintenance, and education of 54 (later 100) poor boys" from the age of eight until their apprenticeship. A charity gave money for eight free places in 1783, raised to 90 in 1830, after which the school declined. A Girls' Charity School was established in 1786 for 60 girls (8 to 16 years old) training them mainly in domestic subjects. There are records of other such foundations in Wadsley (1712), Fulwood, Crookes (1724), Broad Oak Green (1729), Sharrow (1782), Grimesthorpe (1793), and Upper Heeley (1801). Undoubtedly the most important of these foundations was the so-called Free Writing School (1721) built near the Grammar School and evidently run in conjunction with it at times: John Eadon, an author of well-known school textbooks, taught in both in the later 18th century. Indeed, it may be that the tail was wagging the dog, for in the Grammar School, it was said "an acquaintance with the classics, if not wide yet accurate, was caned into (the sons of the townsfolk). They were well grounded in Latin, and for mathematics and penmanship they had the advantage of capable instruction from the master of the adjoining Free Writing School. The result was that our forefathers, if shaky in their spelling, often wrote an exceedingly good hand."[5] T. A. Ward was an old Grammar School boy and remembered sharing the churchyard as a playground with the "Charity Boys." His Latin was reasonable, but he was so conscious of the deficiencies in the rest of his education that he spent much of his private time in later life improving some portions of it, notably the French and Italian languages—and much of his public time in fostering societies for mutual adult education.

For the rest, some teaching was carried on by individuals for gain, often in their own dwellings. Such "schools" ranged from what was little more than a baby-sitting service to the solid instruction given by learned men. Not all of it was full-time. One intriguing entry in the 1774 Directory describes one John Swan, of Hollis Croft, as "scissor maker of various sorts and Teacher of the Mathematics." More reasonably, John Richardson who ran a school in Paradise Square, combined it with a circulating library open before and after school hours and in the dinner break, as well as giving evening classes for apprentices and free Sunday school for poor widows' children, while his wife also managed a girls' school.

When Sheffield, in common with other industrial towns, had to absorb unprecedented numbers of a largely working-class population in this phase, the inadequacies of the existing educational facilities were only too obvious. Two needs in particular stood out: the need for a modicum of literacy and for an understanding of some of the properties of the materials on which the men worked, as well as of the care and maintenance of machinery; and the need for religious, moral, and political indoctrination in order to make it easier to keep a turbulent and underpoliced town under control. In order to perform these functions, two characteristic types of school were developed: the Sunday School, and the denominational day school on the monitorial principle.

The first Sheffield Sunday School was opened in 1780 in Carver Lane. The Wesleyan Sunday School, opened in 1785, stood under the general direction of Daniel Hinchliffe, a scissor manufacturer; James Vickers, the inventor of Britannia metal used in local industries; Thomas Holy, button-maker; and Henry Longden, ironfounder. Within five years, 750 children attended such schools in the town, and in the new century, progress was even more rapid, particularly among the nonconformists. The Unitarians established theirs in 1811, with T. A. Ward as a prominent supporter and collector of funds, attending regularly once or twice a day in the early months. In 1812, the Wesleyans opened the largest of all, Red Hill Schools, catering for 1,200 children, and the Sheffield Sunday School Union was formed. Although the established church stayed away from it and there was a good deal of rivalry between the denominations, the Sheffield Sunday School Union became not only a strong force of indoctrination and education, but also of entertainment and color in the drab lives of numerous children: for many, the annual Whitmeet was the only occasion when they were given new clothes. It is important to remember that Sunday schools covered a larger proportion of the town's children than any other form of education. From just over 3,000 in 1813, numbers rose to 8,500 in 44 schools in 1820, when there were 3,000 also in Church of England schools: this would represent 75–80 percent of the eligible children of their age groups. The proportion was to fall somewhat in the following decades: the S.S.U. recorded 10,500 attenders in 1831 and 12,900 in 1841, or an increase of 50 percent over 1821, while the child population had risen by 70 percent.

The strength of the Sunday School in the industrial towns was its availability even to the children who worked during the week — possibly the most deprived group of Sheffield citizens at that time. Its weakness was the concentration on religious topics which in the hands of untrained and often ignorant teachers (there were 1,859 teachers in the S.S.U. schools alone in 1820) either became meaningless dogma or legends and fairy tales of a distant people whose environment and whose problems bore no relationship to the experienced environment of the children. Moreover, its teaching was intermittent and absenteeism was hard to combat.

Some of these weaknesses were overcome by the denominational day schools on the Lancasterian principle. Joseph Lancaster visited the town to propagate the monitorial system in February 1809 and four months later a Lancasterian school was opened. "The factory system applied to education was a success: the original 320 boys had more than doubled by the time Sir Thomas Bernard wrote an account of it in 1812. All in a room 99 by 63 feet they passed at the command (transmitted by a telegraph) of the single master from monitor to monitor through the carefully organised phases of the three R's."[6] The Anglicans were not far behind, their "national" school, run on Dr. Bell's lines and opened in 1811, having 1,000 pupils in 1814 when the Lancasterian still had only 700. T. A. Ward, president of the Lancasterian School for Boys in 1811, was at that time active in raising money for a Lancasterian school for girls, which was duly established in 1814 in the Red Hill Sunday School premises and, because of overcrowding in the "National" school, took some of their overflow also. With the increase in population both these systems expanded, but did not substantially increase their coverage of the poorer children. In 1830, Ward was on the committee of the new Infants Department of the Lancasterian School. In 1870, when a new Education Act provided for local School Boards to fill the gaps left by private endeavor, there were 28,000 places for 40,000 children requiring elementary education: among working-class children, therefore, the coverage was probably around one half.

The provision for middle-class education was increasing at a faster rate. It has been estimated that there were 10 private academies in Sheffield in 1800 and nearly 60 in 1830. By 1836, a Church of England (subscription) Collegiate Grammar School opened its doors, and in the following year the first stone of the Wesleyan Proprietary School was laid. To the three grammar schools for boys (including the old Grammar School) was added the first Girls' High School in 1878. To this list should be added a growing provision of elementary teaching facilities for adults who had missed their opportunities earlier. In 1840 the Unitarians opened an Adult school, the Quaker in 1845, and the Church of England in 1853, but of these, only the Quaker school had some continuing success.

It is not easy to sum up the consequences of such patchy and varying educational provision in a period of rapid social change and substantial population growth. As far as the middle classes were concerned, new worlds opened out for them. The most successful sent their sons away to the ancient Public Schools or to the newer foundations, modelled on them but pervaded by a 19th century ethos. For the rest, the local grammar schools not only increased the numbers of places available, but greatly raised their standards. By the mid-19th century, Sheffield was educationally on the map.

The lower orders also certainly achieved a much higher level of formal education than at the beginning of the Industrial Revolution, and it is clear that around half the artisans were literate by the mid-19th century. Certainly there seemed to be no difficulty in getting political messages across to them, if only by some man reading out current newspapers to groups in public houses, and whatever else might have hampered the periodic religious and evangelistic crusades, inability to read the bible was not among the commonly quoted obstacles. Similarly, trade unions, cooperatives and friendly societies had no difficulty in finding highly literate office bearers—at least one local secretary having a command of shorthand—and employers found as much education among their hands as their jobs demanded. The foundation of the School of Design in 1843, becoming in 1857 the "School of Art," showed, like the Mechanics' Library of 1824, the flexibility of local provision when a clear industrial need was felt to exist.

PHILANTHROPY: MOTIVES AND ACHIEVEMENTS

This education was not given, and possibly not even received, without a purpose. Did it alter the picture of the world held by the men and women of Sheffield? Did it affect their political and religious outlook? Did it make them quiescent, thankful for the British constitution, or more restless, more revolutionary as they could read and grasp the meaning of the critical literature available to them? Did they become more efficient, more obedient cogs in the economic machine?

No doubt, much education provided by the rich for the poor represented a form of philanthropy. A man like T. A. Ward believed that knowledge was almost as precious as life itself and should not be withheld from anyone: the inner confidence of the stable society of his youth, into the upper echelons of which he was born, left no room for fear that education might be subversive. Inasmuch as the churches or their congregation had an influence on these matters, their commands to be charitable could not be ignored and were added to local pride, humanitarian feelings, and tradition, among other motives, to keep the local stream of philanthropy flowing.

The foundation of the provision for the poor was the Elizabethan

Poor Law. Like so much else, it was affected by the absence of a local elite in the 18th century. In 1871, a scissor smith named Benjamin Blonk wrote:

> It is much to be lamented that the great trust or office of Overseer of the Poor should generally be so little attended to, but it will no longer be a wonder why it should be so when tis considered that the persons mostly elected thereto are tradesmen without experience in time or inclination and who are owing to the clamors and many disagreeable circumstances at present attending the office most heartily tired before their term is expired being deprived of that most useful assistance which the officers of other towns experience — that of the attendance (at the poorhouse) on publick days of many of the principal inhabitants."[7]

Nevertheless, the Poor Law stood up extremely well to the great pressures to which it was subjected by the fluctuations in prosperity during the years of war and the postwar slump until 1820.

Extremes of Expenditure (Easter to Easter)

1792–93	(low)	£ 4,234
1796–97	(high)	10,156
1797–98	(low)	8,685
1801–2	(high)	14,323
1802–3	(low)	9,922
1808–9	(high)	18,831
1810–11	(low)	16,453
1812–13	(high)	27,005
1814–15	(low)	16,715
1819–20	(high)	35,166

In the process, a number of the town's more prominent citizens, like T. A. Ward came to take the place of the lowlier, if more representative Overseers of earlier times, as part of their growing domination over local government. Although Sheffield had in Samuel Roberts, a silver and plate manufacturer, one of the most fanatical and eloquent national opponents of the new Poor Law of 1834, the law was introduced into the city in 1837 with little trouble and none of the violence that occurred in some other industrial towns of the north. Partly, this was because of excellent friendly payments provisions of local trade unions and friendly societies which kept the Sheffield artisans out of the clutches of the Poor Law except in the very worst slumps. Another reason may have been the attitude of the local guardians who were less inclined than elsewhere to administer the law with the inhuman harshness demanded from London.

Typical philanthropic institutions which were founded as the town's industrial population began to grow included the Female Benefit Society (1795), the School of Industry (1797), and the Royal Infirmary (1797). The latter was not strictly philanthropic, since those unable to pay were normally taken to the Poor Law hospitals. Subscribers to the Infirmary could, however, nominate patients on the basis of their subscriptions, and some nominated their servants or even their employees, while trade unions and friendly societies who had contributed largely to its erection, also continued to subscribe and obtain places in the Infirmary, and later other city hospitals, for their members.

T. A. Ward took an unusually, and perhaps even an untypically prominent part in the town's philanthropic endeavors, including the Infirmary and the Aged Female Society. We find him as a leading sponsor of the efforts to relieve distress during the slumps, as in 1809 and again in 1819. In 1810 he was associated with a scheme to employ poor children in pin-making and to raise the wages of certain workmen while attempting to prevent prosecution of some trade unionists by the masters under the Combination Acts. In the same year he also attempted to found a Humane Society, and he was connected with the Society for Bettering the Lot of Chimney-Sweeping Boys, a mainly Quaker group founded in 1807. He acted for a time as the Chairman of the Board of Health, set up in 1831–32 to deal with the threat of the cholera.

Even in the case of an exceptionally kindhearted person like T. A. Ward, however, the attitude towards his less fortunate and less affluent fellow townsmen, including those of the artisan and laboring classes, was not purely altruistic or divorced from a drive to influence, improve, alter, or dominate. The ambivalence implied in this attitude is one of the most difficult to grasp, but also one of the most rewarding if we wish to understand the social reality and social dynamics of a city in the Industrial Revolution.

One of the most enlightening institutions in this context was the Sheffield branch of the Society for Bettering the Conditions of the Poor, established in 1803: Ward was associated with it at least from 1809 onward and possibly earlier. Its objects, defined in 1812, were "to promote the comfort and welfare of the poor by the encouragement of industry, economy, and order and by assisting them in their distress," as well as benefiting their children by the provision of schools of industry. Young women employed in manufactories were to be helped by supplying religious and moral tracts to them. Vagrancy and begging were to be suppressed, and visitations of the houses of the poor were to be organized. The task of the visitors was "the reminding of cleanliness, order, care of families, the disadvantages of debt or dealing with pawnbrokers." Those found without bibles in their homes "are recommended as to where they may be supplied." Finally, thrift was to be encouraged, and those making weekly deposits to the Society's visitors were to have one quarter of the sum put by, added to by the Society.[8]

It would be difficult to better, in so small a compass, the remarkable mixture of genuine aid and compassion with the overwhelming suggestion that all poverty was the fault of the poor and not in the least of those who employed them, or failed to employ them, or of society as a whole. Moreover, while somehow implying that religion would overcome the poverty or other misfortunes of the poor, the approach manages to suggest at one and the same time the moral superiority of the middle class philanthropists and visitors, and the thorough inferiority of the moral codes of the victims, so wholly inferior in fact that it could be doubted if they could ever free themselves of their self-induced poverty and inferiority. The poor, by their very behavior, typical for the lower orders, showed themselves to be sinful and nonelect. However, a way out was suggested: to model themselves as closely as possible on the alleged virtues of the middle classes, especially their religiosity, thrift, and respectability, without a mention that if the advice were taken seriously and large numbers of the poor became middle-class owners of capital, the social system would break down as there would then be no one to do the work of the world at low wages.

Thrift was the main aim of another of Ward's interests, the Sheffield Savings Bank. It opened in 1819 with the subscription of a number of wealthy well-wishers, the object being to encourage savings by "industrious mechanics and labourers." Ward became a governor in 1819 and a trustee in 1827. As in most other towns, its depositors were not so much found among artisans—though rather more so in Sheffield than elsewhere—as among domestic servants, white collar workers, and small shopkeepers. Regularity of income was clearly a more important aid to saving than its sum total, and it did not occur to the members of the town's elite who were behind such schemes that the logic of the irregular income of the normal artisan, his job insecurity, and the very close approach to mere subsistence even when in work, was to eat as well as he could and provide other necessities to preserve himself in health as long as he could, and then to hope for charity or to live off his fat in bad times, rather than to undermine his health by starving himself even in good times in order to put something by for the inevitable setbacks.

Another drive to convert the lower orders to respectability was the attack on drink. The campaign here was much more ambivalent, not only because the consumption of alcohol was so obviously a middle class failing, but also because the drink trade was a highly vocal pressure group, generally organized for the Tory Party. Although it was not difficult to point to evident examples of families impoverished and ruined by drink, it could be argued that in the abject housing conditions of the day the public house was an important center of social intercourse and of recreation and that beer contained some nourishment. In retrospect, what strikes the historian most about the Temperance and Abolitionist campaigns, in which Sheffield played a leading part, is on the one hand the theatricality and obvious dishonesty of the conversion stories with which the crusades were enlivened, and on the other their ineffectiveness. But perhaps here, too, the basic and possibly unconscious objective of the campaigns was not so much to convert, but to imbue the lower orders with a consciousness of their own moral inferiority as the just and self-induced cause of their economic and social inferiority.

RELIGION

Education and philanthropy, the inculcation of thrift and of sobriety, important though they were, were possibly overshadowed by another, even more potent means in the drive to make the lower orders respectable and integrate them into society without giving them greater political power or higher economic reward. This was religion, in its many manifestations. The support for organized religion in that era of rapid transformation had numerous different components. But the fear of revolution, and the awareness of the dark beast that lay in waiting just below the surface, unknown and unknowable despite many efforts to discover its secret, were never far from the consciousness of the urban, middle classes of that period. Inevitably, the power of religion, since it was available, was used to help to tame it; and in turn, the role of religion as a tamer of the beast accounts for much of its popularity among the middle classes.

Sheffield, like most other underprivileged industrial towns, had been strongly Parliamentarian and Puritan in the 17th century, and the tradition had survived the Restoration and the Clarendon code. The established church had its privileges, its endowments, and the Parish Church: a second large town-center church, St. Paul's, was built in 1719, but characteristically not used until 1740 owing to internal dissensions. But the Old Dissent was strong in Sheffield: by the end of the 18th century, the Presbyterian, later Unitarian Upper Chapel, built in 1700 and largely rebuilt in 1848—even today one of the neatest and most dignified in the city—the Nether Chapel of 1715, both in Norfolk Street, the Quaker Meeting House, first erected in 1705, and the five new chapels built between 1774 and 1790, contained the greater part of the Sheffield respectable citizenry in their congregations every Sunday.

John Wesley first visited the town in 1742 and was appalled by the violence which greeted him. The mob destroyed two meeting houses before a third was firmly established in Mulberry Street in 1757, allegedly the largest nonconformist chapel in the town. But when the sect moved into its grander Norfolk Street Chapel in 1780, it was already ceasing to be a truly popular group and becoming, like the others, an expression of the spiritual aspirations of the lower and middle, middle classes. Yet Sheffield showed some significant deviations from the norm here: because of the imperceptible social gradations, there were still many artisans left in the Methodist connection, and in consequence a strong local countercurrent to the conservatism in politics and religion increasingly associated with its leadership. Three times did schisms have very active support from Sheffield, in each case for a more democratic or populist variant: in the case of the Kilhamites (Methodist New Connexion) who split off in 1797, the primitives who broke away in 1811 and made their first large inroads in Sheffield in 1819, and the Free Methodists who split off in 1849. "There can be no doubt that Primitive Methodism embraced more of the artisan class than any other church in the second half of the (19th century). . . . The Primitive Methodist picture in Sheffield is of a denomination largely made up of the most respectable of the working class, always appearing well-dressed, devout, enthusiastic, with an admixture of the lower middle group, small tradesmen, and such people, not without a handful of wealthier families in some chapels, who had made money and retained their old associations."[9]

Two movements affected the religious practice about the turn of the century. One was the move to Unitarianism and rationalism which was part of the scientific groundswell. T. A. Ward, for example, left the Church of England for the Unitarians in 1809. He was associated with a group who called themselves "Rational Dissenters" and later with the Hackney circle. Somewhat later, a more extreme version was to be propagated by Owenists who opened their Sheffield "Hall of Science," the name again linking rationalism and the trust in science, in 1839.

The second, more powerful one, was the Evangelical drive of which Methodism had been a portent but which affected also the established Church of England. Somewhat belatedly it bestirred itself to take cognizance of the new urban population which it had hitherto pointedly ignored. In Sheffield there were only 3,600 sittings in three large Anglican churches (St. James' had been built in 1789) and two chapels in 1800 for a population of 46,000. Four large churches were built under the Million Act in the inner suburbs and consecrated between 1825 and 1830, another six were built with State funds, and four by private subscription by 1850. In 1846 the town had been divided into 25 parochial districts, and after incumbents had been appointed to each of them, great efforts were made to build the churches for them. According to the religious census of 1851, there were 23 Church of England places of worship in the city and 47 other churches and chapels. In all, 44,000 sittings were available, of which only 14,300 were free ones, or a little over one in ten for the 135,000 inhabitants. The morning of the test Sunday, 20,300 attended; 4,600 in the afternoon, and 18,500 in the evening. During the morning service, one third of the Anglican places were filled, one half of the Dissenters, and 100 percent of the Roman Catholics. Between 1850 and 1900 another 30 new churches were built by the Anglicans while nonconformist building was even more active, but a second religious census in 1881 showed an attendance figure of 31 percent of the population, or about the same as in 1851. This represented a high point, and attendances as a proportion of the population declined thereafter.

Detailed studies have confirmed the impression derived from these statistics, and especially those of free sittings, that church attendance was limited to the minority of the respectable classes, the majority of the poorer members of the community staying away, and that this accurately reflected the hold which religion had over the people of Sheffield. Perhaps the high point of the class-oriented nature of the church was reached during some of the most critical weeks in the Chartist period in 1839, when the Sheffield Chartists asked the vicar to preach to texts chosen by them and announced their intention of attending the Parish Church *en masse*. They were met by the constables who preserved the traditional decorum of the Anglican Church by the simple expedient of excluding by force all those whose dress showed signs of poverty. The churches might be used for the high points of life: baptisms, marriages, burials, and for ceremonial occasions as at Easter or Whitsun. Most children would have passed through the Sunday Schools, and many through denominational day schools at some points in their lives, and most townsmen were familiar with biblical phrases, biblical systems of thought and at least some of the legends and historical descriptions of the Old and the New Testament. Yet to most of them it was an alien and irrelevant culture. On the other hand, there was a highly significant minority of leaders who were deeply religious, and who had found their self-confidence to speak in public, to advise others, and to manage organizations, within their chapels, usually among the more democratic and obscure sects. In so far as these men were of significance, the confidence placed in organized religion as a preserver of the social order was not entirely misplaced.

SHEFFIELD'S POLITICS

It has been pointed out above that the large majority of the town's population, the artisans and laborers and their wives, were excluded not only from the church, but also from political government. Indeed, until the Reform Act of 1832, which gave Sheffield two members of Parliament and the middle classes the vote, and even until the local adoption of the Municipal Corporations Act which gave Sheffield a

Town Council in 1843, the middle classes had little political influence, though the elite among them had gradually taken control over the Church Burgesses, the Town Burgesses, the Cutlers' Company, and the police powers under the Act of 1818. Between them these authorities had many of the functions of local Government. T. A. Ward, for example, held prominent office in all of them except the Church Burgesses, as well as being an Overseer of the Poor, the Town Collector in 1828 and 1829, and a magistrate of the West Riding from 1836. Thus, with the early weakening of aristocratic and traditional power in the town, and against the background of an important, but numerically weak Tory minority, Sheffield politics in this phase were largely played out by the middle classes in power versus the majority of propertyless citizens without rights, all within the framework of a crystallizing Whig-Liberal-Radical party allegiance. The underlying current of change was economic and social, drastically shifting the meaning and role of "class" over time. The piquancy of local politics is based on the fact that unlike the majority of towns, Sheffield had no clear-cut class differences at the margin, and the strata of workers, artisans, shopkeepers and manufacturers shaded imperceptibly into each other.

As there was no ancient corporation and no other center of privilege and wealth without function in the town, most townspeople right up to the Reform Act could make common cause in their demand for political reforms in the direction of greater democracy. However, the heady years following the Revolution in France saw the last occasion when artisans, shopkeepers, small masters, and struggling professionals could see themselves as "the people" unjustly deprived of their rights by the corrupt and unrepresentative oligarchy which then governed Britain nationally and locally. Henceforth the growing economic antagonisms between masters and journeymen, and the emergence of the claims by laborers and others ignored by the Robespierran democracy, would gradually transform that unity into an uneasy coalition at best, and after the Reform Act of 1832 into outright opposition between those who had the vote and those who did not.

Riots in the town in July 1791, occurred ostensibly over some enclosures at Crookesmoor and Hallam, while the attempt to burn down part of the vicar's residence was clearly caused by resentment over his role in widening Church Street (by reducing the size of the graveyard), as well as by his bias and ruthlessness as a magistrate. What was perhaps equally significant on that occasion, however, was a rash of bills posted all over the town "with the words *NO KING* in large characters," and these words were also shouted by the mob who added, for good measure, "No Taxes" and "No Corn Bill," two ever popular slogans in a manufacturing town. The immediate result was the quartering of troops in the town and in 1792, the erection of Barracks in Sheffield to overawe and intimidate the townsfolk. Significantly, it was built well outside the outer perimeter of houses, to prevent fraternization and to emphasize that government in Britain was *over*, not *by* the people.

The Sheffield Society for Constitutional Information, formed later in 1791, quickly grew to an astonishing membership of 2,000, probably larger than any other similar Radical Society anywhere in the country, London included. Formed largely by artisan-craftsmen and small masters, it felt strong enough to send missionaries to other towns in 1792 to celebrate the victory of the French revolutionary army at Valmy; to assemble 5,000 inhabitants to deplore the declaration of war on revolutionary France, and to send a petition for political reform, signed by 10,000 to Parliament. Sharp Government repression in the next few years reduced the membership and overt activities of the Radicals, and drove some of them to the left and ultimately underground. It is now known that a strong, clandestine, democratic group continued through the years of war and persecution, while the population reacted to the periodic food shortages and fluctuations in employment by open rioting. In one riot in 1795, when the soldiers mutinied, the volunteers fired into the crowd, killing two and later wounding several more with their sabers. There were riots again in 1800 and in 1812, both associated with high food prices, but the protracted disturbances in the latter year included a violent raid on the militia depot and an affray in the theater, when the gallery objected to the singing of "God Save the King." The proliferation everywhere of democratic, radical, and revolutionary societies after the war included strong local plants in Sheffield's fertile soil. There were further riots in the town in 1816, a conspiratorial plot in 1817 and an attempted insurrection (part of the nation-wide armed rising) in 1820 which ended with an abortive march on the barracks by the insurgents.

Many of the popular views, like hostility to the Corn Laws and to high bread prices, to government corruption and high taxes, and in favor of a representative Parliament, could be supported by middle-class reformers but there was always sooner or later a parting of the ways when economic aims of a fairer distribution of incomes, guaranteed work, or higher wages were mentioned. T. A. Ward, who was far to the left of most manufacturers but still a long way from the extreme Radicalism of his day, exemplifies this ambiguity very clearly. In 1810, he had joined the "Friends of Parliamentary Reform" and became their vice president, and had himself, largely drawn up the petition for parliamentary reform (in support of Sir Francis Burdett) which was passed at a mass meeting in Paradise Square on June 6. But in 1812, he stayed away when the "Friends" entertained the old Radical Leader, Major Cartwright—having been frightened off, in common with "the most respectable gentlemen," by the preceding riots. He rejoiced later at having stayed away, for, since "the dinner tickets had been priced so low that the company, with few exceptions, were of the lowest rank," it "was a shabby, and, if some accounts may be credited, a disreputable, nay even a disgraceful meeting," coming out in favor of Annual Parliaments and Universal Suffrage.[10]

In 1813, he was one of the Sheffield delegation to London to oppose the continuation of the monopoly of the East India Company, an issue which had the whole spectrum of Sheffield opinion behind it; whereas in 1814, as noted above, he objected to the unfairness of sending workers to prison for joining trade unions, an issue in which he found himself opposed by most other manufacturers who had formed the "Sheffield Mercantile and Manufacturing Union" to organize the prosecutions. In 1817 he objected to the suspension of *habeas corpus* and the prosecution of Sheffield workmen on the evidence of government spies and *agents provocateurs*, while yet at the same time assisting in the proceedings to increase the number of special constables from 200 to 1,000. In 1819, he joined those who protested in strong language against the Peterloo massacre, but in 1820, he admitted not only that very slow parliamentary reform was the "utmost we must expect," but also that "I am almost sure it is preferable to Radical reform, the effects of which we can scarcely foresee, and which, though irrefutable in theory, might not 'work well'. Is it not better to be cautious, and to change by degrees, as far as experience may prove to be eligible?"[11]

No doubt the name of one of the societies in which he became active in 1823 had his full approval: this was the "Society for the Gradual Abolition of Negro Slavery." In 1824–29 Ward supported numerous other liberal causes, from free trade to Catholic emancipation, and as the agitation for parliamentary reform mounted again, this time to lead to the limited Reform Act of 1832, he became president of the Sheffield Political Union, the chief reform association in Sheffield. Under the new Act, Sheffield was given two seats. At the first election no Tory considered it worth his while to stand, but there were four Whigs/Radicals of various shades, T. A. Ward being the most progressive of them. His platform included disestablishment of the State Church, a free press, free trade, the ballot, the abolition of colonial slavery, the reform of corrupt local bodies, and promises to look after local interests. At a public show of hands he was the popular favorite, but as the working classes still had no vote, he failed to be elected. When this became known, a riot ensued in which the soldiers, ordered by the magistrates to fire, killed three men and two boys and wounded many more.

This, in effect, ended Ward's party political career, but for Sheffield party politics had only just begun. As long as Sheffield was limited to two parliamentary seats, these were generally held by men on the Radical, not to say eccentric, wing of the Liberal Party, and this continued after the franchise was extended in 1867 to urban skilled workers. But what was particularly significant was the local reaction to the exclusion of working men from the vote in 1832.

In a town like Sheffield, where there were large numbers of householders in houses valued at £9, £8 and all the way down, the limit of the right to vote at the line of the £10 householder—drawn with great care to include the middle classes, but exclude the wage earners—seemed particularly illogical and indefensible. Thus the national campaign which was to challenge this injustice in the years 1838–48 under the name of the Chartist movement found at first very widespread local support including even the *Iris* newspaper and Ebenezer Elliott, the "Corn Law Rhymer." When it became clear that Chartism had a working-class base and as such represented implied revolutionary social demands, such middle-class support largely dropped away. At its peak, particularly in the years 1839–42 and 1847–48, Chartism represented the apogee of the old populist-artisan tradition with its mass meetings in Paradise Square or on the dramatic hilltops near the town, with its class meetings on the Methodist model and its conspiratorial groups, its brilliant and influential press, and its rhetoric couched in terms of abstract justice and ancient rights while making up-to-date economic demands. Yet it also represented the first chapter in the new history of working-class politics operating within a developed industrial capitalism. In Sheffield, significantly, there was less hostility between the contemporary anti-Corn Law campaign and Chartism than elsewhere; although the town in the winter of 1839–40 became, once more, one of the few places in the country where armed rebellion had reached an advanced stage of preparation, the local middle classes were less afraid of revolution than elsewhere—even during the great strike wave of 1842—and the nominal aims of the Chartist, as distinct from the social programs superimposed on them, had more widespread support. Despite the limitations of the franchise, the Chartists won 8 of the 14 Town Council seats in November 1849, and then held 22 out of a total of 56, and therefore a majority of the 42 seats which were elective. Many of their proposals, on public relief for example, enjoyed widespread support. Local Chartism began to decline in 1852, but the political integration of the lower orders into established society was not interrupted, and the extension of the franchise to the bulk of the working classes in 1867, passed with scarcely a ripple in local political waters. By 1869 the majority of Borough electors were working class, but before 1884 there had been only one Town councillor of true wage-earning status, and he a rather conservative-minded Liberal.

The independent, and indeed anarchical, tradition remained, however. During the trade-union enquiries of 1867, Sheffield was almost the only place in the country to express some support for the trade union "outrages," the use of violence to enforce the kind of union policies which had earlier on been legally enforced by the guilds. The *Free Press,* later a national radical paper, was started in Sheffield in 1851 and the *National Reformer,* later acquired by Bradlaugh, in 1860. The Sheffield Labor Association (1885) and the Socialist Club (1887) were early socialist manifestations, and, in the 1890s the Anarchists, recalling in some ways the traditions of a century earlier, had one of their strongest bases in the city.

What were the main outlines of the picture of the world held by Sheffielders, those lines which were held so firmly and unconsciously that they did not even need any formal articulation? The overwhelming impression was one of progress: growth everywhere, growth of the town, of its wealth, its technology, and its markets. A part of this progress was also the growing power of individuals to control their destinies, the growing understanding of their environment, their widening horizons in discovering the world. Perhaps means of transport and communication were the most obvious symbols of this progress. It was noted earlier how the expansion of markets by new roads and waterways in the 18th century led to a dramatic growth in the town's industries which in turn brought technical breakthrough and growth of population in their wake. A canal reached the center of Sheffield finally in 1819, but the fundamental change was that brought about by railways. At first, Sheffield's hills had defeated the railway engineers, but a link to the main South-North line was completed in 1838, and the main East-West line, the Manchester, Sheffield, and Lincolnshire was opened in 1845 to Manchester. With the railways came the power to move vastly greater quantities of coal and iron, a mass demand for steel that was to transform the local steel industry, an easy extension of the labor market, cheap trips to the seaside and cheap visits to the Great Exhibition of 1851 where Sheffielders could compare their own products and methods of manufacture with those of the rest of the world.

T. A. Ward who had held some canal shares, had bought large quantities of railway shares, of local and more distant lines: in 1836–37, he had been secretary of the Sheffield to Manchester line. Together with shares in the Water Company (1827), the Gas Company (1818), the Fire Office (1808), and the General Cemetery Company (1834), they enabled him to lead a comfortable life, devoted to public interests and educational advance in middle age while reducing still further his active interest in the family cutlery firm. Thus on this personal level, too, the great public utilities contributed to wealth, to civilizing life, and to opening up new horizons, setting the seal on the staggering signs of progress viewed in one lifetime.

Yet Ward remained a rebel. He never ceased to demand reforms, to right wrongs, and to help those who were underprivileged. For together with the signs of progress, the age also had its staggering social failures, the poverty and insecurity, the soot and dirt and lack of sanitation, the ugly urban sprawl, and oppressive class system. Victorian Britain was full of the success stories of local worthies, of missionaries to convert the rest of the world to its peculiar form of civilization; but those who understood the potentialities of progress were also appalled by its breakdowns, its mental cruelty to children and to the poor, its bleakness of spirit. Man had created splended opportunities, but then had gone on to miss them. This must remain the epitaph on Sheffield in the Industrial Revolution.

NOTES

1. R. E. Leader, *Sheffield in the Eighteenth Century* (Sheffield, 1901), p. 41.
2. A. B. Bell and R. E. Leader (eds.), *Peeps into the Past* (London and Sheffield, 1909), p. 6.
3. Ibid., p. 318.
4. Ibid., p. 55.
5. R. E. Leader, *Sheffield in the Eighteenth Century* (Sheffield, 1901), p. 120.
6. W. H. G. Armytage, "Education in Sheffield (1603–1955)," in D. L. Linton (ed.) *Sheffield and its Region* (Sheffield, 1956), p. 203.
7. Quoted in Mary Walton, *Sheffield. Its Story and Its Achievements* (Sheffield, 3d ed. 1952), p. 144.
8. Quotations from the Report by Mrs. Kibham to the Society in 1812.
9. E. R. Wickham, *Church and People in an Industrial City* (London, Lutterworth, 1957), p. 134.
10. *Peeps into the Past*, p. 191.
11. Ibid., p. 264.

BIBLIOGRAPHY

Bell, Alexander B. (ed.) *Peeps into the Past, being Passages from the Diary of Thomas Asline Ward* (Sir W. C. Leng & Co., London and Sheffield, 1909).

Holland, G. C. *The Vital Statistics of Sheffield* (Sheffield, 1843).

Hunter, Joseph *Hallamshire, the History and Topography of the Parish of Sheffield in the County of York* (London, Virtue & Co., 1869 ed.)

Linton, David L. (ed.) *Sheffield and its Region: A Scientific and Historical Survey* (British Association, Sheffield, 1956).

Lloyd, G. I. H, *The Cutlery Trades. An Historical Essay in the Economics of Small-Scale Production* (Longman, London, 1913, repr. Frank Cass, London, 1968).

158

Pollard, Sidney   *A History of Labour in Sheffield* (Liverpool University Press, 1959).

Walton, Mary   *Sheffield. Its Story and Its Achievements* (Sheffield Telegraph and Star, 1948).

Chapter 4

*T*he dramatic growth in urban population, both in absolute numbers
and as a steadily increasing proportion of the total, was a significant
development in 19th century Europe. Sheffield's statistics (20,000
in 1750; 40,000 in 1800; 120,000 in 1851; 240,000 in 1871) are not
exceptional; they are matched by the data from other industrial communities. For example, the city of Essen in the Ruhr valley of western
Germany grew from a small provincial town of 4,000 in 1810 to a
city of 230,000 in 1905, an increase of 5,874 percent in a century
(*A. and L. Lees, eds.,* The Urbanization of European Society in
the Nineteenth Century [*Lexington, Mass., 1976*], p. x). In 1851,
one half of the population of England and Wales was classified as
urban; 40 years later, the proportion had risen to 72 percent (A.
Weber, "Urban Growth in England and Wales in the Nineteenth
Century," in Lees, op. cit., p. 7). Between 1801 and 1891, the number
of English urban dwellers had increased from 2.3 million to 19.8
million. The expansion of urban populations on the continent occurred somewhat later than in England, but the pattern of growth
was similar. In Germany, 23.7 percent of the total population lived
in communities of 5,000 or more in 1871; by 1910, that ratio had
increased to nearly one half (W. Kollmann, "The Process of Urbanization in Germany," in Lees, op. cit., p. 31). The proportion of
Germans who lived in large cities (over 100,000 in size) increased
during this period from 4.8 to 21.3 percent.

Urbanization did not proceed at the same pace in every country or region in the 19th century; its progress was highly irregular and uneven. In areas that were intensively industrialized (Lancashire and the Midlands in England, the Ruhr valley in Germany), the urban population grew most rapidly. But in districts that were not affected, or touched only lightly by industrialization (the south of England, the mountainous districts of central and southeastern France, the plains of East Prussia), cities grew very slowly or not at all. Ancient provincial towns like Winchester in southern England and Arles in southern France were scarcely larger in 1900 than they had been in Roman times. However, industrialization was not the only stimulus to urban development in these decades. The great capital cities of Europe — London, Paris, Berlin, Vienna, St. Petersburg — expanded greatly throughout the century, becoming so large — in territorial extent and in numbers — as to form a unique and historically unprecedented, urban type. In 1809, London's population was just over one million; that figure rose to 2,350,000 in 1850, and to over four million in 1890. In that year, Paris was the second largest city in Europe (2,500,000), followed by Berlin (1,600,000), Vienna (1,300,000) and St. Petersburg (1,000,000).

These metropolitan centers had long exercised a magnetic attraction for the inhabitants of their respective countries, and that pull grew stronger during the 19th century. As political and administrative centers, the capital cities housed throngs of civil servants who found employment in the proliferating national bureaucracies. Men with political ambitions flocked to the capital from the provinces, to sit in newly created or expanded legislative assemblies, and to be close to the centers of power. Capital cities played a key role in the economic life of European states. They were the major financial centers, the hubs of road and rail systems, the largest market for goods and services. They usually attracted some industry, more commonly in suburbs and outlying areas than in their centers, which were reserved for government buildings and for mercantile activity. The capitals were also the major centers of national cultures; they housed the publishers of newspapers and books, the theatres and operas, the restaurants and pleasure gardens that provided entertainment for their inhabitants and for visitors.

Industrial cities like Sheffield and Essen experienced severe growing pains, as their inhabitants struggled to forge a viable social order in an environment that was so inhospitable: smoky, grimy, noisy, overcrowded. The problems of living in capital cities were similar, but

with some notable variations. These communities had existed for centuries; their centers were clusters of old streets, churches, and palaces; their social structures and their traditions were ancient. The
waves of migrants that engulfed these cities were partially absorbed
in the central districts, where population densities reached very high
levels, but they also spilled over the ancient urban boundaries and
spread out, in ever-widening circles, into the rural hinterland. Urban
development thus involved the reconstruction of the ancient city
centers, as well as frenetic growth on the periphery. In these vast
metropolitan agglomerations, a very complex society developed.
Nineteenth century Londoners and Parisians experienced the tensions
and traumas of urban living—for example, congestion and street
violence—that had existed in all preindustrial cities, but they also
had to cope with new problems, that could not have been imagined
by earlier generations of city dwellers. The inhabitants of Nineveh
in the seventh century B.C. lived in a smaller, more structured, more
stable society than did the residents of European capitals in the 19th
century. They would not have had to travel a dozen miles, involving
an hour's time or more, from their homes to their workshops. They
would not have experienced the sense of isolation and despair, of
anomie, that motivated thousands of poor Parisians to commit
suicide in the 1800s (L. Chevalier, "Crime and Social Pathology
among the Parisian Lower Classes," in Lees, The Urbanization of
European Society, pp. 168–79).

Of Europe's great capital cities, London was among the oldest,
only Rome and Paris having longer histories. London was also (since
about 1650) Europe's largest urban community and in the 19th century, the most populous metropolitan center in the world. Until the
Industrial Revolution, she had been England's only really large city,
dwarfing her rivals—Bristol, Norwich, Southampton—in numbers
and in importance. London's size and wealth had long been a significant factor in the growth of the English economy, creating a sustained
demand for victuals and raw materials, stimulating (for example) the
production of coal in Yorkshire mines, and contributing to the de-
forestation of the island by her consumption of wood for building and
heating. By 1700, London had surpassed Amsterdam as Europe's
(and the world's) greatest port and commercial center, and she maintained that mercantile hegemony until the 20th century. But industry,
though present in some of her districts, was not as important to the
London economy as it was to that of Paris and Berlin. The administrative center of a kingdom and a worldwide empire, London was po-

litically the most autonomous of Europe's capital cities. The influence of the national government upon London's political and administrative life was minimal, by contrast to the intense concern that the French state focused upon Paris. And despite London's size, and the range and complexity of her urban problems, her inhabitants were less prone to mass violence, to revolution, than were those of any other capital city. The distinctive character of London's modern history is the subject of the next chapter.

Nineteenth Century London

SHELDON ROTHBLATT*

If history begins (like Genesis or Darwin) with origins or beginnings, histories begin (like Homer) in the middle of things. The historian rarely enjoys the luxury of starting at the beginning, and the historian of cities labors under the same constraint, especially if his subject is an ancient capital whose development has occurred over long stretches of time. The urban historian is therefore a Homer, always alluding to what came before and offering, through a series of occasional flashbacks, the background information vital to his story.

The history of London demands such treatment because its story is truly of epic dimensions. Already by the 18th century, London had surpassed in population all the other famous cities of Europe. It continued to grow, spectacularly as well as steadily, until it reached the mammoth proportions it assumes today. So breathtaking was its promise, that well before the Industrial Revolution both foreigners and inhabitants considered London to be a special place. Round about 1700, when the city was merely a fragment of what it is today, that literary man about town and habitué of the coffee houses, Joseph Addison, declared himself a "Citizen of the World" because he was fortunate enough to live in London. He was referring to the urbanity and sophistication of the capital, its cosmopolitanism or international standing. Foreigners were settling into London in increasing numbers

---

* University of California, Berkeley.

Note: The author is grateful to the Keeper of Printed Books, The Bodleian Library, Oxford University, for permission to use illustrations from the Library's collections.

creating new, colorful districts like Soho, which still retains something of its original character. The expansion of English shipping and commerce to the fairest corner of the earth had created a global banking and insurance center in London. The royal court was there and Parliament was there, and the air was thick with political pamphlets, mudslinging, gossip, and excited conversation. London, a dark, cramped merchant's city, was brightening into the center of international finance. And London, a political and administrative city where revolutions had been plotted and judicial murders planned, was becoming a brilliant social world, where a prosperous, mannered, and decently-educated landed aristocracy promenaded in new and spacious streets, walks, and squares.

By the time of the American Revolution the impact of London on European and colonial life was generally acknowledged. There really was no need for the English to look with envy upon the lambent social whirl of Bourbon Versailles or indulge sweet memories of the literary salon life of Parisian hôtels. London was cosmopolitan and elegant too, and it was also an imperial capital, but above all it was itself. The amazed German visitor Von Raumer, repeating Addison, wrote in 1835 that "Paris is more preeminently the Town, Germany the Country, but London alone is entitled to talk of being the World."[1] Nearer to our own time an admiring Danish architect, city planner, and writer has called London "The Unique City."[2]

London has an ancient history, but not all of it is epic. The Romans who marched in with Julius Caesar and founded the port settlement of Londonium, marched out in the course of time, and for many centuries London yielded its trading eminence to other centers. While its economic revival occurred in the medieval period, largely because of the work of foreign merchants—Germans from the cities of the Hanse, Florentines and Lombards from the wealthy, advanced Mediterranean—it is only with the Georgian 18th century that London came of age. Georgian land speculators and builders set the pace for the physical development of the city. Georgian promoters created the urban landscape which the Victorians took over. Georgian impressarios and actors established the pattern of entertainment that remains one of the great attractions of London cultural life. Georgian pleasure gardens and country estates influenced the creation of the marvelous urban parks of the 19th century. The club life and in a minor yet important way the political life of Victorian Westminster was first of all the club life of Georgian St. James. The financial, insurance, and brokerage houses which, while on shaky legs to begin with, became in the long run the anchor of London's and Britain's prosperity, were also Georgian institutions.

If, however, the making of London was undeniably the work of the

Georgians, the city did not remain where they had left it. The trans-forming vitality that had spectacularly affected London in the 18th century carried on through the 19th century, with new phases of de-velopment resulting from new forces and personalities. Today, even after much demolition and clearance, it is possible to spot where Georgian London left off and Victorian London took over, and it is also possible to view this change of management as both disastrous and marvelous, as the destruction of Troy or the foundation of Greater Greece. London is still one of the most written and talked about cities the world has ever known. It is both model and warning.

In the essay that follows, the growth of London in the 19th century will be reviewed in four distinct but interrelated ways corresponding to the paramount shaping forces of the city's history. The first shaping force is the geographical or topographical. It explains certain physical characteristics of the city or changes that can be attributed to its environment. The second shaping force is economic. It establishes the impact of commerce, finance, industry, and transport on the history of London and has a direct influence on the third force, the sociological. Under this heading come the movements of population, either in the demographic aggregate or in such subdivisions as classes, groups, and occupations. The fourth shaping force may be termed cultural. It accounts for the values, beliefs, conduct, and institutions which make up and define daily experience, give meaning to life, and pattern the activities that we find in the city. None of these forces can stand alone, nor can each be absolute master over the other. At certain points in London's growth one shaping force may have achieved an ascendancy over another, but it was never permanent or complete.

In order to understand any historical process we have no choice but to break it down into distinct phases or components, to stop the action as a photograph does, to write history as if it were linear. But the true history of London is one of constant interacting movement and of simultaneous activity that refuses to be contained. London's shape and boundaries, the values of its inhabitants, the plan of its streets, the style of its buildings, the scope of its economic life, its patterns of leisure and child-rearing changed almost with every decade. The phases of change were never synchronized; disharmony and incoherence were more truly the conditions of change than neat dovetailing and coordinated movement.

LONDON'S GEOGRAPHY

If it is rarely possible in history to decide that one single cause was responsible for a particular sequence of changes, it is nevertheless true that geography can play a major part in determining where a particular city will be located and in what directions it will initially spread. The Romans, seeking access to the interior of Celtic Britain, wanted a place where the natural land routes of the island converged and joined up with navigable waterways. The London Basin met their requirements. Coming up from the south and standing on the rise that today is called Shooter's Hill, the Roman legions could view all of the central area that in time became Georgian London. Seen from the air, the topography of the London area confirms the choice of site. London was established in a river valley through which the Thames flows from the western midlands of England to the North Sea, widening as it approaches the city and continuing out of it in a series of estuaries. Water-borne traffic could navigate from the mouth of the Thames inward some 50 miles from the east and here, on a bend in the river at the furthest point of interior penetration, trading centers could be established. London began, therefore, in what are today the eastern port districts. In time, dredging and construction enhanced and extended the economic capacity of the river. In the 19th century the Victoria, Albert, and George dock systems were built in order to improve the flow of trade through London, and the port of London consequently became the largest enclosed space of water anywhere in the world.

Possessing deep-water harbors with ready access to the North Sea and from there to world markets, the London Basin was the logical geographical place from which an island nation could establish a vast transoceanic commerce. But this geographical advantage, while necessary, was not sufficient. For if London was undeniably accessible by sea, it still needed easy communication with the interior in order to create an extensive overseas trading empire. Once again the entrepôt was fortunately situated. The surrounding arcs of hills—the Chilterns to the northwest and the North Downs south of the river—were pierced by natural gaps through which overland trade could come. The new railroads of the 19th century more or less followed these old, familiar land routes, which converged upon London from all the principal directions.

Although the earliest London settlements were in what are today the eastern docklands, these were not actually administratively part of the city until the invention of the "Greater London" idea in the late 19th century. For most of the political history of Britain, the port areas fell under the legal jurisdiction of the adjacent county of Middlesex. The "London" which the Romans named developed to the immediate west of the docklands and in time became known as the "City of London" or just the "City," and by this name it is still known.

The "City of London" was and remains an area of about one square

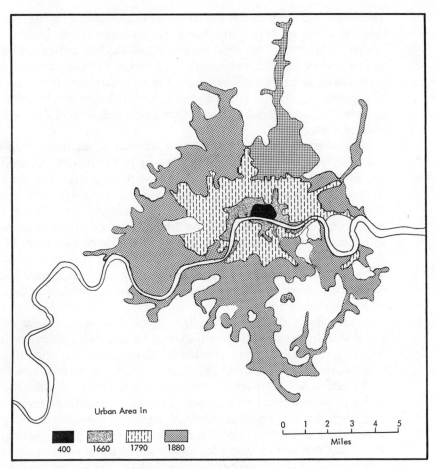

MAP 8.   London's growth since Roman times

mile. It stretches from an eastern district called Whitechapel at a place named "Old Gate" or Aldgate to an impressive arch called Temple Bar. Today Temple Bar is merely a stop on the London Underground, the half surface, half subterranean rail system that is London's inner circulating system. The arch, which was originally wood but was rebuilt in stone by Sir Christopher Wren in the 17th century, is now decaying in the country. In the 18th century it was used for displaying the severed, ghoulish heads of traitors who had risen against the Hanoverian monarchy in 1715 and 1745.

Proximity to the ports gave the City its economic characteristics. It became a financial and commercial center, the heart of British shipping, the center of the world's reexport trade, the core of international insurance, and the home of a currency against which all others would be measured. So powerful did the City become and so jealous of its privileges that as a practical measure the English crown usually observed the ritual of never advancing beyond Temple Bar without the permission of the City's officials. Even to this day the City resists incorporation into the general structure of London municipal government and retains its old guilds or City Companies, its elected aldermen and Lord Mayor.

Upstream from the City perhaps a mile away, another urban center had been long in the making, the "City of Westminster." Around these two nuclei the present London formed, dividing up, so to speak, the city's spoils. The City retained its functions as a banking and maritime center, while Westminster became and remained the political capital of England, Scotland, Wales, and Ireland, the administrative heart of an overseas empire whose boundaries in 1900 exceeded those of Rome in its greatest period of expansion. Westminster was the seat of monarchy, and the mother of all parliaments; the home of a great bureaucracy which increased in numbers, duties, and reputation in the course of the 19th century.

Strung along the northern edge of the Thames between the City and Westminster another urban district formed, which, connecting the two original nuclei, also reinforced their influence and authority. This became legal London. The inns of court, the famous law schools of the late medieval period were established there, as were the great courts of justice, built in massive, foreboding buildings recast by the Victorians in the Scottish baronial style. In the 19th century New Scotland Yard, the home of the new metropolitan police, was given a place near the law courts, a logical siting, and the two were joined in a new partnership. Together they symbolized the orderliness that was supposed to underpin the growth of Victorian London.

There is no necessary reason why a political capital must also be a financial capital or enjoy the status of a major literary or publishing center. Washington, D.C., for example, has never been such a capital: Victorian London was. The concentration of political, economic, and judicial functions made the ancient settlement on the sodden claylands of the river valley through which the Thames flowed the single most important region in all of the United Kingdom.

ECONOMIC STRUCTURES

Victorian London is not commonly thought of as an industrial city. The dubious honor of being the first industrial city in the history of the world goes to a place well to the north of London, to Manchester, where the new textile manufacturing centers developed. The mill town or factory town, where steam engines drove the spindles, is the "Coketown" made famous by the bitter and peculiar fantasies of Charles Dickens' novel, *Hard Times*. Coketown was a new type of city, in the sense that its factory economy was almost the only reason for its existence. The most influential members of the city, those who dominated municipal government, who were its benefactors and philanthropists, established its literary and scientific societies, its hospitals, galleries, and technical institutes, were the leading business families of the communities. They were assisted by local professional families, whose sphere of activity always grows with economic expansion. London, with its Roman and Norman inheritance (the Saxons had put their capital in the south at Winchester), was a commercial, banking, and political city rather than an industrial one. While the merchant community of the City was indeed influential, it was not the

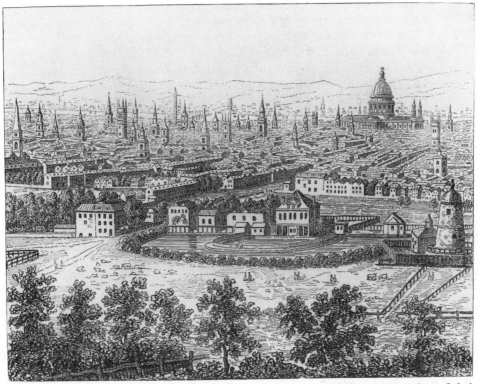

Courtesy Bodleian Library, Oxford

FIGURE 7. The City and East End in 1753. Notice the low elevation, the prevalence of church towers, the interpenetration of open fields, and the bare North Downs in the background.

only source of influence. The City merchants had to share authority with the royal court, with Parliament, with the bureaucracy, and with the social and political leaders of Britain who gathered in the capital.

Yet if London was not a prototypical mill town, a "company town" of the Industrial Revolution, it had certainly long been a major center of manufacturing. When Von Raumer made his visit to London in the middle 1830s there were, besides the enormous expanse of dockyards and shipbuilding facilities, a large center of silk manufacturing at Spitalfields and sugar refineries in Whitechapel. South of the river, in the area of Southwark which was heavily working class in the 19th century, there were tanneries, iron foundries, glass works, dye works, workshops for the manufacture of shoes and hats, and breweries and distilleries to supply the large London drink trade. By the middle of the 19th century, when coal gas was used as the main fuel for lighting, a large gas manufacturing plant was established on the south bank, and its noxious fumes drifted over the eastern districts. The first industrial trade union (as distinct from craft union) was established by the gas workers late in the 19th century.

Other east London districts with a concentration of factories were Woolwich, Enfield, and Poplar. The last, north of the river, had acquired its name from the poplar trees planted to drain the river terraces of the Thames. In the 1850s and 1860s chemical factories were established in Poplar, especially in the part of it known as Bow. (By tradition, anyone born within the sound of Bow Church bells is entitled to be called a "cockney" or native Londoner.) Factories existed for the manufacture of soap, hemp-cloth, matches, rubber, naptha, varnish, and fertilizer, and here as on the south bank, the stink and odors of industrial chimneys were an inescapable part of daily experience.

Factory modes of production, however, were more characteristic of the industrial midlands and the north than of London. It has been estimated that only about one sixth of the adult labor force in London was employed in trades using factory methods and that consequently there was a conspicuous shortage of the kind of semiskilled occupations to be found in the typical industries of mill towns.[3] Small-scale production was the customary manufacturing unit in London. Tucked away in forgotten corners of the city, especially in the eastern and southern districts, small workshops gave employment to the elite of the labor force. At the beginning of the 19th century, London craftsmen had successfully competed with those in other regions, but the progress of industrialism in the north reduced London's national manufacturing importance. Cheap fuel and plentiful inexpensive land on which to build giant factories gave the new industrial cities an insurmountable advantage. London manufacturers were forced to specialize in products designed for local markets. These included luxury and consumer durable goods such as clothing, jewelry, clocks, and stationary for which London's traditional craft structure was preeminently suited. Food and food processing, which expanded with the growth of a restaurant industry in the second half of the 19th century, similarly required highly specialized labor. Another major traditional London industry, the building trades, remained strong. The amazing increase in London's population produced the greatest amount of construction Thameside had ever known. London's Victorian building boom stimulated the furniture and furnishings industries, hardware manufacturing, appliances, plumbing, and lighting. It led to the opening of new brickyards, which changed the face of London from brown or rust-colored brick to the famous red brick of the second half of the 19th century. It created a demand for carpenters and masons, pipefitters and sheetmetal workers, painters, plasterers and decorators, gardeners, and landscapers. The shipbuilding trades, however, were not so successful. The collapse of Thameside shipping in the 1860s virtually put an end to one of London's most famous industries, and the bulk of the engineering trades had to shift over to repair work.

The most distinctive feature of the London employment market, however, was not the existence of relatively privileged craftsmen but the millions of laboring poor—the unskilled workers who struggled in the docklands and worked as demolition crews, the casual labor employed in construction, in the building of railroads and highways, in the digging of tunnels and canals, in the collection of rubbish and other forms of routine maintenance and sanitation. As the century wore on, the numbers drawn into casual work increased. The outward spread of the city produced a heavy demand for scavengers, chimney sweeps, wood choppers, rag collectors, and messengers. The transport industry was a vast employer of unskilled labor. Cabmen were needed to take passengers around the city, coachmen to drive the horse-drawn omnibuses. The railroads absorbed large quantities of manual labor in such jobs as porters and guards and for basic construction. Not only men, but women, too, were brought into the low-paying occupational sector of the economy. The introduction of the sewing machine enabled the East End garment industry, the so-called sweated trades, to employ large numbers of relatively unskilled women without having to resort to factory modes of production. There was no shortage of young women for the clothing industry because the running of the urban household consumed less female labor than did its rural counterpart. Women workers depressed the level of wages even further, but so did immigrant groups like the Irish and the Jews, who were willing to work for less money.

Despite demand, the existence of such an enormous supply of poorly-paid workers constituted a serious social problem, for at any moment thousands could be thrown on the dole. The London economy was characterized by seasonally variable demand, producing sporadic employment. The building industry and the docklands were especially vulnerable. Large builders, who might be expected to weather bad times, were perpetually threatened with bankruptcy by a volatile market. In order to survive, they laid off men without hesitation. In the docklands the situation was particularly acute. London's stature as a major world port made it an unsurpassed center of shipping, but the supply of jobs was influenced by weather, by the famous London fogs and by the seasonal nature of much of the port traffic. Until the use of refrigerated ships in the later 19th century, most of the produce of the warmer regions of the earth were not available to British consumers whatever their income. At certain times of the year the docks were therefore busier than at others, and the cycles of work were interrupted. The situation was exacerbated by the particularly harsh winters of the 19th century. Since unemployment insurance was as yet unknown and the dockers as yet unorganized, the docklands were scenes of frightful misery and destitution.

Alternative work for the unemployed was not always easy to find, as many industries followed the same employment calendar. And even if the cycles of seasonal work dovetailed, many of those who were out of work would not have the requisite experience for another job or would be elbowed out of the way by more qualified workers. The demand for goods and services peaked at different times in different industries, but workers laid off in the winter months suffered greater privation than those dismissed in summer. The cost of living rose in the winter because of fuel, and alternative work such as farming was unavailable until the weather improved.

Small-scale manufacture, industries liable to disruption from many causes, and the vagaries of a market geared to fashion and conspicuous consumption produced the surplus of unskilled labor for which London among all Victorian cities was known. So threatening did the situation become that Londoners, bewildered and frightened by a floating population of unemployed, could only see them at best as an impersonal "residuum," less charitably as shiftless and drifters, and at worst as the "dangerous classes."

Besides being a center of production and distribution, London was also a source of what are called "white-collar" services. As port, banking, insurance, and brokerage activities increased spectacularly in the Victorian period, the numbers required to do office work correspondingly rose. So significant was the increase in the numbers of clerks in the transformation of the City economy that the urban historian, H. J Dyos, has been able to point out that in Camberwell, one of the first new London suburbs south of the river, there were some 7,000 clerks resident in 1901.[4] Almost all clerks were men. Women entered offices very late in the Victorian period, when the invention of the telephone and the typewriter created the familiar occupation of secretary or receptionist.

Clerks were needed in the public sector as well as the private sector. The growing legislative business of Parliament and the assumption of greater social responsibilities by the State expanded the bureaucracy, as did a similar growth in the activities of county and municipal governments. The decline of personal influence in the civil service greatly enhanced the attraction of clerical jobs. The system of administrative appointment through "friends," through patronage or nomination lasted longer in Britain than it did in other western European societies, but it was gradually if unevenly replaced by the principle of merit expressed as recruitment through competitive examinations.

Similar in social and financial standing to the clerks were the new elementary school teachers employed by recently-established school boards. These new public employees did not appear on the London scene until the 1870s, when a state-supported system of primary education was created in Britain. A decade later schooling was made compulsory. Private teachers were also present in London, but the bulk of them enjoyed no greater social esteem than the teachers in state schools. However, those who were masters in smart boarding establishments or historic grammar schools (especially where connected to the Church of England), were in a special category, receiving higher salaries and greater recognition.

Both clerks and elementary schoolteachers were sometimes placed in the category of the lower middle class, which was, in the final quarter of the 19th century, the fastest growing segment of London's population. Occupationally clerks and schoolteachers regarded themselves as members of the professions, an ambiguous category which has never submitted to simple definition. Customarily professional men are white collar workers whose jobs do not involve manual work like those of blue collar workers but depend instead upon a higher level of literacy and numeracy. The growth of the "lesser" professions was one of the most important aspects of the history of Victorian London, so much so that it may be more generally said that the increase in occupations calling themselves "professional" is as much a feature of modern urban life as is the increase in factory workers a feature of industrialism.

The Victorian lesser professions did not require either a university education or some form of very advanced specialized training, and so to begin with they were inferior in social standing to the traditional "higher" or "liberal" professions of law, medicine, and the Church. All three of these historic professions had special London ties. Legal education and the practice of law centered in London. Scotland apart,

London was the home of legal education and the location of the main courts of justice. London also contained the major teaching hospitals in the kingdom and, because of the wealth and diversity of its population, was a desirable place for the practice of medicine. The ecclesiastical hierarchy of the Church of England maintained a large organization in London, and all the bishops and archbishops sat in the House of Lords.

The education, prestige, and occupational opportunities of all branches of law and medicine improved considerably in the 19th century. Solicitors, who had always been inferior to barristers, now found their status rising. The expansion of the economy, of government, and of the London conveyancing or real estate market left them busy and prosperous as never before. What can be said of lawyers can also be said of the medical profession, similarly divided into two branches, the physicians and the surgeons. The former had often appeared as comic figures on the pre-Victorian London stage. Their knowledge of physiology was primitive, and their understanding of chemistry rather hit or miss. Surgeons had also been held in low esteem, as in training and practice they behaved more like artisans than like highly-educated members of a scientific profession. In the second half of the 19th century the reputations of physicians and surgeons rose dramatically, largely because of the advance of medical science, physiology, and bacteriology within the universities and medical schools. The demand for medical services increased when patients realized that medical science could actually ameliorate suffering and increase life expectancy. As a greater emphasis came to be placed on the enjoyment of life in this world, there was a corresponding decline in the belief in the other one. The 19th century, which began with a notable anxiety about an afterlife, ended with a firm commitment to the things of this world.

The decline of belief in a vivid conception of hell did not necessarily lead to a corresponding decline in the services performed by priests and ministers. On the contrary, London population growth increased the need for clergy. Theological instruction improved and professional training was introduced through the establishment of seminaries. New churches were built, both Anglican and sectarian, and the mid-Victorian period especially was one in which the prestige of churchmen and ministers stood high. The desperate poverty levels of so many Londoners produced a major charitable response on the part of all the churches. The Church of England, regenerated from within, was able to loosen its historically close ties to the country's aristocracy in order to assume critically new responsibilities in the urban parishes.

Nineteenth-century London was a dynamic city. Old occupations underwent transformations in purpose and status, and new ones arose in response to economic differentiation. The number of professions recognized as such (or in the making) in the Victorian period especially increased. Civil engineers, architects, clerks and accountants, local government officials, surveyors, teachers, nurses, social workers, and many others entered the ranks of the service occupations in the second half of the century. There was therefore interposed between the skilled workers and the world of finance a wide horizontal band of educated people who were neither blue-collar workers nor businessmen nor traditional leisured *rentiers* living on investments. Ranging from the lower middle to the upper middle class, they formed a large consuming stratum and were conceivably the pivotal sector of 19th-century London, giving the city its special social and economic quality.

LONDON'S GROWTH

Its very early economic importance and its later political importance made London the largest city in the kingdom, and by the beginning of the 18th century, London had already surpassed its rival Paris as the European city with the largest population. London's growth continued through the 18th century. The source of this to about 1780 was migration from other parts of the island. It has been estimated that one out of every six inhabitants of England and Wales visited London in the Georgian period, if only for a short while to sample the pleasures of the capital. Returning to the towns and villages where the overwhelming majority of the population then lived, the tourist may have taken a special pride in having been out in the greater world, at having experienced at first hand the gaiety and splendor of the capital, and he may have carried back with him to the remote corners of the kingdom some special mark of his visit, if only in a shrug or gesture or article of clothing.

The attractions of London were great enough to compensate for its undoubted disadvantages. Unquestionably, if it had not been the case that ambitious and adventurous young men and women were anxious to make their fortunes in the capital, no net increase in population could have occurred, for early Georgian London was a cesspool of alcoholic disease. Children were neglected and often exposed, producing an appallingly high infant mortality rate in the 1740s. The river, which brought prosperity to some, also carried misfortune to others. In the 18th century the London Basin was intersected by numerous rivers and streams that supplied the region with a natural drainage system. A number of these streams, particularly the notorious Fleet River of the City, carried sewage into the Thames from where in another operation filth entered the drinking supply. The stench of the Fleet was a byword of City life. Today the streams have disappeared from view, being largely confined to culverts surmounted by streets and buildings.

Population increase in London was spectacular in the first half of the 19th century, a combination of migration and possibly a high birth rate — scholars still hotly dispute the causes. At no point in the first 50 years of the new century did the decadal rate of growth fall below 17 percent. It was as high as 23 percent in the first decade, and in the 1840s it reached a penultimate increase of 21 percent. After mid-century a falling-off occurred. In every decade of the 19th century, London population growth was substantially greater than national growth, and even the demographic fall of the second half of the 19th century was not as precipitous in the capital as in the country generally.

In 1801, London had just over a million inhabitants. By 1851 London's population had risen two and one-half times, and by 1901 when the great queen died the total population of London was over 4.5 million people. These figures vary according to whether the calculations are based on the city areas of London or on its county size, the peculiarities of its growth making it difficult to disentangle one from the other; but whichever set of statistics is used, the conclusion remains the same. London's rapid demographic increase was remarkable and unprecedented.

Measured by European standards, London's growth was particularly outstanding. Elsewhere in Europe the great capitals also increased in size, but not at the same rate or to the same magnitude as London. The population of Paris doubled between 1801 and 1851; but as we have noticed, London's growth was even greater, and Paris did not reach a million inhabitants until the late 1840s, nor did she attain London's 1851 size until 50 years afterwards. As London experienced a population explosion the pressure exerted on the economy, on housing, and on welfare was unremitting. The population surge added immeasurably to the problems of living in the city by taking up space that had once been used for burials, by increasing surface pollution, and by contaminating the supply of drinking water.

The foul condition of London in the middle decades of the 19th century is almost beyond belief. It is one of the most conspicuous aspects of the city's history. Low standards of personal hygiene, open-air food markets where vegetables decayed in summer, the rather carefree piling of debris in public thoroughfares, and the filth left behind by horses as they pulled delivery wagons and passenger vehicles through ancient lanes and new avenues made early Victorian London an unimaginably dirty, unhealthy city. The westerly winds scattered dust and dirt, along with particles of soot from coal burning in millions of chimneys. A thin layer of grime and grit settled over the entire city but especially in the indigent districts of the east towards which the winds blew. In the winter months, particularly in November, the air-borne dirt mixed with the mists rising from the riverbed to produce the fabled yellow fog of late Victorian London. In such an environment many inhabitants simply could not survive, and many more succumbed to debilitating and humiliating illnesses. Typhoid and cholera, both waterborne diseases, swept through London from time to time with devastating results, especially in the poorer riverside districts. Cholera appeared in Britain in 1831, reaching London early in the following year. Over 5,000 Londoners died, and when the disease returned two years later, another 1,500 perished. The virulence of the disease was greater in 1848 when it returned to claim 14,000 victims. In 1866, when it came again, nearly 6,000 died, of which two thirds lived in the eastern districts. In general the death rate of London was depressingly high. It stood at 25.2 per 1,000 in the 1840s, dropped to 23.6 in the 1850s, and rose again to 24.3 in the 1860s. The death rate elsewhere in the kingdom was not as great.

The problem was two fold, a mixture of the absence of a scientific comprehension of the connection between disease and contaminated water and an impossibly decentralized system of local administration. There was no single authority responsible for the disposal of wastes, and before the discovery of the cholera bacillus in 1884, it was assumed that good drainage alone was sufficient to ensure urban cleanliness. Physicians were held in low repute, and responsibility for establishing adequate measures of urban sanitation went by default to engineers. They made the situation worse. Water closets had come into wide-spread use by mid-century, and the new sewage system installed by the engineers merely guaranteed that the Thames, which was the main source of drinking water, would become a mammoth cesspool as more and more surface and house water was flushed into it. In 1858 Benjamin Disraeli, not yet the famous prime minister he was to become, called the Thames "a Stygian pool reeking with ineffable and intolerable horrors."[5]

The ignorance about how disease was carried was compounded by numerous quarrels. In London there were over a hundred units of local government, each with some vague responsibility for the safety of the environment, as well as privately-operating water companies more interested in profit than the public good. In the parishes with traditional vestry government, the small tradesmen who were in charge resisted any effort to raise taxes to cope with rising needs to stem contamination. Parliament was unable to help as it was nearly paralyzed by a fight between the supporters of strong central government and the advocates of local authority. A social problem quickly became a political one, and delays inevitably ensued. It was not until 1900 that some of the issues were resolved and the annual death rate started to fall.

Of all the shaping forces transforming London in the 19th century none were so cardinal, none came so close to being causal, as the breathtaking population growth that overran the city, interacted with, and often overwhelmed the existing fabric of city life. The historical imagination has always been enthralled by the vision of humanity on the move. It is apocalyptic, a foreboding of terrifying events; or epic, action on the grandest scale. London's population growth produced exactly this mix of terror and challenge. In the background lay the living memory of the French Revolution, of crowds let loose in Paris, and gigantic armies roaming Europe; and in the foreground there were sympathetic radical demonstrations and political reform movements in England itself, reaching a peak in 1848 in the star-crossed Chartist agitation, by then mainly a movement of unemployed workers, unskilled laborers, agrarian populists, and Irish *enragés*. In the foreground too, becoming ever more noticeable and in unhappy syncopation with the trade cycles and structural peculiarities of the London labor market, were the thousands of marginal workers easily set adrift in London. They were the floating population required to build the new boulevards, reshape the Thames embankments, extend the rail facilities, build the huge sheds under which the trains sheltered, bore the London clays for the underground railroads, sewers, and gas and utility lines. Momentous, heroic changes were occurring that called forth the greatest individual exertions to meet unprecedented challenges. These changes astounded those who experienced them and especially astounded, as we well know, the Darwinists just being born.

RAILROADS AND SUBURBAN GROWTH

Persistent demographic pressure on London intensified the salient characteristics of its economy and social structure. A pronounced bias towards handicrafts, a huge mass of casual labor, a large and still growing body of middle and high income consumers, and a large demand for consumer durable goods constituted London's special urban makeup. It is now necessary to explain how demographic expansion affected other aspects of London's history, first of all by showing how population increase decisively contributed to the outward sweep of the city and secondly how the presence of a critical mass of humanity forced the city into a technical revolution in modes of transport.

Not all cities grow and spread in the same fashion. Obviously topographical constraints will exercise some effect on the direction of spread. The valley location of London, intersected by a dominating river fed by smaller rivers perpendicular to it, and two arcs of hills north and south, pulled London growth in a more or less east-west direction. Initially London spread in directions parallel to the Thames, as the logical movement was not over the surrounding hills but along the river which provided a natural road. Otherwise London was difficult to reach, especially in winter when the heavy clays of the valley were gorged with water. At an early date villages appeared along the river ways, and much later fine country houses inhabited by wealthy aristocrats, comfortable landowners, successful merchants (or even a popular Georgian actor-playwright like David Garrick) also followed the cavorting line of the Thames, taming its banks with broad lawns and carefully-placed specimen trees. Houses and villages continued along the Thames right up and even past Westminster. Interspersed between these small settlements were farms and open fields, orchards, grazing lands, flower, and vegetable markets. A glance at a late 18th-century map of London very clearly shows its pattern of interrupted settlement. There was quite intensive habitation in the City and some concentration at Westminster, but otherwise density was light. South of the river deep into Surrey there was meager settlement. Paddington, the site of a busy railroad terminus today and only a short walk from Marble Arch and the Speaker's Corner of Hyde Park, was then set in open areas with only a few houses in the neighborhood. The same was true of the other districts of inner or central London—Holborn, Bow and Bromley, Islington, Mayfair, Bayswater, Chelsea, South Kensington or Battersea. Even today it is possible to see these villages and once-sparse settlements embedded in greater London, drops in amber, stopped in flight like the figures the poet John Keats saw on Greek vases. Villages like Highgate and Hampstead on London's northern heights, or sections of Richmond near the river, retain vestigial village features: winding, narrow streets, a prominent parish church, a village green or a pond where children once sailed boats and still do, as on the Horse Pond in Hampstead.

Urban historians speak about the "leapfrogging" characteristics of London's 19th-century growth. By this they mean that London did not grow by spreading out systematically from a center, clearing woods and forests and filling in pastures, meadows, and wastes as it went (forests in fact had been cleared from the Chilterns and North Downs to be used for fuel long before the 19th century). They point out that London jumped out from the center like an army well in advance of its supply lines, establishing distant centers of potential settlement or setting up command posts in preexisting villages. An arterial would join the outpost to the center, and gradually the intervening spaces would fill in, but in no predictable sequence. London flowed around the earlier habitations, thus to some extent preserving them and the way of life within them. Only gradually did the enveloped rural spaces disappear, as the city negligently or wisely forgot about them in its frantic rush to extend its principal radii.

In the first half of the 19th century it was still possible for Londoners to reach the countryside without difficulty. In 1820, northwest Kensington was open country, and one Londoner recalled hearing there the lark, the linnet, and the nightingale. Hammersmith, a large and heavily populated area on the north side of the Thames, was still very much on the outskirts of the built-up London of 1850. Throughout the century, even within high density areas odd survivals of rural life could be encountered. The poorer inhabitants of London grew vegetables in any available space. They kept animals to provide meat for the tables of the comfortably well-off; the piggeries of Kensal New Town are an example. A famous novel about Jewish life in the thick East End of the 1890s mentions how amusing but natural it was to hear the mooing of a cow while the pious were at prayer in the synagogue.

In the first four decades of the 19th century, then, most of the familiar inner districts of present-day London were still rural parishes, although they were on the verge of becoming urban. Thereafter the practice of leapfrogging suddenly accelerated with the arrival of new modes of transport, especially the two forms of railroad, the surface or mainline train, and the subterranean version which became in time the famous London Underground.

The advent of the London railroads in the 1830s did not, however, produce an immediate impact on city growth. As we have seen, there was a superabundance of land in the central areas north and south of the river, and in the decades before 1850 London's explosive population rise could be absorbed in the spaces between the City and Westminster or in the eastern districts. Only a handful of people were moving into areas more than four or five miles distant from the center, and they could rely on horse-drawn omnibuses introduced in 1829. Fairly dependable, if not overly comfortable or technically impressive, omnibuses could still do about five miles per hour. It was not until the 1860s and 1870s that steam engines became the favored mode of transport for the commuter, now even having sufficient traction for surmounting the surrounding curve of hills.

The commuters of mid-Victorian London were by no means the first in the city's history. In the early 18th century, knots of merchants lived in country houses about ten miles south of London, and they were able to take a stagecoach into the City each day. Trains of course made the journey less strenuous and more rapid, and development at a distance continued but over longer routes, so that London's reach into surrounding counties was lengthened. A certain proximity to the open country was preserved for those who daily worked in London but actually lived some distance from it.

The stagecoach did not affect the regional independence and provincial standing of the old market towns, but the railroads did, braiding them into the burgeoning London economy. The railroads also established new, competitive communities in the country. Wherever railroad termini were established, beginning about 20 miles from the center of London, precursor dormitory suburbs grew up. Shops and services congregated around the new surburban station, and houses were built within walking distance. It took a second technological revolution to push the boundaries of the distant commuter stops another 30 miles into the countryside. The invention of the gasoline engine in the 20th century proved as crucial to the further growth of the suburbs as had the railroads, which in a sense merely continued the erratic and seemingly illogical pattern of settlement that had gone on for about a century in the inner London Basin.

The coming of the railroads furthered the Englishman's desire to live in the country or near it. There had long been an antiurban bias in the kingdom, certainly if Britain's history is compared to that of Italy or northern Germany, where cities were the most important sources of new ideas. Initially the train did not alter the British preference for rural life but instead enabled the ideal to survive in the face of strong demographic pressure. Instead of forcing concentration at the center, the railroads enabled families to disperse, continually draining off those who otherwise would have crowded into the inner districts. But in one special way the railroads did alter the historic pattern of urban growth and population flow. The River Thames was no longer the principal determinant of the direction of development. East-west leapfrogging with subsequent filling in was now supplemented by north-south development, up into and eventually across the Chilterns or, going the other way, deep into the Surrey countryside toward the Channel.

The impact of the railroads on the interior zones of London took a different form. Extensive urban building was already underway when the idea of linking more distant points to the center was first discussed. This meant that the economic costs of railroad construction would be significantly higher and that the social costs as well would be on a scale far in excess of what was encountered in the suburbs.

In some areas of inner London rail lines were able to penetrate without too much difficulty. Since at least the 17th century, a number of the greatest aristocratic families in England, proprietors of land and stately homes in the country, had also been important London landowners. In the 18th century such families contributed to the heated speculation of Georgian urban development, and the streets and squares of central London still bear their family names and titles. In the era of the railroad boom large tracts of land or estates still lay unused or undeveloped. Wherever the great landowner was willing to sell, the railroad companies could acquire rights-of-way rather easily and lay down track through London without encountering physical or financial obstacles. But where land was not owned in large enough parcels, or where it was already built upon, or where the landowner held out for a higher price, the costs of construction naturally rose. By one means or another the London railroad companies of the mid-Victorian period managed to acquire up to 10 percent of the valuable land in central London. Where necessary they engaged in a massive demolition program to clear the land and make it suitable for suburban rail routes.

From the start, however, the railroad construction industry was undercapitalized; building costs soon outraced original projections. Caught flatfooted, the companies found that their penetration of London would only extend to the margins of the central area because they had failed several decades earlier to purchase land closer in. By the mid-Victorian period, property at the very center had greatly appreciated. Not only was this an unforeseen obstacle, but Parliament soon showed a reluctance to allow the companies to indiscriminately toss bridges across the Thames or rip up Westminster, the City, and the intervening West End areas that had by 1860 become filled in. The consequences of this situation may be applauded or deplored, depending upon whether one is a pedestrian and shopper, or a traveller who wants to move as quickly as possible through the geographical bottleneck that London has become. Unlike the lines of many other cities of the world, especially the American, the London railroads do not connect in the center. If a passenger is moving from the north to the Channel, or from the east and southeast to Wales, he must break his journey in London, disembark and cross the city by some other means to a new terminal in order to resume his outward journey.

Because stations had to be dotted around the periphery of the inner areas of London, it was almost immediately apparent that they would have to be linked in some manner by a system of rapid transit. Thus the famous London Underground was born in the early 1860s when the Baker street station of the Metropolitan Railway was opened, connecting the mainline station of Paddington to Farringdon Street and not too long afterwards to Moorgate. The world's first underground rail link had been preceded by over a decade of political and financial discussion. All schemes had to be cleared through Parliament, but there were also technical bottlenecks. Room had to be allowed for the expansion of iron girders, brick arches had to be designed to carry the appropriate stresses, and existing sewers and pipes had to be diverted. Finally there was the public's view. In 1862 the London *Times* wrote with disgust "of dark, noisome tunnels, buried many fathoms deep beyond the reach of light or life; passages inhabited by rats, soaked with sewer drippings, and poisoned by the escape of gas mains."[6]

Despite the considerable technical difficulties of constructing a subterranean transportation system where no precedents existed, the task was made simpler by the soft claybeds which could be bored easily. The claylands south of the river were harder to tunnel through, however, for they were less well drained than those to the north. It was far easier to go along the surface than beneath it, and ever since the middle decades of the 19th century, passenger travel on the Surrey side of London has been more dependent on suburban mainline services than on the Underground.

Until the last decade of the 19th century, tunnels and stations were made by boring and bricking, or by cut and cover construction. Where the tunnels entered the station, they were faced with tiles. In the 1890s an entirely different method of underground construction was adopted, and metal-lined cylinders through which trains could run were laid sectionally under the surface. As a result of this technological break-through, heavily backed by American capital, the Underground acquired its widely-known nickname as the "Tube." Actually metal tube tunnelling had first been tried in the late 1850s, and experiments went on in every decade afterwards; but the success of the innovation depended on a new form of traction, and this occurred, again with American backing, when electric power was introduced as an alternative to steam power in the last years of Queen Victoria's reign. By the end of the 19th century, the Underground managed to complete the process begun by the surface lines. Near the center the railroad termini on the inner circle of London were joined together, and at the periphery the subsurface transport system continued the historic push of London outward and away from its original two nuclei.

The direct and indirect economic impact of the railroads on the history of London cannot be underestimated. The prosperity of many workers was tied to them. The railroads provided direct employment for about 23,000 people in 1861 and for nearly three times as many in 1891. Indirectly it stimulated an ancillary transport industry which employed as many as 48,000 in the last decade of the 19th century. If we add families and dependents, as did the pioneering statistician and social worker, Charles Booth, in his mammoth survey of the working classes of London, we can conclude with him that the transport industry in general accounted for the livelihood of a quarter of a million people when the 19th century finally closed. This was undoubtedly one of the largest industries in the city, and it created subsidiary industries, which gave rise to new services or attracted new users. There was a pattern of economic growth that resembled that of the Thameside docklands, consisting of primary users, indirect users, and services. Originally established to carry passengers from the city to distant residential communities, the railroad immediately attracted consumer businesses of special use to travellers. Hotels, magazine shops, and refreshment facilities sprang up near and around the stations, but so did light and heavy industry for which a rail link was invaluable, and a subsidiary transport industry of moving van companies. Warehouses were built in the vicinity of railroads, and coal and timber yards also were located there.

Despite the railroad's great economic benefits, the aesthetic and social costs were particularly high. To be sure, the architecture of railroad stations is wonderful, whether it is the severe neoclassical sheds of King's Cross, or the Ruskinesque experiments of neighboring St. Pancras, or the playful, airy girder vaulting of Victoria Station. Writers on railroad life and collectors of railroad arcana retain a certain nostalgic fondness for the architecture of the Victorian stations, or for the amenities and style of the greatest of the railroad hotels, which were erected to accommodate passengers breaking their journey or in town for a few days and looking forward to a sumptuous dinner. However, these structures soon became black and sooty. The steam locomotives discharged acids into the London air, and these ate into and discolored the vulnerable Portland stone. Brick withstood discoloration longer, but even brick turned black over the years.

The narrow gothic backs of housing terraces, the endless rows of dwellings which still line the principal rail routes into London, became dark and filthy, as did the laundry hung out to catch breezes and occasional sun. The noise of the steam-fired engine disturbed the peace of the day, and the views out onto the tracks from back windows were not especially diverting, although they may have stirred longings for distant places and adventures. When the steam locomotive was new it was still possible to see it as William Turner saw it in a series of beautiful paintings. The trains were like elemental forces of nature, so rapidly in motion that they joined the winds, so much like the settling mists of a river valley that their enveloping smoke made them at one with them, so powerful that they resembled the storms in the atmosphere. We cannot altogether fault the Victorians for their romance with technology, for the romance is by no means over, although its tone is more ambiguous.

Once released, the steam locomotive tore up the Victorian city. Its appetite for space was voracious. A disgusting Chronos, it swallowed whole some of the most valuable acreage on the fringes of inner London. Land was needed for stations and track, but also for all the other activities of railroad life: for shunting yards and sidings, storage facilities and construction areas, loading platforms and equipment. Space was required for crossovers and connecting lines, and even more space, in retrospect not altogether necessary, was taken up by competitor lines as the various promoting companies each tried to take a healthy slice of the London transport market. If we add to this large area the adjacent land consumed by dependent businesses, we can then completely appreciate what 19th century maps plainly show, that wherever in London the railroads went they severed existing neighborhoods and became gigantic barriers to foot and wheeled traffic. Outside the entrances to the stations, cabs and omnibuses, wagons, carters, vans, and carriers produced an incredible traffic jam, a tangle of animal legs and wheels. Houses nearby or along the track became dilapidated, as owners lost interest in maintaining or improving prop-

Courtesy Bodleian Library, Oxford.

FIGURE 8. A London railroad slum by the French artist, Gustav Doré. Working-class terraces are exposed to the noise and pollution of steam engines.

erty in what had become undesirable residential sections. But since the huge London casual laboring force had to be housed close to cheap transportation and employment, the buildings were full. In time they were subdivided into smaller units, becoming dense and overcrowded. The railroad slum was born.

By the end of the 19th century London, swollen by population growth, was fortunately well-supplied with a wide range of transport services at varying costs to the consumer. Mainline trains ran out to the new suburbs, and the Underground filled in the gaps. Horse-drawn buses were a primary source of ground transportation, and in the 1870s they were joined by horse-pulled trams with a much greater carrying capacity. When the economy of London became dependent upon the railroads, the presence and force of industrialism in the capital could not be denied. Once population expansion and the railroads united, the Georgian city yielded to the Victorian city, the cream-colored stucco of the last years of aristocratic London was replaced by the blackened bricks of the industrial age; and, finally, leisured urbanity was supplanted by the modern culture of timetables.

LONDON'S SUBURBS

It was inevitable that the London population should move out, since room at the center was no longer available and because cheap housing was impossible given the greatly appreciating value of land in the inner districts. Some form of expansion was unavoidable, but this undeniable fact is merely a start in understanding the relationship between center and periphery. Population pressure may have caused London to overspill its original boundaries, but it did not in itself determine the appearance of newer districts or the way of life within them. In these matters Victorian builders and householders were able to express very clear preferences. By examining these the historian begins to appreciate how the suburbs contributed to London's special "urban mentality," if such a bold phrase may be permitted.

Suburbs had existed for centuries. Even the word "suburbe" itself from the Old French was in use in the English language as early as the 14th century. "Suburban" can be found in the 17th century to refer to a place and to someone who lived there. To describe a phenomenon, however, "suburban London" and "suburban growth" are distinctly Victorian words, as is "suburbia," a 19th century neologism from the Latin "suburbium."

In creating the London suburbs Victorian developers were faced with several design possibilities. They could employ the traditional European or "spider" plan or village idea of curving streets, back alleys, half-hidden lanes and unpredictable roads, or they could adopt newer neoclassical ideas of town planning, centering on boulevards and direct thoroughfares. The former increased pedestrian interest, or at least incorporated the principle of locality. Confusing to outsiders and difficult to navigate, the spider plan assumed that the pedestrian was a long-standing resident of the area familiar with its bewildering street plan. The neoclassical or rectilinear grid, on the other hand, was more impersonal. While it served a number of important purposes, one of its primary features was the capacity to carry traffic quickly between designated points without encouraging lingering exploration. Aesthetically the neoclassical plan did not altogether disappoint the traveller, since broad avenues extended both his view and his imagination, like a Claude or Poussin painting or an English estate garden.

Victorian builders employed both types of street plan in the making and remaking of London. New, wide arterials like Oxford Street or Marylebone Road were ploughed through the center in axes roughly parallel to the Thames. Other main roads radiated out from the center, much as did the railroads, either following the lines of older turnpikes or the direction of streams flowing perpendicular to the Thames. The rectilinear grid was also used to develop the southern district of Tooting, parts of which offer the present-day viewer the most astounding uniformity.

Elsewhere, however, once a main thoroughfare connected center and periphery, the spider plan took over. Curving, dancing streets, even lovers' lanes, spread across the open land. These were popular because they recalled the romance of the British countryside, the pleasures of a stroll through grass and under trees and along country paths. They recalled as well the country life of the British gentry and aristocracy. Over and over again the "village in the city," or an adaptation of it called the "garden suburb" was the inspiration of the new suburbs. The Regency architect, Beau Nash, used the curvilinear street plan to great effect when he laid out Park Village East and Park Village West on the Camden Town edge of Regent's Park, and his example has been followed ever since.

To complete the village theme in suburban planning, two kinds of traditional dwellings were also imported from the countryside; the terrace house, called a row house in America, possibly originating in the one-story almshouses to be found in rural parishes, and the single-dwelling or villa house. These could be charmingly sited along the serpentining streets. By far the most popular type of suburban house built, however, was the new Victorian semidetached or duplex as it is known in some parts of the United States, which, more than any other type of house, characterizes the London suburbs. All these forms of

FIGURE 9.   Two scenes of Park Village East, Regent's Park. The origins of the urban "picturesque" or villa suburb style.

house, especially the villa, proved amenable to stylistic invention. Gothic, palladian, Italianate, or chateau designs were available from architects and builders, and the English country cottage proved a lasting favorite. The pre-Raphaelite artists, reacting against industrial civilization, publicized the rural manor house in the second half of the 19th century. Norman Shaw brought the "Queen Anne" style to Bedford Park, the first of the garden suburbs, and a few decades later the Edwardian or "Wrennaissance" architects, Lutyens and Voysey, designed lovely village-style homes, romantic and eccentric, for the next generation of planned neighborhoods. Less impressive semidetached "stockbroker tudor" houses were built for turn-of-the-century businessmen, to be followed in more recent times by large pubs in a reworked Elizabethan half-timbered design. These are to be found today surrounded by asphalt parking lots on choice corners of outer London streets.

From the foregoing description it should be clear that the London suburbs were far more than the vast urban sprawl that the word "suburb" connotes, although some of them did contain endless rows of mean terraces. More characteristically they were pleasant neighborhoods of small houses grouped around or near shopping and attracting in time the range of goods and services needed for the maintenance of ordinary daily life. The "corner store" idea, borrowed from the village, retained its importance in the new suburban setting, the fancy shops and services of the West End being reserved for special excursions. Already in the Victorian period, however, even specialized and expensive shops were moving into the suburbs, following taste and income. Soon other services became available: tea shops and restaurants, circulating libraries, clubs, and after 1870, neighborhood schools. New churches, both Anglican and denominational, were built, especially in the 1850s — another reminder of the traditional English parish. As the range of commercial and social activities increased, many suburbs outgrew their village inspiration, and today they are virtually satellite cities, with movie houses, skating rinks, swimming pools, and franchised firms.

For many sociologists, planners, reformers and historians, past and present, the suburbs represent both a deplorable change in the character of London and an unfortunate trend generally. It is difficult to recall a single feature of the history of Victorian London that has been so savagely criticized. It is pointed out that historically the suburbs were the least desirable part of any town. In the middle ages the suburb was a waste outside the walled town where slop was deposited. Cripples and beggars piteously gathered beneath the walls, and outside the gates disease and suffering prevailed. The suburbs had to be sealed off from view, and so at night the gates were locked to create a *cordon sanitaire* around the town.

In the cities of the 19th century, it is argued, the historical relationship between center and periphery was reversed. The waste outside the gates was transformed into a fertile valley. Now it was the center which had to be kept from encroaching on the suburb. The cold, the hungry, and the miserable were therefore confined within the inner walls of the city where streets served as garbage dumps and sewers. There they were joined by new species of urban insect and animal life: silver fish, carpet beetles, cockroaches, bedbugs, rats, and alley cats. There were, it is true, no actual walls or gates to prevent the unwanted from leaving, but barriers still existed, more insidious because invisible. Metaphorically the gates still closed at sunset as the curfew sounded, and the free movement of individuals ceased for the night.

The suburbs have been accused of sucking out development capital which should have remained in the slums, thus skewing the economy towards the low-wage service sector instead of the high-wage productive sector. The suburbs also have been made responsible for introducing commuting, thus separating work from the family and increasing the tensions between them. Perhaps, above all, the suburbs have been made responsible for the geographical barriers which created separate residential districts for working and middle class families, and for producing a way of life which some have claimed fits the semidetached house—banal and monotonous.

It was the Victorians themselves who first attacked suburbia. The phrase "bored suburban" was introduced in 1887, and it was widely taken up because of the inspired comedy of George and Weedon Grossmith's, *The Diary of a Nobody*.[7] This satire of the snobbish, status-seeking, lower middle class suburbanite, Mr. Pooter, the city clerk who wanted to be considered a gentleman and so moved into the new suburb of Holloway, soon became one of the most devastating stereotypes in the literature of urban London.

THE INNER CITY

It cannot be denied that the social configuration of London altered spectacularly in the second half of the 19th century because of suburban growth. Old neighborhoods turned over, families moved from the center into the suburbs and from one suburb into another, and single dwellings were subdivided or converted into offices. Before the 1860s many inner London districts were more socially heterogeneous than afterwards. The Georgian and Regency terraces of Westminster, Mayfair, or Pimlico backed onto courts where a poor service population lived, and also onto mews or alleys where horses were stabled and carriages kept. By the final third of the century many poor families had been forced out of their former dwellings when the mews and courts were demolished. The establishment of a public system of transport and the availability of cabs had made it largely unnecessary for wealthy households to own carriages and horses, and grooms and coachmen could be let go. The innermost and oldest parts of the West End thereupon began to resemble the new suburbs, which were built without coach houses and stabling yards and similarly did not house the poorer members of London's population.

Other inner London districts, however, did not change quite so drastically but retained or acquired an interesting mix of occupations and classes. Bayswater, the section of London that lies just above South Kensington Gardens and is today another Soho of foreign restaurants and mixed nationalities, was a smart residential neighborhood of palladian terraces in the early 19th century. In the 1840s when moderate-priced houses were constructed there it still had the flavor of a new district. A decade later large town houses appeared requiring domestic staffs of from six to ten servants (Mr. Pooter could only afford one). In the 1860s Bayswater attracted colonial civil servants in need of a London residence. In the next stage of development fancy shops moved into Bayswater, as did a department store in the new style. In the last years of the century some of the older residences were converted into shops and small hotels, and a substantial number of shop assistants settled there. Finally Jewish and Greek families moved into Bayswater, altering its ethnic character, although a number of older men of property still lived there.[8] This does not complete the picture of Bayswater's sociometry, however, for working-class neighborhoods existed nearby. The important rail terminus of Paddington was next door, and characteristically the main line station had created a surrounding colony of workers and rail-related businesses.

Most of the newer northern, southern, and western suburban districts of Victorian London did not possess substantial neighborhoods of working-class workers. For them proximity to work was crucial, walking to jobs was necessary, and commuting far too costly. Only the better-off workers could afford the fares of the horse-drawn omnibuses or trams. The mainline trains did not show an inclination to attract working-class riders until forced by Parliament to add third-class carriages at a penny a mile in the 1860s. By then the Underground was also starting to run special low-fare workers' trains, thus enabling working-class commuters to concentrate in the northeast suburbs of London where train service was best. Another working-class suburb, also relatively close to the center, developed across the river in Southwark where there had been workshops, small masters, and craftsmen since the 16th and 17th centuries. It is probably when the working-class commuting suburb opened up in the 1880s that the better-off workmen ceased to wear the traditional occupational costumes such as leather aprons and special caps and instead adopted the dress of the City clerks and investment brokers. Photographs of Victorian bricklayers show them to be wearing dark suits and bowler hats. Presumably they no longer worked in the old neighborhoods.

It was really only in the 20th century that suburbs created for professional and business families came to be inhabited by large numbers of working-class families. Manufacturing firms were established in a number of the older suburbs, thus transforming once predominantly middle-class areas. A sort of musical chairs occupancy, however, was already occurring in the second half of the 19th century. As middle-class households moved from a suburb closer in to one further out, their former residences were taken over by working-class families also seeking more desirable locations. In the later Victorian period large middle-class houses were subdivided once the original occupants moved out, and working-class families then crowded into the newly-released space.

One of the most extraordinary examples of how the newer suburbs siphoned off London's inner population occurred in the City at mid-century. Small masters, City merchants, stockbrokers and financiers, insurance underwriters and owners of ships who had always dwelled in the City, who had taken pride in their great medieval gilds or companies and in their traditions of self-government, abandoned the City for the suburbs. Outward migration was heavy in the 1860s and naturally coincided with the development of the railroad suburb.

The census returns show the spectacular change in the City's size. Before the 1850s, the City's population never fell below 120,000 people. In 1851, in fact, it stood at 127,000. Ten years later it dropped to 112,000. It continued its astounding decline in the decades following, reaching 31,000 by the end of the century — a four fold drop in less than 50 years! The City became what historically it had never been, a business district, active by day but deserted at night (this did not take place in nearly the same degree in the adjacent fashionable West End; but it is taking place today).

The suburban exodus of the 1860s greatly altered the relationships between London employers and employees. In the pre-Victorian period the prosperous merchants and craftsmen conducted their business from their homes, much as did the Buddenbrooks family in Thomas Mann's great novel of North German life. The counting house was part of the residence, as was the workshop. Employers, clerks, journeymen, and apprentices lived near one another, often on different levels or parts of the same building. How much of a common way of life they shared is debatable, but at least there was a certain daily proximity. Often enough the politics of employer and employee was similar, more because of a shared radical heritage than employer coercion. One social historian has emphasized the importance of the City workshop in creating a work-oriented male culture, much more important than the home, which was only a place to eat and spend the night. All this changed in the second 50 years of the century. Many skilled workers abandoned the central city when cheap trains began to run. For them the home and family became more important than the workshop, especially as the working day shortened, income rose with the fall of food prices in the agrarian depression of the 1870s, and more leisure resulted.[9] Left behind, too abject to join the migration away from the old riverside communities, were the permanently depressed poor.

The changeover of the City from a mixed residential-business area to an office community was reflected in its architecture. In the later 1850s existing structures were torn down. New single-purpose buildings, office blocks belonging to banks and discount houses with space for the numerous clerks who inhabited them by day, went up in place of the former, smaller-scaled units. The new buildings represented the Victorian taste for grandeur rather than the Georgian taste for simplicity. Gothic, Jacobean, and Italian style buildings were put up in stone and brick and faced with terracotta. In the final decades of the century a reviving interest in classicism, partly under the influence of the French Beaux Arts school, which also greatly influenced American and urban styles, gave to the City the heavy, overpowering aspects it conveys today.

Great as was the change in the character and architecture of the City, it was matched by changes of another kind in the adjacent East End, the area stretching from the edge of the City to the dockyards and including within its borders places like Whitechapel, Stepney, Bethnal Green, and Poplar. In the second half of the 19th century the East End became a slum. The word "slum" itself acquired its present meaning of a run-down section of a city.

The areas east of Aldgate did not suddenly become slums, however. Writers on early Georgian London had always commented upon the rookeries and back streets of the narrow medieval thoroughfares of the City and the districts crowding on its eastern borders which gave refuge to thieves. The awesome rate of population growth in the 19th century, however, and the huge demand for irregular employment multiplied the social problems of the East End, as did the high cost of building in the riverside districts. As the years passed housing density increased, sordid tenements replaced the old broken-down cottages; every effort to improve the East End through slum clearance, street improvements, and the construction of railways and docks usually had the effect of reducing the amount of housing space and making a deplorable situation still worse.

The most appalling physical conditions obtained in the East End, but that does not mean it was simply a land of abandoned humanity. The Victorian social investigator, Charles Booth, decided that only a small percentage of East Enders were actually morally depraved and criminally inclined, were habitués of the back alleys and dark dens which afforded protection from the law. The overwhelming majority were poor but decent, in difficult circumstances but respectable. Nor were their lives absolutely barren and devoid of culture. The street life of Victorian London was colorful, with open markets, pedlars and street musicians, with pubs and music halls where friends could meet, drink, sing, and be entertained. In the East End, speaking an Essex dialect, was the famous Cockney—the legendary true, proud Londoner, born within the sound of Bow bells. Even certain strong political traditions survived among East Enders, most noticeably in Poplar, which was a center of socialism in the period before World War I.

The East End also contained substantial communities of immigrants, most notably the Irish and the Jews. The former, disliked by the English, suffered from poverty and malnutrition and unfortunately supplied the eastern districts with juvenile delinquent gangs. Nevertheless, debilitated as they were, the Irish communities of the East End still managed to make some praiseworthy adaptations to urban life, as mothers in particular tried to maintain the stability of the family.

In the decades before 1914 the East End was the principal home of London Jewry. The size of the existing colony was doubled by 1905 when 100,000 refugees escaping eastern European persecution arrived in the docklands. Anglo-Jewry, which had adjusted to British culture in the two centuries following its resettlement in the kingdom, was now exposed to the more creative religious culture of the Pale, as well as to newer secular intellectual movements of Continental origin. If it was a difficult, it was also a challenging period in the history of British Jews, out of which a stronger community emerged.

The East End contained numerous working-class groups, different ethnic and religious traditions, and diverse ways of life. Men, women, and children fought with pride and courage to maintain themselves in bleak and frightful circumstances; but the variety and diversity of their lives and cultures were little understood west of Aldgate. As the century waned, the East End became more and more isolated from the rest of London. So striking was the separation that its inhabitants were not even regarded as ordinary members of the urban population but as strangers and foreigners. They were the denizens of a distant land, tribal, uncivilized, heathens in need of conversion. They had to be studied, as an anthropologist studies peoples and cultures. Their language and their manner of living had to be translated and recorded, even for the sake of science, for it occurred to some investigators that East Enders might represent an earlier state of evolutionary development, like the paleolithic inhabitants of a valley cut off by a landslide. From the mid-Victorian period onward the prototypical urban anthropologists of the day, perceptive journalists like Henry Mayhew, social scientists like Booth, launched expeditions into the East End to study the strange ways of its inhabitants. Their widely-read accounts and studies frightened and disgusted genteel readers, but they also stirred philanthropy.

Increasingly the East End became the scene of numerous excursions — they were often called "pilgrimages" — by charitable organizations (both secular and religious), of fashionable "slumming" by well-dressed ladies, of university-organized religious "missions." Misery was to be alleviated, drunkenness and promiscuity to be eradicated, orphans to be succored, schools and chapels to be founded. These efforts have been received by historians with both praise and sarcasm — depending upon how charity is viewed — as snobbish and condescending, the imposition of an alien moral code, or as devoted, altruistic, and humanitarian. Undoubtedly motives were mixed. The efforts of the missionaries were voluntary and philanthropic because publicly-supported social work and rehabilitation had not yet become the large-scale bureaucratic activity it is today. The Victorian state had erected a series of degrading workhouses to handle the most desperate cases of poverty, and it was only first beginning to legislate in the areas of compulsory public education. Existing institutions for coping with despair on the scale encountered in the East End were inadequate, to say the least, so the slums became an experimental laboratory for private social workers of every description: *grandes dames*, evangelical churchmen, Fabian socialists, economists and sociologists, and high-minded undergraduates.

Interest in the East End picked up in the final decades of the 19th century for another reason as well. By an act of Parliament of 1884 the franchise came close to realizing the radical's dream of universal male suffrage. The gigantic population of two million in the eastern parishes was on the edge of becoming a political force to be reckoned with in a more democratic age. Other events also drew attention to the possible social and political repercussions of the East End on the supposedly isolated and secure sectors of London society. Several major strikes, one by matchgirls led by the famous outsider Annie Besant in 1888, and the still larger dock strike of 1889 centered on Poplar, altered the conventional view of the East End. As the pioneer social worker Edward Denison said in a series of letters published in 1872, the East End may have been a separate city with its own culture, but it was also the creation of the same forces that were transforming the rest of London, and its health was therefore intimately bound up with the health of London generally.

In the last ten years of Queen Victoria's reign the romance of the old East End was utterly finished. Gone forever were sentimental recollections of the old rookeries inhabited by the rogues, adventurers, and charming scoundrels featured in 18th-century plays and picaresque novels. In the East End, as well as elsewhere, Georgian London had been transformed; without any doubt, it was now a totally Victorian city.

URBAN PLANNING AND THE SOCIAL ORDER

The metamorphosis of inner London was made possible by the pull of suburban growth, itself the result of demographic pressure and a revolution in communication. Critics, reviewing this process, still deplore the segregation by social class which followed the decision to adopt the dispersal form of city. For them the model of suburban growth is 19th century Paris, for it involved the idea of the socially concentrated city. While smaller than London, Paris too was a great European capital experiencing the pressures of demographic increase, yet the inevitable outward push of Paris into surrounding open regions occurred at a stage of development later than London's. Instead of immediately dispersing its population into single-dwellings and semi-detached houses, Paris concentrated its population in large blocks of flats or apartments. A single structure therefore contained, so it is alleged, families of diverse social origins, from shopkeepers in the bottom flats to *rentiers* at the top.

The belief in the egalitarian possibilities of the Continental apartment block indicates a peculiar sort of faith in architectural determinism. The architect and city planner, because of the power they exercise over the organization of space, become the platonic guardians of an urban dominion. It is they who prevent segregation by social class by choosing designs and layouts most likely to produce a community of shared interest.

The confidence placed in architecture to create an ideal urban morphology presupposes a willingness on the part of populations to submit to the theories of planners. This is at best optimistic. Just as the stroller will not always keep to designated public paths as he makes his way through a park or field, so the urban resident resists efforts to make his life conform to a particular social pattern. Community results from the culture the inhabitants of a neighborhood or locality bring to it; and no matter what public amenities are provided, separate or distinct social networks will form. [10] These may be based on class, occupation, or style of life, or on religious or ethnic preference, on long-standing identification with a particular street, or simply because there are young families in the neighborhood. The need to provide children with play-mates, the daily outing in the park, the ritual of shopping—all build networks. The physical layout of the city can certainly be involved in these patternings. Residential areas uninterrupted by railroads, parks, and factories are more likely to produce a sense of locality than districts broken up by barriers. In the late Victorian period, Notting Hill had a strong community identity partly because it was working class and partly because its residential character was uncompromised. As a result it was the scene of many neighborhood-generated marriages which in turn intensified local attachment.[11] Nevertheless, no social relationship can be guaranteed in advance, nor can deeply-held values be totally eradicated by urban planning. Privacy, to furnish one instance, is more difficult to acquire under certain circumstances, especially where overcrowding occurs, but it cannot be absolutely prevented if that is what people desire.

Even when catastrophe, demolition, urban renewal, or model towns provide opportunities for planning and zoning the outcome is not usually neighborhoods where values are shared. Families still form attachments for all the customary reasons. In the recent high-rise structures of inner and outer London the only real center of association is very often the elevator, that sarcastic purveyor of enforced leisure; and driven away, no longer welcome, are the sparrows, pigeons, and starlings accustomed to resting on the ledges and ornamentation of buildings of a precurtain wall design.

Historically, the ideal of a class-free community could not have been imposed on London. There was some central direction in sanitation, if belatedly, some minor bits of urban planning by government archi-tects where crown lands could be used. Parliament prevented the rail-roads from carving up the innermost portions of London; but there never existed—and never could have existed—a central planning body with authority to create ideal communities. The Victorians, possessing a fundamental belief in the movement of individuals according to personal and family means, preferred the workings of the open market, even with all its well-known imperfections. Subdivisions, housing projects, and estate development were largely undertaken by private initiative in response to different kinds of demands, actual or potential; and the results were as diverse as the "five percent philanthropy" of the East End multifamily dwellings, the palladian villas and terraces of Chelsea, the Italianate houses of St. John's Wood, and the artists' residences of Bedford Park.

Without doubt social distinctions and snobbery characterized much of suburban life in semidetached London. The Pooters tried to keep the tradesmen at bay, the City men kept the Pooters at bay and were in turn snubbed by families of greater wealth or social position; but it would still be an error to confuse this process of social differentiation with the often-repeated assertion that the London suburbs were socially homogeneous. Victorian suburbia, on the contrary, furnished examples of every kind of social mix and neighborhood network. Religious and ethnic identities often overrode considerations of class, as in the case of the Irish and Jewish immigrants of the East End, or of the Baptists, Presbyterians, and Congregationalists who settled in Hammersmith in the 1860s. Occupation served as a basis for building up neighborhoods in Camberwell, where the clerks settled, and in Bayswater, where colonial administrators built large homes. The political heritage of artisan radicalism accounted for the unique working-class culture of Poplar. Other networks formed for special reasons. Rural migrants coming to London usually settled where their former neighbors did or moved in with people recommended to them before their departure from the old villages. Even among the East End Irish there were subdivisions based on the place of origin: the immigrants from Cork tended to form their own circle. The refugee Jews, separated by religion, language, and appearance from the rest of the East End, apportioned themselves into subgroups according to their countries of birth.

No single social network or reference group provided all the associations of a single family. It was possible to belong to more than one. Certainly movement across social divisions went on, as the right school or success in business altered family circumstances, and as the economy continued to form new occupations and status groups. London was a patchwork of social distinctions and neighborhoods constantly in flux. London's pattern of social dispersal partly resembled the concentric ring theory of urban growth favored by the Chicago school of urbanologists, having an interior ghetto surrounded by bands of wealth increasing in direct proportion to distance. But here the resemblance ended. The newly-developing suburbs did indeed represent bands of wealth surrounding a blighted center, but coming out from the middle, with their apex in the West End, were wedges of some of the most expensive housing in the city, and here and there, along the outer bands, were quadrangles of mixed-income residences. In other words, topographically Victorian London resembled an English dart board.

Finally it must be noted that even much-praised Paris, the model of the concentrated city, did not produce communities of like interest by constructing great apartment blocks, the forerunners of the towers of Le Corbusier. The Parisian poor were not domiciled at the center, as in the case of London, but instead girdled the city with working-class faubourgs. In Paris the rich stayed put, and the poor moved out.

In discussing the history of London's 19th-century suburbs there is need for a balanced assessment. No sympathetic historian would, for example, treat the lives led within working-class tenements or broken-down cottages at the very edge of the street as insipid. The same courtesy has to be extended to the suburbs, which were much more than dreary red-brick terraces and semidetached houses common as a penny. People do not deliberately choose to lead boring lives. Rather they seek comfortable surroundings, where children can be raised in wholesome environments, where desirable playmates are available, where satisfactory schools exist, where the proximity of open space promises a healthier neighborhood, where overcrowding does not make every moment unbearable, where the innocence of childhood can be preserved, and where the streets are not a temptation to crime — where, in other words, the business of everyday life can be carried on with minimum disturbance. These qualities were avidly sought by Victorian suburbanites who, for the reasons given here and elsewhere, selected the dispersal city over the concentrated city and resisted the temptation to build up because historically and culturally they preferred to build out.

LONDON'S CULTURAL LIFE

"Mere numbers are important. . . . There are some thoughts which will not come to men who are not tightly packed."[12] These words of the wonderful historian, Frederic Maitland, remind us that the culture of the city is unique. It shapes the attitudes of its inhabitants and requires of them special exertions or adjustments. Victorian London, containing so much that was unprecedented in the history of civilization, ultimately forced Londoners into adopting a range of values that comprised an urban mentality. City life had a special meaning, if not always a very precise one, and in the search for that meaning city-dwellers defined their relationship to a challenging if impermanent environment.

One of the first places to look for evidence of the meaning of a city is in the paintings and writings of intellectuals. Artists and writers create, in words and pictures, images of the world around them. The intellectuals of Berlin and Paris, the *feuilltonists* of Vienna and journalists of New York have each helped in creating an urban self-conception. Often enough it corresponds to their personal views or circumstances. London, being a restless place, had long challenged the imagination of its inhabitants. Its intellectuals of the 18th century, while sometimes divided in their estimation of the city, were on the whole enthusiastic about it. They were attracted to London from Scotland, Ireland, and the English provinces precisely because it was the center of social and political vitality. They were delighted by its opportunities, by the market it offered for their work, by new sources of income, and by circles of friends. They were the preeminent observers of city life, the purveyors of news, and they were urban cartographers, mapping out novel dimensions of experience. The titles they gave to their magazines —the *Spectator*, the *Tatler*, the *Rambler*—exactly incorporated their stance toward the city. They did not find it necessary to reject London, since the idea of a great city was still fresh, and the countryside was still close at hand. They even thought country and city could fuse together, the best of each to be incorporated into the other, and it is therefore not surprising to find the column in one of the most famous of all Georgian periodicals, the *Gentleman's Magazine*, signed with the hybrid *nom de guerre* "Sylvanus Urbanus."

From the 18th century to the middle of the 19th century London's intelligentsia successfully contended with their city. As London grew, their conception of it, their understanding of its meaning for them, was controlled by a working aesthetic vocabulary which developed late in the 18th century and was based upon classical thought.[13] Both Georgians and Victorians, in confronting awesome city growth, refused to be overwhelmed by size and speed. They called London "sublime," and by that word they meant that a great city was supposed to be grand and disturbing. A city had to charge up the emotions, put the senses on the alert, stretch mind and body to their full capacity. A city had to provide opportunities for the display of energy and for the exercise of individual initiative. The scale and variety of London's buildings: its gigantic Houses of Parliament, its two huge churches, St. Paul's and Westminster Abbey, the miles of docklands accompanied by extensive acres of warehouses, with great arches and vaults, its tremendous estate development, the Thames Embankment project incorporating endless tunnels—this was sensational, thrilling. The noise of London's trains, the din of construction, the dangers of underground tunneling, the shouting in the streets, the sardine-packed humanity, the traffic jams, the crazy rush of life—these too were exciting. Even the East End was sublime. Its criminals made it dangerous, its strange inhabitants made it exotic.

The value of the sublime was precisely that it allowed Londoners to appreciate the special qualities of city life and to approve of them. It made them comfortable in what were increasingly uncomfortable surroundings. It was right to be stimulated, even overawed and perplexed by London, for these were precisely the sensations that a great capital ought to create. Every day brought novelty, new faces, new experiences, for movement from one part of the city to another was like a journey abroad. The discomforts of the city were to be expected, its cacophony to be valued, for the city was a unique kind of place.

In the second half of the 19th century the sublime as a psychological mechanism for manipulating emotion ceased to conceal the disquieting

Courtesy Bodleian Library, Oxford.

FIGURE 10.   A traffic jam in the City. The railroad bridge interrupts the view of
St. Paul's, Sir Christopher Wren's baroque masterpiece. The entire scene is an
example of the effect called the "sublime."

aspects of city life. London was now seen to be a city that Milton had built, Pandemonium, shrouded in yellow mists and fogs, a place inhabited by demons; or it was Babylon, the sensual city of biblical antiquity. London was dirty and unhealthy, full of smoke and soot. Because it was a port, had a migrant dockside population and a plentiful supply of cheap lodgings out of which pimps and prostitutes worked, it attracted the typical riff-raff of the urban underworld. Traditional moral restraints like religion seemed to be an ineffective check on deviants, and so penal theory hardened as the century advanced. Even buildings were not necessarily sublime; they were sometimes also ugly, of monstrous shape and out of all human proportion. The frantic pace of the city was no longer thrilling, and who, anyway, wanted to spend hours tied up in traffic or hurtling through subterranean caverns? It could no longer even be claimed that the city offered excellent opportunities for forming new friendships. On the contrary, London was a collection of strangers, a place where the individual wandered friendless through indifferent streets.

Paintings of London record the loss of grip and sense of place that occurred as the city moved through the 18th and 19th centuries. Artistic conceptions of London and its river show us a city of pikes in the 18th century—a skyline of church spires. The urban landscape is also viewed from a gentleman's terrace: it is sometimes a vernal stretch of water or, more grandly and playfully, an Italian fantasy, the Thames transformed into Venice. In the 19th century such capriccios give way to genre paintings, to scenes of riverside merrymaking, to the activity of ports, and to dreamy nocturnes such as Whistler's. With the arrival of the French school Thameside begins to disappear into an impressionist cityscape, and later, with the Fauvists, there is a sudden burst of "unnatural" color in controlled outlines, as if artists are attempting to regain command of a vanishing environment. Finally, the city becomes the blurred swatches of 20th-century abstract painters. London is too big, too elusive for painters to capture in a single, striking conception.[14]

Photographs of the city taken in the late 19th century tell a similar story even if in a different and contrary way. Photographers, working in a new media, prefer to record the city's reality. At first relatively undiscriminating in their choice of subjects, as if everything that occurred within the city is worth a picture, their photographs become in time more selective, even more focused, as if it is especially necessary to capture details which are in essence impermanent. The city as idea and as reality is disappearing. Buildings vanish and neighborhoods change, and what exists today will inevitably be gone by morning.[15]

By the end of the 19th century, then, the response of intellectuals and artists to the city had changed. No longer was London that mix of country and town that had so delighted the Georgians, no longer was it in easy communication with the countryside, and no longer was it a place which encouraged creative responses. Instead it was an enemy. The East End had turned into a dreadful kind of slum, with a permanently depressed population. The chaos of selfish, unguided development seemed equally permanent. The city was certainly not a place for the helpless and the undecided.

It should be obvious that the suburban city which arose in the 1860s played an important part in furthering this antiurban view of London. The suburbs stood for what the central city had lost, for the stability and virtue of the village and for a close family life. The suburbs were, to use another borrowed Georgian conception, "picturesque," charming and safe, like a scene or picture in miniature.

However, not everyone who lives in a great capital pays attention to its artists and journalists, reads "Atticus," Herb Caen and the "Talk of the Town," or believes what he reads. Nor did everyone who lived in the tangle of late Victorian London see the city in the same way. Despite the writers who turned their backs on London, there were Victorians who continued to love it.

The much-despised suburbanites loved it. Semidetached London gave them privacy, embodying a way of life that the historian would call more Victorian than Georgian. Eighteenth-century culture was urbane or public, a certain amount of social life took place *al fresco*. The world of the Georgian squares and town houses was a world of promenading and showing-off, manners counted, privacy was thought to be antisocial. For reasons that are not completely understood, the Victorians sought and obtained more private conditions. Perhaps because of the spread of an inner-directed evangelical religion, a room of one's own to reflect upon the experiences and lessons of the day suited the greater individualism of the 19th century. The lack of privacy was yet another reason for the general Victorian dislike of the French-style flat, and the smaller amount of living space put families in closer proximity to servants, whose hobby was eavesdropping.

For the affluent the diversity of the city, its novelties, and the range of its pleasures, were irresistible. Since its Georgian days one of the attractions of London had certainly been its social life, but the extent and availability of entertainment was far greater in the final decades of Victorian London than in the last years of its Georgian predecessor. In the late 19th century the city underwent yet another transformation. The West End was converted into a gigantic shopping and entertainment center. New, vast luxury hotels, like Norman Shaw's Piccadilly Hotel, were constructed. Large, modern department stores appeared in Regent and Oxford Streets and in Knightsbridge, like the fabulous Harrod's with its art nouveau windows and decoration. It was the era of the music halls and the revival of the British theater, of smart restaurants, of concerts at the Royal Albert Hall, of the popular comic operas of Gilbert and Sullivan, and of the fancy night life of Piccadilly and Leicester Square, brilliantly illuminated by electric lights. The great museums of South Kensington also date from the end of the 19th century, as do touring clubs and mass-circulation newspapers. Never before had inner London been so crowded with pleasure-seekers. Londoners shopped and stared, dined and danced, and they were joined by numerous visitors from abroad. The tourist industry throve, and the picture postcard industry was born.

But even those who did not inhabit fine houses, did not belong to the carriage trade, or could not afford the new gloves and trousers which the Pooters were so keen on, found pleasure in the animated streets of late Victorian London. The shorter work week produced more leisure time, the Saturday afternoon professional football match made its appearance, and cheaper transport enabled the better-off workers to take in some of the scenic marvels of the capital. There were also free museums and galleries, public lecturers, and Embankment concerts. Life in the city was unquestionably impossible, but where else were such treasures to be found?

Few clichès about the type of personality created in the capital stand up to close inspection. The average Londoner, if there can ever have been such a person, was no more cynical and cosmopolitan, debonair or sophisticated, than he was anomic or suicidal. The numerous patterns of London social life in the 19th century defy stereotyping. Yet when all has been said on behalf of the city, it still cannot be denied that Victorian London made unique demands upon its inhabitants. The growth of the city produced disturbances in the economy and in the culture. It produced new forms of social friction, and consequently required, but did not always get, new forms of social and political cooperation. The stress and pace of London life inevitably created a range of tensions different from those of small-town or village life. The sheer weight of population concentration was in itself an unsettling experience. Since public sanitation was primitive, the population explosion made the tenure of life horribly precarious, especially in the gloomy eastern districts where malnutrition was endemic. So low was the resistance to disease in the poorer sections that even in 1838, before the economic decline of the East End set in, a worker might on the average only live to half the age of a resident business or professional man. So dramatic was the London death rate that evangelical clergymen ministering to the poor in the docklands were once again forced to consider seriously the emotional consequences of early death. Their Georgian predecessors, by contrast, had nearly regarded eschatological questions as largely academic.

The rubbing together of so many different styles of living in the urban environment constantly ate away at inherited beliefs, as did the openness of the port and capital to new ideas. Values as well as clothes were influenced by fashion, and both could be acquired in the open market. The large number of newcomers and the riot of available choices gave the advertising industry a great boost. The inexperienced buyer was fair game, for he who hesitated was not lost, only a better prospect. Change for the very sake of change was part of the definition of urbanism, or to force this thought into some other words of Maitland's, city life requires "a permanent habit of agreeing to differ"; and this is perhaps its most lasting cultural consequence.

Despite the volumes of available information on the history of London, we still do not have a very clear picture of the adaptive process required of Londoners in the 19th century. We can surmise that at best city residents could only expect to make a series of short-term adjustments. They had to be ready to shift with the generations, to think it normal for omnibuses to be replaced by trains and steam power by electricity, to get used to commuting to work, to live with smaller gardens, if any, and to adjust personal standards of morality to new ideas. Moral issues could arise at almost any time. Even so small a matter as the facing on houses could require an ethical decision. The pastel stucco of Regency terraces, for example, as celebrated in these playful lines,

> Augustus of Rome was for building renowned,
> And of marble he left what of brick he had found;
> But is not our Nash, too, a very great master?
> He found us all brick, and he leaves us all plaster,

was denounced by Victorians as "dishonest" (because it merely imitated stone) and even "immoral" (because it appeared frivolous and lighthearted). New buildings were to be done in a sober, brooding style, with "honest" materials like stone and brick. After the craze for gothic building subsided just after the middle of the century, Londoners had to adjust once again to a plethora of competing designs, so that it was no longer possible to choose the "best" one. It was not even easy to decide who the "best circles" were once new occupations and new groups arose, and the historic natural leaders of society, the titled aristocracy, became more or less just another group in the city. All the numerous changes taken together immensely increased the problems of childrearing, for it was barely possible and often not possible at all to raise a family on clear-cut ethical principles that would survive into the next generation. Poor Mr. Pooter, who tried to impress upon his fun-loving son the virtues of his own youth—sobriety, hardwork, patience and caution—not only found out that he had failed but that his son was a far greater business success precisely because he was jovial, reckless, and in a hurry!

Uncertainty may well have been the primary feature of Victorian London—uncertainty of employment, of social status, and of cultural values. Since this was the unavoidable condition of urban living, the only suitable responses were flexibility and independence. Those who, for a hundred reasons, could not muster these indispensible qualities, fell by the wayside. Others, not quite so desperate as, say, the fatalistic drifters of the East End casual labor market, welcomed the challenges of an urban environment. Young persons of both sexes were especially drawn to London. They formed the largest proportion of migrants coming to London in the second half of the 19th century. They were escaping the confinement of village life, tight family control, and the perpetual scrutiny of neighbors. As one Victorian social worker said, London represented the difference between "the contagion of numbers, the sense of something going on, the theaters and the music halls, the brightly-lighted streets and busy crowds" and "a dark and muddy country lane, with no glimmer of gas and with nothing to do."[16] Young people gladly seized the chance to form their own networks and broaden their interests.

Unmarried working-class women particularly found London liberating. It is true that London was not an unmixed blessing for them. The East End sweat shops were not pleasant, and domestic service had its humiliations, the most frightening being the threat of descending into prostitution after having been violated by another servant or the loutish scion of a West End household; but for the typists and office workers, the shop assistants and factory girls, there were opportunities for better employment and money for clothes and entertainment. For economic reasons London parents sent their daughters out to work, no doubt reluctantly, for the consequence was a certain worrisome freedom.

Young people coming to London from rural areas in the second half of the 19th century were highly fortunate in not having to settle in the depressed East End. They found employment in the suburbs, either in domestic service or in gardening, for which they were presumed to have a special competence. Newcomers were preferred because it was generally believed that the typical East Ender was unhealthy and morally debased. Thus the lure of London reinforced East End segregation, making the eastern districts "settlement tanks for submerged Londoners."[17] The statistics bear out the fact that as the Victorian age closed, the London families that fared the worst were those which were native to the East End, that had been there, if not from time immemorial, then certainly far, far longer than was wise.

POST-VICTORIAN LONDON

Today the establishment of the British Welfare State has mitigated most of the greater evils of Victorian London. Bombings and urban redevelopment have cleared out much of the substandard housing, although depressed districts remain. Development is far more firmly controlled, the principle of planning is in force — if not solidly enough for some and too solidly for others. Still, it is the Victorian city that the visitor sees. The central districts are still separated by function from the residential districts and show every sign of becoming still more specialized. The West End, for example, seems to be following the lead of the City. Offices, consulting rooms, shops, consulates, and chanceries have taken over glamorous town residences. The suburbs have continued to grow. Another revolution in transport, this time the automobile, has given the dispersal city an additional boost, and incidentally, has also strengthened the sense of independence that city life provides (or requires). The picturesque villa, a little more streamlined and less ornamented, still holds forth, as does its old neighbor, the garden terrace. It takes a second glance to notice that they are being built without prominent chimneys, as the advent of gas, electric, and oil central heating has removed one pleasant architectural inheritance and at least one historic occupation.

The concentrated city — the new sublime — has put in an appearance. Its predecessor, in fact, is Victorian. It arrived about 1870 in the form of the self-contained flat, but even when established as a minor feature of London's urban landscape flats were still regarded as a French innovation. The new professional families of Victorian London did not find them appealing, and by and large flat-dwellers were either bachelors or rentiers with homes in the country. It was not until after the First World War that the high-rise apartment became a really conspicuous part of London, and not until after World War II did the tower block become the backbone of public housing. Today giant skyscrapers, made possible by steel girder construction, reinforced concrete, and prefabrication, dominate the rebuilt areas of the center and appear in the suburbs as well. Already, however, a reaction has set in, as the traditional suburban houses continue to provide the main residential model. A new generation of county council architects and city planners vows never to go up again; but it is too late to undo existing towers.[18] The highest structure in London is now the telephone building, the General Post Office Tower, in Tottenham Court Road — visible from every point in the city. It remains the symbol of the strangest form of communication ever invented, as Kafka was perhaps the first to demonstrate with chilling fidelity. The GPO tower dwarfs the great cathedrals of the medieval and baroque periods and has broken the unwritten law that secular buildings may not overshadow religious ones. Day in and day out the metropolis renews itself; and in nearly every word or deed of that renewal are recalled the ideas, if not exactly all the values, of Victorian London, the Unique City.

NOTES

1. G. Laurence Gomme, *London in the Reign of Victoria* (London, 1898), 11.
2. Steen Eiler Rasmussen, *London: The Unique City* (London, 1948).
3. Gareth Stedman Jones, *Outcast London* (Oxford, 1971), 32.
4. H. J. Dyos, *Victorian Suburb* (Leicester, 1973), 192.
5. Francis Sheppard, *London, 1808–1870: The Infernal Wen* (London, 1971), 283.
6. T. C. Barker and Michael Robbins, *A History of London Transport*, I (London, 1963), 118.
7. Available in a Penguin edition, 1976.
8. D. A. Reeder, "A Theatre of Suburbs: Some Patterns of Development in West London, 1801–1911," in H. J. Dyos, *The Study of Urban History* (London, 1968).
9. Gareth Stedman Jones, "Working-Class Culture and Working-Class Politics in London, 1870–1900: Notes on the Remaking of a Working Class," in *Journal of Social History*, VII (Summer, 1974) 460–508.
10. For a very useful summary of community formation see R. E. Pahl, *Patterns of Urban Life* (London, 1970).
11. Hugh McLeod, *Class and Religion in the Late Victorian City* (London, 1974), 8.
12. F. W. Maitland, *Township and Borough* (Cambridge, 1898), 24.
13. See the fascinating essay by Nicholas Taylor, "The Awful Sublimity of the Victorian City," in *The Victorian City, Images and Realities*, II, ed. H. J. Dyos and Michael Wolff (London and Boston, 1973).
14. See the catalogue to the exhibition, "London and the Thames, Paintings of Three Centuries," London, 6 July–9 October 1977, Somerset House.
15. G. H. Martin and David Francis, "The Camera's Eye," in Dyos and Wolff, I, 243.
16. J. A. Banks, "The Contagion of Numbers," in Dyos and Wolff, I, 112.
17. H. J. Dyos, "The Slums of Victorian London," in *Victorian Studies*, XI (September, 1967), 30.
18. The recommendation that high-rise blocks "should be progressively demolished because they create more social stresses than the housing difficulties they solve" has recently been made by the chairman of the Greater London Council's management committee. See *The Times*, March 15, 1977. No new tower blocks have been commissioned in London since 1973.

BIBLIOGRAPHY

Few subjects have attracted as much attention as the history of London. The amount of available writing is exhausting. Yet a number of indispensable readings may be singled out. Besides the excellent books and articles mentioned in the notes, the following are highly recommended:

Briggs, Asa   *Victorian Cities* (London, 1963).

Chadwick, George F.   *The Park and the Town: Public Landscape in the Nineteenth and Twentieth Centuries* (London, 1966).

Glass, Ruth, *et al.   London, Aspects of Change* (London, 1964).

Jackson, Alan A.   *Semi-Detached London* (London, 1973).

Kellett, John R.   *The Impact of Railways on Victorian Cities* (London, 1969).

The London Journal

Metcalf, Priscilla   *Victorian London* (London, 1972).

Olsen, Donald J.   *The Growth of Victorian London* (London, 1976), and "Victorian London: Specialization, Segregation, and Privacy," in *Victorian Studies*, XVII (March, 1974).

Pugin, A. W. N.   *Contrasts* (Leicester, 1973), first published 1836.

Tarn, John Nelson   *Five Per Cent Philanthropy* (Cambridge, 1973).

Taylor, Nicholas   *The Village in the City* (London, 1973).

Thornhill, J. F. P.   *Greater London: A Social Geography* (London, 1935).

The Urban History Yearbook.

For contemporary authors, Henry Mayhew, Charles Booth and C. F. G. Masterman are fine starts.

Chapter 5

*A*s the preceding chapters have emphasized, European industrialization was not only, or merely, an economic process involving mechanization, the exploitation of new sources of power, the investment of large amounts of capital, and an enhanced rate of productivity. The pace of industrialization was linked to structures and developments in noneconomic spheres: for example, in the political system of the particular region; in the attitudes and values, the mental set, of people who were caught up in the process. The success of industrialization in any given area depended not only on positive economic factors (the availability of raw materials, capital, and technology), but also on political, social, and cultural contexts that either promoted or inhibited it. As in the British Isles, so on the continent, a political system that was responsive to entrepreneurial interests was an important stimulus to industrialization. Equally important was the existence of cities and of those "bourgeois" activities and values associated with urban life: a dynamic entrepreneurial tradition, habits of saving for investment, the absence (or weakness) of prejudices against trade, industry, and profit. Another basic requirement of industrialization was a large labor supply: workers who possessed (or could be trained to possess) the skills and habits required to operate machines, and to submit to factory discipline. In the early stages of industrialization, the recruitment and training of labor was a main preoccupation of factory owners and managers. Once those problems

211

*were solved, or became less acute, the social and political conse-
quences of industrialization created some of the most troubling issues
confronting European governments and societies in the second half of
the 19th century.*

*Labor problems, and specifically, conflicts between workers and
their employers, were not unknown in preindustrial Europe; they had
a long history. As early as the 13th century in Flanders and Italy,
laborers in the cloth industry had banded together to obtain better
pay and working conditions, to gain a voice in urban government. The
Ciompi revolution in Florence (1378) was only the most dramatic
example of this tradition of association and protest by urban workers
(see volume 1, ch. 6). Before the 19th century, however, these movements were small in scale, relatively weak, and invariably unsuccessful in achieving their goals. Industrialization magnified labor problems, by concentrating large masses of workers into confined spaces,
in the factories and in urban slums, and by creating conditions that
promoted a sense of community, of shared miseries and objectives,
within this laboring "class." Thus, the instilling of factory discipline
in peasants who had previously worked according to loose seasonal
and diurnal rhythms, stimulated an awareness of the need for labor
unity and solidarity, and for tightly organized associations or
"unions" to defend workers' interests. Labor unrest in preindustrial
Europe was characteristically parochial and episodic, involving a
single town, or a single industry or trade within a town. In an industrialized region like Lancashire, the Midlands, or the Ruhr valley,
labor associations were formed which involved hundreds of thousands
of workers. These militant organizations frightened the industrialists
and the politicians who were forced to deal with the "labor question."*

*The most fundamental concern of Europe's industrialized laboring
class was, naturally enough, the earning of a living wage. Generally
speaking, factory workers were miserably paid everywhere in Europe
during the Industrial Revolution. Married men often could not earn
enough to support their families; they had to send their wives and
children to work in the factories as long as 16 hours daily to avoid
starvation. Unemployment was a permanent threat to factory workers,
who could lose their jobs if they failed to work efficiently, or if they
were undisciplined or insubordinate. When demand fell for an industry's product (coal or cloth or cannons), the plant might be closed
down and the workers dismissed. The living conditions for workers
in industrial communities was, by any standard, deplorable. Families
or groups of individuals were crowded together, as many as 10 or*

12 to a room, in squalid houses and tenements. Water and sewage systems in these slums were primitive or nonexistent; rents were high; landlords were ruthless. Nevertheless, these industrial cities continued to attract an unending stream of immigrants from the countryside, which tells us much about the conditions of life and the economic opportunities in Europe's rural areas, where overpopulation, unemployment and destitution were widespread.

In the early stages of industrialization, workers sought to protect their interests and to articulate their grievances in traditional ways, following models that were familiar to them. They might participate in food riots to protest the high cost of bread, as the working poor had done for centuries; they might attack and destroy machines that threatened their livelihood. They formed associations of mutual aid, to assist them through periods of unemployment and to pay for their burial expenses when they died. Workers' strikes for better wages and working conditions were rare before the mid-19th century. They were prohibited by law in most parts of Europe, and workers had not yet developed that degree of cohesiveness and militancy that would eventually motivate them to organize and sustain a strike against their employers. After the great wave of revolutions in 1848, however, strikes became an increasingly common tactic of factory workers, particularly in the more industrialized countries: England, France, the Low Countries. As early as 1839 in England, a manifesto of the Chartists (a society dedicated to political and social reform), called for a general strike of all English working people, "to cease work on the 12th [of August] instant, for one, two or three days, in order to devote the whole of that time to solemn processions and meetings, for deliberating on the present awful state of the country, and devising the best means of averting the hideous despotism, with which the industrious orders are menaced by the murderous majority of the upper and middle classes who prey upon their labour." (J. Kuczynski, The Rise of the Working Class *[New York, 1967], p. 125.) The wording of this proclamation, which antedates the* Communist Manifesto *of Karl Marx by nearly a decade, is clear evidence of the perception of irreconcilable differences separating employers and workers, and of the inevitability of conflict between those "classes."*

How did European governments, and the "upper and middle classes" that controlled them, react to the emergence of workers' organizations and protests? In the initial stages of industrialization, governments were characteristically unwilling to intrude into this area, except to protect property and to control violence. Thus, the authorities might use force to end a factory strike, on the ground that it violated the rights of the owners; or they might dissolve a workers' union because it was perceived as a conspiracy against state and society. But governments were not eager to become involved in questions of wages, hours, and working conditions which, it was felt, should be determined by the market, and by negotiations between employers and individual workers, not groups. But this laissez faire policy could not be sustained, as the social problems accompanying industrialization became more severe. The pressures for change were inspired in part by humanitarian impulses, and partly by a realistic awareness that the tensions generated by industrialization, and specifically, the conflicts between industrialists and workers, were a serious threat to the social order. The 1840s and 1850s witnessed the passage of legislation in England, and on a more limited scale, on the continent, limiting the length of the work day, and imposing restrictions upon the employment of women and children in the factories. More gradually and grudgingly, governments began to accept the concept of workers' associations, and within limits, permitted them to agitate for better working conditions. The culmination of this trend was the intensified participation of the laboring class in the political process, through the broadening of the franchise and the formation of workers' parties that were committed to promoting the interests of their labor constituency.

Each European state developed its particular style of handling the "labor question." In the more backward parts of the continent—the Mediterranean littoral from Spain to the Balkans, the great plain stretching from the Vistula and Dniester rivers to Siberia—social problems arising from industrialization were particularly acute. Though a great power, Russia was one of the most primitive and backward societies in 19th century Europe. Her economy was predominantly agrarian; her largely peasant population was unfree, until emancipated in 1861. Russian cities were few in number, and except for St. Petersburg and Moscow, small in size. The cities did not contain a large and influential group of businessmen, that "bourgeois" class that had been the prime mover of industrialization in Western Europe. The Russian government was autocratic in structure and spirit. Its upper bureaucracy was recruited from the ranks of a service nobility that was generally unsympathetic to Western values and achievements, and particularly hostile to the urban industrial life of Western Europe. Industrialization was literally forced upon this ruling elite, and upon Russian society, by military considerations: the *need to establish factories to produce the equipment needed by modern armies and navies. The defeat suffered by Russia in the Crimean War (1854–56) intensified the pressures for industrialization and was an important factor in the government's decision to emancipate the serfs in 1861. That act contributed significantly to the formation of a Russian laboring class, whose history during the second half of the 19th century is described in the next chapter.*

Factory Workers in Prerevolutionary Russia

ROSE GLICKMAN*

The working classes of the past have been given short shrift by historians. Consisting for the most part of people who neither wrote their own history nor left the kinds of documentation upon which scholars have traditionally relied, they have been overshadowed, in our perceptions of the past, by outstanding people and great events. In recent years, however, the historical field of vision has vastly expanded to include those previously neglected classes, sometimes described as the "inarticulate." The term, however, is somewhat misleading, for these classes were not mute; there simply had been no ear attuned to their particular mode of expression. Historians today are aware that the powerless and the ordinary form the basic fabric of the past, as they do of the present, and a growing body of historical literature attests to the historian's emerging sensitivity to the kinds of evidence which provide insight into their lives.

The "inarticulate" workers who are the subjects of this essay are the Russian workers before the revolutions of 1917. So great has been the impact of the events of 1917 on our view of the modern world, that it is very tempting to discuss Russian workers in the light of the events of that year, when they became the major participants, if not the prime movers, in the first successful revolution since 1789. The hindsight provided by the great event is very seductive indeed. One cannot help but look for evidence of a consciousness that led to the worker's participation in the revolution. Such evidence is easily discovered,

---

* Formerly of Mills College.

for from the end of the 19th century to the eve of 1917, ever greater numbers of workers had been drawn into active, although mainly episodic, struggle for the improvement of their lives. But this in itself is not necessarily an expression of a revolutionary vision and to see it that way is to attribute an intent and a design which, in fact, played no part in the daily lives and expectations of the overwhelming majority of workers before the revolution.

In this essay we shall attempt to depict the Russian workers from the 1880s to 1914, not as the future world shakers of 1917, but as they were at the time: workers whose lives had much in common with working-class life of other European countries at comparable stages of development, yet differed in accord with the specific conditions of the Russian Empire.

RUSSIAN INDUSTRIALIZATION IN THE 19TH CENTURY

The development of Russian industry and the formation of the industrial working class were different from Western Europe in several ways. To begin with, Russia's industrialization lagged far behind the West chronologically. Industry became a significant component of the Russian economy only in the late 19th century, at a time when industrialization already had a firm footing in many parts of the West and had drastically changed the lives of most people there. As far back as the 17th century the energetic and western-oriented Peter the Great had made considerable efforts to stimulate factory production in order to launch Russia into the orbit of the developing western nations. But the vast majority of Russia's population was, and remained, poor, backward, and agrarian, unable to provide the effective consumer demand necessary to encourage would-be entrepreneurs to risk their capital in the production of consumer goods. Thus, such industry as there was, existed to satisfy the needs, mainly military, of the government until the first quarter of the 19th century when the cotton industry expanded rapidly to become Russia's major industry aimed at a growing consumer market.

Another major difference in Russia's industrial development, and the one with which we are mainly concerned, was that factory labor was hard to come by. In fact, it was easier to find capitalists than workers. Unlike the free and often landless peasantry of many western European countries, mobile and potentially available for factory work, Russia's peasantry was not only backward and poor, but until the 1860s, enserfed—legally bound to either the land and the landowner or to the state. These enserfed peasants, approximately 90 percent of the entire population, were completely without legal and personal rights, including the right of movement from the estates to which they were bound. Who, then, in the absence of large cities with sizable lower class populations, was to work in the factories, existing or potential?

Until the emancipation of the serfs, the solutions to populating the factory were piecemeal and inadequate. In some cases the serf's bondage to the land was legally transformed into bondage to the factory. Instead of performing forced labor on the land, this kind of serf did forced labor in the factory. In other cases peasants, whose obligations to work the landowner's land had long ago been transmuted into money obligations, were able to gain the lord's permission to take factory work in order to make his payments. At best such workers provided a seasonal and unreliable work force, and while the number of factories and workers increased in the 18th and early 19th centuries, they did so slowly, making almost no preceptible impact on the economy or on the lives of the great majority.

By the mid-19th century, western technological and industrial development had advanced very rapidly, creating an even larger gap between the West and backward Russia. The recognition that until Russia had a free, mobile labor force and a vigorous industry, she could not maintain her position as a European power, was one of many components in a climate of opinion increasingly favorable to the emancipation of the serfs.

The serfs were emancipated in 1861. The freed peasant was alloted a small parcel of land for which he had to make inordinately large payments calculated to stretch over many years. These redemption payments, as they were called, and the burden of supporting a rapidly growing population on land already exhausted by primitive methods of cultivation, pushed more and more peasants into nonagricultural wage labor and simultaneously provided industry with more than enough work hands. Thus, in 1914 — at the end of our period — Russia numbered approximately 3 million factory workers in a population of approximately 170 million people. This was a small working class indeed, but by comparison with the 1860s, the growth was very impressive.

The concentration of the Russian industrial working class into particular regions gave it a somewhat unique profile compared with Europe's industrial working class. First, the workers were highly concentrated geographically. One area of major industrial concentration was the city of St. Petersburg with approximately 200,000 factory workers in 1910. Another was the city of Moscow and its surrounding provinces, known as the Central Industrial Region. There were other areas of dense concentration such as the oil fields of Baku, the mining areas of the Ural Mountains, and the metallurgy of the Don River basin. But given the vast land mass of the Empire which embraced 8.5 million square miles, factory workers were, so to speak, huddled within relatively few and relatively small regions.

Workers were also densely grouped in the work place. Despite Russia's relative technological backwardness the number of enormous factories in Russia was equal to, and in many cases greater, than factories of Western Europe and America. By the turn of the century, one half of all factory workers were employed in factories of over 500 workers and one third were in factories of over 1,000 workers.

Perhaps more important for our purposes was the concentration of time. Industrialization in Russia, and along with it the formation of an industrial working class, was telescoped into a very short time period. In many western European countries the process stretched out for over two centuries. In Russia the adjustment from the rhythms and patterns of agricultural life (determined by the seasons with alternating periods of work and relative leisure), to the rigidity and monotony of factory work was compressed into roughly half a century.

What mitigated the individual's need to make this rapid and dislocating adjustment was the fact that in Russia industrialization and

FIGURE 11.   A Petersburg metallurgical plant in the 1890s. (Ocherki istorii Leningrada [Izdatel'stvo ANSSSR: Moscow-Leningrad, 1956], vol. 8, p. 21.)

urbanization did not proceed apace. We tend to visualize the factory with its massive structures, its towering chimneys spewing forth smoke and fumes, its sounds and smells as part of an urban scene. We think of the factory worker as an urban dweller returning from plant or mill to an urban slum, living an urban life qualitatively different from rural life. In Russia this was not the case. Aside from the cities of St. Petersburg and Moscow, the majority of factories were not in large cities — not even in small cities — but dispersed throughout the countryside. Sometimes they were clustered in factory settlements large enough in population to be analogous to a city, but containing almost nothing but factories, the workers pouring through the factory gates from their peasant huts in the surrounding countryside. Even the city of Moscow in the early 20th century had only 40 percent of the factory workers in the province of Moscow in which it was located. This distribution remained consistent throughout the prerevolutionary period, so that by 1902, 65 percent of factory workers still worked in rural rather than urban factories.

THE FACTORY WORKER: FROM PEASANT TO PROLETARIAN

This brings us to one of the most passionately disputed problems of Russian labor history. What exactly was the Russian worker — a peasant who happened to work in the factory or a proletarian in the classical sense of the word, i.e., an industrial wage earner, possessing neither capital nor his own tools, earning his living by selling the only thing he possessed — his labor? For in addition to the unusual distribution of factories between city and country, it is not clear to what extent the urban factory worker had severed his ties to his peasant origins.

Throughout the 19th century the great majority of factory workers were seasonal, that is, they worked in the factory during the dormant agricultural periods, returning to their land for planting and harvesting. The peasant was very reluctant to abandon his land entirely, and he did so only when he could no longer scratch minimal survival from the earth. Therefore, the male factory worker frequently left elderly kin, wife, and children behind to care for the land during his seasonal, or even full-time, work in the factory. This meant that although the larger portion of his work life and income may have derived from the factory rather than the farm, his emotional commitments and an important part of his social life remained in the countryside. Even workers who abandoned the land completely, living year round within the factory radius, who had married in the factory or brought their families with them, returned to the village for the important rituals

FIGURE 12.   Seasonal road workers in the early 1900s. (Ocherki istorii
Leningrada [Izdatel'stvo ANSSSR: Moscow-Leningrad, 1956], vol. 8, p. 121).

of their lives—births, marriages, deaths, and all the numerous holidays
in the Russian religious calendar. This category of worker increased
in the 20th century. And by 1914 the number of hereditary workers,
second or third generation workers with no ties at all to the countryside had also increased. Yet the rapid growth of an industrial labor
force from the late 1890s to 1914 could not have occurred by utilizing
only the labor of hereditary workers, and new peasant recruits were
therefore constantly nourishing the factory's growing appetite for
working hands. We do not have sufficiently reliable statistics to state
with any confidence the numerical relationship of hereditary workers
to workers with strong peasant ties. We can only say that side-by-side
with a small but growing percentage of fully assimilated workers—
who thought of themselves exclusively as workers—there continued
to be those with fully peasant self-images or with ambivalent and
fluctuating identities, depending on the actual physical contact and
emotional commitment to their peasant roots.

It is important to keep in mind that at whatever stage in the worker's transformation from peasant to proletarian, the serfdom of his ancestors was still a vital, living memory. The adult worker at the beginning of our period—the 1880s—had been born a serf and may even have lived his formative years under serfdom. Even by 1914, a worker in his early 50s had been born a serf, and although he may never have experienced serfdom directly, the expectations of oppression, the humiliation of servile status were not obliterated in one generation.

Even at the beginning of our period, peasants who resolved to take work in the factory were not likely to have suddenly and dramatically plunged into the world of the factory. Their own parents may have worked occasionally in nearby factories or even traveled some distance. If not their immediate families, then there were other villagers who had done so, affording glimpses into city ways or tales of factory life. Of course, it is one thing to be exposed to occasional vignettes and stories and quite another to participate in the entirely new rhythms and demands of the factory system. Nevertheless, the *notion* of factory work was not entirely new and alien. Moreover, new workers attempted to alleviate the adjustment to the new life by following well-trodden paths, by seeking work in factories or in towns where people of their acquaintance had been before. Even those who ventured quite far from home gravitated toward their fellow-villagers when they reached their destinations. In fact, given the enormous excess of demand for jobs over supply, often the only way to get a job was through such contacts. Looking for work was extremely unpleasant under these conditions. Here is how one worker described his experiences in the city of Ekaterinslav in the 1890s:

> Usually the job-seekers gathered in the early morning and at lunch-time at the factory gates, waiting for the factory administrators whom they would ask for jobs. Almost always the seekers exceeded the number of jobs. . . . The bosses, feeling themselves in command would speak to no one, or worse—when the seekers gathered at the gates in a crowd of 100 or more, the bosses, for their own amusement, would order the watchman to pour water on them.[1]

This worker, as most others, preferred to find work through his contacts: "It seems that in this business many of my countrymen were very useful. . . . Although I did not know them, they had been acquainted with my grandfather and grandmother or were related to them in some way." Barring direct contacts, as another worker wrote in his memoirs, "In order to get my job, my father gave a bribe of five rubles to the foreman's wife."

While there were workers who with perseverance and time found work without contacts and bribes, it was more common to count on one or the other. The pervasive custom of seeking work through contacts with fellow-villagers was only the first link in a chain that re-inforced the ties of workers to their rural origins. For, as we shall see, not only did new workers rely on their fellow-villagers for admission to the factory world, they tended to cluster with them for long periods of time, sometimes for the whole of their work lives. The pattern, however, was not universal. For some workers these village allegiances were gradually replaced by new occupational and geographical bonds. The long-time St. Petersburg worker who had become a fully urban person, for example, regardless of his point of origin would invariably seek out other urbanized St. Petersburg workers, feeling himself to be very different indeed from his recently arrived fellow villagers.

WORKING CONDITIONS IN THE FACTORIES

Once having found work, the worker was very much at the mercy of the factory owner. Until the mid-1880s factory labor was largely unregulated by law and even thereafter there were very few rules which the factory owner had to observe in any aspect of his relation-ship with the worker. Further, in a buyer's market where the demand for work far exceeded the supply of jobs, the employer's free hand in controlling the worker's life was facilitated by the illegality of workers' unions. The late 1870s and mid-1880s witnessed the first large-scale strike efforts on the part of workers to force changes in their situation, but neither these strikes nor subsequent regulatory legislation made significant differences in the conditions under which they toiled.

The length of time for which a worker was hired reflected his peasant ties. Generally, work contracts were drawn up twice a year; one period ran from the autumn after the harvest to Easter; the second ran from Easter to July, the month of the greatest exodus of workers back to the fields. Within these contractual periods the work day was extremely long. Until 1897 a 16 to 18 hour workday was not uncommon, and, as many factories ran 24 hours a day, night work was a standard feature in the worker's life. Sometimes a worker would work a day shift one week and a night shift another week. Other contracts broke each shift into six-hour periods. This meant the worker worked for six hours followed by a six-hour rest interval and worked again for six hours. If a worker lived a long distance from the factory, as was often the case in rural factories, it might take him the entire six hours just to walk back and forth between factory and hut. In 1885 a law was passed prohibiting night work for women and children under the age of 17. As the night shift was defined as 10 P.M. to 4 A.M. the arduous day for this category of worker was only minimally mitigated. More-over, employers felt they had an excuse to lower women's and adolescent workers' wages on the basis that day work was less taxing and therefore deserved less remuneration.

In 1897 the work day was reduced by law to $11\frac{1}{2}$ hours. As great an improvement as this was for the worker, the gain was offset by the employers' virtuosity in extracting the maximum work for the minimum reward, by the many covert ways that were perfected for adding to the length of the worker's day. Perhaps the least offensive was demanding that workers clean their machines before leaving the factory, a procedure that was carried out *after* the work shift had allegedly ended. Another more serious extraction of unpaid labor was to demand overtime work. Although on the surface overtime was presented as a voluntary option, a worker could not refuse without incurring the risk of losing his job. According to the law of 1897, the amount of overtime expected of a worker had to be written into the contract and paid. Most often observed in the breach, this stipulation left workers who were paid piece-rates untouched.

The most devious and widespread method of bringing down the workers *de facto* wage considerably below the nominal wage was the system of fines which most factories imposed on workers. Let us look closely at some of these fines, for they convey more than just information about wages; they tell us something about the kinds of pressures to which the worker was subjected.

Most factories were constructed like walled fortresses, guarded by watchmen and surrounded by gates which opened only to swallow up or disgorge their human contents at the beginning and end of each factory shift. A Moscow pattern-maker writing in the 1890s relates:

> Order at the factory was strict. . . . Let us begin with the enormous metal factory gates which, like a clock mechanism, slammed in the morning at the beginning of the work day and again after lunch. If you did not run in on time the heavy gates would rattle to a close before your very nose — and then you had to wander about for half a day, losing about a ruble as a fine for tardiness.

Such fines for tardiness could cost the worker a significant portion of his daily wage. But tardiness was only one form of "truancy" as it was called. There was an entire category of fines for truancy which included, in addition to tardiness, illness not verified by a doctor's report, absence for drunkenness, absences for unauthorized holidays, marriages, births, and deaths, absences to care for ill family members, and for women workers, absences for going home to feed nursing infants.

Even more onerous were fines built into the production process. As one factory inspector noted, "It would actually be hard to imagine a worker who could fulfill all the demands set for him, no matter what his effort and skill, who would not be subject to fines and deductions." In many factories, especially textiles, impossibly high production quotas were set for full wage payment, and deductions were made for the portion of work which was incomplete. Workers were fined for damaging or losing tools, for imperfections in the finished product, and in textiles, for dirty materials. Sometimes the worker had to pay what in effect amounted to a fine for the use of a tool whether or not it was lost or damaged. By law, the kind of behavior subjected to fines was to be stated in the so-called work book given out to the worker when he was hired, but it was not unusual for factories to innovate fines for infringements never mentioned in the books. An ironic example was a factory which forced workers to pay for the work book itself.

In addition to imposing specific economic hardships on the worker, the system of fines was symptomatic of the factory administrations' contemptuous attitude towards workers, of the assumption that workers could — and should — be treated as something less than adults. When a government commission suggested that fines for "rudeness and disobedience" be made illegal, employers retorted that this would "undermine discipline and deprive factory owners of the possibility of maintaining necessary order and respect for the stewards of their establishments."

This condescension toward workers was manifested in the infliction of countless daily humiliations. At many factories workers were subjected to a body search as they entered and left the factory premises. Experienced as an abasement by all workers, it was especially painful for women workers who were searched by men to the accompaniment of jeers by their fellow male workers. Especially humiliating was the absence of what workers called "polite address." Russian, like other European languages, has a polite form of address used in formal situations and to superiors and a familiar form used to address intimate friends, children, servants, and animals. Workers were obliged to address supervisory personnel in the polite form, while they themselves, as a matter of course, were addressed in the familiar — a practice which they felt to be demeaning and probably experienced as a vestige of the former master-serf relationship. Related was the normal abusive behavior of supervisory personnel, both verbal and physical. For women the abuse was frequently sexual. Perhaps the atmosphere of the shop is best conveyed in the words of a woman textile worker at the turn of the century.

> When you come to work you hear only curses and swearing . . . He [the foreman] does not permit us to go to the toilet; if he sees you going, he puts his hand in your way, pulls you by the hair, fines you, and threatens to fire you. If a woman worker pleases him he calls her to his office and is not shy about making the most foul propositions. If the woman refuses, she is subjected to pressure, oppression, and even firing. Once a girl ran

from his office screaming, and the very next day she was fired. We are supposed to take breakfast while we work. But the machines do not stop, and if you sit for a moment to drink tea, [he] pulls your hair and breaks the dishes which we bought with our pittance. . . . The boss pays no attention to our complaints. He only knows how to curse and fine.[2]

Except for the obvious sex-related incidents, this ambience was common for all workers. That they tolerated it as long as they did speaks for their own low self-image and expectations, reinforced by the hard economic facts of life in a market glutted with working hands. However as labor unrest gained momentum in the mid-1890s, demands for "polite address" became as frequent as complaints about low wages, long hours, and other abuses. This, in turn was symptomatic of the slow changes that were occurring among Russian workers who, by the turn of the century, were becoming less willing to tolerate disregard for their status as worthy human beings.

Servile expectations, however, were not universal to all workers. There was a hierarchy among industrial workers clearly felt by them and reflected in certain external manifestations as well. The hierarchy was roughly based on whether they worked in heavy industry or light industry, whether they were skilled or unskilled, as well as whether they were seasoned, long-time workers or new arrivals to the factory. For the most part, jobs in light industry required few skills and very short training periods, calculated in days or weeks. A worker did not have to read, write, or calculate to perform these jobs. On the other hand, many jobs in heavy industry, especially in engineering and metal processing factories, required literacy, long training periods and often considerable skills. As a result, skilled workers in heavy industry commanded far better wages, a more comfortable life, and more respect. A skilled metal worker, for example, could not be threatened so easily with fines or loss of job, because he was not so easily replaced as was the unskilled laborer, whose place in the factory could be filled from the ranks of illiterate, unskilled peasants seeking employment. Moreover, the skilled worker in heavy industry was more likely to be urbanized, having gone through a long period of apprenticeship. In other words, the highly skilled workers in heavy industry constituted a kind of labor aristocracy.

Thus, the basic distinctions in the workers' hierarchy were skill, literacy, and urbanization as opposed to lack of skill, illiteracy, and retention of strong ties to the countryside. As one worker remarked:

The working population of Nevskaia Zastava [a huge working class district on the outskirts of St. Petersburg] was divided into two parts by external existence; the *plant* workers [heavy industry] and the *factory* workers [light industry].* The former were more cultured, had higher earnings and the majority of them were no longer tied to the land. The *factory* workers, many of whom were women with meager earnings, lived in barracks, strictly protected from outside influences by their "benefactor-bosses." Although their ties to the countryside were weak, they still retained peasant superstitions and the uncultured peasant style of life.[3]

The "factory" worker was even distinguished by dress from the more assimilated and better paid "plant" worker. He was more likely to dress as he had in the village, as one skilled metal worker of many years in St. Petersburg observed when he ventured into a factory for the first time on a kind of anthropological expedition:

> The whole crowd of lads and girls clearly reminded me of a village in the provinces. The girls were striking for the colors of their attire which was completely different from city wear, especially of the capital, and the boys wore their trousers tucked into high boots . . . grey homespun shirts cinched at the waist by raggedy belts.[4]

The "plant" worker, on the other hand, especially one who had lived for a long time in the city, was barely distinguishable from other lower class city dwellers; he was more likely to wear his shirt with its starched collar tucked into neatly pressed, narrow trousers. "On holidays some even wore derby hats. . . . They carried themselves solidly with an awareness of their own worth, swore only indoors under circumstances of great pressure or on payday when they got drunk, some not even then." One member of the "worker aristocracy" remarked on the stratification even among the skilled workers based on whether the worker had acquired his skill through a "proper apprenticeship" in an urban plant or whether he had been a "village carpenter, doing simple, coarse work who had become skilled by chance or through his contacts; either a foreman did them a favor in hiring him or a fellow-villager arranged things."

These differences were profoundly internalized by workers and reflected real differences of work experience, income, urbanization, and ultimately interests and life-style. The worker whose family still lived in the village, to whom he sent the greater part of his already meager wages and to whom he returned at every opportunity, was more likely to be illiterate, to think and converse about village matters — the land, the weather, the harvest. Longer working hours and lower income afforded such a worker less time and energy to develop an

---

* The words in Russian used to distinguish the factory engaged in light industry from the one in heavy industry are here translated as "factory" for the former and "plant" for the latter.

interest in city culture, broadly defined, and city mores; the skilled worker with more time, money, and independence from the brutalization of humiliating treatment was more likely to develop a feeling of pride and identification with his occupation and his immediate urban environment.

In a certain sense women workers can be considered a special subcategory on the lowest rungs of the hierarchy just described. Whatever their relationship to the land, however long they worked at the factory, whatever the degree of literacy or urbanization, they were consistently shunted to the less-skilled, lower-paying jobs in all industries which employed women. The majority of women worked in the textile industry although they were dispersed throughout other light industries as well.

The female sector of the labor force grew slowly but relentlessly throughout our period. In 1880 one out of every four workers was a woman and by 1914, one out of every three. By the early years of the 20th century, factory owners showed a positive preference for women whom they began to hire wherever possible at the expense of men. The underlying reason for this preference was that women were a consistently cheaper source of labor, especially after 1882 when the employment of children in factories was severely limited by law. They were a cheaper source not only in the sense that they were more likely to be employed in jobs which required little skill, but because in all jobs they were paid less than men. The notion of equal pay for equal work was entirely lacking among entrepreneurs, male workers, and women workers themselves, as it was in all industrializing countries. Survival for women workers was thus complicated by lower wages,

FIGURE 13.   A group of textile workers in the 1890s. (Istorii Moskvy [Izdatel'stvo ANSSSR: Moscow, 1955], vol. 5, p. 41).

greater illiteracy and, for married women workers, by the double burden of work and domestic responsibilities.

They had to cope not only with these specific physical and economic hardships, but shared with women of all classes in Russian society a lesser status in general. This status was low not only in the eyes of industrialists who had no compunctions about exploiting them, but also in the opinion of their fellow male workers who carried with them the deeply ingrained patriarchal attitudes of their peasant origins. As a woman worker lamented in 1908: "We women have two burdens. At the factory we serve the boss and at home the husband is our ruler. Nowhere do they look at the woman as a real person." Furthermore, the traditional attitudes of male workers were compounded by the threat that cheaper female labor posed to their own access to work and wages. In the words of a woman worker in 1907:

> Heavy, dismal, joyless is the woman worker's life at work; yet even sadder, even more bitter is her life when her fellow male worker thinks of her with suspicion and hostility. Women workers, have you not ever heard the insulting bitter words that the woman is a harmful, evil competitor with the male worker? And this reproach is hurled at you who toil at heavy work from morning till night. . . . Has not even your own husband reproached you with the insulting, unjust words, "Ah, if it were not for women who sell themselves for almost nothing and lower our wages, would we have such a wretched life?"[5]

We must be cautious, however, about overestimating these intraclass differences. It is true that the various gradations of status among workers were deeply experienced reflections of their reality. But the differences of income, style, and status were, in fact, not objectively great and did not negate the similarity of burdens which all workers had to endure.

At the work place, whether technologically primitive or sophisticated, physical conditions were notable for the absence of all elementary safeguards for the workers. Factory inspectors repeatedly spoke of the noxious fumes or dust in certain industrial processes unrelieved by adequate ventilation, of the overcrowding of machinery so as to present a hazard to the worker's body, of the primitive toilet facilities which contributed to the odoriferous and unhygienic atmosphere of the workshop. Factory owners were often reluctant to provide adequate lighting for the workers; indeed, some even demanded that workers provide their own candles. While knowledge of advanced industrial processes and machinery were known and understood in Russia, it was not unusual for factories to prefer outmoded and more physically demanding hand processes because labor power was more plentiful and cheaper than investment in machinery.

LIVING CONDITIONS OF FACTORY WORKERS

The worker's home was rarely a refuge from the filthy, overcrowded, and dangerous work place. The worker in a rural factory who worked close enough to his peasant hut generally lived in his native village. Otherwise, regardless of skill or income, the rural factory worker lived in factory housing. Most rural factories, especially in large factory settlements, were obliged to provide some kind of housing for their workers and, as more workers abandoned the land at the onset of the 20th century, for workers' families as well. But factory owners were as reluctant to invest in housing as they were in safe, hygienic workshops. In the 1880s one factory inspector in the Central Industrial Region enthusiastically reported that several factories had constructed small stone houses for married workers, each with a small kitchen garden, chicken house, and little courtyard where the worker and his family could carry on a domestic economy as they had in their native village. He observed that the workers were very content with these arrangements and implied that therefore factories would be inspired to build more. Contrary to his optimistic prediction, this kind of dwelling, which was certainly no worse than the average peasant dwelling — indeed better than most — tended to disappear.

The majority of factory dwellings, urban as well as rural, were barracks. The barracks contained several large rooms, crammed full of wooden bunks, sometimes free standing, sometimes in tiers. There were countless factories in which workers slept in a bed in shifts. Bedding was unheard of and workers slept on hay or on their own clothing. Inside the barrack rooms there was no other furniture, no toilet facilities, no amenities, not to speak of the total lack of privacy. "In the majority of factory housing there is totally indiscriminate mixing of sexes and ages, most often all sleeping next to each other in the same barrack room . . . married and single, children and adolescent girls . . . in extremely crowded and dirty conditions." To be sure, in many factories families slept in special rooms separate from single workers, but always several families to one small room with nothing but makeshift curtains to divide one family from another.

Worse than the barracks were barns built by the workers themselves which were, in the opinion of one factory inspector, "more like dog kennels or chicken pens than like dwellings for human beings." To be housed at all, however badly, was still an improvement over the conditions in some factories, notably in the textile industry but in other light industries as well, where the workers worked, ate and slept at the side of their machines. Factory owners justified this by claiming that the workers were "village people who have not yet lost their country habits and attitudes; they view sleeping on the loom as reminiscent of their own homes."

Factory workers in cities had some greater choice in housing, for they could rent rooms in private dwellings. But as public transportation was not an amenity which most workers could afford, they tended to live in the neighborhoods that had grown up around the factories, in other words, factory slums. A typical factory neighborhood in St. Petersburg was described as

> an entire forest of factory chimneys, throwing out clouds of black smoke obscuring the already grey Petersburg sky. The factory buildings, houses, streets and the bustling crowds of people were all covered with a thick layer of soot. From everywhere rushed the massive rhythmical sounds — the rattle of huge rollers, the penetrating clank of iron bars, the heat of steam hammers which shook the earth . . . and above all these sounds in the air hung the uninterrupted hum of huge steam boilers lying on the ground like gigantic caterpillars.[6]

In this neighborhood, perhaps not too different from factory districts elsewhere in Europe, the worker sought out what he could afford: a room shared with many others, a small corner of a kitchen rented from a family of workers who could not afford to keep an entire apartment for themselves. As in the factory barracks, to share a bed was not uncommon. A skilled metal worker from St. Petersburg of the 1890s described his quarters in the following way:

> My room and board was not far from the factory in a huge stinking house populated by haulers, cabbies and day-laborers. We were 15 men renting the apartment as a collective. Some were bachelors, others had wives in the countryside who looked after the land. I was put in a small dark room without windows — in other words, a closet. It was filthy and stuffy, full of cockroaches and bugs and smelled acutely of "mankind." In this closet stood two wooden cots. My fellow villager and guardian slept on one and his son and I on the other.[7]

The housing situation grew even worse in the 20th century. In St. Petersburg, for example, although the number of apartments doubled between the 1860s and 1900, the number of inhabitants per apartment increased. Rents began to escalate in the 1890s and continued to rise thereafter. Although city and governmental authorities were well aware of the acute nature of the housing problem, the various proposals for low-cost housing never left the drawing board. It should come as no surprise that there were twice as many people per apartment as in Berlin and Paris, and the "corner habitation," the subdivision and re-subdivision of apartments making corridors and even kitchens into quarters, became a uniquely Russian phenomenon. In 1904 in the city

FIGURE 14. A worker's apartment in St. Petersburg of the early 1900s.
(Ocherki istorii Leningrada [Izdatel'stvo ANSSSR: Moscow-Leningrad,
1956], vol. 8, p. 132).

of St. Petersburg, two thirds of the single workers and two fifths of
married workers lived in such "corners" and conditions were similar
in Moscow and other cities.

Still one notch lower than the "corner" was the flophouse which
began to emerge on a fairly large scale in the late 1870s. Originally
intended by charitable organizations to provide cheap night shelter
for the temporarily homeless, by 1910 the flophouse had become a
permanent institution, often housing people for long periods of time.
In St. Petersburg they provided 6,200 beds, and entirely against city
ordinances, in fact housed many more people than the number of beds.
The bedding consisted of bare slats constructed like stalls: filthy and
overcrowded, the flophouse was a breeding ground for contagious
diseases and was often blamed for the recurring typhus and cholera
epidemics.

The highest priority in the urban worker's income was housing,
and as income rose so did the quality of housing within the limits

FIGURE 15.   A worker's house in a factory district of Moscow in the early 1900s.
(Istorii Moskvy [Izdatel'stvo ANSSSR: Moscow, 1955], vol. 5, p. 233).

described. Clearly, then, this was one of the differences between the
skilled and unskilled worker: again not a great difference, for even the
highly skilled worker often had difficulty making ends meet. From the
1880s to the outbreak of World War I, nominal wages rose considerably,
but the cost of living rose faster. In 1910 budget studies showed that a
family in St. Petersburg required 600–700 rubles per year to maintain
a tolerable standard of living, yet the average wage of a metal worker,
the "aristocrat" of labor was 516 rubles per year, and in the lowest
paying industry — food processing — the average wage was 268 rubles.
The wage scale in St. Petersburg was higher than elsewhere as was the
cost of living, but the relationship of one to the other was similar
throughout the Russian Empire. It should be noted that women workers, regardless of the industry in which they were employed, earned
one half to two thirds of the male income. The discrepancy between
income and expenses meant interminable indebtedness for many.

Normally, the rural factory ran a shop in order to provision its
workers with necessities unobtainable elsewhere because of the distance from town facilities. From the standpoint of the factory owners,
however, these shops were profit-making endeavors. Prices for food
and other basic necessities were considerably higher than the current
prices elsewhere, but workers had no choice but to buy. They were

advanced credit for their purchases to be deducted from their wages. The higher prices and poor quality of food, compounded by indebtedness, often made the company store the first target of looting and destruction during periods of labor unrest.

Both rural and urban workers attempted to ameliorate the problems of survival by forming living and eating collectives, known as artels. They were frequently comprised of workers from the same village or province, another example of the way workers sustained allegiances to their birthplace. The members of the artel pooled their money and hired a worker's wife or retired older worker to do the marketing and prepare the daily meals. As quantity and quality of food was determined by the wages of the artel's members, within the village groupings there was a further division into workers earning roughly the same wages. Women and adolescent workers who earned far less than adult men had separate artels. Studies of workers' budgets and eating habits revealed that those who lived as families ate best, followed by skilled workers in artels. The single worker who provisioned himself fared worst and, among them, women trailed at the end of the continuum. It was not unusual for a single woman worker to survive on bread and tea for two meals a day with a bit of meatless soup at night augmented by an onion and a bit of potato. Even the most affluent workers had an inadequate and extremely monotonous diet, as the following description by a well-paid St. Petersburg worker illustrates:

> At 11 A.M. every day, as soon as the bell for dinner break rang, we ran eagerly to the apartment and immediately sat at the table on which already steamed an enormous basin of cabbage soup. All 15 of us ate from the same common bowl with wooden spoons. Bits of meat floated in the soup. First we gobbled the liquid and as it disappeared we waited tensely for the signal. Someone tapped a spoon on the rim of the bowl and pronounced the awaited "Go to it!" Then the race for the few floating bits of meat began. The most adroit got the most meat. After the cabbage soup we had buckwheat groats with pork fat or fried potatoes.[8]

The Russian worker's ability to maintain family life intact was severely limited by the conditions we have described. Fortunate indeed was the worker who retained close ties with his village, for he could send his children there in their early years to be brought up by kin. However disruptive this arrangement was of family life, it was the only alternative for many workers who could afford neither the housing, the feeding, nor the time to care for their children. The government exhorted factory owners to provide nursery facilities for factory women as well as schools for school-aged children. But exhortations were never written into the law and were therefore provided only by the rare benevolent factory owner, primarily in the Central Industrial Region.

FIGURE 16.   A workers' lunchroom in St. Petersburg of the early 1900s. (Ocherki istorii Leningrada [Izdatel'stvo ANSSSR: Moscow-Leningrad, 1956], vol. 8, p. 133).

So unusual were minimally adequate facilities for child care at the factory that they provoked great outbursts of admiration from the factory inspectors where they did exist. Needless to say, the entire burden of child care in those families which remained intact was borne by the woman worker. The most common way to care for children who stayed with the family during the woman worker's long working day was to hire an older child or an elderly woman, neither of whom were particularly qualified or reliable. A system of baby-farming, common in England as well, began to flourish in Russia as a way of caring for children. Originally intended to be homes for foundlings, workers took considerable advantage of them. It was the least desirable of alternatives; families in the countryside were paid a small sum by the government to care for children who were not relatives, and mainly the poorest peasant families ventured into what became an industry in its own right. The system had unfortunate consequences for the children, since profits could be increased by economizing on the youngsters' food. Deprived of nourishment, squeezed into the already overcrowded peasant hut, baby-farming contributed to Russia's very high infant mortality rate.

LITERACY AND LEISURE

The conditions of the Russian workers' lives, the squalor and poverty in which they lived, the long hours of arduous labor for which they were so miserably remunerated left them with little time and energy for recreation. Nor were amusement and social amenities readily accessible. To begin with, literacy which can be the door to a more pleasurable as well as a more comfortable life, was very low in the Russian Empire, lagging far behind most other European nations. According to the only Empire-wide census taken in our period, in 1897 only 21.1 percent of the entire population was literate: 29.3 percent of men and 13.1 percent of women. To be sure, literacy among industrial workers was considerably higher: 56.5 percent for men and 21.3 percent for women — 50.3 percent for both sexes taken together, and there is no question but that by 1914 literacy among workers had increased. However, literacy rarely meant more than the ability to scratch out one's name and read a simple text, for few but the most skilled workers went beyond the three year primary schools scantily dispersed throughout the countryside. Workers in cities were more literate than their counterparts in rural factories. Still, in St. Petersburg in 1910, one third of the children between the ages of 8 and 11 were not accommodated in schools. It is not clear to what degree schooling, which was more available in the cities, actually contributed to the higher degree of literacy among urban workers. Some may have come to the city factory already literate, since such workers were more likely to risk the new life than illiterate peasants. The main advantage of the city over the village was that educational opportunities were available for adult workers. The liberal educated classes in Russia, as elsewhere, were convinced that education was strong medicine for the ills of the lower classes, and various civic and philanthropic organizations organized Sunday schools and evening classes for city workers. For the most part the teachers were drawn from the leisured or idealistic groups in Russian society, whose members donated their time to teaching the poor the rudiments of literacy, arithmetic, religious subjects, and sometimes offered more advanced technical training. The schools were a bright spot in the lives of those workers with the energy and the motivation to pursue learning. Indeed, it took a very special and highly-motivated worker to endure the average six-day, 14-hour-a-day work week and then devote his evenings or day off to school. Many more male than female workers attended the Sunday schools. Even in this most enlightened sector of public philanthropy, the old patriarchal attitudes persisted and Sunday schools for women were fewer and slower to increase. Nor were women workers encouraged by their families or peers; in the peasant and worker milieus, education for women was considered a useless frivolity and inappropriate to the woman's role in life. Indeed, in this sphere attitudes and reality were mutually reinforcing. Discouraged by her acculturation, constrained by the double burden of work and domestic obligations, the woman worker in reality had no concrete reward for sacrificing her few leisure hours to education. There was a high correlation among male workers between literacy and wages—the more literate, the higher paying job —but not among women. Throughout our period women were relegated to the less skilled, lower paying jobs regardless of their degree of literacy.

One of the fundamental assumptions of the founders of Sunday schools was that literacy would wean the worker from the alcoholism which was endemic among factory laborers. A great problem among the peasantry as well, alcoholism was probably more clearly observable among workers, clustered as they were in their factory ghettos. The dislocations produced by factory life were blamed for the enormous consumption of vodka, especially by male workers who sought release in the tavern from the routine of their pinched, drab lives. One worker described the Smolensk tract, a factory ghetto in St. Petersburg, in the following way:

> The entire working class population of Smolensk tract lived in crowded, filthy, and primitive conditions. . . . Throughout the tract there were innumerable taverns, inns, beer halls, and churches, but not a single cultural establishment. For the 60,000 inhabitants there were only two shabby theaters.

It is not surprising then that "Twice a month on Saturday payday, our artel became the scene of a wild debauch. Some, getting their wages, went directly from the factory to the tavern and the saloon; others, more dandyish, came home to change clothes. Everyone would return home late at night or on Sunday morning morose, sullen, frequently battered, and with hangovers."

The violence of working class life was not confined to the tavern and the street, however, but extended into family life as well. The worker's wife, whether she was a fellow-laborer or a wife at home, had an unending struggle to prevent the husband from frittering away his inadequate wages on vodka and the concomitant struggle to avoid being beaten in the attempt.

HEALTH CARE AMONG THE WORKERS

Another experience common to all workers was the poor quality of medical care and, until 1903, the almost complete absence of medical insurance or pension plans for invalidism and old age. Throughout Russia, medical care for the poor was inadequate and the standards abysmally low. An index of the combination of wretched living conditions, poor nutrition, and inadequate medicine was the rate of infant mortality which remained consistently twice as high as the rate of infant mortality for other European nations. In the countryside, local governments lacked the resources to provide the rural population with regular professional medical personnel, not to speak of hospitals and medication. The low cultural level of the peasantry bred superstition and suspicion of medical and scientific cures, so that peasants were inclined to trust age-old folk remedies and local people endowed with alleged curative powers and wisdom. In the cities, where the general sophistication and level of culture was somewhat higher, the poor should have had better access to medical care; in reality much of the medical care available to them was private and beyond their means.

The deprivation of health care which workers shared with the entire poor population of Russia was only part of the problem. They were also vulnerable to the health and safety hazards in the factory, the many varieties of work-related diseases, the easy and rapid spread of disease within the factory enclosure, and industrial accidents which could lead to temporary or permanent work disabilities.

In 1866 in anticipation of recurrent cholera epidemics, the government had issued an edict requiring factory owners to provide one hospital bed for every 100 workers. Implementation of the regulation had been slow and half-hearted. The factory owners' reluctance to comply with it was facilitated by the fact that there were no provisions for enforcing the decree. Such was the fate of countless "obligatory rulings" on medical care enacted by local arms of the central bureaucracy which, on paper, set reasonably high standards for medical care. Twenty years after the first regulation, factory inspectors found that medical care for workers was a fiction. Whether or not a factory worker was provided with minimal first aid, diagnosis, and medicine or hospital care for enduring illness continued to rest entirely with the factory owner's discretion. In the Central Industrial Region, where factory owners had a greater tradition of paternalistic concern for workers than elsewhere in Russia, some form of medical care was more common, although the properly trained doctor was rarely available on a regular basis. Usually workers were treated by the "feldsher," a kind of paramedic who was only slightly more knowledgeable about disease and treatment than the patient. St. Petersburg factories were scandalously derelict in providing medical care. By the turn of the century only one large factory employed a doctor on a regular basis; he received patients two hours daily which meant, of course, that he was not available to treat accidents which occurred in his absence. Among 662 Moscow city factories in 1904, only 246 had outpatient clinics and of these only 179 had fully trained doctors.

Care for pregnant women workers was entirely lacking. One factory inspector in the 1880s polled factory owners and managers in a Moscow province about their facilities for pregnant workers and found that "they even expressed bewilderment [at such a strange question]. Convinced of the total absence of need for it, they answered frankly that they simply pay pregnant workers and release them to the four winds." The most generous provisions in the province were to be found in one factory that exempted pregnant workers from fines for tardiness, and in another at which the woman worker was permitted to take three days off after delivery.

Venereal disease, especially in the cities, was a grave social and medical problem in our period, affecting women in factories as well as men who probably served as an effective transmission belt back to the countryside. Both diagnosis and treatment were woefully lacking, as the following description of a factory medical examination in the 1890s indicates: the worker-narrator tells how the workers were required to submit to an examination specifically for the detection of venereal disease before their periodic pilgrimages back to the country.

> The examinations were made primitively and coarsely and can hardly be said to have yielded results. When we went to collect our earnings at the bookkeeper's office, a doctor was waiting there. We lined up, pulled down our trousers and showed the necessary part of our bodies to him. He poked around with a pencil, conveyed the results of his "examination" to the bookkeeper, and if we were clean we were given our pay. Certainly at the plant there were many workers with venereal disease, but I do not know of a single case discovered by that doctor during the examination.[9]

Before 1903 only 28 percent of Russian workers were covered by some kind of accident insurance for, like medical care, the provision of accident benefits and pensions was at the discretion of the individual factory owner. The fortunate workers whose employers joined private insurance companies were nonetheless poorly remunerated for temporary or permanent disability. Payments were so low that, as one observer remarked, they were less than the selling price of a medium sized cow. In 1903 an accident insurance law was promulgated. While it covered the worker for loss of the ability to work due to bodily injury on the job to the tune of two thirds of his wage, it was not applicable to workers at state enterprise or to transport, construction, and agricultural workers. Worse, if a factory owner could prove that an accident was the result of the worker's "malicious intent" or "carelessness," he was relieved of all financial obligation. The worker then had to go through the courts to receive compensation, a long and costly process which left him and his family bereft of support in the interim. Nonetheless, it was the first legislative attempt to remove the worker's health and well-being from the whim of the employer.

INDUSTRIAL CONFLICT IN RUSSIAN FACTORIES

There were, of course, many complex reasons for the reluctance of government and industry to provide minimal amelioration of the worker's condition and detailed analysis of these complexities is beyond the scope of this essay. We will discuss here only two major impediments to the formulation of workable solutions to the problems of the burgeoning working-class.

The first obstacle was the widely held, if not unanimous, opinion that Russia's workers were not a proletariat in the real sense of the word. Given the relationship of many workers to the land, it was argued, they did not constitute a distinct class for which it was necessary to legislate separately. Persistent, if sporadic, labor unrest dispelled this notion by the turn of the century, and from then on government and industrialists accepted labor legislation as necessary and inevitable. The second impediment, once the inevitability of legislation was acknowledged, was the serious discord between government and industry regarding the direction that legislation should take.

For centuries Russia's autocracy had been the sole source of legislation in every area of life, at every turn resisting infringements on the Tsar's arbitrary rule. The intellectual and theoretical justification of monarchical rule was the notion that the monarchy and its representatives were a nonclass element whose task it was to stand above and reconcile society's class dissensions. What this meant in practice was that while the government was always anxious to encourage and support industry, it also perceived itself as the protector of the worker against the selfish aims of the industrialist. Thus, the government was not averse to enacting legislation designed to benefit factory workers. Moreover, the government felt that attending to workers' economic grievances was a way of siphoning off actual or potential political discontent which might threaten the political primacy of the autocracy.

The industrialists, on the other hand, were adamantly against economic concessions which threatened their purses or their power over workers. After the revolution of 1905, however, when workers began to make political as well as economic demands, they sometimes gave mild support to workers' political demands, in part because they themselves coveted political freedoms which the tsarist government did not make available to them.

The fundamental conflict between government and industry remained unresolved throughout our period. The result was that despite a plethora of government commissions, despite proposals and counterproposals and despite (in some cases) reasonable intentions on both sides, labor legislation was enacted with great difficulty. Nor did these laws improve significantly the living conditions of the factory workers.

Workers in western European countries and America devised ways to help themselves in some of the important areas of their lives for which there was no protective legislation. In some countries they formed mutual-aid societies, pooling their resources to see workers and their families through illness, to provide survivors with some support after the death of the primary wage earner. The Russian government was suspicious of such manifestations of private initiative, perceiving it as fertile ground for potential competition with its own all-embracing control over the lives of its subjects. However, in line with its general policy of seeking ways to prevent political discontent by making economic concessions, it embarked on a curious experiment in the early 1900s known as "police socialism." First in Moscow and then in Odessa and other towns, workers were permitted to form a kind of union under the tutelage of government agents, designed to give workers some carefully controlled scope for the expression of economic grievances. The experiment was a failure. Extremely irritating to industrialists, the police unions were rejected by the workers as well, once they understood them to be ineffectual facsimiles of channels for the expression of discontent. That there was a hunger among workers, however primitive, for autonomous organization was manifested in their eagerness to join yet another such organization in St. Petersburg in 1905. Led by a charismatic priest concerned primarily with the workers' moral improvement and under covert police surveillance and control, this police union was, in a sense, taken over by the workers at the grass roots level. Its denouncement occurred on January 22, 1905 in the form of a massive demonstration of workers and their families coming to *petition* the Tsar for his ear. In other words, St. Petersburg workers, the most urbanized and sophisticated in all of Russia, were still prepared to supplicate, not demand. The Tsar's response to the demonstration was a massacre of the peacefully assembled workers in an event aptly called Bloody Sunday, which inaugurated the revolution of 1905.

Although strikes were illegal, in the absence of effective legal channels for peaceful settlement of grievances, the Russian workers' only weapon was to withhold their labor. From the beginning of our period workers engaged in strikes, even though to strike was to risk severe punishment, ranging from loss of job to prison terms at hard labor. Strikes ranged from short-lived spontaneous outbursts of rage against living conditions, methods of wage-payment, illegal firings, and all the other abuses of the existing order, to longer and more organized protests demanding substantive changes in the system of industrial relations. Strike activity increased both quantitatively and substantively in the 1890s, breaking out with particular vehemence during the revolution of 1905. That revolution, which has been described by Lenin as the dress-rehearsal to 1917, culminated in an Empire-wide general strike of factory workers as well as of workers of every description. These dramatic events provoked a grudging recognition on the part of autocracy and industry that Russia's workers, whatever their ties to the land, whatever their degree of illiteracy, ignorance, and naiveté, were growing impatient with dilatory and half-hearted legislation.

The energy engendered by the 1905 upheaval resulted, among other things, in the formation of 600 local unions. The union movement, however, was not destined to play the same critically important role in the Russian worker's fate as it did in the West. In part this was due to continuing repression. Once the revolutionary fervor of 1905 abated and the state no longer felt threatened by acute unrest, the continuing formation and existence of unions, although now recognized in principle, was hampered by the government and the industrialists. The militant union worker, like his striking predecessor, was vulnerable to loss of job, to administrative exile, to blackballing, and even to prison. The economics of the workers' lives, unchanged by the 1905 revolution, similarly served as an impediment to the success of unions, and after the initial burst of courage, fewer workers were prepared to jeopardize their jobs and their freedom by vigorously pursuing union organization and membership. By 1908 the number of local unions had dwindled to 300 and by 1914 most of them existed only on paper.

Unions in the West faced similarly oppressive obstacles in the decades of their formation and evolution. Yet, workers persisted and, with varying degrees of success, wrested from government and industry a recognition of the union's legitimacy. But we must be cautious in making direct comparisons. The mentality of the Russian worker, and the rigidity of his employers and rulers, did not permit unions to play the same role in Russia as they did in the West.

To be sure, the government and industry attempted, in the years between the revolutions of 1905 and 1917, to hammer out their differences and legislate in a way which would pacify workers without, however, undermining either the government's or the industrialists' basic positions. The resulting legislation was an open but feeble acknowledgment of the inevitability of worker participation in the institutions which affected his life. In 1912 a law was passed that provided workers with insurance against illness. The great innovation contained in the law was the right of workers to form their own representative bodies to administer the illness funds jointly financed by workers and employers. Union leadership attempted to encourage workers to organize around the illness funds, to take advantage of the legality of worker representation in this narrow sphere, hoping to revive some of the activism of the 1905 revolution. The response was minimal, no doubt because participation in the administration of illness funds promised so little to the worker; it did not affect the hours he worked, his scanty wages, his insecurity in old age nor, indeed, most features of his difficult and cheerless life. In other words, the efforts for active participation were incommensurate with the rewards.

His rage and discontent found more satisfying and direct release in strikes which once again gained momentum in 1912. The outbreak of World War I interrupted all aspects of Russian life and for a while held workers' discontent in abeyance. But the dislocations and economic privations brought on by the war were especially trying for workers and their dissatisfaction once again surfaced in the form of a revitalized strike movement culminating in the Revolution of 1917.

NOTES

1. K. Norinskii, "Moi vospominaniia," in *Ot gruppy Blagoeva K "Soiuz Bor'by" (1886–1894).* Gosudarstvennoe Izdatel'stov, 1921, p. 24.
2. Leningradskii Gosundarstuennyi Istoricheskii Arkhiv. Fond 1229, op. 1, d. 146, 1. 3.
3. S. Kanatchikov, *Iz istorii moego bytiia* (Moscow-Leningrad, 1929), p. 80.
4. I. V. Babushkin, *Vospominaniia Ivana Vasil'evicha Babushkina, 1893–1900* (Moscow, 1955), p. 30.
5. *Stanok,* 1908, no. 3, p. 2.
6. Kanatchikov, *Iz istorii moego bytiia,* pp. 68–69.
7. Kanatchikov, ibid., p. 10.
8. Kanatchikov, ibid., p. 11.
9. Kanatchikov, ibid., p. 44.

BIBLIOGRAPHY

The quotations as well as the major part of the information in this essay were taken from Russian language sources: factory inspectors reports, workers' memoirs, archival documents. The literature on the Russian worker in English is sparse. What follows is a selected bibliography dealing with some of the major themes presented in the essay.

Bater, James H.   *St. Petersburg. Industrialization and Change.* London: 1976.

Blackwell, W. L.   *The Industrialization of Russia.* New York: 1970.

Glickman, Rose L.   "The Russian Factory Woman, 1880–1914" in *Women in Russia.* Stanford University Press, (forthcoming).

Haimson, L.   "The Problem of Social Stability in Urban Russia, 1905–1917" part 1, *Slavic Review,* no. 4, December 1964. Part 2, *Slavic Review,* no. 1, March 1965.

Sablinsky, W.   *The Road to Bloody Sunday.* Princeton, 1976.

Schniederman, J.   *Sergei Zubatov and Revolutionary Marxism: The Struggle For the Working Class in Tsarist Russia.* Ithaca, 1976.

Tugan-Baronovsky, M. I.   *The Russian Factory in the 19th Century.* Irwin, Inc., 1970.

Von Laue, T.   "Russian Labor Between Field and Factory," *California Slavic Studies,* vol. 3, 1964.

———   "The Russian Peasant in the Factory," *Journal of Economic History,* vol. 21, March 1961.

Zelnik, Reginald.   "Russian Bebels: An Introduction to the Memoirs of Semen Kanatchikov and Matvei Fisher" part 1. *Russian Review,* vol. 35, July 1976. Part 2, *Russian Review,* vol. 3, October 1976.

———   *Labor and Society in Tsarist Russia, 1855–1870.* Stanford, 1971.

Chapter 6

*T*he experience of Russian factory workers in the decades before
World War I reveals the human cost involved in the rapid "modernization" of a traditional peasant society. Yet hundreds of thousands
of men and women were willing to abandon their native villages for
a miserable existence in factories and urban slums, driven by hunger
and despair to seek a better life for themselves and their children.
They were part of a vast internal migration that included the shift
of more than three million Russians across the Ural mountains to
the undeveloped lands of Siberia. Thousands of Jews left their rural
ghetto settlements in Poland and western Russia for America to
escape the pogroms that were sporadically organized by the government. But the vast majority of rural Russians remained in the
villages where their parents and grandparents had lived in serfdom.
They formed the bulk of the Russian army—some 15 million—
mobilized during World War I. And though the factory workers in
St. Petersburg played a crucial role in the Russian Revolution of
1917, the flight of the peasant soldiers from the military front to
their villages in search of land contributed significantly to the
success of that revolution.

For no European country, from the most "progressive" to the
most "backward" was modernization a simple or easy process. With
her huge territory, her authoritarian but inefficient government, and
her primitive economic and social structure, Russia experienced the

greatest trauma in her transition to the 20th century. No part of Europe was immune from the tensions and strains of adjustment, and from pressures to reform antiquated and dysfunctional structures, to align them more closely with the new realities. Every government had to respond in some fashion to the economic and social problems spawned by industrialization and urbanization; every regime had to contend with forces seeking to liberalize and democratize the political process. Three general considerations shaped the responses of governments to the demands for reform: first, the rapidity and scope of the economic and social changes; second, the receptivity of ruling elites to foreign influences and models (e.g., the example of the French Revolution or of England's parliamentary system of government); third and most important, the historical experiences which had formed the institutions and shaped the habits and values of the society. The following essay describes the particular experience of one country (Italy) and one city (Milan) in its difficult and painful passage to the modern world.

Italy's modern history began with the political unification of the peninsula in the 1860s, under the aegis of the Piedmontese monarchy. For the first time since the disintegration of the Roman Empire in the West (fifth century, A.D.), Italians were all—or nearly all—united under one government, one rule. But this development did not automatically lead to the integration of the various parts of the peninsula into a cohesive whole. Nor did it promote, at least in the short term, the modernization of Italy's economic and social order. The problems were admittedly great. Italy was not well provided with natural resources like coal and iron ore that had fueled industrialization elsewhere in Europe. The peninsula's geography—its mountainous terrain and the paucity of navigable rivers—hampered trade and communications. These natural features inhibited the expansion of commerce and industry, and of economic growth generally. It has been argued that unification was actually a deterrent to modernization, because it created a forced marriage between the more advanced north and the very backward south (including the islands of Sicily and Sardinia). Energies and resources that might have been utilized to create a modern society in the northern and central regions of the peninsula were instead expended on sustaining that creaky political structure. It required, for example, an army of 100,000 soldiers and the expenditure of millions of lire to "pacify" the rebellious south in the decade after unification.

This tenacious resistance by southerners to the monarchical regime that was imposed upon them in the 1860s suggests that the greatest barriers to unification and modernization were not physical but mental and psychological. For more than a thousand years, Italy had been politically fragmented into dozens, even hundreds of small units; nowhere in Europe were local and regional loyalties stronger than in this Mediterranean peninsula. Most Italians identified first with their city or province—with Milan or Lombardy, with Siena or Tuscany—and only weakly and grudgingly (if at all) with the nation. Only 2 or 3 percent of the population "had Italian as their first language at the time of national unification: to most Italians, the 'national language' would have been unintelligible, and the word Italy unknown." (Denis Mack Smith, "Regionalism," in Modern Italy, ed. E. Tannenbaum and E. Noether [New York, 1974], p. 127.) After Rome was occupied by Italian troops in 1870, Pope Pius IX declared himself to be a prisoner in the Vatican, and refused to have any official contact with the state. The papacy forbade Catholics to vote in elections, or to participate in the political process. Devout Catholics thus joined alienated southerners and other provincials in denying their allegiance to the regime, which had never been popular with the peasantry, the largest and poorest segment of Italian society.

To understand Italy's problems in the postunification period, a local focus—the historical experience of one community—is as illuminating as a national perspective. Milan was, in the 19th century, one of Italy's most populous and prosperous urban centers: a city with a glorious past, the capital of the rich province of Lombardy. Milan had been an autonomous city-state since the 11th century; her citizens had led the Italian opposition to the efforts of German emperors to control the peninsula. While Florence was achieving a dominant position in Tuscany in the 15th century (see volume I, chapter 6), Milan established her control over Lombardy, and under the rule of her ducal dynasties, the Visconti and the Sforza, became one of Italy's great Renaissance states. Milan's glory faded after her conquest by Spanish armies in the early 16th century, though she remained the political and administrative center of Lombardy during three centuries of Hapsburg rule. She was also the capital of the Cisalpine republic established by Napoleon in 1796, and later of the French-dominated Kingdom of Italy. After the collapse of the Napoleonic empire (1814–15), Milan and Lom-

bardy were again occupied and governed by Austria. Except for a few months in 1848, when the Milanese expelled the Austrian garrison and established an independent government, the city remained under Hapsburg rule until 1859, when Piedmontese troops drove the Austrians from Lombardy. Milan and its province became part of the new kingdom of Italy, whose capital was first Turin, then Florence (1864), and finally Rome (1871). Though not destined to be the center of the national government, Milan did play a very significant role in Italy's political, economic, and cultural life after unification. The nature of that role, and of Milan's transformation into a "modern" city, is the theme of Professor Lyttleton's essay.

Milan 1880–1922: The City of Industrial Capitalism

*ADRIAN LYTTLETON**

MILAN'S GROWTH AFTER 1880

The citizen of Milan in 1880 was conscious of belonging to a city which had both a glorious past and a promising future. During the course of a brief promenade in the center he would be reminded of the city's multiple functions and meanings. On the right of the great Gothic cathedral, dating from the time of the Visconti dukes in the 15th century, there now stood the Gallery. Named after King Victor Emmanuel II and decorated with statues of Italian worthies, it commemorated the integration of Milan into united Italy. But it was loved by the Milanese for other reasons; it was convenient, luxurious, and modern. It symbolized the new Milan of the bourgeoisie. A wide-spanning glass roof, an exciting novelty in Italy, gave shelter from the rain and dank fog which so often afflicted the city. Inside the Gallery the visitor was plunged into warmth and light; the brilliance of the shop fronts drew his admiration. If he wished to stay longer, one of the equally splendid cafes might detain him. The Gallery preserved many of the functions of the classic Italian piazza; it was a meeting place, a focus of social life, and conversation. The more casual sorts of business deal could be initiated here; musicians, singers, and their agents congregated to discuss opportunities and terms for employment. The attractions of vice, too, were not lacking: but only the most elegant and discreet of the city's many prostitutes frequented the Gallery. The prevailing tone

---

* University of Reading.

was one of bourgeois decorum, spiced with fashion and bohemian gaiety. However, in times of trouble the Gallery was a focus also for political demonstrations, and the unemployed would gather to force an indifferent city to take account of their miseries.

Very near the Gallery and the Cathedral the Scala opera house was another potent attraction. Opera was the favorite sport of the Milanese, and all other subjects of conversation took second place. The Scala also served as the showcase for the conspicuous consumption of the city's wealthiest inhabitants. The Scala was built under the Austrians; but it had attained perhaps its greatest splendor during the brief period when Milan was the capital of the Napoleonic Kingdom of Italy. After 1860 the capital of Italy moved in succession from Turin to Florence to Rome; but Milan had in a certain sense preceded them, and consciousness of this was an important component of the city's civic identity.

These key monuments and the public spaces associated with them were like powerful magnets drawing the life of Milan into the center. No new quarter or fashionable suburb could compete with their glamor. Consequently the new structures of the age of business, the head offices of the great banks, and the first large department stores, clustered thickly around the Piazza del Duomo and the Piazza della Scala. The most powerful of the banks, the Banca Commerciale, eventually built itself a new headquarters in Piazza della Scala itself, flanked on one side by the opera house and on the other by the town hall. The development of a modern "downtown" business center brought about the piecemeal destruction of much of the fabric of the old Milan. The most important demolitions had already taken place before 1880, to clear the ground for the Gallery and the new, unnecessarily large, piazza in front of the cathedral. Later on, a new street, the Via Mercanti, was pushed brusquely through one corner of the city's medieval center, the Piazza Mercanti, destroying its character as a closed and intimate space. However, even after 1880 there was for a long time no clear segregation of business and residential quarters in the center. Indeed the prestige and attractions of the center exercised a contrary tendency; as in other Italian cities, the rich still wanted to live there. It would have been unthinkable for the successful Milanese businessman to desert the heart of the historic city for a quiet new suburb, as his counterpart in Manchester had done. The civic tradition was too strong for that. G. B. Pirelli, the founder of the famous rubber manufacturing firm, at first lived in a house next door to the factory, on the outskirts of Milan. But this was from necessity, not choice. When he had made his fortune and could delegate the responsibility for the day-to-day management of the factory, he moved into the center. Such a move was a prerequisite for acceptance into the city's ruling elite.

The social geography of Milan was in large part dictated by the con-

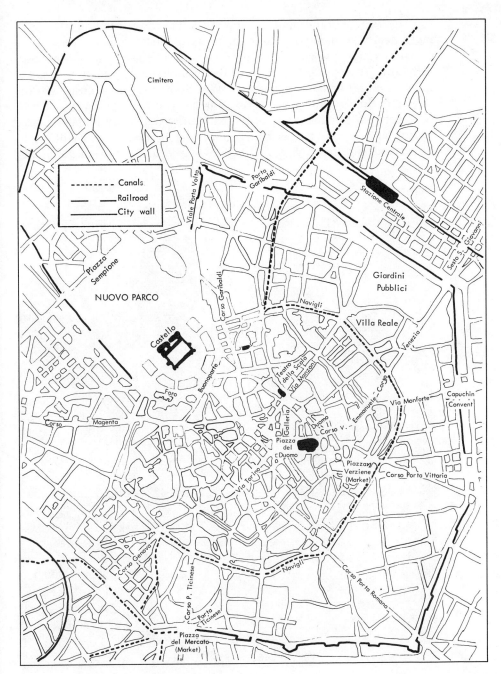

MAP 9.   Milan about 1910

tinued prestige of the center. Although Milan was the Italian city which most nearly imitated northern patterns of development, the way its social divisions were projected onto urban space was nonetheless different. As in other Italian cities the fundamental opposition was not (as in London or Paris) between "West End" and "East End," but between periphery and center. In 1860 the inner ring of the old city, contained within the circle of the Navigli (canals), still housed a large artisan and working-class population. The inner city was still an ordered and familiar environment, known and loved by its inhabitants.

FIGURE 17.   Social contrasts: the poor and old on benches in the piazza; the bourgeois in the Gallery. (Raccolta Civica Bertarelli, Castello Sforzesco, Milan).

FIGURE 17   (continued)

There was squalor and great poverty in the back streets and alleys,
although standards of hygiene and medical care compared favorably
at least with those of Paris. More than half the houses were rebuilt
during the period between 1815 and 1860, but there had been little
change in the pattern of narrow streets and courtyards inherited from
the medieval city, or in the social life which went with them. Building
styles remained fairly uniform. The typical house in the inner city had
two or three stories, and was built round an inner courtyard. There was
little difference in style between the housing of the middle classes, the
petty bourgeoisie and the artisans; economic distinctions made themselves felt through subdivision of houses and overcrowding. Working-
class dwellings seldom had more than two rooms, and many lodgings
were shared by more than one family. In these conditions, the ideal

of "domestic life" held up by paternalistic reformers was a mockery.
Even after 1860, streets not far from the Duomo, like the Via degli
Armorari, contained some of the worst pockets of poverty in the city,
as evidenced by the large numbers of foundlings which they contributed to the city's hospital.

By 1880, however, slum clearances and rising rents had begun to
reduce the number of workers who lived in the heart of the city. One
of the first casualties of modernization is the sense of familiarity.
Toward the end of the century, in his evocative *"Milanin, Milanon"*
(Little Milan, Big Milan), the writer Emilio De Marchi lamented that
he could no longer recognize the city he knew, "our dear Milan of the
Milanese . . . with so many fine drinking-places with good wine and
good company," which "huddled around the cathedral, like a family
warming itself at the hearth." The Milanese were now ashamed to
speak their own dialect, "that sincere language of true weight," and
spoke a colorless Italian instead. The new Milan had swept away the
intricate variety of narrow streets, courtyards and loggias which offered
protection against both summer heat and winter cold, and replaced
them with "great white houses, all straight, all wall."[1] Complaints for
the vanished scenes of one's youth are, of course, commonplace, and
one should not forget that, as we have seen in the case of the Gallery,
the new too could inspire affection. Some quarters of the city had been
much less affected by change than the center. But the transformation
of Milan was a continuing process in which the demolition of old habits
and old ties along with old buildings would become a recurrent feature.
In 1864 the French historian and sociologist Taine had observed that
Milan was "animated, without being feverish like Paris or London."
Thirty years later, the city was full of people "who go, who run, who
shove, on and off the trams . . . day and night." Milan now clearly
aspired to rival the great capitals in the ceaseless pace of its many
activities, from business to shopping to night life.

The years after 1880 were those of the city's most rapid growth. In
one decade the population grew by almost a third, from 321,000 to
424,000. Nearly 120,000 immigrants entered the city during this period,
while only 31,000 left; migration thus accounted for almost nine tenths
of the city's increase. Economic crisis put a brake on expansion after
1890. In 1892 net immigration was under 5,000, compared with an
average of almost 9,000 during the 1880s. It was only at the very end of
the decade, in 1899–1900, that the rhythm picked up again. The majority
of newcomers to Milan were, of course, peasants and artisans; shoe-
makers, tailors, and seamstresses followed their clientele to the city.
However, commerce and the professions also attracted large numbers of
middle-class immigrants. In 1894, when the industrial crisis was still
at its most severe, they actually outnumbered the workers.

The city drew in more migrants than it could absorb. The exceptionally rapid growth of the 1880s was as much the result of rural desperation as of urban opportunity. These were years of deep crisis for the agricultural economy of Lombardy, hit by disease and falling silk prices as well as by the general slump caused by the competition of American and Canadian wheat. When the crisis spread to industry, mass unemployment was bound to result. Another serious consequence of the economic crisis was in its effect on the housing market. The general loss of confidence in the building industry was reflected with disproportionate intensity in the provision of working-class housing. The ratio between the number of new rooms built for the workers and for the middle classes fell from roughly 1:1 to 1:4 between 1890 and 1898. A vicious circle had been created. Builders doubted the workers' ability to pay for new housing, and the scarcity of accommodation forced up rents. The numbers forced to take refuge in squalid lodging-houses, on the streets, or in farm buildings on the outskirts of the city, grew continually. In 1900 it was estimated that there were four unhoused workers looking for each new room. After 1900 there was certainly some improvement. Overcrowding in the central areas at least diminished, although in some parts of the periphery it may have got worse. Even in the more buoyant conditions of the early 20th century the city could not fulfil all the hopes it aroused. In the years before the war the percentage of new immigrants to the city was higher than ever before; but in some years as many as two people left the city for every three who arrived. Probably these included many of the new arrivals, disappointed in their hopes of a better job, who had given up the struggle after one or two years. In spite of these problems of absorption, immigration radically changed the composition of Milan's population. In 1901 native Milanese were outnumbered 56 to 44 percent by those born outside the commune. Most of the latter, however, had travelled only short distances. The majority came from other districts of Lombardy. The peasants of the South, who emigrated in such vast numbers to the Americas during this period, were not as yet attracted by the cities of northern Italy. Although by this time the majority of workers in manufacturing were first-generation immigrants, the highest concentration of recent arrivals were to be found in unskilled service occupations (porters, transport workers), or as laborers in the building trade. Women from peasant families tended to go into domestic service.

The majority of the immigrants to Milan did not settle in the center, where new housing was in short supply. They congregated instead in the suburbs outside the walls. The suburbs, known as the Corpi Santi, had benefited during the 19th century from their exemption from the city tolls and taxes. Workers could buy bread more cheaply outside the city limits, and taxes on property were also lighter. The Corpi Santi were annexed to the commune in 1873, but their opposition was so strenuous that they kept their fiscal autonomy and separate representation in the communal council for another 20 years. New large-scale industrial enterprises found in the suburbs not only a cheaper and more abundant labor force but low land values, room to expand, and easier access to the railways. As early as the 1870s population growth in the suburbs far outstretched that of the area within the walls. The innermost city, within the canals, was almost saturated; there was no space for new building and commerce was taking more room. However, the next ring, between the Navigli and the walls, had not been entirely built over even in 1880. Some areas were still occupied by the gardens of the patrician palaces. More important, the proprietors of some areas, notably in the southeast towards Porta Romana, preferred to hold onto their land and wait for values to rise before building. Instead, in the suburbs it was easier for small investors to buy land and build a few houses cheaply.

By 1914 the process of social segregation had advanced considerably. There was a clear contrast between the inner city within the Navigli, where the working class now numbered less than one fifth of the total population, and the outer periphery, where they numbered almost 70 percent. However, there were still large and important concentrations of workers in some old quarters between the Navigli and the walls. The two most important of these quarters were those around Porta Garibaldi in the northwest and Porta Ticinese in the southwest. Both of them were prolonged outside the walls by the ancient *borghi* which served as the nucleus for the development of new working class quarters. In these areas, therefore, there was no sharp break between the old and the new. The recent immigrants were absorbed into established popular communities and rapidly assimilated their customs and culture. The solidarity of the new working class was grounded in the informal "life of the quarter," in the neighborly gossip of the courtyards and the drinking circles of the *osterie* (inns). It was in these quarters that Milanese dialect put up the strongest resistance to the inroads of Italian. They preserved the old, combative traditions of the barricades of 1848, when the people had driven the Austrian army out of the city in five days of bitter fighting. Fifty years later in 1898 the barricades went up again, only this time it was the Italian army which was the enemy.

Already by 1900 a somewhat different type of working-class quarter had developed around the main railway station and to a lesser extent in the southeast, outside Porta Romana. These quarters were in the immediate vicinity of large factories and attracted a high concentration of industrial workers. The influence of previous popular traditions was less marked.

The new working class was not housed for the most part in large tenements or in model factory estates. Many were accommodated in converted older housing. In the distant suburbs, laborers' houses and farm buildings were turned into lodgings for industrial workers, and in the older borghi near the gates the courtyards were filled in, and rooms subdivided, as the pressure of population became more intense. It was in this way that the most dilapidated and run-down slum areas were formed.

New housing for the workers followed traditional building patterns. The typical block of workers' dwellings presented a facade to the street which differed only subtly from that of a block of middle-class apartments. The balconies would be fewer and ornament more sparing. The social reality of the buildings was revealed instead in the back courtyard, encircled by the *ballatoio,* a narrow wood or iron balcony which ran the length of each floor and which served instead of a corridor. The ballatoio was also the place for washing and gossip. This arrangement directly copied that in use in the farmhouses of Lombardy; the only difference, aside from the greater height and density of occupation, was that the ground floor of the courtyard would be given over to small workshops instead of farm animals. As a whole, these blocks were a compromise between semirural squalor and urban decorum. Their builders probably hoped that in time the new areas of the city would become more respectable and that the apartments could then be converted to a higher class of residence. Milanese workers remained badly housed even when economic conditions improved after 1900. Wages were still too low to allow most workers to purchase adequate housing on the free market, and even the better-off were generally reluctant to increase their expenditure on rent, putting other needs first. The proportion of working-class incomes set aside for rent seems not to have changed much before the first World War, and it was low by London standards. The only solution could come through the development of public subsidized housing. This was almost negligible before 1900; after 1902, under socialist pressure, the commune at last embarked on a serious program of building. Nonetheless, by 1914 the total number of rooms provided by public housing was only about 7,000, or less than one year's immigration to the city.

Overall, it would probably be wrong to think of loss of community as one of the major evils suffered by Milanese workers. Informal neighborhood life remained vigorous and merged without difficulty into the new and more formal solidarity of the cooperative, the union, and the political party. This generalization, however, would not apply to the settlements of the extreme periphery, inhabited by a transient population of very poor rural migrants in unstable occupations. In every sense, these were people who lived on the margins of the city.

A profound gulf existed between the perception of the city shared by the ruling class and the inhabitants of the center on the one hand, and the working class and the inhabitants of the suburbs on the other. The elite's love and attention were lavished on the center; this was still the true Milan. On the other hand, even before the hardening of class boundaries around 1890, the Corpi Santi had a long tradition of hostility to the city and its governors. When the mayor Negri tried in 1886 to reduce the ration of bread which the workers of the suburbs could bring within the gates free of tax, in the interests of the city bakeries, he was rapidly forced to withdraw the measure by violent rioting. The petty bourgeoisie and even many of the industrialists of the suburbs tended to hold radical views in opposition to the conservative *consorteria* which ruled the city. Their criticism, however, which concentrated on the commune's extravagance, did not always make it easier for the municipal government to meet the needs of the city. The suburbs were short of essential facilities. Working-class leaders complained that the commune was ready to close one of the few existing public nurseries on grounds of economy, yet spent lavishly on museums, the Scala, racing, flower shows, and other amusements for the rich.

It would be unfair to forget that there was a positive side to municipal action. It is easy to take for granted the enormous practical problems involved in the equipment of a modern city. The expansion of the city was profoundly influenced by new developments in urban transport and technology. In 1881 the first horse-drawn trams appeared in the streets. The network was rapidly extended and even stretched out beyond Milan to neighboring cities. Throughout the next 40 years the tram remained the essential means of communication for most Milanese; 1893 saw the first experiments with electric trams, and five years later the horse-drawn tram was a thing of the past. Although highly utilitarian, the tram could also be a source of pleasure. A board game based on the Milan-Monza ride was marketed with success. In the 1900s the futurist artists took the tram, with its noise, jolting motion, and blurred, changing vision of the world outside, as the symbol for the whole metropolitan experience.

The rapid electrification of the tram system was made possible by the early appreciation of the possibilities of electric power by a group of Milanese businessmen. The first experiments with electric street lighting date from the 1880s, although it only gradually replaced gas during the next 20 years. In 1885 the city began to build raised pedestrian pavements. The separation between street and pavement, traffic and pedestrians, is an important moment in the change of urban life styles. The practical and social functions of the street are divorced, and the unimpeded circulation of traffic becomes a norm to be upheld by the authorities and the police. Milan was readier than most Italian

FIGURE 18.   Trams and haycarts coming into the city. A reminder of the continuing importance of Milan's relationship with the surrounding countryside. (Raccolta Civica Bertarelli, Castello Sforzesco, Milan.)

cities to sacrifice the old patterns of civil intercourse to the modern concern with speed. The Milanese shared the northern suspicion of "loitering." The creation of new drains and a new system of water supply in 1888–89 completed the work of a decade of improvement. This was reflected during the 1890s, in spite of worsening economic conditions, by an improvement in public health. Both birth and death rates began to fall, but the latter fell faster. For the first time in history, the city actually became healthier than the countryside. Admittedly, there was still little room for complacency. Infant mortality, though below the national average, was still high. Down to 1910 about one in seven Milanese babies died in their first year.

As in so many 19th century cities immediate and pressing practical needs preoccupied the governing elite to the exclusion of long-term strategy. Business interests were hostile to any form of public intervention. The municipal government saw its task as that of mediating between private interests, not of assuming initiatives. To a large degree the city relinquished control over its own future shape and appearance. The first comprehensive plan of the city was drawn up between 1883 and 1885 by G. Beruto. The plan had grave faults; it failed to solve the problem of providing for adequate radial roads and of linking them to the main streets. However, it was the more progressive features of the plan, such as the building of a new piazza to relieve the Cathedral square of excessive traffic which drew opposition. The commission appointed by the commune to examine the plan rejected the proposal on the grounds that "it was not necessary and indeed might be harmful to take away from the Piazza Duomo the bustle, flow, and movement which is afforded by the tram service." More significant for the shape of the city as a whole was the decision to reduce the size of the building plots. The final report, drawn up by the industrialist Pirelli, argued that the rapid rise in the price of land dictated more intensive building. Yet by designing a larger number of minor streets, left unsettled by the original plan, the commission ensured that the value of the street frontages would rise still more rapidly. The arguments of the speculators had won.

Neither the modified Beruto plan nor its successor, drawn up in 1912, attempted to solve the problem of the diversion of traffic from the city center. By allowing the city to expand in all directions at once and by failing to reserve land elsewhere than in the center for civic uses they ensured by default that the problem would not be met. The planning of the center of Milan was bedevilled by the awkward alignment of the Cathedral square (east-west) with the main streets which ran southeast-northwest. Failure to resolve this difficulty meant that the *piazze* or *larghi* where streets met were mostly of polygonal shape, aesthetically unattractive and awkward for traffic.

The Beruto plan had tried to provide the city with adequate open space. Beruto wanted to protect the spacious gardens of the patrician palaces from building. The expectation was that they would pass to the city and become public parks. Here too speculative interests, not least those of the patrician landowners themselves, were responsible for cancelling one of the best features of the original plan. It is true that the surrender to the speculators was not total. A powerful property company, the Fondiaria Milanese, had planned intensive building development on the whole area surrounding the ducal castle. The commune refused to sanction the development and eventually concluded an agreement with a rival company, which preserved the large area behind the castle, formerly used as a parade ground, for use as a park. The Foro Bonaparte, fronting on the castle square, became one of the most fashionable locations for the residences of the new bourgeoisie. It was the commune which was responsible for ensuring that the houses were of uniform design; they were "solid, with severe and regular facades, high ceilings and massive doors." This liking for weight and solidarity was characteristic of Milanese bourgeois taste. Here, and in the neighboring area of Corso Magenta, the commune was successful in laying the foundations for the development of a residential quarter of high prestige, the only one which succeeded in rivalling the old center. The care taken here contrasts with the lack of interest in the working-class quarters. The new city outside the walls was left to grow haphazardly and without a plan.

MILAN'S ECONOMIC STRUCTURE

In 1880 manufacturing in Milan was still prevalently on a small scale. There was about one owner for every four workers. It was dependent on the city's thriving trade and its importance as a center of consumption. In Milan, as in Paris or New York, the city created the factories, not the factories the city. Writing in 1881, Giuseppe Colombo, one of the most intelligent and far-sighted entrepreneurs of the time, could still doubt the necessity and wisdom of developing big industries in Milan. First and foremost the city should remain a commercial and business center, the heart of a vast region fed by a network of "great arteries from the valley of the Rhine . . . to Egypt and India."[2] The opening of the St. Gothard railway tunnel in 1882 made Milan once again the center of trade with Germany and Switzerland. Italy was as yet in the first stages of the Industrial Revolution and had to import the machinery for the new factories. A great part of these essential imports came through Milan. Colombo, of course, did not deny the importance of manufacturing for Milan. Even in 1871 the proportion of industrial workers in the population was higher (29 percent) than in any other Italian city. What Colombo argued was that the small scale of Milanese industry was an advantage and that the success of Milan's economy was guaranteed by the diversity of its crafts. Prosperity could be more securely founded on a myriad of small, specialized workshops than on a few large factories. The clothing industry, which needed close contact with its customers and an intelligent, adaptable, working-force, was more suitable for the city than the large-scale production of basic textiles. A whole variety of tools and precision instruments could also be manufactured in small back street workshops. Social and political fears reinforced Colombo's preference for small industry over large. The former was less subject to sudden and catastrophic crises of unemployment, and a dispersed, highly skilled working class would be more manageable than the gray, undifferentiated masses of factory workers. Domestic and workshop industries would, it was believed, reinforce family ties, while factory industry destroyed them, and conservatives put great faith in the family as a bulwark against disorder and socialism. Colombo's version of the future of Milan was by no means wholly fallacious. In some respects he predicted its ultimate destiny. Eventually, like other great cities, Milan would become a city of offices rather than factories. Already by 1880, firms with factories in other parts of Lombardy preferred to have their head offices in Milan. The largest industrial firm of the day, Alessandro Rossi's wool manufacturing company, had its main factory far away at Schio, in the Veneto, but its headquarters were in Milan. Rossi was an indefatigable propagandist and lobbyist for the whole Italian textile industry, and his belief in the superior docility of rural workers was matched by an equally sharp perception that finance and politics required a base in the city.

However, Colombo in a sense saw too far ahead. In the period with which we are concerned, from 1880 down to the 1920s, Milan did develop as an industrial city. The number of workers employed in manufacturing increased from 47 percent of the active population in 1881 to 55 percent in 1911. Moreover, an increasing number worked in large factories, particularly after 1900. In the 1880s the largest category of workers were those in the clothing industry. They numbered about 30,000, five women to every one man, and nine out of ten worked either in small shops or at home. The greatest concentration of factory workers was in the textile industries, which employed about 9,000 workers all told, two thirds of them women. But the biggest and most modern textile plants were located in the satellite towns to the north of Milan, not in the city itself. Certain industries, like the great Pirelli rubber factory, had taken on symbolic importance. In times of trouble the news that Pirelli was laying off men, or that the Pirelli workers had come out on strike, would be regarded as of special significance. Increasingly the large factories set the tone for the whole economy, since much employment in the smaller firms depended on their orders.

At the same time capitalism modified the conditions of work even in the artisan enterprises. This was probably the major change in the city during the first 20 years after 1880. Tailors, cobblers, leatherworkers, and craftsmen in the furniture trade all found their livelihood threatened by cheaper methods of manufacture. Many town cobblers were out of work during the crisis years of 1890–94, thanks to the competition of large shoe factories using machinery. In 1891 the tailors complained that "the introduction of the machine and of the ready-made clothing trade is producing a serious alteration in the respective interests of employers and workers." Unemployment was rising and wages were falling, as unbridled competition forced small firms to cut wages in order to survive. Women dressmakers were even more bitter in their complaints. The peculiar demands of fashion meant that in the high season they might be forced to work halfway through the night, while in the dead season they could get no work at all. They were particularly prone to eye disease from working in bad light, and to tuberculosis from generally unhealthy working conditions and malnutrition. The only consolation was that many seamstresses gave up work when they got married.

WORKERS AND LABOR CONFLICT

Italian industry was backward and it was hampered by a shortage of raw materials and above all of coal. Employers were able to argue that it could only compete if wages were kept down to a minimum. They strenuously opposed any limitation on the hours of work, even for women and children. In 1877 the average length of the working day in the factories of Milan was calculated at 12 hours in winter and 14–15 hours in summer. Laborers in sand quarries, whose work was particularly heavy, might nevertheless do a 15 or 16 hour day. Moreover, the length of the day's work was often irregular and entirely at the discretion of the employer, who might either send his workers home early with reduced pay, or force them to work overtime without paying special rates. Even at the Pirelli works, generally cited as the model factory, the normal working day was 11 hours, not counting breaks, and the management reserved the right to shorten or lengthen it at their discretion.

Working-class militancy grew rapidly during the 1880s. The first big strikes among factory workers and builders had broken out during 1872, but they had been suppressed by the government. The victory of the Left in the general elections revived political activity among the working class. In 1881, following agitations in Milan and elsewhere, the suffrage was extended. A literacy test replaced the previous property qualification. In Milan the number of voters trebled, and many workers qualified. As union activity had been made more or less illegal, the most important form of working class organization had been in the "societies for mutual help" (friendly societies). Their aim was to provide a measure of insurance against calamities like sickness or prolonged unemployment. They were usually presided over by rich philanthropists. Extension of the suffrage made these societies of obvious political importance. Conservative and democratic patrons competed for their support. The General Workers' Association was headed by Visconti Venosta, an aristocrat and one of the leaders of the Right. It was rapidly outclassed by the *Consolato Operaio* (Workers' Consulate), which supported the radicals. In 1882 the type-founder Maffi ran for parliament in Milan and became the first working-class deputy. In time, however, during the 1880s a third tendency developed. Working-class leaders protested that they were only interested in bettering their condition, not in the political contest between different sections of the bourgeoisie. The influence of the radicals and of the Consulate itself rapidly declined. The *Partito Operaio* (Workers' Party), founded in 1882, refused even to admit bourgeois sympathizers to membership. It was organized on a federal principle and sought to give leadership to the various working class organizations. As a political party it was unsuccessful; in the 1889 local elections its candidates got only 780 votes. However, the principles for which it stood gained ground. The workers' societies became increasingly suspicious of all middle-class influence. The crucial question was whether the working-class societies would subsidize strikers. It was on this issue that many societies parted company with their patrons. Many of the societies, by agreeing to support strikes, turned themselves into "leagues of resistance," another name for trade unions.

The crisis years from 1889 to 1892 were decisive for the development of the working-class movement. The well-educated and well-organized printers were influential in Milan as in many other industrial cities in setting the pattern for working-class organization. They formed part of a national trade union founded as early as 1872, and it was their statutes which served as a model for the "leagues" founded in the 1890s. In 1890 the crisis forced the large engineering factories like the Elvetica and the Miani Silvestri to lay off workers. Unemployment spread to the small firms and it was reckoned that as many as a third of the 10,000 workers in engineering were out of work. At first the hostility of the workers was directed more against the government than the employers. Some of the workers' leaders accepted the latter's explanation that it was the government's failure to provide industry with orders, particularly for railway equipment, which was the cause of the crisis. However, as unemployment persisted and as the employers seized the opportunity to lower wages, this attitude changed. In 1891 the dismissal of forty workers by the Elvetica factory, which offered to re-employ them at a lower wage, triggered off a strike of all the engineering workers which lasted 12 days. The strikers complained that the employers were manipulating piecework rates to lower wages, and demanded the abolition of this method of payment. They also complained about the exaction of fines by the employers for faults in production which were not their responsibility, and about their attempt to impose a faster rhythm of work without compensation. The strike failed, and the engineers' union collapsed due to unemployment and to disputes between the various trades, but a precedent had been set. During the later 1890s, agitations in the engineering factories forced the employers for the first time to recognize workshop committees which could discuss grievances directly with them. The worker was no longer entirely at the mercy of the employer's interpretation of the rules.

One group of workers who had a particular sense of grievance were the bakers. Night work, which was general, ruined their health, family relations, and sex life. Very few got married and among those who did many were betrayed by their wives. "Crimes of honor" and suicide were both frequent among this group. It was a primitive, small-scale industry; few employers hired more than three workers and in a number the labor was supplied by the proprietor's own family. Most Milan bakeries were hot, dirty, and airless and it was the usual habit of employers to lock their workers in for the night. One of the most combative leaders of the Workers' Party, Casati, was a baker; and they were one of the earliest categories of workers to found unions. But these were generally either short-lived or ineffectual, and their attempts to abolish night working failed. This failure illustrates the general difficulty of organizing the poorer and more unfortunate sections of the working class. The bakers' occupation segregated them from the rest of society, and they had a bad reputation for honesty and reliability. Most were children of peasant families, originally recruited by labor contractors when they were less than ten years old. Bakers, builders, and some other groups of workers suffered particularly from the humiliating conditions in which they had to seek employment. They were hired in the piazze, often by intermediaries who had to be paid. It was largely to remedy this situation and to provide an honest and free employment exchange that the *Camera del Lavoro* (Chamber of Labor) was created in 1891. The Camera was modelled on similar French institutions, the *Bourses du travail*. At first it was a very moderate organization, whose aims, apart from serving as an employment exchange, were to collect statistics, and to arbitrate in labor disputes in order to avoid strikes and aid cooperation between workers and employers. Most of its funds came from a subsidy granted by the commune. However, very soon the bourgeoisie and the government grew nervous about the success of the Camera in Milan and elsewhere as meeting-places in which the workers of all trades could discuss their common problems. The Camera was dissolved by the government a first time in 1894, and although it was soon allowed to open again, from 1896 onwards the attitude of the authorities became much more unfavorable and the subsidy was cut off. After the 1898 riots it was closed again for 18 months. These government actions probably achieved the opposite of what was intended. They transformed the Camera from a semiofficial labor exchange into the central institution of working-class politics. After 1900 it was the Camera which had the main role in directing the strategy of labor, in deciding whether or not to negotiate with employers or to call sympathetic strikes. Its attitude was usually more radical than that of the major trade unions, which tended to represent the interests only of the skilled workers.

It is difficult to say how far the working class standard of living improved in the years down to the war. In the first two decades the chief influence on the standard of living was still the price of bread, with wage levels not altering much. Down to 1893 the worker benefited from cheap bread; but between 1894 and 1898 bread prices increased by 50 percent and he was reduced to misery. An indication of this is that the consumption of meat in the city as a whole fell by almost a third. After 1898 there was certainly some improvement. However, an inquiry in 1903 revealed that the majority of the workers earned less than two and one half lire a day, which was about the minimum needed to feed a family with two small children. As many as a quarter, moreover, earned less than one lira. It was vital for most families to have more than one cotton wage-earner. Women were much worse paid than men. At the Cantoni factory in 1892 the average daily wage for a woman cotton spinner was one and one fourth lire; for a man, two lire. The assumption was that a woman's wage was only a supplement to that of her husband or father. This was convenient for the clothing and textile industries, in which the majority of workers were women. Although women did sometimes play an active part in trade union movements, their poverty and dependence on their menfolk made it difficult for them to maintain membership of trade unions over a long period. The only strike in the large Cantoni textile factory at Legnano, between 1880 and 1900, for example, took place in the two departments where men were in the majority, and not in the others, mainly staffed by women. The industries in which female labor was predominant were also those in which unions were weak, which tended to accentuate their inferior condition. However, married women did perhaps benefit indirectly after 1900 from the higher wages earned by men. Men had never liked their wives going out to work, and as they earned more the number of married women working in factories declined. Even domestic service became less popular, and after 1905 the bourgeoisie of Milan for the first time had to come to grips with a servant shortage. This is one of the few unequivocal signs of a higher standard of living. Even on the eve of the war there had been little change in the patterns of working-class consumption. Two thirds of the budget of an average family still went for food, and another quarter on rent, heating, lighting, and clothing, leaving very little over for needs. For the Milanese working man to buy a newspaper was an extravagance. Better wages were absorbed to some extent by the necessities of modern city life; the worker spent more on tram tickets and gas heating, though the latter was perhaps a real benefit. In the meantime the prosperity of the bourgeoisie and the middle class grew more steadily. An indication of this is that the last two decades of the 19th century saw an increase of 67 percent in deposits in the Milan savings bank. A vast middle class clientele laid the foundations for a new consumer culture. By the war, thriving shopping areas had developed in the suburbs, like Corso Buenos Aires, as well as the center. This inequality underlies the political conflicts of the period.

MUNICIPAL POLITICS

During the years from 1880 to 1922 Milan cannot be identified with the dominance of any one political force. It was in turn a conservative city, a radical city, a socialist city, and even, at the end, a Fascist city; and from 1890 on, though never dominant, the Catholic movement was a political force whose importance no other party could overlook. Down to 1882 Milan was securely controlled by the conservative liberals, or "moderates." They, alone among the Milanese, had welcomed Cavour and the new kingdom of Italy without reserve. Their ideals were free enterprise, order, and representative government, confined however to the propertied and the educated. They were not too troubled by the "Piedmontization" of Lombardy's laws and institutions, or the subordination of local government to a centralized state. At least, this was true until 1876, when the Right lost national power. This had serious repercussions for the Milanese moderates. They lost control of the city's greatest center of financial power, the Cassa del Risparmio (Savings Bank). Henceforth the moderates too learned to look with distrust on government interference and to champion local liberties.

Their opponents called the moderates the *consorteria*. This indicated a tightly-knit network of powerful families. They called themselves "the aristocracy of birth, wealth, and talent." The Milanese nobility were not exclusive as a class. Rich industrialists, at least in the second generation, adopted the patrician style of life, competing for the best chefs and the best boxes at the Scala. Some, like the textile industrialists Cantoni and Ponti, married into the aristocracy. The heart of Milanese high society, and the moderates' true political headquarters was the Union club. When money was to be raised for their newspaper, *La Perseveranza*, the owners would simply hold a quiet get-together in the club, and their friends would be sure to oblige.

In the absence of strong parties, newspapers had great importance as centers of political activity. The conservatives had the *Perseveranza*; the radicals had the *Secolo*. The two newspapers were bitterly and totally opposed. In 1898 the *Perseveranza* approved and perhaps even instigated the closure of the *Secolo* and the arrest of its staff. While the *Perseveranza* was exclusive and old-fashioned (its circulation became something of a joke), the *Secolo* was popular and forward-looking. It owed its popularity not so much to its radical political campaigns as to the fact that the paper regularly ran two serialized novels at the same time. However, during the last decade of the century the *Secolo's* circulation (about 100,000) was rapidly being overhauled by that of a third newspaper, the *Corriere della Sera*.

The entry of the working class into politics shifted the balance of power within Milan and posed new political problems which the city's elite were ultimately unable to solve. Yet divisions among their opponents prolonged the tenure of power of the moderates, who had controlled the commune ever since 1860. In 1876 the Left were already successful in the general elections; they elected three deputies out of five including two radicals, and one of the Right's leading figures, Visconti Venosta, was defeated. It seemed likely that the democrats would soon capture the town hall, but instead they had to wait another 23 years. One reason for this lay in the peculiar position of the Catholic Church and its supporters. After the annexation of Rome in 1870 the Pope forbade his loyal supporters to vote in general elections. Although not all obeyed, the effect in Milan, a city of powerful Catholic traditions, was considerable. However the prohibition did not apply to local elections; in consequence the radicals were never as successful in these as they were in elections to parliament. In addition, it seems likely that many middle-class Milanese preserved their shrewd and cautious business sense when voting. They were willing to send radicals to parliament, but they were not quite so certain that they wanted to see them in control of the city. One curious device probably helped the moderates to maintain power. The rules allowed voters to vote for "mixed lists" of candidates from opposing parties, and the newspaper which had the greatest influence among the bourgeoisie, the *Corriere della Sera*, regularly published its own list of recommended candidates. It favored the election of businessmen, even if they supported the radicals, and opposed both the more extreme left and the Catholic candidates.

Milanese businessmen played an active part in city politics. The commission appointed by the commune to discuss Beruto's 1884 town plan included three leading industrialists, Colombo, Pirelli, and Prinetti, and it was Pirelli who drew up the final report. In the 1895 local elections 19 out of 84 candidates were either industrialists or bankers, and 16 were elected. No other profession was so successful: the lawyers had 26 candidates, but fewer won. Although the leading industrialists usually supported the Right, the smaller employers, particularly in the suburbs, generally backed the radicals. Taxation was an ever-present grievance. Particularly in the years from 1887 to 1896 when the prime minister of Italy, Crispi, embarked on an ambitious program of high military expenditure and colonial expansion in Africa, the Milanese bourgeoisie regarded the central government with considerable hostility. These were also the years of the great bank scandals, with leading politicians heavily implicated. These events greatly reinforced the Milanese conviction that their city was the "moral capital" of Italy, with the implication that Rome was the immoral capital. It would be hard to deny that Milan had the most varied, lively, and representative political life of any Italian city at this period; the newly founded Italian socialist party made Milan its headquarters.

The radicals and the socialists were best placed to take advantage of the mood of hostility to the government; they were not afraid to attack the state, the army, and the monarchy. But most of the moderates also opposed the imperialist policies of Crispi, all the more since the latter claimed to be a man of the Left. The opposition of the "state of Milan" played a great part in weakening Crispi. After the disastrous defeat of the Italian invasion of Abyssinia at Adua, mass riots in the streets of Milan more or less forced his resignation. On this occasion for once the Milanese elite were in agreement with the aims if not the methods of popular agitation. Crispi's fall, however, ruptured the unity of a front which had stretched from the moderates to the socialists. In 1897–98, as the rapidly rising prices of bread and rice brought social tensions to a new pitch, there was no longer a scapegoat to divert popular hostility from the city's rulers. The Milanese moderates fully supported the national government of Di Rudini. Both the city and the national government, faced with the steady advance of socialism and the revival of the republican party, increasingly gave way to panic. They became convinced that Milan was the center of the subversive opposition and that it was there it had to be crushed. In 1898 they mistook the outbreak of bread riots and other disturbances in various parts of Italy for the beginnings of an organized revolution. It was the government's own action in recalling two classes of conscripts to the colors which finally caused popular indignation to boil over. The call-up deprived many families of their most active wage-earners at a time when hardship was already acute. The socialists issued a manifesto attacking the government, but warning the workers not to be pushed into a revolt which would only end in massacre. It was the arrest of the socialists who were distributing this manifesto among the workers of the Pirelli factory during their lunch break which sparked off the conflict.

THE RIOTS OF 1898

The 1898 riots were the result of a complicated interaction between the working class of the factories, traditional forms of popular protest, and official reaction. The trouble started with the workers of the Pirelli and the neighboring large factories in the quarter near the station. Three years before Pirelli had complacently boasted that his workers were drawn from ignorant women and peasants who were unresponsive to socialist influence. Pirelli's confidence was misplaced. He had had a relatively good reputation among the employers of his day. Nevertheless in 1898 the Socialist Dell'Avalle wrote him an open letter in which he refuted his claim that only "outside agitators" could disturb the harmony of the factory. "The agitation is produced by life inside, which is hell." Discipline was rigid and sometimes brutal, and "our miserable pay does not allow us enough food to make up for the exhaustion of the organism."[3] In consequence, more than half the factory's workers had been affected by illness during the year. In spite of great difficulties put in their way by the management, the socialists had finally succeeded in organizing a league of rubber workers on May 3, only three days before the outbreak of the riots. The socialist message had appealed particularly to the women workers at the Pirelli, aided by the eloquence of Turati's companion Anna Kuliscioff, who had addressed meetings there. In the labor force as a whole, women only slightly outnumbered men, but in the league they contributed 700 out of 1,000 members. It was the novelty of this militancy which made it particularly explosive.

On the second day of trouble, May 7, a column of workers tried to penetrate from the suburbs to the center of the city. On being turned back by the troops, a group of demonstrators seized hold of a couple of trams to build a primitive barricade. This set off three days of sporadic fighting between rioters and the army, after the city had been placed under martial law. Fear of the authorities led them greatly to exaggerate

FIGURE 19. Trams used as barricades: Corso Venezia, 1898. (Raccolta Civica Bertarelli, Castello Sforzesco, Milan.)

the gravity of the outbreak. In the whole four days of disorders, only one soldier was killed and about 12 wounded, while civilian casualties probably amounted to about 500. A grotesque incident took place on the last day of the riots. Wild rumors were by then current of bands of students from Pavia or exiles from Switzerland on their way to attack the city. The army, on the strength of one such rumor, bombarded and stormed the Capuchin convent outside Porta Monforte under the impression that it was a revolutionary stronghold. Inside they found only the monks and 30 or 40 terrified old beggars, whom they solemnly arrested and escorted to the police station.

There was much controversy at the time about the nature of the riots and the responsibility for them. To some they were the work of outside agitators; others, like the editor of the *Corriere della Sera*, Torelli Violler, argued that the rioters came prevalently from the ranks of the recent immigrants to the city, employed in low-paid industry or casual labor, and that women and boys outnumbered grown men, while the main body of the organized working class remained quiescent. As a study by Louise Tilly has shown, neither assumption was correct. Among the cobblers immigrants, working in the cheap trade, were better represented than older residents. The brick makers, an underpaid and marginal group, living on the edge of the city, were also heavily involved. On the other hand, the skilled workers in printing, the making of precision instruments, and the luxury trades (all trades which were still carried on in the center of the city) were less affected. Native Milanese were admittedly only a minority among the rioters, but then so they were in the labor force as a whole. Many of the rioters were comparatively well-paid metal and engineering workers. What emerges is the breadth of working-class participation. The riots were neither the work of the mob, nor, unlike the great revolutions of 1789–1848, were they prevalently the work of the skilled and native urban artisans. It was the refusal of the government to allow the industrial working class to organize freely which drove them into a form of protest which the socialist leaders regarded as archaic. In spite of the differences in social composition, reminiscences of 1848 must have been important; the fiftieth anniversary of the rising had been celebrated not long before. The barricades were most numerous in the popular quarters of Porta Garibaldi and Porta Ticinese, where, as we have seen, popular traditions were strongest.

MILANESE SOCIALISM: FROM TURATI TO MUSSOLINI

The socialist leader, Turati, had tried to avoid the outbreak because he quite correctly saw that the authorities and a part of the bourgeoisie were looking for an opportunity to outlaw his party. Indeed the bourgeoisie's initial reaction to the events was one of "ferocious jubilation"; they had terrorized the rank and file of the popular movement, and the leaders, not only socialists but also radicals, were all in jail. Martial law was maintained for six months. Even the Catholic opposition was charged with complicity. The leader of the intransigent Catholics, Don Davide Albertario, was jailed; the articles he had written in defense of the peasants had made him particularly unpopular with the aristocracy. But divisions soon emerged among the Milanese elite as it became clear that the strategy of repression was meeting with great resistance. The moderates had overreached themselves, and in the 1899 municipal elections they lost control of the commune for the first time.

Neither side was anxious to repeat the experience of 1898. The rebels had learned the futility of direct action without prior organization; while from the moderates' point of view repression, though successful in immediate terms, had been a political failure in long-term perspective. A new economic upswing took the edge off both popular desperation and bourgeois apprehension. In the violent years after the war, men would look back on the prewar era with nostalgia as an untroubled peaceful time. However, even the prosperous years from 1900 to 1914 were by no means free from crisis. Milan was a divided city, in which class conflict always threatened to get out of hand. In the years 1901–1904 the troops were called out nine times to aid the police in dealing with disturbances, and the ten years from 1904 to 1914 saw four general strikes. Nevertheless, Milan became identified with the growth of a reasonable socialism, which put its faith in reforms rather than immediate revolutionary action. In the late 19th century socialists and democrats shared a common belief in the inevitability of progress. They believed in the doctrines of men like Herbert Spencer, who had tried to transfer Darwin's evolutionary schema from the natural to the social world. They felt that science as well as sentiment was on their side. Their world was one in which literature shaded off into politics. Rebellion against bourgeois conformity, and the conviction that literature, even poetry, must be realistic, "positive," and take the condition of the people as its theme, were the stages by which one passed into the other. The painters, too, shared this frame of mind. Paintings like Pellizza da Volpedo's splendid *The Fourth Estate,* or Pusterla's "*Porta Nuova soup kitchens,*" are documents of their social commitment. The leader of Milanese socialism, Filippo Turati, came out of this environment, and for some years aspired to be a poet, though without great success. Turati's background was an unusual one for a socialist; he was the son of a government Prefect. The father also wrote verse and seems to have been tolerant of the son's political views. Turati first came to sympathize with socialism when, as a 19 year old student at

Bologna university, he attended the trial of the Internationalist Andrea Costa. But the event which really changed his life was his encounter with the beautiful Russian revolutionary, Anna Kuliscioff, in 1884. She did much to clarify his political beliefs, and her love enabled him to overcome the suicidal melancholia which had previously afflicted him. For the next 40 years they formed an extraordinary partnership, in which Anna was often the directing influence. Both had a merciless eye for the pretentious and the insincere, the demagogue and the careerist. The young Mussolini, who impressed many, failed to conquer their salon.

Turati enjoyed enormous popularity because he combined great intelligence with equal warmth and passion. However, although he was the leading figure in Italian socialism for 20 years, his hold over the socialists of his own city was insecure and frequently contested. Many complained that he made too many compromises with the government and the bourgeoisie, that his belief in a peaceful evolution toward socialism was too optimistic, his culture too remote from the people. The other side of Milanese socialism can be personified in the journalist Paolo Valera. Unlike Turati, Valera came from a very poor background. His father sold matches and his mother was a seamstress. Turati, who was quite fond of him, nonetheless thought his politics were those of "a rabble-rouser and a mountebank"; Valera, on his side, accused Turati of not being, like him, a true "man of the crowd." An effective writer, who specialized in lurid and somewhat prurient exposés of vice, crime, and degradation — particularly prostitution — seen as the consequences of capitalism, Valera knew how to rouse indignation. He had more serious gifts as a reporter as well; he was effective in publicizing cases of low wages and bad work conditions, and he wrote the best journalistic account of the repression of the 1898 riots. In the years before the war the young provincial from the Romagna, Benito Mussolini, at first awkward and ill at ease in the big city, suddenly shot into prominence as the rising hope of the revolutionary left. He and Valera cooperated in publishing a review, and Mussolini's characteristic rhetoric would seem to have owed something to the older man.

For some years the small minority of Milanese factory workers who were active members of the socialist party accepted Turati's strategy of gradual reform. Another revolutionary outsider, the Neapolitan intellectual Arturo Labriola, briefly fired the Milanese proletariat with his syndicalist enthusiasm for the general strike, but the failure of the 1904 general strike dampened their enthusiasm. It was Giolitti's decision to invade Libya, and the hardship and unemployment caused by the financial results of the Libyan war, which led the Milanese socialists to swing from Turati to Mussolini's brand of revolutionism. Turati never recovered his grip on the party, although when the socialists won the municipal elections in 1914, the mayor and administration of the commune belonged to his reformist group. Mussolini broke with the party in 1914 over the issue of Italy's entry into the war. Unlike Turati, Mussolini was unquestionably "a man of the crowd," and though the socialists had the backing of the majority they were vulnerable to his new, violent style of street politics. In May 1915, when Mussolini and his friends roused the traditionally patriotic petty bourgeoisie of clerks and shopkeepers, together with dissident groups of workers, to demonstrate for Italy's entry into the war, the socialists lost control of the piazza. This was a forewarning of postwar defeat by the organized strong-arm tactics of the Fascists.

Fascism had its headquarters in Milan. It is clearly not possible here to analyze the phenomenon as a whole, and its local roots have unfortunately received curiously little study. What one can say is that Fascism was a blow to the order and traditions of the native Milanese bourgeoisie, although the latter had a decisive part in promoting its victory. The Milanese business elite retained the substance of property and power; but a bourgeoisie which embraced Fascism could no longer claim to exercise its hegemony in the name of thrift, prudence and respectability. Fascism was largely a movement of the uprooted, of the thousands of provincial immigrants in search of fortune; several of its leaders came from the bohemian milieu which had formerly contributed so much to the left. The values of such men were profoundly different from those of the old Milan. What kind of men were responsible for the fortunes of Milanese industry? We know little, unfortunately, about the host of small businessmen who made a vital contribution to the Milanese economy. But without surrendering to the mythology of the "heroes of industry" we can still recognize the importance of the leaders of Milanese business in seizing and creating new opportunities.

INDUSTRIALISTS AND MERCHANTS

In the earlier 19th century the merchants of Milan had been notable for their staid traditionalism. Contemporaries complained that they were too slow to take advantage of the new opportunities offered by international trade, let alone to invest in industry. It was not among them but rather among the lesser country merchants that the nucleus of the future class of entrepreneurs was to be found. These men, dealers in cloth, silk, and corn, usually with a farm or two of their own, continually on the move between the thickly clustered small towns and villages of the Lombard plain, first organized domestic production by handloom weavers and spinners and later built the first factories using machinery. The industries were concentrated north of Milan, in and near the foothills, where water power and labor were cheap.

Costanzo Cantoni, the founder of one of Milan's largest textile firms, started out in this way. In 1820, on inheriting the capital accumulated by his father through trade and agriculture, he invested part of it in the purchase of looms which he hired out to the domestic cottonworkers in the neighborhood of Gallarate. Fourteen years later he was able to buy a mill and install machinery for cotton spinning. The enterprise prospered, and by 1845 the original 500 spindles had been increased to 3,500. However, the 1848 revolution and the war between Piedmont and Austria which followed caught the firm at a difficult moment, when Costanzo had invested heavily in new machinery of English make and imported skilled workmen from Switzerland.

Costanzo, shaken, withdrew from the direction of the firm in favor of his son Eugenio. Eugenio, as was typical of the second generation of entrepreneurs, had travelled in Switzerland, Germany, and England to acquire technological expertise. He was an ambitious and ruthless businessman who managed to combine constant attention to technical improvements in the cotton industry with involvement in many other kinds of enterprise. He invested heavily and successfully in the construction of the local railways. Later in life, he even interested himself in the import and sale of English lavatories. In 1868 he set up a small factory on the outskirts of Milan to produce handkerchiefs. This he entrusted to the management of Ernesto De Angeli, who was to become another one of Milan's leading industrialists. In 1872 he allied with other leading industrialists to found a joint stock company, although he and his father retained a majority shareholding. His plans for expansion required fresh inputs of capital, but he did not intend that going public should in any way restrict his prerogatives as chief of the firm. In fact, success at this point seems to have gone to his head. He started buying up small and inefficient factories with the intention of modernizing them, and ignored the first warning signs of recession. By 1877 he was in serious trouble; criticism by the smaller shareholders of his total failure to observe the rules of a public company had become more and more vociferous, and in the end forced his resignation. Among other things, he had sold one of the company's factories to another firm of which he himself was a co-owner without obtaining the approval of the board, and they now sued him for damages. Cantoni had been defeated, in spite of his majority shareholding, because under the rules of the company no single shareholder could control more than five votes. However, this defeat was only temporary; Cantoni solved the crisis by the simple expedient of distributing a large block of his shares to faithful supporters who gave him a secure majority. This, too, was quite illegal. Led by Alessandro Rossi, the cotton industrialists got a protective tariff from the government in 1878, and this helped to revive prosperity. By the end of the century the company could compete successfully with the most modern cotton firms, and it was exporting 60 percent of its production.

Cantoni, like several other second-generation industrialists, made it into the aristocracy. Although in 1848 he had been seized by patriotic enthusiasm and had briefly volunteered to serve with Garibaldi, in 1857 he married an Austrian baroness, the daughter of the emperor's private secretary. In 1871 he was made a baron himself by King Victor Emmanuel. Cantoni's attitude to labor was one of rigid and obstinate conservatism with paternalist overtones. He was willing to spend money on providing his women workers with a rudimentary education, but he was a leading opponent of legislation to limit child labor. He even opposed a compromise suggested by the more progressive Pirelli, making it at least illegal for children to work at night, on the grounds that it would make it impossible to resist foreign competition.

Commerce as well as industry was revolutionized during the later 19th century. By the 1890s, as we have seen with Cantoni, the Lombard textile firms were looking beyond Italy for their markets, but in many cases they lacked the expertise needed to market their goods effectively. One entrepreneur, Enrico Dell'Acqua, was struck by the unexplored possibilities of the South American market; the larger number of Italian immigrants would aid the diffusion of Italian goods. Dell'Acqua was another entrepreneur whose methods were often somewhat too unorthodox to meet with the approval of his shareholders, and he went through some bad moments during the crisis of the early 1890s. But he won success by sending his commercial travellers deep into the interior of Brazil and Argentina, thus bypassing the old commercial houses of the coastal cities. Nearly all the Lombard textile firms came to use his sales organization.

The pioneer of Milan's retail revolution was another country merchant of humbler origins than the Cantonis. Ferdinando Bocconi joined his father and his brother as a travelling cloth salesman, based on the town of Lodi, after spending only three years in school. The family began to sell ready-made clothing in Milan in 1850, when Bocconi was 14. In 1865, after patriotic service against the brigands in the south of Italy, he married and opened his first shop. Twelve years later he risked his big coup when be bought and adapted a hotel in the center of town. At first it had a French name, *Aux villes d'Italie*, to suggest kinship with the great Parisian department stores, although nationalistic criticism soon forced him to translate the sign into Italian.

By 1879 the store had 300 assistants in 30 departments. Ten years later he opened an even more grandiose store in the Piazza Duomo itself at a cost of 5.5 million lire. Although clothes were its main specialty, the store also sold toys, scent, and furniture. The department store, moreover, was only one facet of Bocconi's activities. He developed a huge mail order business, again imitating the French, and his illustrated catalogues were diffused throughout Italy. He was an industrialist as well, employing 1,200 workers to make clothes for his shops; counting the shop assistants, now nearly a thousand, as well, he was the largest employer in Milan in 1890.

Bocconi's unpopularity matched his importance. He was widely hated, though also admired, not perhaps because he was more ruthless than other employers, but because his activities were particularly influential in bringing about the ruin of small men. Many small shopkeepers were driven out of business by his more modern methods, and it was his ready-made clothes which were cutting into the custom of the small tailors and dressmakers, whose complaints we have heard. He was violently attacked by Paolo Valera for exacting one year's unpaid work from his apprentices. Perhaps as a means of disarming criticism, Bocconi was prodigal in his gifts to charity, and in 1902 he founded a "commercial university" in commemoration of the death of his son, killed at Adua in Africa. In his blend of avidity, patriotism, and philanthropy, Bocconi was one of the most representative figures of the age. Men like him identified with the city, as the source of their fortunes; but their allegiance was to a new Milan built in their image and they were as impatient of tradition as of other obstacles. When the clearance of the old houses in front of the cathedral was finally about to be completed, the enthusiasm of Bocconi was so great that he rushed up, seized a pick from the hands of a worker and gave a symbolic blow to the ruins. As he said, "It seemed like working for myself, like preparing the scene in which my excited imagination already saw the future kingdom of my activity." It was hardly just fantasy, since Bocconi had already bought up a large plot of houses due for demolition, on which he later built his store.

The retail revolution in some respects did more to change the face of the city than the industrial revolution itself. In 1860 the great majority of purchases were still made in open markets or from travelling salesmen. Slowly, however, the development of shops, particularly in the fashionable center, began to change the habits of Milanese society. By the 1880s the old markets were being complained of as "indecent sheds which still pollute many parts of the city": street salesmen became suspect to the police as semivagrants who obstructed the traffic. Journalists were already writing sentimental pieces about their disappearance. Here, too, the working class preserved old habits longer. For them the market was still essential, and the shop remained a part of bourgeois living.

In the early days of Milanese business (since 1848) another group had been even more important than the provincials in making up for the city merchants' lack of enterprise. Foreigners, mainly Swiss and Germans, were quick to sense the possibilities of the city and its hinterland for industrial as well as commercial enterprise. Many settled in Milan and became part of its economic elite. The Falcks were among the most successful of these immigrant families. G. E. Falck came to Lombardy in the 1830s from Alsace, then one of the most advanced industrial regions of Europe. His technical advice had been sought by local iron manufacturers, and he soon became a partner of one of the leading industrialists in the field, G. Rubini. Although the partnership lasted only ten years, the alliance of the Falck family with the already established Rubini remained a cornerstone of their rise to wealth and power. G. E. Falck's son, Enrico, was converted to Catholicism and married Rubini's daughter. In 1871 he entered into partnership with another local family, the Redaelli, to purchase a factory near Lecco, in the mountains north of Milan. In the third generation, with the second G. E. Falck, they became one of the most important families in the city. Falck had the intelligence to perceive that changed circumstances had made it more profitable to locate factories near Milan rather than in the mountains, the traditional center of the Lombard iron industry. Foreign competition had rendered the old methods based on the use of charcoal and local iron ore hopelessly uneconomical; it was therefore no longer necessary to be near the forests and mines of the Alpine region. Instead factories in the environs of Milan, using scrap metal and imported German coal, would benefit from reduction in transport costs and from the easy access to the market provided by the city's engineering industries. Even so, most industrialists were hesitant to take the risk. They were afraid to lose the traditional skills of the workers of the mountain districts, but Falck trusted that the railway would bring the ironworkers of Bergamo and Como to Milan. He was fortunate in making his move at a time (1895–96) when the economy was about to revive after a severe slump, and he seized the opportunity to introduce the latest technology. His factory was the first in Italy to manufacture basic steel by the Martin-Siemens process on a large scale. By 1905 his ambition had grown further. The original site of his factory to the east of Milan had grown too small and he chose a new one, at Sesto S. Giovanni, halfway between Milan and Monza. This was the axis of the city's most rapid development, and had the best rail services. Not only Falck, but other leading industrialists, Breda (locomotives) and Morelli (electrical engineering) built factories in the area. Sesto became the industrial heart of the new conurbation. It had no links with the past. Its whole existence was bound up with the factory. Formally Sesto is not part of Milan even today, but with the multiplication of such settlements in the hinterland, the whole definition of the city was called into question.

By the 1900s it was clear that heavy industry could only prosper through concentration and combination. Falck carried out a merger with two other firms in 1906. The new company had four factories and 2,400 workers, about half in the Milan area. At the same time Falck became a public figure: he was the leading spirit in the foundation of the association of metal manufacturers. In both these initiatives the Rubini connection was again of vital importance. The Rubini firm was one of those involved in the merger, and Giulio Rubini was an important politician who twice became Minister for the Treasury. As such, he could do much to help Falck and his association, who recorded that "he always used his legitimate influence in favor of our industry."

There was nothing flashy about the Falcks' rise to fortune. It was a success story of the kind that most pleased the Milanese. They prided themselves on their hard-headed caution, and distrusted the ambitious speculator who made money too rapidly. For a long time, indeed, Milanese investors had been reluctant to lend money on any security except land. Only gradually was their distrust overcome. In 1860, the organization of capital in Milan had still been backward in comparison with that of some other regions of Italy; there were fewer joint stock companies in Milan than in Turin, Genoa, or even Florence, and they were mostly small. Most new companies were in utilities rather than industry. After 1870 the confidence of investors grew, and an active market in industrial shares developed. By 1880, the mentality of the Milanese business world had changed profoundly. A new generation of true industrialists was beginning to achieve prominence. It became more and more necessary to receive a solid educational grounding before setting out on a career in industry. The era of the self-taught man was drawing to a close. The famous *Politecnico*, founded in 1863, was the nursery of Milan's entrepreneurial class, and Giuseppe Colombo, who became its rector, their tutor and guide. The complacency and lack of curiosity of which earlier observers had complained was now replaced by an eager desire to profit from the latest foreign innovations. A period of foreign travel, in Germany, England, and now frequently also the United States, was more than ever an indispensable feature of the aspiring industrialist's apprenticeship. The importance of formal education in the industrialist's career is reflected in the way that *l'ingegnere* (the engineer) came to be a standard way of referring to the boss.

G. B. Pirelli was the most brilliant representative of the new type of educated industrialist. He studied with Colombo, and owed much to his encouragement. They remained close friends and business associates. In 1870 he won a scholarship to study abroad. The secrets of the new rubber industry were at this time jealously guarded, and Pirelli could only discover them by methods bordering on industrial espionage. At one time he tried to enroll as an ordinary worker in a foreign factory to learn the processes but was refused employment by a rightly suspicious management. At first he employed a French technician in his factory, but he proved incompetent and had to be dismissed. It is a sign of the readiness of the Milanese to take calculated risks that Pirelli was able to find investors willing to risk 200,000 lire to back a new industry and to make him managing director at the age of 24. Nevertheless the early years of the firm were very difficult. He overspent on putting up his factory, which employed 40 workers, and had trouble raising the extra capital. His associates were discontented and he had to explain to them that in a new line of industry immediate profits were not to be expected. As a condition of their continued support, they forced him to give up the teaching job which he held at the *Politecnico* and to go and live next door to the factory. His son and successor, Alberto, recalled that "as children, we heard the throbbing of the machines on the other side of our bedroom wall." In 1874 Pirelli admitted that "the labor force is disorganized; a part of the capital has been lost, and a fraction of our clientele has been alienated." However, under Pirelli's day-to-day personal supervision conditions improved rapidly. By 1882 the firm had a turnover of 1.5 million lire and had won its first export markets in Switzerland. Even the most grudging partners could hardly complain when the average profits for the decade worked out at 7.5 percent. Pirelli knew how to appeal to the Milanese mentality. His 1880 report declared that "Our industry by nature progresses in stages. We started by taking small steps, wisely and prudently," only when progress was assured did he move on to "new conquests."[4]

Pirelli's success continued to be helped by Colombo. It was the older man who realized the importance of Edison's inventions and obtained the patent to exploit them in Italy. Pirelli became Colombo's partner in the enterprise which in 1883 gave Milan the first electric power station in Europe. It was the expansion in the use of rubber for insulating electric wires and telephone cables which ensured the immense fortune of the industry. In 1884 Pirelli bought a ship from England for laying underwater cables with money provided by the government. State patronage provided him with many lucrative contracts for linking Italy by cable with Sicily and Sardinia, South America, and her African colonies. The enterprise won Pirelli not only profits—but applause— for patriotism and "the promotion of civilization." One would be wrong to mock at Pirelli's sense of public and patriotic duty, even if he did make it coincide with profit. Like several other entrepreneurs, Pirelli had fought for Garibaldi in his youth, and it was his interest in the navy which had first involved him in the uses of rubber for pumping out sunken ships. Cables and wires were only part of the Pirelli business. The needs of modern life and leisure were turned to account in all sorts of ways. Milanese rain helped to swell the sales of rubber mackintoshes, and in 1890 the development of the bicycle tire started Pirelli off on the line of manufacture which was to make the company a household word. It was not without difficulty, however, that Alberto Pirelli convinced his fellow industrialist Giovanni Agnelli to use Pirelli tires on his new Fiat cars. But by 1914 success was assured.

By 1919 Pirelli had become Italy's first "multinational" company. It had subsidiaries in England, Spain, and Argentina, and rubber plantations in Malaya. It was a characteristically modern firm in the use which it made both of scientific research and of advertising. Pirelli's interests extended into banking, with part control of Milan's second largest bank, the *Credito Italiano*, and into the electrical in- dustry. Alberto Pirelli, the founder's son, was one of the oligarchy of industrial and financial magnates who were to dominate Italian business between the wars.

Whatever the national or international concerns of Milanese busi- nessmen, they remained strongly tied to the city. Their outlook re- mained Milanese rather than Italian; they were confident, often with good reason, that other parts of Italy would have to conform to what they thought and did. Up till World War I, the record of the involve- ment of Milanese industrialists in politics and civic affairs is impres- sive. Some of the leading political personalities of the city, like Colombo or Prinetti, were men with direct experience of industry. Colombo's influence on Milan, as we have seen, was multifarious. He was director of the Polytechnic for 46 years; he represented Milan in parliament for 14 and became Minister for the Treasury; and he was responsible for bringing electric power to Milan. Ironically, it was this last achievement which was responsible for overcoming one of the major difficulties which Colombo had foreseen would hinder the development of large- scale industry in the Milan area. The possibility, developed at the end of the 1890s, of transporting hydroelectric power, for example, was as much a legislative as a technical problem; it raised very complicated issues about water rights, and landlords demanded compensation for the passage of cables across their lands.

Another leading industrialist, Ponti (wool and hemp manufacture), became mayor from 1905 to 1909, when the moderates recovered power. This was the Indian summer of the industrialists in politics. By now, some industrialists had become aware that unrestrained speculation on building land was not to their advantage. It raised the costs of building factories and contributed to working class discontent. Ponti's administration in fact carried out an enlightened policy of public purchase of building land, and did at least more than its predecessors for working-class housing. Here was a sign that the more enlightened industrialists, under pressure from the socialists, had come to see that they could not simply unload the social costs of industrialization onto the workers and the community. In national politics, however, the influence of the Milanese industrialists remained extremely conservative. They opposed the more progressive policies of Giolitti, who instead received much support from the industrialists of Turin.

THE PRESS AND PUBLIC OPINION

The Milanese industrialists' hostility to Giolitti was shared and expressed by the city's major newspaper, the *Corriere della Sera*, and its editor, Luigi Albertini. The *Corriere* was conservative in its outlook, but its conservatism was of a more open and modern kind than that of the *Perseveranza*. It aimed to be the newspaper not of a small elite but of the wide middle-class public. Like the *Times* it sought to reflect public opinion as much as to influence it and was careful not to get too far out of step with the prejudices of its readers. The ownership of the *Corriere* from 1895 onward was in the hands of a group of industrialists; half the shares belonged to the textile industrialist Silvio Crespi, while Pirelli and another textile industrialist, De Angeli, held most of the remainder. In the later 1890s the owners disagreed with the founder and editor of the paper, Torelli Violler, over the wisdom of the repressive policies pursued by successive governments. Torelli was strongly opposed to these policies, but shortly after the 1898 riots, feeling perhaps that his readers were out of sympathy with him, he gave way and surrendered the editorship to the reactionary Domenico Oliva. Oliva's reign, however, was shortlived. The Milanese elite, as we have seen, started to have doubts about the wisdom of repression. Although the former mayor Negri and the *Perseveranza* wanted the emergency restrictions on political activity to be made permanent, Colombo took a much more enlightened line. He pointed out that "no one reasons on an empty stomach," and that repression without a search for remedies to poverty would be bound to bring disaster. By 1900 the owners of the *Corriere* could see that the political climate was changing and that Oliva's outlook was out of date. They replaced him provisionally with a young man, Albertini, whose previous experience had been on the business and technical rather than on the journalistic side of the paper. This was an unusual background for an editor at the time, but Albertini soon revealed great gifts. Under his editorship the circulation of the *Corriere* increased from about 85,000 to 350,000 on the eve of the war; during the war itself it reached 600,000. Although the *Corriere* still looked to Milan for much of its readership, it had become Italy's first true national newspaper. Although Albertini was not a native Milanese, the qualities which brought him success were very much those of his adopted city. He lived in the Foro Bonaparte, in the heart of bourgeois Milan. He imposed the standards and criteria of industry on the still leisurely and Bohemian world of Italian journalism. No industrialist was more insistent than Albertini on precision, efficiency, and punctuality. Like the industrialists, he travelled widely to acquaint himself with the latest inventions. In the period before he became editor he had already revolutionized the printing of the *Corriere* by buying a rotary press of the type used by the *Times*, which had to be installed by English workers. With this he was able to print a 12-page Sunday supplement with 2 pages in color, and to this he soon added a supplement for children. But all this would not have been enough if Albertini had not had a keen sense of his public and their demands, and an eye for talent. He learned and improved upon Torelli's perception that, in order to succeed, the *Corriere* had to be a family newspaper, and that family newspapers are not sold by politics alone. Sport, exploration, prize competitions, and fashion all had their place and the leading writers of the day, like D'Annunzio, wrote for the literary third page. Albertini was a cultured man who once confided that, after all, the "inner life" was more important than work, ambition, or money; he married the daughter of the poet Giacosa. His major interest, however, was in the world of politics and history; he ended his life by writing a standard history of the origins of the first World War. As editor, his first concern was the improvement of the news service. He was the first Italian editor to have a regular telephone service from London, and he encouraged a "star system" among his foreign correspondents.

The *Corriere* had serious limitations, but they were those of Milan itself, or at least of her bourgeoisie and middle class. The newspaper reflected a city open to the wider world, international in its interests, but still provincial in its values. Albertini's editorials rejected social and political change in the name of the virtues of an idealized bourgeoisie, modest, sober, and prudent. The *Corriere* was the epitome of a closed civilization, which was to be destroyed by the First World War, as confident in rejecting the music of Richard Strauss or the art of the futurists as it was in combating socialism. No one perhaps believed more strongly in Milan's mission as the "moral capital" of Italy than Albertini, and no one did more to make the phrase a reality. But in the end he was to be tragically disappointed, when so many of his friends in the Milanese business and political world compromised with Fascism. Albertini was a conservative who had often been rigid and unyielding in his attitude to reform, but he would have nothing to do with dictatorship.

MILANESE CULTURE

The *Corriere* under Albertini was compared by contemporaries to a smoothly running machine. The same ideals of efficiency and exactitude can be seen at work even in the field of music. In opera too, technical innovation was required to adapt local tradition to new international standards of performance. The reforms carried out at the Scala by the great conductor Toscanini can be seen in this light. Italian opera in the earlier 19th century had been an essentially social occasion in which the music was not expected to interrupt conversation. Already by the 1880s this had changed. When Berlioz visited Milan, he complained that he was unable to hear the music at all, because of the audience, who talked loudly and turned their backs on the stage; but the novelist Fogazzaro reported that at the first performance of Verdi's *Otello* in 1886 the audience preserved "a religious hush." The genius of Verdi, in fact, had transformed the expectations of the audience and had established the preeminence of the composer over the individual performer. However, the old traditions of informal audience participation were by no means wholly extinct. If the public now kept silent during the singers' arias or ensembles, it still claimed the right to interrupt the performance whenever it chose, to demand encores. Most operas, on the other hand, were performed in heavily cut versions. The *palchettisti* (owners of boxes) were a privileged corporation, whose members had the habit of coming onto the stage in intervals to make assignations with the girls of the *corps de ballet*. It was only in 1906 that Toscanini put a stop to this.

Toscanini during his years at the Scala had a hard battle with the audience. He walked out of a performance of Verdi's *Masked Ball* in 1902 when the public demanded an encore, and returned only four years later, after posing stringent conditions. He insisted on strict silence in the audience and equally strict discipline from the performers because he conceived of the operatic performance as a unity. The conductor was no longer to be a mere executor but the "organizing intelligence" directing the whole: he was to have the final say on costumes and scenery as well as musical interpretation.

The conception of opera as a total, quasi-religious experience, was German in origin, and some of Toscanini's innovations directly copied those of Wagner at Bayreuth. Wagner achieved great popularity in

Milan for the first time during the 1890s, when his operas were performed more frequently at the Scala even than those of Verdi. No doubt this shift in taste prepared the audience for Toscanini's new style of performance. Nevertheless, it met with stubborn resistance from traditionalists who complained that his conducting was too austere. He was described as a "human metronome," and accused of substituting a "rigid and mathematically exact" interpretation of the music for "the fluid and melodic genius" proper to Italian opera. We can see in Toscanini's stress on mathematical precision, as in the notorious and bitterly resented severity of work discipline which he imposed on his orchestras, a cultural analogue of the spirit of Milanese industry. When in 1920 Toscanini reduced the time available for rehearsals, the *Corriere* commented that "the rhythm of life . . . pulsates with unheard-of rapidity. The orchestra has already arrived at a degree of productivity which makes possible notable economies of time. By abolishing the dress rehearsal Toscanini has cut out the superfluous and intensified the necessary."[5]

Opera in Milan was not just an elite amusement. It was the one genuinely popular art form, and Verdi was universally appreciated. But the management of the Scala generated fierce hostility. The commune subsidized the theater, and this was seen as the most salient example of the willingness of the rich to spend public money on their own amusements while neglecting the necessities of the poor. Criticism was exacerbated by the tendency of the palchettisti to regard the opera house as their private property. They were compensated for their investment by paying an almost nominal price for tickets to the individual performances, and some of them made a good profit out of reselling their boxes. In the critical years of the 1890s, the radicals and socialists demanded the abolition of the commune's subsidy, on the grounds that "while the struggle for existence rages all around us, we need to think of questions of quite a different degree of urgency." They were successful, and during 1897–98 the theater had to close. However, more money was raised from the shareholders, and in 1900 the duke Visconti di Modrone, who owned four boxes in the first row, personally paid off the theater's 80,000 lire deficit for the season.

The Scala was not the only place in Milan where opera was performed. The city, in fact, was rich in theaters of all kinds. They ranged from the Scala and the luxurious Dal Verme in the Foro Bonaparte to humbler establishments like the Cannobbiana, which opened only during the carnival season for a public of shopkeepers and bank clerks, or the Fossati near Porta Garibaldi, where the audience always demanded that proceedings end with a hymn to the hero himself. The Porta Ticinese alone of the Milanese quarters was too poor to support a theater except on Sundays, when it was mainly reliant in the custom of prosperous farmers who had come to Milan for the day to sell their cattle. The margins on which most workers lived were too narrow to allow more than very occasional expenditure on entertainment.

Nevertheless, there are some indications that by 1914 the workers' feeling of estrangement from the cultural life of the city had significantly weakened. Socialist criticism of the Scala in the years before the war was no longer purely negative, as it had been in the 1890s. The socialists now complained not that the commune spent money on music, but that none of it went to improve the musical education of the people. In 1912, in response to this demand, Toscanini himself conducted a series of popular symphony concerts. One was even reserved to members of the *Camera del Lavoro*. The *Corriere* drew the moral that music had shown its capacity to overcome class distinctions: "Petty-bourgeois, reformists, syndicalists and revolutionaries forgot their differences faced with the majesty of art . . . music knows how to reconcile the most diverse environments and publics."[6] However, the socialist *Avanti* drew attention instead to the advance in working class culture demonstrated by the audience's appreciation of Wagner, a composer previously considered inaccessible to popular taste. This was another proof of the ascension of the proletariat. In 1918, in fact, the socialist town council produced a highly successful scheme for the reorganization of the Scala. It became an independent public corporation, presided over by the mayor Caldara, and the subsidy was continued on condition that the popular symphony concerts become a regular institution. Largely thanks to the help of Albertini, 6 million lire were raised from banks and industry. The new board of the Scala was unique in that it brought socialist deputies together with leading representatives of the plutocracy. This harmony was short-lived. Fascism forced the resignation of the socialist councillors, ended the popular concerts, and restored undisputed control of the theater to the industrialists and the aristocracy.

Toscanini, a fierce patriot, was briefly persuaded in 1919 to lend his name to the nascent Fascist movement. The man who is said to have convinced him to do so was Filippo Tommaso Marinetti. With Marinetti, we are once again in the presence of a man who applied the techniques of the entrepreneur in an unexpected direction. Marinetti was the creator, financier, and organizer of the literary and artistic movement of futurism. His whole ideology was centered around the exaltation of the new machine age and the condemnation of the provincial past. Electricity, where Milan was in the forefront of development, particularly fascinated Marinetti. So did the new invention of radio; the ideal of the new poetry should be "imagination without wires," to be achieved by the abolition of conventional syntax. Marinetti's view of technology was romantic. His admiration was for the showy and the spectacular, for speed, sport, and the destructive potential of the new weapons; he had little interest in the details of production, and his understanding of industry was far more superficial than that of the German reformers of the *Werkbund* or the *Bauhaus*. Yet Marinetti's showmanship was in its way extremely practical and characteristically modern. He fully appreciated the importance of publicity and advertisement; the Futurist movement progressed through a series of manifestos, each one more provocative than the last. By these methods, he drew to himself a small group of artists and helped them to achieve international fame, although to most Milanese art lovers, shocked by his call for the destruction of all museums, his name remained anathema. The success of the futurist revolution in rescuing Italian art from provincial obscurity was yet another example of the successful appropriation of foreign techniques, in this case those of the Parisian avant-garde. As in the world of fashion, Milanese taste followed and interpreted Parisian taste in order to capture the market from its products. At first, the futurist revolution interested only a minority even of those interested in art; but after the war they found a clientele among the wealthy bourgeoisie of Milan and Turin. In the long run, the futurists had a considerable effect on taste through their influence on advertising and industrial design.

The Futurists produced the most memorable images of an urban environment subject to radical and violent transformation. They were painters of civil conflict, of the riot and the fight, as well as of the factory, the railway station, and the motor car. The greatest of their artists, Boccioni, was particularly fascinated by building sites, where men and machines worked together in an alternating rhythm to demolish and to build anew. They revelled in change and confusion; they dealt with the dilemma we mentioned at the outset of this essay by denying its existence. Yet the pleasure which they took in rejecting and offending tradition was perhaps only possible in a city in which the framework of inherited values was still so strong. Vice versa, the pace of change, accelerated by the war, increased the yearning for order and stability. But the order imposed by Fascism was only apparent. The undirected expansion of the city rendered its shape increasingly unrecognizable, and the contours of the urban experience itself became ill-defined and hard to grasp.

NOTES

1.   E. De Marchi, *Milanin Milanon* (Milan, 1902), pp. 4–9.
2.   L. Cafagna, *Il Nord nella Storia d'Italia: antologia dell'Italia industriale* (Bari, 1962), pp. 28 ff.

3. S. Merli, *Proletariato di fabbrica e capitalismo industriale* (Florence, 1972), II, pp. 710–11.
4. A. Pirelli, *La vita di una azienda industriale: la Pirelli* (Milan, 1946), pp. 7–18.
5. G. Barblan, *Toscanini e la Scala* (Milan, 1972), p. 47.
6. Barblan, *Toscanini e la Scala*, p. 189.

BIBLIOGRAPHY

Seton Watson, C. *Italy from Liberalism to Fascism* (London and New York, 1967).

Tilly, L. "I fatti di maggio: the Working Class of Milan and the Rebellion of 1898," R. J. Bezucha, ed., *Modern European Social History* (Lexington-Toronto-London, 1972).

——— "Urban Growth, Industrialization and Women's Employment in Milan, Italy, 1881–1911," *Journal of Urban History*, 3 (1977).

Chapter 7

R *eading about World War I (the Great War, as it was called by con-temporaries) is a profoundly depressing experience. There have been few major conflicts in European history which began over such petty issues, or which were so ineptly managed. In every country involved in the struggle, political and military leadership was, at best, barely competent, and at worst, incredibly stupid. On the Western Front, the strategy of the German and Allied generals was simple and unvaried: to send hundreds of thousands of soldiers to their deaths in futile attempts to dislodge the enemy from entrenched and impregnable positions. The admirals who commanded the fleets were more cautious; they preferred to keep their ships in safe harbors instead of risking battle. Consequently, both the British and German navies were largely intact at war's end, and except for the submarine crews, the sailors who manned the ships suffered few casualties. Georges Clemenceau, the premier of France in the later stages of the conflict, once remarked that war was too serious a business to be left to the generals. But the political leadership was generally no better than that provided by the high commands; it was particularly weak in thinking about, and implementing, peace negotiations. The only heroes of this war were the 10 million dead and the 20 millions of multilated survivors, and that tiny handful of pacifists who spoke out against the war and refused to participate in the slaughter.*

It is easy, too easy perhaps from hindsight, to excoriate the leaders of the warring nations. There had been no major conflict in Europe for 50 years; wars that had involved the European powers had been fought in Africa and Asia, and were of limited scope (the Russo-Japanese war of 1904–1905 was an exception) and short duration. Still, making allowances for lack of experience, the conservatism of the military leadership was striking. "The generals had little interest in new weapons," A. J. P. Taylor writes. "They had accepted the rifle, though mainly in order to stick a bayonet on the end of it. . . . They resented the machine-gun as a defensive and therefore cowardly weapon. They regarded the tank and the aeroplane with suspicion. They were even indifferent to motor transport for their men, though not for themselves." (From Sarajevo to Potsdam [London, 1966], p. 31.) Like the generals, the political leaders were not prepared for a war of such magnitude and longevity, since it was universally believed that any conflict among the Great Powers would last only a few weeks or months. As the struggle dragged on without resolution, the governments had to recruit more soldiers to replace the mounting casualties, to train, supply, and transport them, and to mobilize civilian populations in support of the war. Political leaders of every belligerent power sought to stimulate support for the war by patriotic appeals, and by depicting the enemy as the incarnation of evil. The popular passions thus unleashed were not easily controlled, and they certainly contributed to the prolongation of the conflict. The leaders of the autocratic states (Russia, Germany, Austria-Hungary, Turkey) realized that their regimes, and their underlying social structures, would not survive a military defeat. In the parliamentary governments of the West—France, England, Italy—statesmen were not willing even to consider a negotiated settlement with no victors or losers. Only victory could make up for the lives lost, the sacrifices made, in this first European "peoples' war." Before 1918, only Lenin and a few Bolshevik leaders in Russia were willing to end the war between states, so that the international conflict between capitalists and workers could begin.

Nationalism had been a factor in beginning the war, with the assassination of the Austrian crown prince Franz Ferdinand at Sarajevo by a Serbian nationalist, and it was a guiding principle in redrawing the map of Europe at war's end. If all European peoples were united under their own flag and with their own government, it was argued by President Wilson and others, then a major source of conflict would be eliminated and Europeans would live in peace forever. The concept was attractive in theory, but difficult to imple-

ment; as the Versailles peacemakers discovered. Ethnic boundaries were not clear-cut; peoples of different cultures, languages, and religions intermingled with each other, particularly in a broad zone of east central Europe stretching from the south Baltic coast to the Adriatic and Black Seas. As finally constituted, the Slavic state of Czechoslovakia contained a large German minority in its northwestern region, and enclaves of Ruthenians and Magyars in its eastern and southern districts. The victorious Allied powers violated the principle of national self-determination by refusing to allow Austrians to unite with Germany, and by seizing large blocs of the dismantled Turkish empire for themselves. The new states that were created by the peace treaties lived precariously and insecurely after 1919. They lacked a tradition and the mechanics of self-government, and their economic structures were fragile. Of the newly established European states, only Czechoslovakia appeared to be a healthy polity, with a viable parliamentary government and an expanding economy neatly balanced between agriculture and industry. No other state in central and eastern Europe was so prosperous or so stable.

President Wilson had believed that his program of Fourteen Points would provide the basis for a just and durable peace, but his hopes were unrealistic and he contributed himself at Paris to their non-realization. Europe did not solve her major political problems at the peace table; more seriously and fatefully, her leaders failed to see that economic problems could be as dangerous to peace and stability as political issues. The leaders of the Allies were not known for their mastery of economics, and they did not listen carefully to their advisers who were specialists in the "dismal science." The war had been funded by borrowing, not taxes, and every belligerent power had incurred enormous debts by 1918. The Bolshevik regime in Russia resolved that problem by repudiating all of the obligations of the Tsarist government, but this option was not readily available to the other European powers. In his prophetic book, The Economic Consequences of the Peace, the English economist John Maynard Keynes had made a strong plea for treating the defeated states, and particularly Germany, with leniency. His arguments were ignored, and Germany was saddled with reparations of $33 billion, an enormous sum that was several times larger than her Gross National Product. The folly of this vengeful policy was quickly demonstrated; it contributed significantly to the collapse of the Weimar Republic and the triumph of National Socialism in 1933.

The history of Germany in the first half of the 20th century forms *the background for this final chapter: the biography of the Ruhr industrialist Paul Reusch (1868–1956). Reusch was a small child of three when Germany was united under the leadership of Bismarck. He grew to manhood while Germany was establishing herself as the most powerful state on the European continent; his political ideas were formed during that intensely nationalistic age. He was loyal to his emperor and to the authoritarian political structure over which he ruled. He believed that Germany deserved to be the preeminent power in Europe, indeed, in the world. Reusch was very much a man of his age and his class. As one of Germany's leading industrialists, he accepted the values of her bourgeoisie. Like his counterparts in Sheffield, St. Petersburg, and Milan, he believed that capitalism was the best economic system. He was himself instrumental in the organization of German heavy industry into its distinctive "cartelized" form—highly centralized and coordinated. As this chapter makes clear, Reusch was the epitome of the capitalist "boss," hated and feared by the workers who were employed in his mills and factories. His economic and social views were as conservative as his politics. Like many contemporaries whose values had been formed in the 19th century, he did not adapt easily to the post-World War I era. Paul Reusch's life is a story of political and economic power, its triumphs and failures, in this turbulent period of German and European history.*

Chapter

7

Paul Reusch and the Politics of German Heavy Industry 1908–1933

*GERALD FELDMAN**

PAUL REUSCH, INDUSTRIALIST (1868–1956)

In the spring of 1908 when the Second German Empire of William II was at the height of its power, Paul Reusch became General Director of the Good Hope Mining and Smelting Company (Gutehoffnungs-hütte = GHH), one of the oldest and most important producers of iron and steel in Germany's chief industrial region, the Ruhr. He was 40 years old at the time. When he was born in 1868 in the town of Königs-bronn in the South German Kingdom of Württemberg, Germany was still divided between the North and the South along the river Main. Three years later Prussia, under Bismarck's leadership, completed the unification of the country after defeating France in the Franco-Prussian War. Although Reusch's career was made in the Second Empire, his greatest and most lasting achievements as general director of the GHH came after Germany's defeat in the First World War and the Revolution of 1918 which created the Weimar Republic, a democratic regime which he loathed with all the passion he had once devoted to the support of the authoritarian empire. When Reusch finally left the general director-ship of the GHH or, more accurately, was forced out by the Nazis in 1942, the Third German Empire of Adolf Hitler ruled all of Europe. At

---

* University of California, Berkeley.

Courtesy of the Historisches Archiv der Gutehoffnungshütte

FIGURE 20.   Paul Reusch (1868–1956). A drawing by Professor Fritz Erler.

the time of his death in December 1956, Germany was once again divided, now between the East and the West along the river Elbe. The 88 year old Reusch did have the satisfaction of knowing, however, that his son, Hermann, had succeeded him as General Director of the GHH after World War II and that the basic strength and fundamental structure of the company which Paul Reusch had forged during his 34 years as its general director had survived through two world wars and four regimes. It continues to survive to this day, and those who wonder if there is any continuity to modern German history might find some answers in the career of Paul Reusch, the company he directed, and the Ruhr industrial region in whose heart it lies.

When Reusch became the *Herr Generaldirektor* of the GHH, he joined a small, highly select group of top managers who administered the great German industrial enterprises whose technical achievements and productivity had enabled Germany to overtake England as Europe's industrial leader and hold a position second only to the distant United States. These top managers were not the owners, let alone the founders, of the companies they served. Reusch and the directors who served under him on the GHH Board of Directors were the paid employees, albeit the very well paid employees, of the GHH who were permitted to control the company so long as the owners of its stock (who sat on its Supervisory Board) thought they were doing a good job and saw fit to renew their contracts. Nevertheless, it would be false to think that the GHH directors and their counterparts in the other great enterprises simply worked to keep their jobs or increase their salaries. Reusch thought of himself as the captain of a great ship for whose welfare he was ultimately responsible, and it was this sense of calling and responsibility that explains his complete and total devotion to his work. Naturally, the chief owners of the GHH, the Haniel family, whose forbears had helped to found the GHH in 1810, expected performance from Reusch when they appointed him General Director. Reusch was instructed to undertake major reforms of the company in three areas: its economic structure, the technical development of its plants, and its labor policy. It was Reusch's success as well as his devotion that caused the GHH ownership not only to retain him for 34 years but also to give him a virtually free hand in determining the fate of the GHH and becoming one of the most influential and powerful leaders of German industry.

Reusch was well prepared for the tasks assigned to him. Although somewhat untypical of the top managers of the Ruhr in his South German origins, Reusch was by no means untypical in his social background and professional training. His father had been the director of state owned mining and smelting works in Württemberg, while his mother came of a family of high Württemberg officials. Following in his father's footsteps, Reusch was trained as an engineer in the Stuttgart Polytechnical Institute and began his practical training in the works managed by his father. He then took positions in the old Austro-Hungarian Empire, working first in a major machine construction plant in Budapest and then in a coal and steel plant in Moravia. In 1901, he finally came to the Ruhr where, after working in the Friedrich-Wilhelm Smelting Company in Mülheim-Ruhr, he was invited in 1905 to come to nearby Oberhausen as a member of the GHH Board of Directors before assuming the general directorship three years later. Apparently, Reusch was a first-rate engineer with a specialty in foundry technology, and he produced a series of technical articles on such topics as the "magnetic qualities of cast iron" for the industry's superb technical journal, *Steel and Iron* between 1902 and 1908. They were the last such articles Reusch was to write, however, for then as now, the upward mobility of engineers was determined by their managerial promise and ability to go beyond technical questions and handle the economic and labor problems Reusch was instructed to solve by the GHH Board of Supervisors. Thus, it was no accident that when Reusch next appeared in print it was as the author of an article on the formation of trade associations in the machine construction industry in 1908 and as the interviewee in the local Oberhausen newspaper on the great miner strikes that took place in 1912.

THE GROWTH OF HEAVY INDUSTRY
IN THE RUHR VALLEY

The German coal, iron, and steel industry, that is, German heavy industry, was the most concentrated and highly organized industry of its type in Europe, and the GHH was one of about 25 leading heavy industrial concerns which controlled most of the production in the industry. Nearly all of these were located in the Ruhr, although quite a few of these Ruhr concerns had important branches in the closely associated region of German Lorraine. Germany had two additional heavy industrial regions besides the Ruhr; the Saar and Upper Silesia, but the Ruhr was predominant, producing 60 percent of Germany's coal and, in combination with German Lorraine, 61 percent of Germany's pig iron and 65 percent of her crude steel production in 1913. It was the Ruhr which made Germany a great industrial power, both then and now, and the chief reasons for its crucial role were its enormous coal reserves and its favorable location from the standpoint of transportation. It had the best and most concentrated supplies of anthracite coal in Europe and this was the coal needed for producing the coke used to fuel the production of iron and steel. The one big disadvantage of the Ruhr was that it did not have its own iron ore supplies, but here its favorable location in the West and proximity to the Rhine and its tributaries gave it easy access to the rich minette ore fields of Lorraine while the Swedish and Spanish ores used by German heavy industry could also be shipped easily by barge from Dutch and German North Sea Ports.

The entire situation of the Ruhr encouraged the concentration of heavy industry in mammoth concerns which would be in a position to

Courtesy of the Historisches Archiv der Gutehoffnungshütte

FIGURE 21.   The Gutehoffnungshütte at Oberhausen in the Ruhr.

combine the production of coal and its coking with the smelting of the iron ore into pig iron and the processing of the latter to produce crude steel as well as the rolling of steel to produce more finished steel products. The more that these processes could be coordinated and the more that could be produced in "one heat," the greater the saving in cost per unit. These were the technical considerations which encouraged vertical concentration, the effort by the concerns to combine the various stages of production in order to maximize production at the lowest cost. Often, however, their success in achieving this goal got them into trouble by producing a glut on the market during times of depression and potentially ruinous cutthroat competition among the concerns. Such dangers induced the concerns to engage in horizontal concentration, that is, to join together in cartels and syndicates aimed at limiting production and maintaining profitable prices for the basic products of the industry, coal, pig iron, and crude steel. The most famous of these horizontal organizations were the Rhenish-Westphalian Coal Syndicate, founded in 1893, and the Steel Works Association, founded in 1904. Their goal was to maintain the stability in the industry that was demanded by the great bankers and stockholders who preferred a sure, albeit reduced, profit to the kind of all-out competition that could threaten their enormous capital investments in heavy industry.

Courtesy of Historisches Archiv der Gutehoffnungshütte, Oberhausen

FIGURE 22.   Smelting plants of the Gutehoffnungshütte at Oberhausen.

The cartels and syndicates were much less popular among the customers of heavy industry in the machine building, bridge, locomotive, and other manufacturing industries who did not see why they should have to pay high prices that increased the costs of their products at home and abroad while heavy industry was protected by high tariffs at home and exported at reduced prices abroad. The national economy, critics of the cartels pointed out, benefitted much more from the sale of quality manufactured goods produced by skilled but cheaply paid German labor than it did by the less finished products of heavy industry. The heavy industrialists responded by arguing that without a healthy German heavy industry, German manufacturers would become dependent upon foreigners for their raw materials. At the same time, however, leading heavy industrialists were becoming altogether too well aware that the greatest profits were to be found in the sale of manufactured goods. The notion of using their own iron and steel to produce machines and bridges became increasingly appealing as the profits on the cartelized basic products decreased. Horizontal concentration thus promoted new ventures into vertical concentration, as the heavy industrial concerns sought to make up for the restrictions cartels imposed on their production and profits by producing and selling more finished products and even going into competition with the manufacturers themselves. The GHH had produced machines, boilers and other manufactured products from a very early stage of its development, but this was a trend which Reusch was to push even more. It was fundamental to his policy, and the key to the economic strength of the GHH through the turbulent years ahead.

If Reusch strove first and foremost for the success of the GHH, however, he was no less convinced that the German business community had to stick together and combine healthy competition with the avoidance of internecine conflict. The heavy industrialists had always been very good at this. One of the advantages of the concentration of heavy industry in the Ruhr was that the general directors and their subordinates could easily get together both formally at the meetings of associations like the Association for the Protection of the Common Interests of Rhineland-Westphalia — appropriately nicknamed the Long-Name Association by Bismarck — and the Northwest Group of the Association of German Iron and Steel Industrialists, and informally at social gatherings. In short, they were friendly competitors and even more friendly collaborators in their efforts to get the government to lower freight rates, give large contracts for its fleet building program, keep down taxes, and keep up tariffs. Reusch, however, also believed that it was necessary for heavy industry's customers in machine building and other industries to get together in good organizations. This may sound strange given the tension between the two branches of industry over tariffs and prices, but one must remember not only that the GHH and some of its fellow heavy industrial concerns like Krupp in nearby Essen were engaged in manufacturing themselves, but also that it could be very dangerous if German manufacturers aroused public opinion against heavy industry and pressured the government into reducing tariffs or taking action against cartels and syndicates. From Reusch's point of view — and most of his colleagues agreed — it was preferable to have the machine builders organize so that they could bargain collectively with heavy industry to their mutual benefit and to the exclusion of public and governmental interference with business. If manufacturers, for example, could be assured that they could compete in the sale of their machines abroad by receiving a rebate on the iron and steel they bought from the cartels that they used in producing for export, then they would be less hostile to iron and steel tariffs and to paying higher iron and steel prices on their production for the domestic market. In a protected German market, after all, the higher prices could be passed on to the consumer. If "production policy" triumphed over "consumption policy," to use the favorite slogans of industrialists like Reusch, then the "national labor" would be protected and all of industry would prosper and, with it, the nation. This was one reason why Reusch encouraged organization, cooperation, and collective negotiation throughout industry. Another reason was the growing power of organized labor. Collective bargaining between industry and labor, after all, was quite a different matter, and he was extremely anxious to mobilize industry against this danger.

In this respect, Reusch was the typical great Ruhr industrialist and did not partake of the more moderate, democratic attitudes of the Swabians, as the people from Württemberg were called. He did, to be sure, have many of the personality traits ascribed to his fellow Swabians. He was serious, austere, and very blunt and forthright. His correspondence, which he carefully preserved, was enormous, but his letters were always laconic and to the point. In Württemberg, however, these characteristics, as in neighboring Switzerland, were tempered by a measure of egalitarianism and liberalism. Reusch, in contrast, was elitist and authoritarian, and he was quite at home in the Ruhr and the state of Prussia of which the Ruhr was a part. He firmly believed in the political system under which the Reich and Prussia were governed.

INDUSTRY AND LABOR IN GERMAN POLITICS, 1871–1914

Under this system, the Imperial Chancellor and Minister-President of Prussia as well as the chief administrators of the Empire and of Prussia were appointed by the Kaiser, who was also the King of Prussia. They were responsible to him and not to the Reichstag or the Prussian House of Deputies. Unlike England or France, there was no parliamentary system because a parliamentary majority could not overthrow the government and put a new government in its place. The government could not simply disregard parliament in Germany because budgets and laws had to be approved by the parliaments, and the government constantly sought to buy off various parties and form friendly coalitions to support government programs. Nevertheless, the Kaiser retained sole control over the army and foreign policy, and while the parliaments could criticize and obstruct, they were barred from playing a role in ruling the nation. The regime's worst problems were with the national parliament, the Reichstag, which was elected on the basis of universal manhood suffrage. In 1871, Bismarck had made the mistake of thinking that universal suffrage would favor the cause of conservatism in the still predominantly agrarian Germany of that time. By 1890, his mistake had become pain-

fully obvious thanks to Germany's rapid urbanization and industrialization and, by 1912, the Social Democrats, whose strength among
the workers had grown persistently and who were formally committed
to Marxism and the creation of a democratic republic, were the largest
party in the Reichstag. Fortunately for Bismarck and his successors,
however, the Prussian Chamber of Deputies was elected by a gro-
tesquely plutocratic suffrage system that insured a steady conservative majority and the predominance of the so-called Junker-industrialist
alliance. Since Prussia was the largest and most important state in the
Empire and, under the complicated system created by Bismarck, was
able to dominate the policies of the imperial government, this Junker-
industrialist alliance was able to serve as an effective block to major
political and social reform until the Revolution of 1918.

The alliance between the large landowning East Elbian nobility and
the great industrialists had been forged in the late 1870s when the
industrialists agreed to support high agrarian tariffs in return for
Junker support of iron and other industrial tariffs. It was then re-
cemented in 1902 when the Junkers agreed to support the Kaiser's
naval building program with its lucrative contracts in return for new
and higher agrarian tariffs. It was, in short, an alliance of the most
powerful industrial groups against the consumers founded on the basis
of political and social authoritarianism and imperialism. In England
and France, during the crucial periods of development of those countries into parliamentary states, industry had stood on the side of
liberalism and political reform. In Germany, however, the big industrialists traded government support of their economic interests in
return for the acceptance of Junker domination of the army and upper
bureaucracy, and the acceptance of the authoritarian and militaristic
values which this implied. Reusch supported this system unstintingly
and enthusiastically so long as it lasted and looked back to it with
nostalgia after it had gone.

When it came to labor relations, this meant that the employer was
to remain "master in his own house." The labor contract was viewed as
an individual matter between employer and worker, and the conditions of work, that is, wages, hours and working regulations, were to
be set by the employer alone. Reusch and his colleagues did not want
any trade union secretaries from outside their plants negotiating on
behalf of the 22,000 persons employed by the GHH, raising inappropriate demands, ruining discipline by their agitation and bringing
the workers out on strike. This is not to say that Reusch and his fellow
industrialists were indifferent to the welfare of the workers. They
were anxious to maintain a stable and loyal labor force, and firms like
Krupp and the GHH were proud of the fact that many generations of
workers from the same families worked for them. These concerns

sought to bind the workers through low cost housing, social clubs, pension and insurance schemes and other welfare devices. Nevertheless, they expected gratitude and obedience in return and, quite appropriately for militaristic Prussia, they always made an analogy between the officer and his men and the boss and his workers. Indeed, when hiring workers, a distinct preference was shown for workers who had done their military service and who presumably understood that questioning the rule of those in command of a factory was no more appropriate or tolerable than questioning the orders of a superior on the battlefield.

By the beginning of the 20th century this attitude had become utterly anachronistic. The notion of the individual labor contract made little sense in huge enterprises with masses of workers, and while the patriarchalism of family owned enterprises like the GHH and Krupp might have some hold on the workers it was artificial and unconvincing in the more impersonally controlled companies like the Rhenish Steel Works, the Phoenix concern, or the Deutsch-Luxemburg Mining and Smelting Company which were the products of recent mergers of various companies and which could boast very little individual history or character that might earn the special loyalty of their workers. Men like Hugo Stinnes, the dynamic "merchant from Mülheim," as he styled himself, who had expanded into the iron and steel industry from the base of his huge coal mining and marketing organization, or the iron merchant Peter Klöckner, who decided to expand into the industry itself, necessarily viewed their holdings much more impersonally than did members of the Krupp family. Similarly, Stinnes' General Director at the Deutsch-Luxemburg works in Dortmund, Albert Vögler, was much more impersonal in his attitudes toward both his works and his workers than Paul Reusch with his direct commitment to the GHH and the Haniel family. Thus, while all these men could agree on the virtues of the existing system of labor relations and fight together to maintain it, there was a latent conflict between the kind of industrial system they were building and their conception of what labor relations should be like.

At the time when Reusch became General Director of the GHH, the heavy industrialists had come to feel very threatened by the increasingly powerful trade union movement and by the sympathy which had been shown for the cause of the workers among influential intellectuals and in certain government circles. When the Ruhr miners struck in 1905, for example, public opinion was clearly on the side of the exploited miners, and the pressure of this opinion led to the passage of legislation reforming conditions in the mines and compelling the employers to discuss problems with worker committees. Of course, the mine owners still refused to deal with the trade unions, but the influence of the three big trade unions, the Socialist Free Trade Unions, the Christian Unions, and the liberal Hirsch-Dumcker Unions remained very strong among the miners. The progress of unionization in mining was encouraged by the special skills required of the miners and the solidarity induced by working in that dangerous occupation. By contrast, the unions had made no significant inroads among the largely unskilled iron and steel workers despite the very harsh conditions in the continuously operating plants of the industry where workers were employed in twelve hour shifts in plants that combined the intense heat of the blast furnaces with the cold drafts that surged through the huge work halls during the long winter. The employers argued that the workers really worked only ten hours since they had two hours of pauses, but such a working day hardly left either strength or time for leisure, and the situation was made worse every other Sunday for the workers when they had to change shifts and thus worked a full 24 hours. Little wonder, therefore, that the eight-hour day was one of the great goals of the unions both for these workers and for the rest of German labor which normally worked a ten- or nine-hour day before the war. Prior to 1914, however, the Ruhr industrialists did not confront an organized labor force of iron and steel workers because they had the strength to keep the unions out of this part of their industry. In fact, taking the nation as a whole, the unions had been most successful among craftsmen and skilled workers in medium-sized and small plants, where the employers had neither the financial strength nor the organizational ability to resist the unions and thus preferred to engage in collective bargaining.

Many social reformers, particularly noted economists in the universities, argued that collective bargaining was inevitable and pointed out that the Socialist trade unions, like the Socialist Party itself, was becoming increasingly reformist and that they would give up their revolutionary goals entirely, if given the opportunity to concentrate on "bread and butter" issues. This view was also shared by some enlightened bureaucrats in the government, and this was a situation which truly alarmed the heavy industrialists. The latter argued that all these suggested concessions to labor were a mistake that would tear down the existing political system by strengthening the Social Democrats to the point where social reforms would have to be followed by suffrage reform and the introduction of a parliamentary system. As Reusch reported to Franz Haniel at the end of 1913: "For as long as I have been engaged in economic life, I have always devoted the greatest efforts to undermining the Social Democrats and their trade unions, and I have not refrained from frequently fighting them ruthlessly, not only because I considered this to be my duty, but also because I am of the view that even the slightest retreat by industry before the demands of social democracy must have incalculable political and economic consequences."[1]

"Ruthless" was indeed the right word for the tactics employed against the trade unions by Reusch and his colleagues. Known trade union members and Social Democrats were fired outright and blacklisted. This system was perfected when the employers set up labor exchanges to control the hiring of workers in heavy industry and thus insure that only workers who went through the exchanges would be hired. After the turn of the century, the employers engaged in a massive organizing effort of their own in which heavy industry, alarmed by the growth of trade unionism, took the lead. Not only did these organizations make it possible for the employers to formulate a common policy, but they also made possible the development of collective mechanisms to fight against strikes. The most important weapon against labor demands and strikes was the lockout. In preparation for lockouts, employer organizations would set up funds for which every employer would be assessed according to the number of his workers so that financially weak firms would not suffer for their solidarity with their stronger colleagues. The industrialists were not only interested in measures of self-help, however, and they demanded that the courts and the government act on their behalf by banning or restricting picketing and protecting those "willing to work." The courts were, indeed, quite harsh in fining and imprisoning workers who insulted scabs or committed the slightest violation of existing ordinances, but the government and the Reichstag were not easily won over to new legislation against the trade unions that might increase social tensions. On the whole, the years before the First World War were years of prosperity, and at such times trade unionism can make considerable progress because industry is reluctant to lose the advantages of good business conditions by having its plants idle. The mobilizations against the workers, therefore, were most successful during downswings in the economy when high unemployment weakened the effectiveness of strikes, strengthened the resistance of employers who were anxious to cut costs anyway, and won government sympathy for employer arguments that Germany could not compete successfully abroad if wages and social costs were increased through trade union successes. Thus, during the recession of 1913–14, heavy industrial demands for an end to social reform and legislation against picketing was greeted with particular friendliness by the government and even in the Reichstag where alarm over Socialist victories in the 1912 elections and the bad economic conditions were swinging the pendulum in favor of the employer point of view.

The industrialists did not only count upon repression, however. Increasingly they also turned to manipulation. Obviously, it was easiest to manipulate friends and potential friends than enemies, and the industrialists and their organizations poured large sums of money into the support of Conservative, National Liberal, and Catholic Center Party candidates for the Reichstag and Prussian Parliament who were friendly to industrialists' interests. This tactic of supporting the "right" people in a variety of parties and trying to make all the respectable parties beholden to industrialist money was regularly practiced by the industrialists in their battle against the left wing liberal Progressive Party and the Social Democrats. Similarly, the industrialists became financially involved in a number of newspapers which could thus be counted upon to give publicity to the industrialist positions on various matters. At the same time, the industrialists, like their agrarian allies, associated themselves with all kinds of patriotic causes and leagues — the racist Pan-German League, the Colonial League, the Naval League, the Reich Association against Social Democracy — in an effort to ally themselves with the entire bourgeoisie and to have the entire bourgeoisie associate itself with them in support of a strong foreign policy and the maintenance of the existing domestic order. Often, these efforts were frustrated since large segments of the German bourgeoisie were hostile to the economic power of heavy industry and skeptical of its views. In bad times, however, as in 1913, heavy industry found it easier to rally important segments of the middle class, particularly craftsmen and lower middle class groups resentful of growing Socialist power and fearful of being proletarianized, to the general cause of imperialism and conservatism in a so-called "cartel of the producing estates."

At about the time Reusch became General Director of the GHH, however, the heavy industrialists became increasingly active in a cause that was to become particularly dear to Reusch's heart, namely, the effort to win over the workers through the creation of nonstriking company unions, "yellow unions," as they were called by their enemies. Krupp led the way in 1908, and Reusch followed four years later, when growing worker support for the Social Democrats in Oberhausen and a bitter strike in the coal mines convinced Reusch and his colleagues that greater effort had to be made to influence the workers. A company union was set up in 1912 which, by 1914, encompassed about 20 percent of the workers. It was subsidized by the GHH as was the propaganda which it distributed among the workers and, in combination with the various welfare programs of the company, was designed both to increase identification with the company and management and also to influence the workers in a more politically conservative and nationalist direction. For this reason, the GHH, under Reusch, gave substantial financial support to conservative Catholic organizations seeking to educate the workers away from supporting the Christian trade unions and to strengthen the right wing of the Catholic Center Party. Indeed, by the eve of World War I, Reusch had assumed a prominent position among the Ruhr industrialists seeking to mobilize and organize a right wing defence against the growth of Social Democracy, the powerful left wing of the Center Party, and the intellectual and governmental circles inclined to temporize with trade unionism and Socialism. Whatever the long-term results of such efforts might have been, they seemed to be heading for new successes in 1913–14 before they were abruptly and surprisingly interrupted by the outbreak of the first World War.

GERMAN INDUSTRY DURING WORLD WAR I, 1914–1918

The First World War was greeted with much greater enthusiasm by the general public than it was by the great German industrialists. It was not that they were not patriotic and did not believe that Germany deserved the "place in the sun" that the "encirclement" by England, France, and Russia denied her. It was rather that the war was necessarily unwelcome in its immediate consequences for businessmen. It interrupted international trade, removed valuable workers from the plants because of the military draft, created raw materials shortages and, in general, made life difficult in every way. With the exception of Krupp and one or two other major private companies, very few firms produced for the army and, since the war was expected to be short — indeed, to be over in six weeks — companies like the GHH anticipated little by way of war contracts. Insofar as they undertook any reconversion for war production, they expected it to be on a small scale and therefore relatively unprofitable.

Their great consolation in all this disruption of their normal business activity was the anticipation that Germany would emerge from the war victorious and that it would use its victory to strengthen not only its military and political position but also its economic position. From the early days of the war, the leading Ruhr industrialists looked forward to Germany's annexing the Briey-Longwy iron ore region of France in order to secure this vital raw material; they hoped to see Germany dominate Belgium, whose neutrality Germany had violated at the outset of the war; they expected Germany to impose trade treaties on Belgium and France that would reduce the competition from those countries while at the same time opening up their markets even more than before the war to German exports; they anticipated that Germany would make colonial gains in Africa and elsewhere at the expense of England and France. As before the war, so now, they acted in collaboration with their agrarian Junker allies and, in a meeting of December 15, 1914, at which

Reusch was present, these war aims of the industrialists were combined with Junker and Pan-German war aims for vast annexations in the East to increase the German Empire's agrarian resources and thus maintain some balance between industry and agriculture. As enthusiastic as Reusch was about the alliance between industry and agriculture and an annexationist peace, however, he found himself somewhat at odds with his colleagues when it came to annexations in the East: "If we want to pursue a world policy, then we must punch England in the nose and expand our territory to the West. But on the other side we cannot have the entire world as our enemy permanently, and therefore we have to come to terms with Russia."[2]

Reusch's relatively sober view of what Germany should take in the case of total victory seems to have made little impression on his colleagues, but they found him quite congenial in all other matters pertaining to the war effort. Reusch particularly shared their concern about what they held to be the weak policies of the Chancellor of the Empire, Theobold von Bethmann Hollweg, who they deemed not to be the man to bang his fists upon the peace conference table and whose promise to give a new orientation to German domestic policy (because the Social Democrats had proven their loyalty to Germany and voted for war credits) truly alarmed the industrialists. In order to maintain domestic harmony in the crisis, the industrialists could not at this point attack either the Chancellor or the promise of a new orientation, but they agreed on the need to arm against it and hoped, as the Pan-German director of the Krupp firm, Alfred Hugenberg, openly put it "to distract the attention of the people and to give phantasies concerning the extension of German territory room to play."[3]

Had the war ended with a rapid German victory, this might have been possible. Instead, it turned into a long and unprecedentedly brutal war which made immense demands upon the entire German economy. Trench warfare transformed the war into a battle of materiel, and the industrialists were increasingly called upon to produce for the war effort and convert to war production. Naturally, they did their patriotic duty, but they did not do it without complaining. They found the military authorities unsteady and confused in their procurement policies, wanted their old workers back, and demanded that industry be properly compensated for producing under such trying circumstances. They were happier after the summer of 1916 when a new military Supreme Command under Field Marshal von Hindenburg and First Quartermaster General Erich Ludendorff took over and launched a massive munitions program in which questions of cost were made secondary and under which substantial numbers of workers were returned from the front. Reusch agreed with many of his colleagues' criticisms of the previous military administration and also welcomed the new Supreme Command, but he was quite unhappy about the profiteering of some of his colleagues who wanted to charge what he held to be excessive. He was fearful that this lack of moderation would lead to government action in response to the growing public criticism, and he therefore wanted no "responsibility for the consequences of a pricing policy such as the one conducted recently by short-sighted industrialists."[4] Similarly, as the food shortages increased, Reusch, who was appointed to the Advisory Council of the government's War Food Office, sought to persuade his colleagues not to use the black market to procure food for their plants since this would lead to the total collapse of the government's efforts to ration the food supply, control its distribution, and control prices. Such effort to restrain the growing economic dislocation, immorality, and breakdown of authority produced by the war were unsuccessful, and by 1917, the domestic political truce in Germany had broken down and opposition to the war and demands for reform from the left were rising just as the forces supporting annexationism and the maintenance of the old order were becoming more vociferous.

The truth was that Reusch's own honorable business practices, strong respect for authority, and sense of civic responsibility in no way changed his basic political attitudes on either foreign or domestic affairs. He was utterly horrified as the government made one concession after the other to the Social Democrats and trade unions, in order to encourage them to keep the working masses in line despite food shortages and other privations. When the Supreme Command asked for the compulsory mobilization of the civilian population for work in the winter of 1916–17, the left wing coalition in the Reichstag took advantage of the situation to set up arbitration and mediation committees throughout the country based on parity between industry and labor. Industrialists were now forced to sit at the same table on such committees with trade union secretaries appointed to these positions. Also, worker committees had to be elected for all plants with more than 50 employees, and trade union people were not only allowed to come and speak to the workers in connection with these elections but actually encouraged to come and organize the workers by the government which felt that only the trade unions stood between the workers and the increasingly organized opposition to the war effort. Under conditions of labor shortage, the workers had the upper hand in demanding higher pay, and Reusch and his colleagues blamed the continuous demands for higher wages and the high turnover in the plants on left wing agitation and the failure of the Reichstag and the government to take a firm hand with the workers. They were in no way convinced by government arguments that the unions were helping to keep the domestic situation stable, and they petitioned the government to stop giving the unions "undeserved compensations" for their support of the war effort. Reusch and his colleagues were particularly resentful over the way in which the government was neglecting the company unions and various nonstriking unions in favor of the more powerful independent organizations. Naturally, they were extremely alarmed when Chancellor Bethmann Hollweg promised reform of the Prussian suffrage system after the war and was supported in his efforts by General Wilhelm Groener, the head of the army's agency for economic mobilization, the Prussian War Office. Groener not only argued that the workers had to get ballots when one could not give them bread, but he distressed the industrialists even more by suggesting that industrialist demands for control of wages should be accompanied by an acceptance of the control of profits. Reusch thought Groener, who came from his native Württemberg, a "splendid person," but when Groener was brought down in August 1917 by the intrigues of right wing military leaders and big industrialists, Reusch blamed the event on Groener's "idealism and failure to understand the economic realities."[5] He had no such sympathy for Chancellor Bethmann Hollweg, who was forced to resign in July 1917 by the Supreme Command, and his opposition in the Reichstag, and Reusch hoped that the new leadership in Berlin would pull the country together behind a program of total victory against left wing demands for a peace of understanding and compromise.

In order to promote his cause, Reusch not only played a leading role in the effort to strengthen the yellow unions, but he also lent his support to the Fatherland Party. Established in September 1917, this movement, inspired by the Supreme Command and various annexationist groups, was not really a party but rather an effort to rally Germans of all parties against a "lazy peace" and in support of Hindenburg and Ludendorff's drive for total victory and the maintenance of the existing domestic order or perhaps even the establishment of a dictatorship of the military. At its height, its membership numbered three million, and many historians view it as a proto-fascist organization because of its effort to mobilize a mass movement in favor of imperialism and authoritarianism. As shall be shown, Reusch did not share the racist and more extreme proclivities of the Pan-Germans, who were very prominent in the party's leadership. For him, support of this party was one of a continuous chain of efforts to lend financial and personal encouragement to every promising attempt to rally the German middle class in defense of a strong state and a conservative order.

In supporting the Supreme Command's effort to attain total victory, however, Reusch and those who thought like him were undermining the very conservative order they sought to preserve because, on the one hand, Germany did not have the manpower and material strength to attain the desired victory and, on the other hand, the increasing privations created by the blockade and the demoralization provoked by the protracted and ever more hopeless conflict were destroying the authority of the existing order and paving the way for revolution. Although large numbers of workers had already been radicalized by the severe food shortages in 1916–17 and despite the fact that there were serious strikes throughout 1917 which were strongly influenced by the Russian Revolutions of February and October as well as by the democratic propaganda that accompanied America's entry into the war, the workers remained quiescent in the spring of 1918 when Ludendorff launched a series of major offensives designed to bring about a decisive breakthrough on the western front. They failed and, by the end of the summer, as the allies began their counterattacks and two million fresh American troops began to pour into the front, a new demoralization set in accompanied by ominous manifestations, the most important of which was the demand by the exhausted workers that the hours of work be shortened, and their growing practice of walking off the job after working a certain number of hours. Naturally, the industrialists and government authorities tried to remind the workers of their patriotic duty and stepped up propaganda, but no amount of "enlightenment" could overcome the total unwillingness to hold out once Ludendorff, overreacting to the difficult situation in which he had placed his armies, suddenly demanded that the German Government conclude an armistice with the enemy immediately. Ludendorff entertained the fantasy that the German armies would be allowed to conduct an orderly retreat, regroup, and then fight on if the terms were not acceptable. At the same time, he cynically acquiesced to the proposal that a reform government be set up in Berlin under Prince Max von Baden that would include Social Democrats and would appeal to President Wilson's democratic instincts. It would be given the task of concluding the armistice and making peace, thereby relieving the military of all responsibility. The burden of the military's failure to inform the people of the real situation and of the prolongation of the war for annexationist purposes would thus be deflected from those truly responsible.

THE REVOLUTIONARY PERIOD, 1918–1919

In industrial circles, the deteriorating situation in the summer of 1918 presented dangers of a very material nature that could not be evaded by such devices. Even under the best of circumstances, the industrialists anticipated that the end of the war and the demobilization would bring horrendous problems of settling the masses of men streaming back from the front in search of jobs, but the growing prospect of having to conduct the demobilization under conditions of defeat and blockade with the authority of the state in doubt and the horrendous model of Bolshevik Russia to inspire the embattled and radicalized masses was nothing short of terrifying. In Berlin, leaders of the electrotechnical and metal industries began negotiations with the Socialist trade unions in July 1918, with the intention of collaborating to make sure that the demobilization was orderly and that the government would be induced to provide contracts to employ the returning soldiers. These industrialists recognized that the trade union leaders were moderate men, who feared revolution as much as the employers and who wanted to preserve their organizations from a radical takeover and to preserve the economy from collapse. The more prescient and forward-looking industrialists recognized early that the Majority Socialist Party and the trade unions constituted their most effective barrier against the Independent Socialists, who had split off from the party in 1916–17 in opposition to the war, and the revolutionary Spartacists, who were to form the German Communist Party in January 1919. By contrast, the Ruhr heavy industrialists were very slow to accept this view, although a few heavy industrialists, Hugo Stinnes, Albert Vögler and Alfred Hugenberg, had been secretly discussing a trade of recognition of the trade unions in return for trade union acceptance of annexationist war aims in 1917. The trade union leaders had never been willing to accept such an arrangement and, in any case, the situation in the fall of 1918 was such as to make these same heavy industrialists more than happy to join with their Berlin colleagues in any effort to win the trade unionists over to an alliance with industry to prevent revolution and preserve private property in return for an employer surrender of the "master in his own house" principle.

The patriarchal and authoritarian Reusch remained aloof from these negotiations, although he certainly must have realized that recognition of the trade unions and collective bargaining were unavoidable under the circumstances. Throughout the revolutionary period 1918–19, he was almost olympian in his contempt for the political events taking place and in his conviction that what was most necessary in the emergency was a strong hand and the strength of one's convictions. Thus, on October 31, 1918, he urged a high government official that "the military authorities should take care to create a few unconditionally reliable divisions which are to be recruited largely from the rural population and are to be available for maintaining order in the interior."[6] Unhappily for Reusch, it proved impossible to prevent revolution. When the naval authorities decided to implement a harebrained scheme to send the battle fleet out for a final glorious encounter with the British in the North Sea, the sailors and workers in Kiel revolted on November 4 and set up Soldiers and Workers Councils. By November 9, the Revolution and the councils had spread across Germany and to Berlin, where the Emperor abdicated and a Republic was proclaimed under Socialist leadership.

The Revolution did not disrupt the negotiations between the industrialists and the trade unions, for the latter were now more fearful than ever that the popular movement would get out of hand, destroy the economy, bring about an Allied invasion, and deprive them of the expert industrialist help they felt they needed to keep things going. At the same time, the unions were in a position to force new concessions upon the industrialists involving not merely recognition of the unions and collective bargaining but also the introduction of the eight-hour day throughout German industry, and a promise by the industrialists to cease giving financial support to yellow unions. On November 15, 1918 an agreement to this effect was signed between Hugo Stinnes and the head of the Free Trade Unions, Carl Legien, which also provided for concerted action by the trade unions and employer organizations in matters of economic and social policy. Reusch was not enthusiastic about the partnership idea, which he regarded as excessive, and he was honestly chagrined by the employer betrayal of the yellow unions. As he told the chemical industrialist, Carl Duisberg, "I cannot betray a cause which I have promoted for years. For the moment, I have not lost my self-respect."[7]

From Reusch's point of view, all the disturbances from which Germany and the Ruhr suffered in the winter and early spring of 1919 were the fault of the people in Berlin, who were constantly trying to pacify the masses. He showed little appreciation of the degree to which the Majority Socialist leaders there headed by Friedrich Ebert and Philipp Scheidemann were seeking to quell the radicalism within their ranks, take over and eliminate the workers councils, and create order within the country. Much to the chagrin of the Independent Socialists, who wished to purge the army and the bureaucracy and socialize major industries with the help of the councils, the Ebert government hastily announced elections for a National Assembly to create a new constitution, held them on January 19, 1919, and then felt justified in denying all legitimacy to the workers councils. Despite worker demands for the socialization of the coal mines in order to break the power of heavy industry, the new regime insisted that the matter be carefully investigated first, warned against actions that might reduce the already low coal production, and called upon the miners to work as hard as possible to increase production. As historians now generally recognize, the chief source of the strikes, uprisings, and attempts at spontaneous socialization — that gripped the industrial areas of Germany in the winter and spring of 1919 — was the disappointment of the workers over the failure of their moderate leaders in Berlin to impose a more thoroughgoing democratization upon the institutions of German society. It was this that enabled radical agitators to win over large numbers of workers to their cause, and the radicalization was only increased when the Majority Socialist Minister of Defence, Gustav Noske, instead of creating a democratic people's army to replace the old regular army, created Free Corps units composed of bourgeois troops led by radical right wing officers hostile to the republic. Many of these officers and their followers were later to find their way into the ranks of the Nazi Party and its paramilitary organizations, and their vicious and brutal behavior in suppressing the worker uprisings across Germany in 1919 gave a foretaste of things to come.

Reusch, however, could only see the rowdyism and disruption represented by the Spartacists, and he complained constantly that the government was using the Free Corps too little and too late. The strikes in Oberhausen and at neighboring GHH plants were seldom protracted or violent, and Reusch was certain that a combination of firmness and persuasion could succeed with his workers if only the government would not have continuously negotiated with the radical leaders and thus encouraged agitators from radical nests like neighboring Mülheim/Ruhr to intensify the problems at the GHH. This was what bothered him, and he was singularly indifferent to the National Assembly Meeting in Weimar, which he called a "debating club," just as he was utterly disgusted by the lack of "energy" shown by the regime. As he told a Württemberg industrialist more sympathetic to the regime than himself, Philipp Wieland: "We need energetic men at the top, and you cannot deny that energy is something Ebert and Scheidemann do not have. Until now, Noske is the only person who has accomplished something positive. His creation of the Free Corps was a deed which saved us from complete collapse."[8] Reusch's positive view of Noske and the Free Corps was widely shared among the industrialists, who were happy to supplement the pay of these troops in order to increase their enthusiasm and effectiveness. Thus, millions of marks of industrial money were poured into the Free Corps from Bremen, Hamburg, Berlin, and the Ruhr, and Reusch authorized such expenditures by member companies of the GHH.

Aside from such contributions and contributions to friendly political candidates and to newspapers and publications supportive of his point of view, however, Reusch maintained a relatively low political profile during the first three years of the Weimar Republic. In contrast to leading industrialists like Hugo Stinnes and Albert Vögler from heavy industry, or the electrotechnical industrialists Carl Friedrich von Siemens, Reusch showed no disposition to enter the Reichstag or speak out much on purely political matters. He did not play a particularly prominent role in the successful industrialist fight against socialization, and although he joined his colleagues in attacking the acceptance of the

Treaty of Versailles in June 1919, opposed the creation of factory councils in January 1920, and criticized various social legislation measures, he remained politically in the background. Unlike the speculator Hugo Stinnes, he was not prepared to play every political possibility. As things turned out, he was laying the foundation for a period of intensive political activity and leadership of heavy industry after 1923, but during the early years of Germany's first experiment with political democracy, Reusch tended to view domestic political developments in Germany with simple disdain: "In general so much nonsense is written and spoken today that one does best to read no newspaper at all any more. Hopefully mankind will return to reason in the foreseeable future."[9] Politically, Reusch's day was yet to come.

Ironically, however, these very years of political disillusionment, when Reusch sought solace in the gloomy, pessimistic philosophy of Oswald Spengler's *Decline and Fall of the West* and invited his colleagues to join him in hearing and supporting Spengler's depressing message, were the years when Reusch made his most lasting and important achievements as General Director of the GHH. Reusch's successes were part of the general and remarkable reconstruction of German heavy industry after the debacle of the First World War, but Reusch's accomplishments, in contrast for example, to those of the most famous industrialist of the period, Hugo Stinnes, were notable for their solidity and durability. The GHH emerged from the inflationary period between 1918 and 1923 permanently strengthened while heavy industry as a whole came out of the reconstruction as an artificially overexpanded and undeservedly influential sector of the German economy.

GERMAN INDUSTRY IN THE 1920S

If heavy industry was not the industrial sector hardest hit by the war, it certainly was the sector hardest hit by the Treaty of Versailles which brought the peace. The war had created problems in the coal industry by depriving it of manpower, encouraging overexploitation of the mines, and thus promoting a serious diminution of productivity and a severe coal shortage and energy crisis that lasted until the end of 1920. The Peace Treaty seemed to deal a crushing blow to the iron and steel branch of heavy industry. Instead of annexing Briey-Longwy, the German industrialists were deprived of German Lorraine, which was returned to France, and lost major ore concessions in Normandy. They ceased to control any French minette ore sources, and they were compelled to divest themselves of the very modern plants and productive facilities they had set up in Lorraine before 1914. Furthermore, Germany's productive capacity in iron and steel was also diminished when the French assumed control over the Saar for 15 years and the newly created Polish state received important industrial regions of Upper Silesia in 1921. In sum, Germany lost 43.5 percent of her pig iron producing capacity and 38.3 percent of her steel-making capacity, and was thrown back upon a Ruhr industrial network disrupted by the loss of Lorraine. Germany was thus threatened by severe short-term shortages of coal, iron, and steel at the end of the war and seemed to face a long-term diminution of her competitive position vis-à-vis the greatly expanded French industry which, under the Treaty of Versailles, was insured against any increase of the old German iron tariffs until 1925. Nevertheless, by that year, German heavy industry had nearly attained prewar production levels and had reemerged as the dominant heavy industrial power in Europe.

The truth was that France's advantages were more apparent than real, and that the Ruhr industry was in an excellent position to overcome the liabilities imposed by Versailles. Germany had never been as dependent on French minette ore as people claimed — including the annexationist German industrialists. The same industrialists who insisted during the war that minette was a vital necessity demonstrated in a few years that, once the German iron and steel industry employed higher quality Swedish ores and made greater use of the Siemens-Martin open-hearth process to make steel, which employed scrap rather than ore, the French could — as one German industrialist gracefully suggested — "choke on their minette."[10] If the iron ore was not the asset the French thought it was, however, France's short supply of anthracite coal was a liability it could not really remedy despite German obligation to pay large amounts of reparation coal under the treaty. France depended upon Ruhr coal and upon the willingness of German miners to produce it and German industrialists to surrender it. Insofar as there was a coal shortage, the Germans could not practically be compelled to deliver coal to France until German minimum needs were satisfied. Also, insofar as Germany was required to pay large reparations in money, she had to be in a position to make the necessary money by exporting, and Germany could not export unless she produced, and she could not produce until she had the coal to keep her plants running. After 1919, England and the United States persisted in making this point to the French since they were more interested in restoring economic stability than they were in French anxieties about German recovery, and the German Government and the Ruhr industrialists took advantage of the divisions in Allied ranks to evade many of their treaty obligations. Finally, German heavy industry had the money necessary to reconstruct its plants thanks to its high war profits, the compensation it received for its lost holdings in Lorraine, and the advantages it was able to take of shortages and inflation at the expense of other industrial branches within Germany.

German heavy industry had never been overly popular with its customers in the manufacturing industries, but its practices during the first years of the Weimar Republic made it so detested by small and medium-sized business and even certain large manufacturers that some businessmen actually would have welcomed the socialization of heavy industry while many others called for government control of heavy industrial pricing and distribution policies. The great heavy industrial concerns hoarded their coal, iron, and steel for their own use and for export at great profit abroad, delivered only to favored customers, or delivered only to those willing to pay outrageous prices payable in foreign currencies. Because the heavy industrialists had been compelled to import huge quantities of Swedish ore which they had to pay for in kronen rather than marks, they were among the first businessmen to discover how seriously the German mark had depreciated during the war because of the government's high expenditures and its use of the printing press. They came to understand how important it was to secure high valued foreign currencies from foreign customers and that a special profit was made when they paid for their supplies and labor at home in depreciated marks and then sold abroad for foreign currency. That is, they paid wages, taxes, debts, mortgages, and material costs in German marks, the real value of which had deteriorated. Because of these low domestic costs, they were in a position to undersell their foreign competitors and make a profit not only on what they were selling but also on the money market. When they procured foreign exchange, they either hoarded it in speculation against further deterioration of the mark, or purchased marks which they immediately disposed of either by paying debts or by "fleeing into real values," i.e., expanding their plants or buying up companies. In this manner, the heavy industrialists led the way in the recovery of Germany's position on world markets and in the plant expansion that characterized the inflation between 1918 and 1923.

Naturally, the manufacturers were most anxious to make full use of the export advantage provided by the inflation also, and they argued quite cogently that the German economy would benefit even more if they—and not the heavy industrialists—did the exporting, since the profits on the export of manufactured goods was particularly high because of the value added by the relatively underpaid German skilled laborers. The heavy industrialists could not deny the truth of this argument, but they insisted that their solvency had to come first if German manufacturers were not to become dependent upon foreign raw materials producers and that the recovery of German heavy industry required sacrifices from its domestic customers. The real goal of many of the great heavy industrial concerns, however, was to secure these profits from manufacturing for themselves, and the inflation greatly intensified the drive toward vertical concentration that had begun before the war.

As noted earlier, the GHH had long been involved in manufacturing, but Reusch's desire to push much further in this direction was increased during the war and afterward by the realization that other nations had developed their iron and steel industries during the war, and that the market would be best for manufactured products rather than basic iron and steel. The GHH would be advantaged if it could consume its own iron and steel in the production of high quality manufactured goods for export. The postwar situation gave Reusch and other heavy industrialists significant advantages in the pursuit of this goal. On the one hand, manufacturers suffered from the raw materials shortages and came to the conclusion that they could best assure their supplies of coal, iron, and steel by allying themselves with large heavy industrial concerns. On the other hand, the manufacturers were in desperate need of operating capital because it took them a long time to fill their orders for complicated machinery. They needed constant supplies of liquid capital to pay for their raw materials and to keep operating until paid for their products. Only heavy industry had the kind of capital that would permit the flexibility necessary in the unstable and insecure postwar world, and only alliances with heavy industrial concerns seemed to insure that the necessary raw materials and capital would be forthcoming. Also, heavy industry was often in a position to offer important marketing opportunities since many of the great concerns had built up large and highly efficient marketing organizations in Holland and other neutral countries with worldwide connections. Such considerations drove many old, established machine construction and manufacturing firms in Germany to surrender their independence and permit large heavy industrial concerns to take over control of their works in whole or in part. The Ruhr concerns, anxious to increase profitability and spend their profits before their money could either be taxed or depreciate, were quite ready to take advantage of the situation.

The most famous and spectacular examples of vertical expansion during the inflation were provided by Hugo Stinnes who, between 1918 and 1920, forged a combination between the great mining, iron, and steel works of his Deutsch-Luxemburg Mining and Smelting Company and Germany's largest coal producer, the Gelsenkirchener Mining and Smelting Company. Then, he created a "community of interest" based on mutual stock participation between this combination and Germany's largest electrotechnical concern, Siemens. Siemens was too big to be absorbed by its heavy industrial partners, but the cooperation of these giants was supposed to last until the year 2000, and it was intended to create an economic unit that would be in a position to build whole factories from the foundations of the plants to the keys to the factory gates and that "ought not to go unnoted and unasked for any project that comes up in this world. . . ."[11] The Siemens-Rhine-Elbe-Schuckert Union, as it was called, was by no means Stinnes' only interest since he had his own giant concern of coal marketing and shipping operations, paper companies, hotels and, indeed, almost anything he could lay his hands on.

Reusch had considerable distaste for Stinnes' mode of operation, which he correctly viewed as too speculative, and Stinnes' enthusiasm and extraordinary powers of persuasion seemed to have made little impression on Reusch. Nevertheless, Reusch was pursuing many of the same policies more modestly but no less tenaciously, and he was to demonstrate that Stinnes could be beaten at his own game. Under Reusch's direction, the GHH expanded rapidly during, and after the war. It took over Haniel and Lueg in Düsseldorf with its foundries, steel plant, hammer and press work, machine plant, and mine shaft building facilities; it controlled the shipbuilding facilities of the Deutsche Werft in Hamburg, acquired the steel wire works of Boecker and Co. in Gelsenkirchen, and took over the Osnabrück Copper and Cable Works. Reusch was not only interested in expanding within the Ruhr and into northern Germany, however, and he looked to his native South Germany for important new acquisitions, gaining control of a Württemberg machine building firm in Esslingen and a Bavarian iron works in Nürnberg. In 1921, the GHH was to enter into a partnership with the State of Württemberg to operate the mining and smelting works once managed by Reusch's father. These were all substantial gains for the GHH, but the great prize was South Germany's largest and most important machine and diesel motor construction company, the Bavarian Maschinenfabrik Augsburg-Nürnberg or MAN.

Stinnes had been desperate to bring the MAN into the Siemens-Rhine-Elbe-Schuckert Union. He viewed the Bavarian firm as the linchpin in the alliance of great companies he had brought together, and he counted upon the traditional cooperation between the MAN and the Siemens-owned Schuckert works in Nürnberg to make great strides in motor and turbine construction. Consequently, Stinnes had employed all his persuasive powers with the General Director of the MAN, Anton von Rieppel. Rieppel was oppressed by the thought of surrendering the independence of the MAN but was convinced that the company would be left "hanging in the air" if it did not team up with some giant Ruhr producer. From Rieppel's point of view, all the Ruhr industrialists were dominating and threatening, and his goal was to enter into that arrangement which was least threatening to the autonomy of his company. Reusch, who bluntly stated his intention of "placing the entire finishing of his own iron and steel production in his control as effectively as possible" seemed nothing short of "ruthless and crude" to Rieppel. Stinnes, however overwhelming in his plans and goals, seemed to Rieppel to be a person who "counts less upon the power at his disposal than upon a conviction of the necessity of his proposals and intentions."[12]

Unfortunately for Rieppel, Reusch and his agents in South Germany were more skillful and persuasive than Rieppel imagined, and they took advantage of the latter's illness in the summer of 1920 and the confused management of the MAN to play upon the conservative attitude and distaste for Stinnes felt by the head of the MAN supervisory board and major stockholder, the Baron von Cramer-Klett. At a critical moment, Reusch took advantage of the baron's fears of a Stinnes takeover, and the GHH purchased a large packet of stock from the Baron which it then used as a foundation for gaining majority control of the company by the end of 1921. The entire affair caused much bitterness within the MAN and anger in South Germany against Ruhr "imperialism," but it was a great triumph for Reusch and the GHH. In contrast to Stinnes' Siemens-Rhine-Elbe-Schuckert Union, which disintegrated after his death in 1924, the structure constructed by Reusch during the inflation did not fall apart with the coming of stabilization and has lasted unto this day.

In reality, the various companies which became attached to the GHH in one form or another during this period benefitted considerably from the connection. Reusch and the Haniel interests behind the GHH were in a position to provide operating capital and credit, to supply needed raw materials, and to give them access to the superb marketing organization based in Holland that Reusch had built up during this period. It certainly was not always easy to work for Reusch, who once stated that "my people are not in the habit of acting in violation of my instructions, and I am not in the habit of putting up with violations of my instructions."[13] The evidence shows, however, that Reusch was more interested in competence than servility and that he was a superb manager who believed in decentralization and who gave the directors of the various member companies of the GHH a great deal of freedom within the framework of an increasingly rationalized and coordinated national and international business organization. Reusch's business achievements, therefore, were truly admirable, and he used the opportunities provided by the inflation with great skill. It would be a mistake, however, to view his achievements and those of his fellow heavy industrialists from an economic perspective alone. They were no less important from the perspective of domestic and international politics.

To begin with, vertical concentration was a way of making sure that the manufacturing industries would not turn against heavy industry with success and possibly join with unfriendly politicians or bureaucrats in an effort to control heavy industry. On a number of occasions after 1920, for example, the MAN joined the GHH in threatening to leave the association of German machine builders when that organization's leadership seemed to pursue policies favorable to small and medium-sized business. Similarly, great manufacturers like the MAN could now be counted upon to pursue social and political policies in line with those desired by the heavy industrialists. The MAN took a harder line with its workers after 1920 and backed up Reusch in matters of foreign policy.

Heavy industry stood in almost unanimous opposition to the fulfillment of the reparations arrangements of the Treaty of Versailles which, under the London Ultimatum of May 1921, stood at 132 million gold marks. Its leaders argued that Germany's loss of wealth during the war and under the Armistice and Treaty made payment of such a large sum impossible — and demanded that an amount be set in accordance with Germany's capacity to pay. Also, they insisted that nothing significant could be paid until Germany received a large loan from the United States. The Weimar governments tended to agree with the industrialists' view of reparations, but some of them also took the position that Germany had to pursue a "policy of fulfillment," that is, make every effort to carry out the terms of the treaty in good faith in order to show that it was impossible. This meant a policy of rigorous taxation aimed at balancing the budget and stabilizing the currency, as well as the willingness of industry to employ both its credit and to mortgage some of its assets on behalf of stabilization and fulfillment. This was all the more necessary because neither the United States nor England were prepared to lend money to Germany until that country made an effort to stabilize its currency and put its own house in order. The heavy industrialists were not convinced, however, because they saw no point to a policy of stabilization at home when it would be disrupted by impossible reparations demands and payments. Furthermore, they insisted that before industry could accept any obligations connected with a businesslike settlement of the reparations question, they had to have operating conditions that would enable them to produce as much as possible, as cheaply as possible, so that they could compete on world markets under the much more difficult conditions that would exist once the mark was stabilized. That is, the heavy industrialists demanded that the eight-hour day be abrogated because the German workers could not expect to work fewer hours under the miseries of Versailles than they had during the prosperity of the Empire. Furthermore, not only would the workers have to work 10 or 12 hours a day, but they would have to do so for less pay because Germany was less wealthy than she had been. Pay increases would have to be tied to increased productivity. Similarly, all available capital would have to be used for Germany's industrial plant, and the government would have to keep social expenditures to a bare minimum. Such was the industrialist stabilization program.

Until these goals were attained, however, that is, until the Allies "came to their senses" and there was a strong government in Germany capable of reversing the gains made by labor in the Revolution, Reusch and his colleagues were quite prepared to use the inflation as a means of exerting pressure on the Allies as well as to improve their economic position at home. Thus, while most of the world suffered from a depression in 1920–21 thanks to the policies of deflation pursued in an attempt to balance swollen wartime budgets and reduce wartime productive overcapabilities, the Germans pursued a policy of inflation in order to fight revolutionary ferment by maintaining high employment as well as to gain export advantages and thus recover old market positions. Naturally, Germany's export drive and dumping policies intensified the economic difficulties among her customers, and Reusch heartily approved of this policy because "Germany must export as much as possible so that the enemy states find themselves in worse and worse circumstances and are thereby finally brought to reason."[14] Reusch and many of the heavy industrialists also took a tough line concerning the dangers of a French invasion of the Ruhr to enforce the Treaty, a danger which they viewed with remarkable equanimity given the fact that it would be their mines and factories which would fall under French control. Reusch persistently advocated that Germany should let the negotiations with the Allies "break down without regard for the consequences if the Entente does not significantly reduce its demands."[15] An occupation of the Ruhr would show the French that the Germans could not be forced to produce for them with bayonets, would ruin the French economy, and would drive a greater wedge between England and her Anglo-Saxon allies than the one that already existed. For these reasons, Reusch opposed any conciliatory gesture toward France but was himself actively engaged both officially and unofficially in efforts to win over British bankers and industrialists to a policy sympathetic to the German point of view.

When the French finally decided that they had enough of German treaty evasions and bad faith and invaded the Ruhr in January 1923, Reusch became one of the staunchest supporters of the passive resistance policy pursued by the government of the shipping industrialist Wilhelm Cuno, with whom Reusch seemed to have friendly and close relations. While workers and industrialists in common patriotic outrage joined in a policy of noncooperation with the French, Reusch urged that everyone hold out at all costs. He rejected isolated suggestions that the Germans try to compromise with the French by offering them stock participation in German enterprises and said that any industrialists who proposed such a thing "would be justly beaten to death by the local population and the workers."[16] In an interview with the American journal, *The Nation*, Reusch declared that "we will go to the extreme and transform ourselves into Communists and deliver our goods to the workers before we surrender ourselves in the face of French machine guns. . . ."[17] He was convinced that the French would bleed themselves to death financially in the Ruhr if given enough time and opportunity and that the franc would soon suffer the fate already being suffered by the mark.

By the summer of 1923, however, it was becoming clear that the German mark was going to be ruined first since the entire passive resistance struggle was being financed by the printing press and credits from the government to pay wages to workers for employment in an industry increasingly unable to produce, let alone to export. The privation and misery experienced by the masses throughout Germany incited radicalization on both the right and the left that was to culminate in Hitler's Beer Hall Putsch in Bavaria, and Communist threats in Hamburg and Saxony. As the mark plummeted to a level that, by November, was to reach 4 trillion marks to the dollar, firms like the GHH began printing their own emergency money, and the wives of workers waited anxiously outside the factory gates to receive and immediately spend the one or more daily wage payments that were necessary to keep up with the depreciation. Much to Reusch's chagrin, support for passive resistance had diminished greatly by early in the summer, and in late August, the Cuno Government fell and was replaced by a new coalition government—which included Socialists—under the liberal People's Party leader, Gustav Stresemann. This government was committed to ending the hopeless struggle, and Reusch attacked Stresemann as the "chancellor of capitulation"[18] and resigned his membership in the People's Party. Reusch was no less angry at many of his fellow industrialists for signing separate agreements with the French to deliver coal and money in return for French cessation of the seizure of their stocks of iron and steel.

Reusch could hardly conduct passive resistance by himself, however, and there were some favorable developments to compensate for its unhappy termination. The heavy industrialists took the opportunity offered by their agreements with the French to unilaterally abrogate the eight-hour day on the grounds that the agreements could not be carried out unless prewar working hours were restored. There were strikes, protests, and even some violence by the workers, and the 1918 partnership with the unions was dealt its death blow, but ultimately the sullen and beaten workers returned to work and the middle class government of Wilhelm Marx that took over in November issued a decree permitting the return to prewar hours of work. Also, the workers were forced to labor for wages paid in a new stabilized currency that were set below prewar levels. The workers, after all, did not have the credit or the resources of their employers, and the revolution had long been defeated. The GHH had, for example, expended valuable resources and had lost money during the Ruhr occupation, but it had important holdings outside the occupied areas, substantial stores of material that could be sold someday, and sufficient reserves of foreign exchange. No wonder, therefore, that Reusch could report confidently in September 1923 that "for the moment the affairs of the Gutehoffhungshütte are not in a bad way" and that he could "steer the ship Gutehoffnungshütte through the coming storms without suffering serious damage."[19] As for the workers, they were to row. The rewards for their deprivations during the passive resistance were longer hours, lower pay, and a harsher tone from the GHH directors. When they complained about this tone, they were told that "the behavior of the workers in the factories since the beginning of the Ruhr struggle has been a much less satisfactory one than before" and that "the sloppiness must come to an end."[20]

The truth was that the policies of Reusch and the heavy industrialists had worked, albeit at a very high cost. In 1924 a new reparations settlement, the Dawes Plan, was worked out based on Germany's capacity to pay and there began a period of large-scale American loans to Germany that ushered in a period of recovery and economic improvement that was to last until 1929. The price of this stabilization had been the destruction of the old mark and of the savings and investments of important segments of the middle class, great political bitterness and social tension throughout German society, and a retreat from the social reforms of the Revolution. While some of the economic empires created during the inflation collapsed, most notably that of Hugo Stinnes, the more solidly founded concerns survived the stabilization crisis of 1925 and began the process of rationalization, that is, the shutting down of old and obsolete mines and plants and the standardization and modernization of those that remained. This process of rationalization greatly increased their production, and Germany once again assumed economic leadership, but it also caused technological unemployment and promoted dangerous overcapacities. In order to keep up prices, Germany took the lead in developing a complicated system of national and international cartels that regulated prices and production within the industry.

PAUL REUSCH AS SPOKESMAN FOR GERMAN INDUSTRY

At this time, Reusch came to assume a major and notable position of leadership in heavy industry and served as the most outspoken representative of its policies. Although prominent in the directorship of the Reich Association of German Industry, Reusch found this so-called peak association too moderate and compromising for his tastes and concentrated his efforts on strengthening the old Long Name Association in the Ruhr and using it to keep the Reich Association in line. In his capacity as chairman of the Long Name Association, Reusch spoke out with great regularity against the policies of the various Weimar governments, even though most of these were quite sympathetic to industrial interests. Particular venom was reserved for the Labor Ministry which, under the leadership of the Center Party social reformer Heinrich Brauns from 1923 to 1928, pursued a policy designed to restore the eight-hour day as soon as possible and to introduce important social legislation, particularly unemployment insurance. The Ministry shared the trade union view that the workers were entitled to benefit more fully in the prosperity of Weimar's best years, 1926–28. For Reusch, however, Weimar had no good years. He warned, not incorrectly, that the prosperity was a very shaky one based on short-term loans from America that could be cut off the moment conditions there deteriorated. He insisted that the economy had to be left in peace if it were to function properly and objected to the "misuse" of money on public works projects, municipal improvements, and social measures and complained that industry was being overtaxed. While economists today would argue that such expenditures by government often "prime the pump" and improve business conditions and create employment that is productive and although trade unionists then insisted that the economy would benefit if purchasing power were increased through wage increases, Reusch concentrated on the need to produce for export at the lowest possible cost. He did not think that the American consumer-oriented economy was applicable to Europe and, after a trip to the United States in 1926, he returned to argue that Europe did not have America's great domestic market, could not count on its domestic consumers, and had to produce quality goods for a foreign market rather than cheap goods for its people. Too much attention was being paid to the demands of the masses, and there was no doubt in his mind that the day of reckoning would come. Reusch fumed and raged when his own colleagues behaved otherwise. Thus, when Peter Klöckner, one of the most influential Ruhr industrialists, gave an optimistic speech about the future of the economy and even suggested that hours of work might be reduced, Reusch launched a campaign against him. He was gentler but quite firm in organizing opposition to the proposal of his friend, the lignite industrialist Paul Silverberg, who in 1926 suggested that industry reestablish the working partnership of 1918 with the trade unions. Reusch agreed with Silverberg that it was impossible to rule against the workers and without the workers, but he refused to accept the idea that the independent unions were the only true representative of the workers. As before and during the war, so in Weimar, Reusch strove mightily to support and strengthen worker organizations that would follow employer leadership and would abjure the strike. Were it not for government concessions and coddling of the Socialists and the unions, he was convinced, the workers would turn away from the unions and their insidious demands for "economic democracy."

In 1927–28, Reusch and his fellow heavy industrialists became convinced that the drift toward higher wages, shorter hours, and increased social legislation had to be fought with more than words: petitions to President von Hindenburg, the various ministries, and the Reichstag, and campaigns to influence public opinion. The government and trade unions were acting, and they had to act too. They objected strongly to the government practice of mediating labor disputes and then arbitrating them with prolabor decisions that were declared binding on the employers. The passage of an unemployment insurance law and an hours of work law in 1928 alarmed them, as did increased union militancy and a left wing election victory in May 1928 that brought the Socialists back into the government for the first time in four years. By late 1927, Reusch, Albert Vögler of the United Steel Works, the mammoth trust that had been created in the stabilization crisis of 1925, and other heavy industrial leaders had organized a huge fund and a series of secret agreements among the major producers in the Ruhr in preparation for a decisive battle against the pro-labor policies of the government and binding arbitration in favor of the workers. In late 1928, the opportunity came, and they proceeded to lock out 250,000 workers in the Ruhr in what became the greatest lockout and labor dispute in the Republic's history. The industrialists succeeded in changing the terms of the government's decision and dealt an important blow to the binding arbitration method, but Reusch, in his usual manner, wanted to hold out for total victory and resigned his position as Chairman of the Long Name Association in protest against the unwillingness of his colleagues to fight on in the face of government, Reichstag, and public criticism of the ruthlessness of heavy industry.

Indeed, as successful and important an industrial leader as he was, Reusch felt continuously frustrated in his struggle to gain acceptance for his views and programs. Neither the Reich Association nor the Long Name Association kept industry on as conservative and steady a course as he would have liked. In 1927, he tried a new method of organization by setting up an exclusive club of 12 of Germany's leading industrialists to meet monthly to coordinate policy and, hopefully, influence their colleagues and organizations. The Ruhrlade, as it was called, was a very formal affair, and its members met in tuxedos, but if they all looked alike, they did not all think alike and unanimity was not always easy to attain. Naturally, Reusch and his fellow industrialists continued their old practice of giving substantial support to candidates in the bourgeois political parties who could be counted upon, but here too there were great frustrations. Reusch had no confidence in the leader of the German Nationalists after 1928, Alfred Hugenberg; and while he sympathized with this party more than any other after 1923, he found it too extremist in matters of foreign policy and too prone to radical racist and lower middle class anticapitalist resentments. The People's Party, which was strongly financed by big business, was led by Gustav Stresemann until his death in 1929, and Reusch objected to Stresemann's liberal politics and desire to compromise with and work with the Socialists. Industry constantly struggled to move it to the right, and faced a similar problem with the Catholic Center Party which had a strong pro-labor element. In short, politics was always standing in the way of economics, and Reusch strongly advocated a reform of the constitution that would reduce the power of the parliament, establish an upper house representing economic interests and increase the strength of the executive so that the true needs of the economy could be met.

THE GREAT DEPRESSION AND THE CRISIS IN GERMANY, 1929–1933

In this context, the depression which rapidly spread from the United States to Germany in late 1929 was an opportunity as much as it was a disaster. The withdrawal of American loans seemed to prove that Reusch's warnings about the shaky future of the German prosperity were absolutely valid. Increasing unemployment brought about a government crisis in March 1930, since the costs of unemployment insurance soared and the People's Party could not come to terms with the Socialists on how these costs were to be met. A new Chancellor, Heinrich Bruning, came on the scene who was committed to fiscal and economic conservatism. New elections were held in September 1930 and while these elections had the disastrous consequence of bringing 107 National Socialists into the Reichstag, they frightened the Socialists into tolerating Bruning's economic decrees which reduced wages and cut government spending enormously. To some extent, therefore, Germany had returned to the kind of government she had before 1918 in which the Chancellor, protected by President von Hindenburg, was able to act with relative freedom from parliamentary control under the emergency decree provisions of Article 48 of the Constitution.

Reusch's goal, throughout the Great Depression was in complete consonance with his past political aim, namely, to create a united bourgeois conservative front in favor of an authoritarian reform of the constitution. It was precisely the creation of such a bourgeois coalition that proved impossible in the political crisis of 1930–32, that accompanied the depression, and that culminated in the appointment of Adolf Hitler as Chancellor on January 30, 1933 and the Nazi seizure of power. The Nazis were the chief beneficiaries of the fragmentation and radicalization of the German middle class which, among other things, was reflected in the virtual collapse of voter support for the middle class parties. Through his lobbyists in Berlin, Reusch sought to keep contact with various party leaders and the conservative veterans organization, the Stahlhelm, which he viewed as the mass base for his proposed coalition, but he was constantly frustrated in his goal of forming a united bourgeois front against the Socialists, Communists, and Nazis.

With a few prominent exceptions like the aging coal industrialist Emil Kirdorf and the somewhat politically romantic and very confused Fritz Thyssen, the great German heavy industrialists disliked the Nazis and were reluctant to support them albeit often for the wrong reasons. Reusch had been approached to support the Nazis as early as 1921, when the party was confined largely to Bavaria. He rejected the notion and reacted strongly against the party's anti-Semitism and the radical nationalization points of its economic program. He could see no reason why industrialists should give support to their "grave-diggers."[21] Reusch viewed Hitler's Beer Hall Putsch of November 1923 as a particularly "idiotic" move that hurt rather than helped the national cause, and he referred to General Ludendorff as a "political imbecile" for participating in the affair.[22] Although Reusch remained well informed about the Nazi program and Nazi activities through his agents in Bavaria and Berlin, his distaste for them persisted. The only positive remark he could make about Nazi political successes in 1930 was that "it was a not undesirable phenomenon" from the standpoint of foreign affairs, presumably meaning by this that it would induce the Allies to terminate reparations more quickly. From the standpoint of domestic politics, however, the Nazi successes were "highly undesirable."[23] For Reusch, the Nazis were dangerous radicals with crazy economic ideas, and he viewed their rowdy lower middle class following and leaders with considerable contempt. As the crisis deepened, however, and Nazi strength grew, it became impossible for the industrialists to evade all contact with the Nazis or efforts to "tame" them, and Reusch not only met twice with Hitler in an attempt to sound him out and encourage him to pursue a "sound" economic policy, but also supported efforts by the ruthlessly ambitious former Reichsbank President, Hjalmar Schacht, to cultivate the Nazis and improve their economic program. For his part, Hitler, ever in search of funds, sought to cultivate the industrialists and assure them that he would not touch their property or interfere in their leadership within their own enterprises. By early January 1933, Reusch was prepared to see the Nazis enter a conservative government in order to increase the pressure on France and other nations to make concessions to Germany in matters of foreign affairs, but Reusch considered a Hitler chancellorship "out of the question."[24]

The man who received Reusch's strongest support in the crisis was the chancellor from May to December 1932, the conservative Centrist, Franz von Papen. Reusch had become disenchanted with Bruning in the course of 1931 as the crisis became worse and Bruning began to take measures to lower prices as well as wages, and to interfere in industrial affairs in return for government financial support of various enterprises and banks facing bankruptcy. Reusch always opposed industry turning to the state for subsidies and other forms of assistance on the grounds that it would lead to government controls of the free market. Evidently, Reusch paid only limited attention to reports from members of his own staff that the cartels had so rigidified the iron and steel market that it was impossible to speak of a free market. He did begin to understand, however, that the crisis could not be overcome without government "pump priming," and this led Reusch and his colleagues to promote an authoritarian solution to the political crisis that would place in power a strong government favorable to industrialist interests and willing to give private industry the lion's share of the contracts designed to stimulate employment. Franz von Papen, who was Chancellor from May to December 1932, pursued precisely such a policy. Private industry received huge government contracts and tax breaks while being allowed to reduce wages once again.

Not surprisingly, von Papen was the favorite Chancellor of the industrialists. The mass of the German people, however, detested the "Cabinet of Barons" over which von Papen presided. The industrialists poured huge sums of money into the pro-Papen candidates for the Reichstag elections of November 1932, but their money was not transformed into political power. When von Papen failed, the military intriguer, General Kurt von Schleicher, became Chancellor and proceeded to irritate the industrialists by trying to promote public works programs in collaboration with the trade unions.

Reusch played no role in the final intrigues of von Papen and a small clique of Junkers, businessmen, and plotters who persuaded President von Hindenburg to appoint Hitler Chancellor at the end of

January 1933. What was "out of the question" in Reusch's view had taken place, and while Reusch undoubtedly consoled himself with the thought that von Papen was Vice-Chancellor and would be the real power in the new regime, Reusch and the numerous conservatives who took this position were to learn otherwise. Hitler may have exceeded the expectations of the industrialists by dissolving the trade unions on May 1, 1933, but his regime also compelled industry to "coordinate" itself with the new order and, as one of Reusch's correspondents noted, industry's days of making "economic policy resolutions and great protest demonstrations will be over." Reusch's days as a major spokesman for German industry certainly were in the past, and while he continued to play an influential role within his industry and to have the ear of the relevant ministries in Berlin, his major attention was devoted to the GHH after 1933. Unlike Gustav Krupp von Bohlen und Halbach, Reusch refused to play up to the new political order or pretend to ever have had much sympathy with Nazism. As always, he was unwilling to betray his principles and made no secret of his continuing friendship with Paul Silverberg and other non-Aryans. Reusch was too conservative and old-fashioned for the New Order, and he was driven out of office in 1942 when his international prestige and connections no longer counted. While never an important figure in the resistance, Reusch did have close associations with some of the prominent conservative figures who were to play an important role in the German opposition to Hitler.

A man like Reusch thus poses serious dilemmas for the historian. His accomplishments as a businessman are undeniable and long-lasting, and whatever one thinks of his views, he held them with conviction and sincerity. Had this not been the case, he never would have preserved his enormous collection of correspondence and papers which contain not only a remarkable record of his life but also of the activities of his colleagues and of German heavy industry over half a century. Clearly, Reusch never overcame the authoritarianism and nationalistic environment within which he was nurtured, and one of the tragedies of German history was that such persons were permitted to assume so prominent a political role. Reusch did not support Hitler, but he opposed democracy and was allied with the people whose selfishness, authoritarianism, and miscalculation brought Hitler to power.

However overbearing, Reusch was willing to tolerate and befriend persons with political views different from his own like Paul Silverberg and the democratic Württemberg industrialist Philipp Wieland. He was not willing to tolerate differing views from those who were not his social equal, however, and his patriarchal concern for the workers and refusal to deal with trade unionists unless forced to do so was anachronistic. He embodied that rigid class spirit that played such a devasting role in German social and political life. It was more than appropriate that his son, Hermann, who succeeded to his position after the war, should have distinguished himself as the most outspoken opponent of codetermination, that is, giving organized labor a formal participation in the management of heavy industrial concerns. Even Hermann Reusch, however, no longer dreamt of smashing the unions. If son was like father, Bonn was not like Weimar, and the complete legacy of Paul Reusch did not and could not survive.

NOTES

1. Quoted in Klaus Saul, *Staat, Industrie, Arbeiterbewegung im Kaiserreich* (Düsseldorf, 1974), p. 57.

2. Quoted in Dirk Stegmann, *Die Erben Bismarcks, Parteien und Verbände in der Spätphase des Wilhelminischen Deutschlands* (Cologne, 1970), p. 452.

3. Quoted in Gerald D. Feldman, *Army, Industry and Labor in Germany, 1914–1918* (Princeton, 1966), p. 136.

4. Reusch to H. Boecker, May 18, 1916, HA/GHH, no. 300193003/3.

5. Reusch to P. Wieland, August 25, 1917, HA/GHH, no. 30019390/29.

6. Reusch to A. Müller, Deutsches Zentralarchiv Potsdam, Reichswirtschaftsministerium, no. 7287, Bl. 160–61.

7. Reusch to Carl Duisberg, December 1, 1918, HA/GHH, no. 30019390/7.

8. Reusch to Wieland, May 25, 1919, HA/GHH, no. 30019390/29.

9. Reusch to Duisberg, December 1, 1918, HA/GHH, no. 30019390/7.

10. Quoted in Feldman, *Iron and Steel in the German Inflation, 1916–1923* (Princeton, 1977), p. 204.

11. Quoted in Feldman, *Iron and Steel*, p. 222.

12. Ibid., p. 230.

13. Reusch to Director Müller-Nico, October 2, 1921, no. 300193022/1.

14. Statement at concern meeting of October 21, 1921, HA/GHH, no. 3001900/1.

15. Feldman, *Iron and Steel*, p. 203.

16. Reusch to A. Cossmann, February 17, 1923, HA/GHH, no. 30019390/6.

17. January 26, 1923 interview, HA/GHH, no. 300193008/21.

18. Reusch to A. Haniel, September 25, 1923, HA/GHH, no. 300193000/5.

19. Ibid.

20. Discussion with worker representatives on December 27, 1923, HA/GHH, no. 3000035/3b.

21. Reusch to Dr. Glaser, May 8, 1921, HA/GHH, no. 30019393/5.

22. Reusch to Director Endres, November 11, 1923, no. 300193010/14.

23. Quoted in Henry A. Turner, *Faschismus und Kapitalismus in Deutschland* (Göttingen, 1972), p. 139.

24. Reusch to Dr. R. Kötter, January 8, 1933, HA/GHH, no. 400102024/7.

BIBLIOGRAPHY

This essay is based largely on the author's work with the Reusch papers and GHH documents in the Historical Archive of the Gutehoffnungshütte (HA/GHH). I wish to thank the archivist, Herr Bodo Herzog, for his many kindnesses as well as for sharing with me his great knowledge in this area. Insofar as secondary literature is concerned, I have made particular use of the works listed.

Feldman, Gerald *Iron and Steel in the German Inflation, 1916–1923* (Princeton, 1977).

———— and Heidrun Homburg *Industrie und Inflation. Studien und Dokumente zur Politik der deutschen Unternehmer 1916–1923* (Hamburg, 1977).

Maschke, Erich *Es entsteht ein Konzern. Paul Reusch und die GHH* (Tübingen, 1969).

Stegmann, Dirk "Zum Verhältnis von Grossindustrie und Nationalsozialismus 1930–1933," *Archiv für Sozialgeschichte*, vol. 13 (1973).

———— "Kapitalismus und Faschismus in Deutschland 1929–1934" in *Gesellschaft. Beiträge zur Marxischen Theorie 6* (Frankfurt, 1976), pp. 19–92.

Turner, Henry A. *Faschismus und Kapitalismus in Deutschland* (Göttingen, 1972).

Index

This book has been set in 10 point and 9 point Palatino, leaded 2 points. Chapter numbers are 60 point and 84 point Caslon #540 italic (on chapter opening page, 24 point Palatino italic and 84 point Caslon #540 italic). Chapter titles are 20 point Palatino italic. The size of the maximum type page is 30 by 46 picas.